THE BALTIC SEA
2022-23

Super New Edition

CONTENTS

INTRODUCTION	2
TIPS FOR TOURING THE BALTIC SEA	7
CURRENCY OF THE BALTIC STATES	12
BALTIC SEA GEOGRAPHY	15
A BRIEF BALTIC SEA HISTORY	21
ENTERING THE BALTIC VIA THE KIEL CANAL	27
PORTS CLOCKWISE AROUND THE BALTIC SEA	33
* Copenhagen, Denmark	34
* Bornholm Island, Denmark	66
* Malmö, Sweden	82
* Borgholm, Öland, Sweden	104
* Visby, Gotland, Sweden	113
* Stockholm, Sweden	127
* Helsinki, Finland	167
* St. Petersburg, Russia	193
* Tallinn, Estonia	252
* Riga, Latvia	274
* Klaipéda, Lithuania	297

* Gdańsk, Poland	**314**
* Warnemunde & Berlin, Germany	**340**
AROUND THE GULF OF BOTHNIA	**381**
* Sundsvall, Sweden	**384**
* Luleå, Sweden	**394**
* Kemi, Finland	**403**
* Oulu, Finland	**416**
* Vaasa, Finland	**433**
* Mariehamn, Åland, Finland	**443**
* Turku, Finland	**456**
About the Author	472

The author took the majority of photos used in this book. Where another photographer's material was used, proper credit is given.

Many of maps used in this book comes from Open Street Map contributors and are so noted for each map. For further information contact:www.OpenStreetMap.org/copyright

All other maps have the author's reference cited.

INTRODUCTION

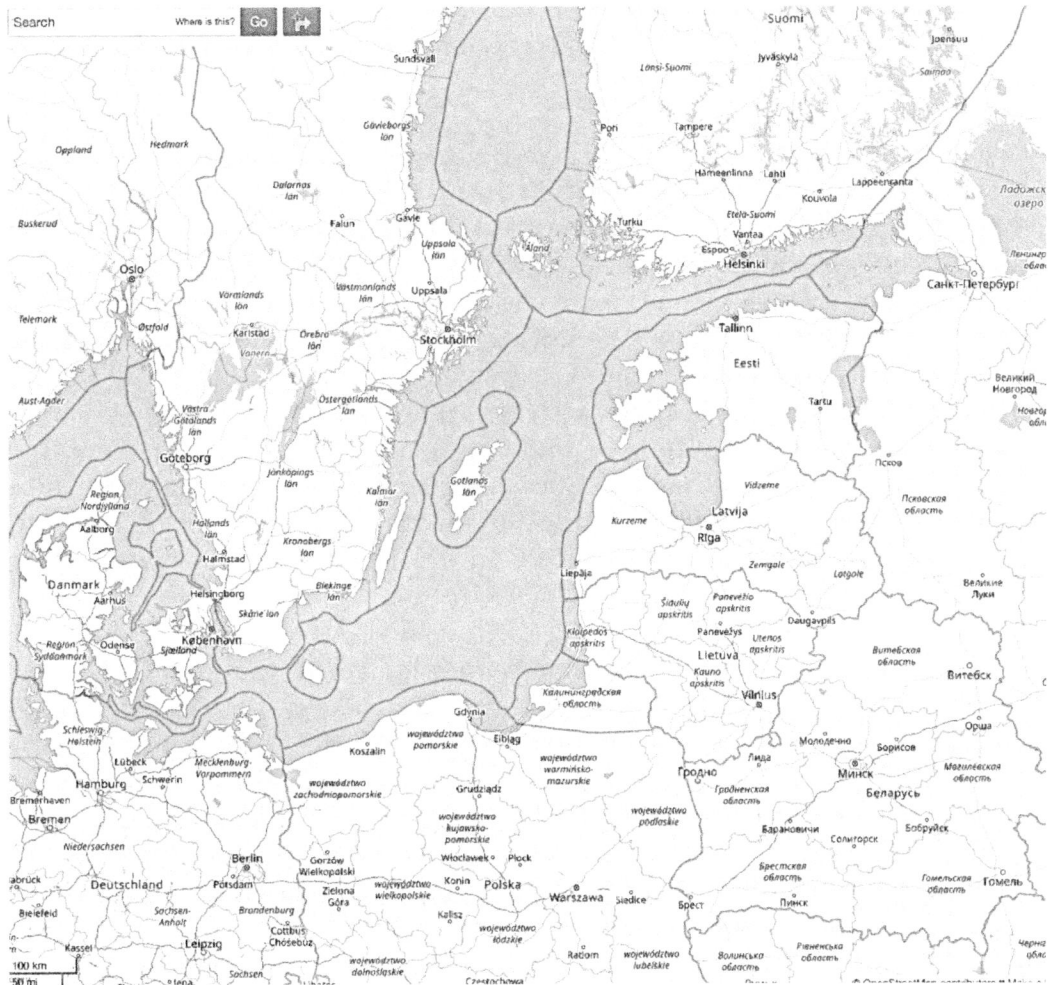

A map of the Baltic Sea countries (© OpenStreetMap contributors)

This book is a new concept emerging from several successful versions of my single volume title *Cruising the Baltic Sea* that I first wrote for Kindle in early 2015. Today Amazon publishes this book in paperback 8.5 x 11-inch format, both in standard black and white as well as a deluxe color edition, updated every other year. As the years have gone by, I have found that readers want more and more detailed information, photos and maps. Thus, to accommodate requests for more detailed information, this super edition enables the expansion of text, maps and photographs. In this new single book I am able to expand the text by adding additional material on the geography and history of the Baltic Sea, enlarging each of the chapters on the ports of call to include more details about each location as well as limited, but specific dining and shopping information. I have also added numerous lesser ports of call, especially those around the Gulf of Bothnia that are visited by the smaller cruise ships, most often representing the higher end companies. I also included a transit through the Kiel Canal of Germany since many cruises on smaller or medium size vessels that begin or terminate in England or The

Netherlands use the canal for entering or departing the Baltic Sea. Of course, not all cruise itineraries include every one of the ports of call listed in this book, but I have managed to include all possible Baltic destinations. If you are not cruising the Baltic, but just visiting various major cities on your own, you can still find a lot of valuable information in this book.

The popularity of the Baltic Sea has grown each year and today it is one of Europe's most popular destinations. Summer in the Baltic Sea of northern Europe is a delightful season, especially for anyone who loves cool weather, as there are few days that could be called hot. The days are long, especially between mid-June and the end of July, and the farther north one travels they increase in length. In places like Saint Petersburg, Helsinki and Stockholm the days are up to 19 hours in length and the farther north one goes, they are even longer. Daylight hours will reach their maximum above the Arctic Circle to where there are approximately six weeks of total daylight. The Gulf of Bothnia, that long arm Baltic Sea reaches almost to the Arctic Circle and in ports such as Luela, Sweden or Kemi, Finland you will have almost a full 24 hours of daylight in June. In the major cities of Stockholm, Helsinki, Saint Petersburg and Tallinn the maximum daylight during this period is around 21-hours.

This region is one of the most popular venues for cruise ships, and all the major lines offer itineraries that vary from one to as much as two weeks. Some more up market cruise lines using smaller ships also include the Gulf of Bothnia on their longer Baltic Sea cruises. The highlight of any Baltic Sea cruise or a visit on your own by air is Saint Petersburg, Russia. Some of the more upmarket cruise lines stay in port for as long as three days, but if traveling on your own I recommend staying longer. Apart from visiting Saint Petersburg, all of the other Baltic ports are rich in historic sites and offer distinctive cultures presented in spotlessly clean settings, thus making for a grand tour that has become one of the most enticing in the cruise industry and that is why this area is now so popular.

The main purpose of this edition is to introduce you to the individual coastal ports and the countries they represent. It will provide you with background information to help you better understand the places you will be visiting. To best appreciate one's surroundings, it is always advantageous to know something about the geography, history, social life and customs and major sites. Yet so many cruisers do not read up on the countries they are visiting, and as a result they miss so much of the true value of international travel. The better informed the traveler is, the more rewarding the experience of visiting new places.

This is the latest update for 2022-23. One new feature is that for each port it describes the various touring options available such as ship tours. private excursions with a car and driver or taxi, use of hop on hop off busses or local public transportation. And it offers direct links to many important resources. Those links will, however, only activate in the Kindle version since the paperback edition is printed and not available as an on line resource.

In this new edition, I have updated my select recommendations as to my favorite restaurants where you will experience local cuisine. I have also updated information regarding shopping for the major ports of call. I do include select hotel information for Copenhagen and Stockholm, as these two cities are the starting or ending points for the majority of Baltic Sea cruises with the exception of those that originate outside of the region in either Amsterdam, London or one of the English Channel ports of the United Kingdom. Even if not cruising the Baltic, both Copenhagen and Stockholm are important air destinations for arriving or departing the Baltic.

I must advise that this is not a mass market guidebook similar to what you can find in a bookstore travel section. The aim is not to provide hotel, restaurant and shopping detail as a primary focus, along with suggested walks or driving routes. When you are on a cruise, you will generally only have eight to 10 hours in port, sometimes even less. Therefore, this book is designed to make sure you can maximize your visit and see and experience as much as possible. The main focus is upon helping you to plan an itinerary or select among the ship's tour offerings or to venture out on your own with enough background to make the best choice possible. This will maximize your understanding and enjoyment of the ports of call on your itinerary. If you need the finite detail of a guidebook then I highly recommend that you look into publications by either Frommer of Fyodor, especially if you are traveling on your own and not by ship.

The region of the Baltic Sea is one of the most beautiful and historic parts of Europe. Settlement dates back to before historic record keeping. Most visitors have heard or read stories about the Vikings who spread outward from the western margins of the Baltic Sea and terrorized the more sedentary peoples of the British Isles and the western coastal margins of Europe clear down to the Mediterranean. But few realize that Vikings also were great colonizers. Russia owes its very existence as a European society to early Viking settlers who pushed inland, utilizing rivers as a means of settling the vast interior forests and steppes. And Vikings were responsible for the settlement of Iceland, Greenland and even for a brief time the shores of what is now Newfoundland in Canada.

The Germanic tribes also played a major role in the development of this region, and their cultural impact has been very profound in historic times. Likewise, the Poles, and the Lithuanian people also expanded their nations and once dominated not only their neighboring peoples in the greater Baltic region, but extended their rule as far south as the Black Sea. During the middle ages, the Hanseatic League played a major role in the establishment of trade routes and port cities all around the margins of the Baltic Sea. And their architectural impact is virtually impossible to overlook in many Baltic ports.

Today with the breakup of the Soviet Union, the nations of the Baltic Sea are finally able to trade and interact with one another on a level that has been absent for nearly a century. Most of the Baltic nations have joined the European Union, thus giving them a unity of purpose with regard to trade and economic development. Yet the Western news media constantly warns of danger from Russian expansionism that could threaten the Baltic Sea region. Such factors will be brought out in several of the chapters to help you in asking important questions or looking for telltale signs of the political climate of the Baltic Sea, thus expanding your personal knowledge. Travel around the sea is no longer hindered by lengthy border crossings with the exception of entering Russia where the visa issue still is a factor to contend with for the majority of visitors. In Russia today, tourism has come to play an important role in its economic development and its relationships with other nations bordering the Baltic Sea.

Most of the capital cities of the nations bordering the Baltic Sea are coastal ports with the exception of Germany, Poland, Russia and Lithuania. But in each case, the capital cities, which are located inland, have close ties to the ports on the Baltic Sea that are vital to national commerce.

This book is designed to introduce the reader to the major cities of the Baltic Sea, with the inclusion of Berlin, capital of Germany because it is so closely associated with its coastal port of Warnemunde-Rostock where the majority of cruise lines stop and provide tours into the German capital.

Although I have written a specific book for those venturing to the city of Saint Petersburg, much of that text is included in this volume because it is such an important Baltic Sea port city and has played such an important role in the history of the region since its inception. For cruises around the Baltic Sea, Saint Petersburg is always the major highlight. I have also written a special book just on the two arrival and departure cities of Copenhagen and Stockholm.

If after reading this book you still have questions about any particular port or aspect of the region, you can contact me either through my web page, which is www.doctorlew.com or on Facebook. I will be pleased to respond. It is important to me to see that my readers maximize their knowledge of the Baltic Sea region before taking their cruise. This is a region that is so diverse, unlike the Mediterranean, and there is a lot to learn about the lands and peoples.

Dr. Lew Deitch,
January 2022

TIPS FOR TOURING THE BALTIC SEA

Almost all major cruise lines offer summertime Baltic Sea itineraries. These cruise lines vary in price and of course in the levels of quality service and cuisine being offered. Most of the itineraries are very similar with the major ports of Copenhagen, Stockholm, Helsinki, St. Petersburg and Tallinn included in the one-week cruises. Longer itineraries may include Warnemunde/Rostock, Gdańsk and Riga. More specialized cruises often add Bornholm Island, Visby on the island of Gotland and Klaipéda, Lithuania. And still more specialized cruise itineraries may include the ports of the Gulf of Bothnia such as Sundsvall and Luela, Sweden along with Kemi, Vaasa and Turku, Finland as well as other lesser ports of call. The length of the itinerary and the number of ports visited is commensurate with the price for the cruise. And in some instances, a cruise line will either precede or follow a Baltic Sea cruise with a Norwegian fjords itinerary thus enabling guests to book them back to back for a longer excursion.

The higher end cruise lines offer smaller ships and their staterooms are generally larger and better appointed than the mega ships belonging to the major mass market companies. There is also a higher ratio of crewmembers to passengers, thus giving more personalized and attentive service. Likewise, the cuisine on the smaller up market lines is gourmet oriented, and often provides a taste of the countries being visited.

The greatest disadvantage for many in traveling on a smaller ship that carries fewer passengers is the lack of lavish entertainment because their theaters and casinos are relatively small. One must choose between having a more sedate and elegant atmosphere or "glitz" and glamour of the larger vessels.

The greatest advantage of traveling on a smaller vessel is in its ability to access ports of call the mega liners cannot visit, and even in the major ports of call, smaller ships are able in many instances to dock at facilities closer to the city centers rather than in the commercial port areas. This is a definite advantage when it comes to not having to spend valuable time riding shuttle busses to and from each city. The large mass market ships provide shuttle busses, usually at a fee for each transfer, and the hordes of people gathering to board the busses can be rather daunting. You also waste valuable time spent transferring to and from the heart of each port. It is an advantage when you can depart the ship on foot and in a matter of minutes be in the heart of the city. This is especially true in such ports as Copenhagen, Stockholm, Helsinki and Saint Petersburg where the smaller high end cruise ships can avoid the large commercial port, docking in or adjacent to the city center.

The higher end cruise lines also have a price schedule that is more all-inclusive, resulting in there being no additional charges for alcoholic beverages, bottled water, shuttle transfers in ports and in end of cruise gratuities. One up market line even includes all tours in the fixed price of the cruise, a trend that is likely to spread.

For those who are new to cruising, here are some basic tips that will help to maximize your voyage:

* **Always book an outside cabin** if traveling on one of the larger ships that offer less expensive interior cabins, which have neither a window nor a veranda. Interior cabins can be quite claustrophobic because it is always necessary to use artificial illumination. At night these cabins are totally dark to where a nightlight is needed in the event you want to get out of bed for any reason. And if the weather is stormy, which on occasion occurs, it can be an intimidating feeling to be in the interior of the ship with no ability to look out the window.

* **If you wish to economize,** you can book an outside cabin with a window, as these are generally on the lower passenger decks where a veranda is not provided. One advantage if the sea should become rough or even moderately choppy is that being lower down in the ship equals more stability when the ship begins to pitch or roll.

* **Although forward cabins are offered lower prices,** be aware that the ship's maneuvering thrusters and anchors are forward. You will be exposed to a fair amount of noise when the ship is docking or leaving port, and this can often interrupt your sleep, especially if you tend to be a light sleeper.

* **Veranda vs no Veranda.** If having the opportunity to enjoy fresh air at any time, even if the weather is very mild or downright chilly is important to you, then it is wise to book a cabin with a veranda.

* **Whenever possible book a cabin in mid ship,** as when a ship begins to pitch the mid-section acts like the fulcrum in that it experiences far less movement than either forward or aft cabins. Most often the Baltic Sea is quite calm during summer, but on occasion squalls can cause the sea to become choppy. For those cruises beginning or terminating in England or The Netherlands you may experience rough seas in the waters of the North Sea or Straits of Dover. And if you are doing back-to-back cruises that include the Norwegian fjords, the waters along the Atlantic coast of Norway can become rough at any time of year. Climate change has definitely had an impact upon the sea with regard to there being more days with chop than in the past.

* **If you should become queasy** during periods of rough weather and pitching or rolling sea, it is best to go up on deck and breath some fresh air. Also, by staring off at the horizon the body surprisingly is less stressed by motion. But if you are unable to go out on deck because of the danger presented during really inclement weather, it is still possible to sit near a window and from time to time look out to

sea, toward the horizon. Fear also plays a role in the way you feel during rough seas. If you become frightened that the ship may capsize or sink, it will only heighten your feeling of uneasiness. Remember that ships can take a lot of punishment, and it is almost unthinkable for a modern cruise liner to go down in rough weather.

* **Starving one's self when feeling queasy will only make the condition worse.** Dry crackers or toast along with hot tea is one way to calm an irritated stomach. And there are patches, pills or injections available from the ship's medical office to calm extreme discomfort.

* **Be prepared for sudden changes in the weather.** During summertime, the average temperatures in the Baltic Sea region are between 15 and 26 degrees Celsius or 62 and 82 degrees Fahrenheit. Occasional summer rainstorms can drop temperatures and it is easy to become chilled or soaked if not properly dressed or carrying an umbrella. Dressing in layers is the best way to accommodate the changes that can occur on a given day. And yes, there are occasional hot, humid days when the sky is blue, the sun feels strong and temperatures can climb up to 31 degrees Celsius or 90 degrees Fahrenheit, but these are the exception rather than the rule.

* **Do not over indulge in eating or drinking.** It is best to pace yourself and try and eat normally, as you would at home. Overindulgence only leads to discomfort and added weight gain. The same holds true for overindulgence in drinking, which many attempt to take advantage of on the more high end cruise ships where beverages are included in the total fare.

* **Electric voltage on board most international cruise ships** is both the 110 North American standard and the 220 European standard. But in non-international brand hotels prior to or post cruise, you will often find only the European standard. Thus, for hair dryers or electric shavers and all battery chargers, you may wish to have an adapter along to expedite use of these appliances.

* **When in port,** weigh the option of going on organized tours against freelancing and visiting on your own. If you have any sense of adventure, a local map, public transit information and the names of basic venues make it possible to see as much, if not more, in a relaxed atmosphere in contract to being shepherded around as part of a tour group. Also, by striking off on your own you have more opportunity to mingle with and meet local residents. With the exception of Russia, English has become a widely spoken second language. Unfortunately in Russia a much smaller percentage of the local people speak English or for that matter other European languages.

* **When visiting Russia,** you cannot venture off on your own unless you have a visa in your passport or come from a handful of countries that do not require a visa. Without having a visa or being from a country not requiring one you are limited to

being on shore only when participating in ship sponsored tours or private excursions arranged through a travel company licensed to provide the proper documentation required by the Russian authorities. Further visa information will be found later in this chapter. My recommendation to anyone who likes the freedom of venturing off on your own is to go through the rather lengthy process of obtaining a Russian visa. I always use Travel Document Services at www.traveldocs.com .

* **When starting a cruise, arrive at least 24 to 36 hours ahead of the departure** and spend a minimum of one night in the port of embarkation. This enables you to recover from jet lag and to become acclimated to a new environment. Likewise, this may be your only chance to experience the flavor of the port of embarkation which is often either Copenhagen, Stockholm, London or Amsterdam. Normally the cruise line will not offer tours in cities where the cruise begins or terminates.

* When disembarking, it is also recommended that you spend at least one night in the final port of call before flying home. Two nights is preferable, as most cruises end in one of the major ports where there is a lot to see and do. Again, the ports of disembarkation generally will be Copenhagen, Stockholm, London or Amsterdam.

* **When on shore in the Baltic Sea countries,** it is safe to eat without fear of gastrointestinal upset. The countries of the Baltic maintain a high degree of sanitation, and good restaurants abound. There are no specific cautions against eating raw fruits and vegetables. Only in Saint Petersburg, Russia is it recommended not to drink tap water because of an endemic local microbe that our bodies cannot tolerate. Elsewhere in the region, local water supplies are safe. Most restaurants, however, provide bottled water throughout the Baltic region.

* **Violent crime in the Baltic Sea region is minimal.** The ports of call on the itineraries of most ships are exceptionally safe. However, pickpockets are found almost everywhere that tourists will be seen in greater numbers. So wise precautions always apply regarding not keeping a wallet in a back pocket, not showing large sums of money and for women to keep a tight rein on their handbags. But you should feel totally comfortable walking even in areas that are not regularly frequented by tourists. There are very few local neighborhoods in any of the Baltic ports of call that might be considered moderately risky.

* **The use of credit cards is widespread** at all major restaurants and shops. However, in Europe data chips are the norm. If your credit card has a data chip, insert it into the front of the credit card machine and follow the prompts. You will either enter a pin code or wait for the receipt to be issued and then sign it. Cards without a data chip will require a special pin code. Check with your credit card service before leaving home.

* In the Baltic Sea region there are still numerous national currencies in use. And in most of the region's countries American or Canadian dollars are not readily

accepted. However, in many of the countries that use their own currency, the Euro will sometimes be accepted. Most small vendors do demand their own local currency for purchases. To date, Denmark, Sweden, Russia and Poland still use their own currency, as does Norway if you happen to be adding a fjord segment to your itinerary.

* **Returning to the ship is normally expedited** by having your cruise identification card handy to be swiped by the security officers. Packages and large handbags are generally put through an x-ray machine similar to what is used at airports. And passengers pass through an arch to screen for any major metal objects.

* **Most ships offer hand sanitizers** at the gangway and recommend that you sanitize your hands upon return. This is not mandatory, but it never hurts to be cautious. The Baltic Sea region is one of the cleanest parts of the world, but still a bit of extra precaution is a good policy. This is especially true in the Covid 19 era.

* **For countries in the Western Hemisphere, visas are not necessary** for any of the Baltic countries except Russia. For nations such as Argentina, Chile, Brazil, China, Hong Kong, Kazakhstan and Israel no visa is required to enter Russia. Without a visa, you will be forced to remain on board except when you hold a bona fide tour ticket issued by the cruise line or a reputable tour company authorized by the Russian government. With a visa, you have the freedom to leave the ship at any time and explore, dine or shop at your leisure. I strongly urge you to secure a Russian visa before departing home. Saint Petersburg is a vibrant city and you will find that once you are there, you will want to get off on your own, especially in the evening to enjoy a meal or just to walk during the long "white nights." But without a visa, you will essentially be held prisoner on board the ship, as you may only depart with an authorized ship's tour ticket or a prearranged tour through a reputable, licensed company. Securing a Russian visa is a somewhat complex process, but it is not that difficult. You can use the services of one of the travel service companies that secures visa for travelers, and then the amount of work you need to do to obtain the visa is minimal. And once in Russia, it is not possible to obtain a visa. Over the years I have always had a visa for Russia. It has afforded me the opportunity to explore in ways that you cannot do even with a private tour because you will still have a car and guide. Saint Petersburg has a good transportation network of busses, trolley cars and a Metro. Yes, it is daunting to use, but there are limited signs written in English to help visitors. The advantage of the visa is to give you freedom to get to know Russia and its people. And you can also explore its cuisine by having meals on shore, which is a gastronomic treat.

CURRENCY OF THE BALTIC STATES

The currency of any country is both a reflection of its national pride as well as a look at the people that have played a prominent role in its historical development. However, with the impact of the European Union, many of the countries in the Baltic have switched over to the use of the Euro, which is essentially very nondescript and does not give one a feel for the country.

At present, there are still several diverse currencies in use around the Baltic Sea. This is definitely a drawback for foreign visitors because of the need to maintain so many different currencies while traveling. In countries that use their own currency, it is next to impossible to use American or Canadian dollars for local purchases. Street vendors and small restaurants generally will not accept credit cards, and thus you will need to have local currency. If you go on tours provided by your cruise line or have private arrangements, it is customary to tip the driver/guide, and they prefer their own currency so as to not be forced to then go to a currency exchange office. However, there are currency exchange bureaus in most major ports, but their rates of exchange are not always the most favorable. It is best to purchase small amounts of the currency you will need from your own bank prior to departure. An alternative is to use a local ATM in the country where you wish to purchase their currency, as the rates are more favorable than a currency exchange bureau.

At present the following countries do not use the Euro and have no future plans to switch to a unified currency:
  Denmark uses the Danish Kroner
  Norway uses the Norwegian Kroner
  Poland uses the Złotych
  Russia uses the Ruble
  Sweden uses the Swedish Kroner

Euro banknotes used in Finland, Estonia, Latvia, Lithuania and Germany

Sample Danish Kronor

Sample Norwegian Kronor

Sample Polish Zlotych

Sample Russian Ruble

Sample Swedish Kronor

BALTIC SEA GEOGRAPHY

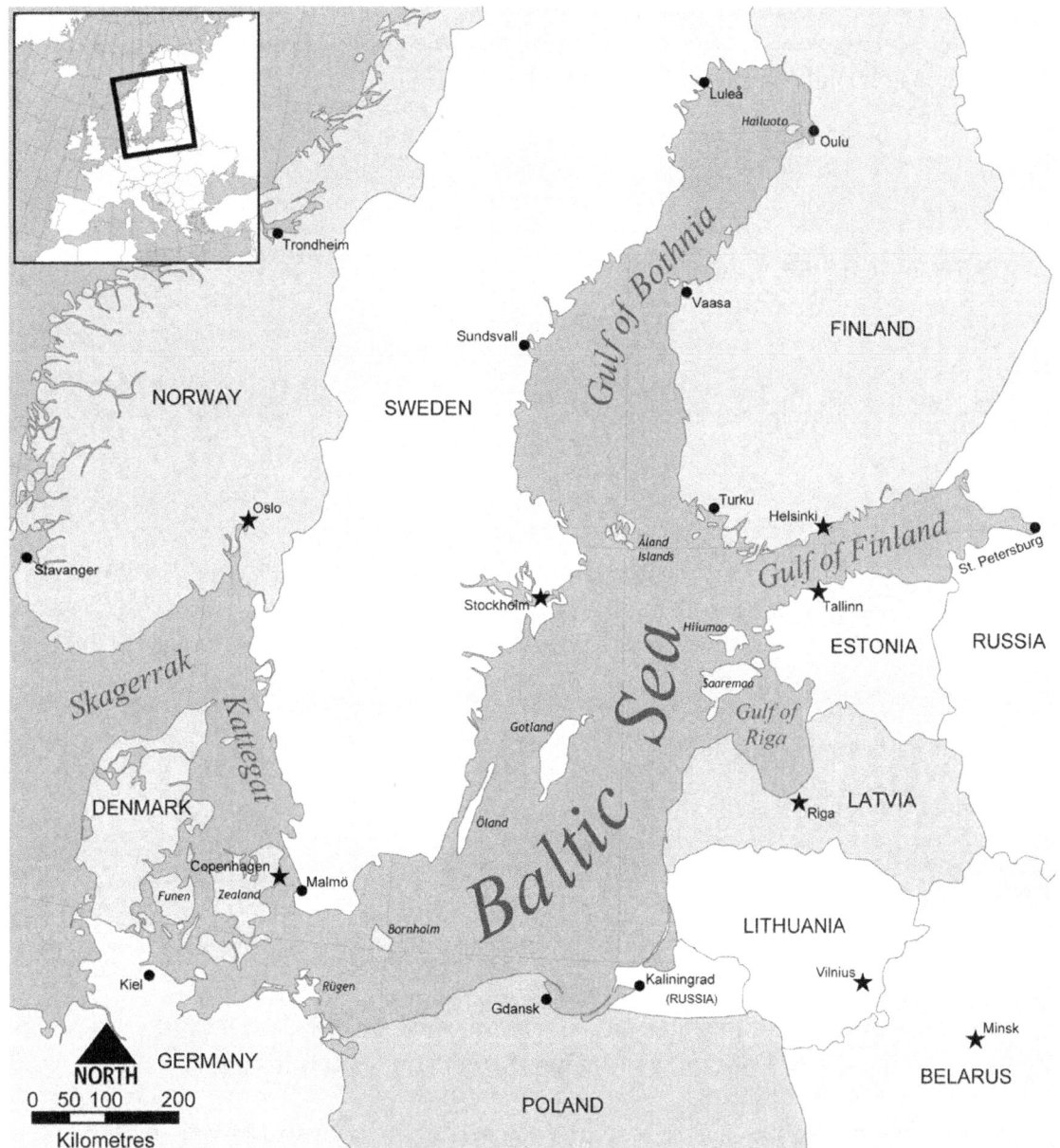

A political map of the Baltic Sea (Work of NormanEinstein, CC BY SA 3.0, Wikimedia.org)

Many people do not have an appreciation for geography as a result of the way in which it was taught, especially in North American schools. Having to memorize which mountains were the highest and which rivers were the longest was what most of us remember. I found the topic captivating even the way it was taught in grammar school. As a professional geographer, I have always believed that such rote memorization for most people takes the joy out of learning about new places, their landscapes and people. Modern geography is a discipline that examines the natural landscape as the home of mankind. It then proceeds to explore how groups

of people have come to develop their culture in a given locale, how they have interacted with other people and how they have molded the natural landscape to create what we see, that being a combined physical and cultural landscape. And for anyone who travels, it is essential to have some understanding of the visual and historic aspects of the places being visited.

The Øresund region between Denmark and Sweden where the Baltic Sea meets the North Sea (© OpenStreetMap contributors)

Essentially the Baltic Sea is a semi-enclosed arm of the northern waters of the Atlantic Ocean. To the northwest, the Scandinavian Peninsula containing Norway and Sweden separates the Baltic Sea from the open waters of the Atlantic Ocean. To the east and south lies the main body of the European continent. The Gulf of Bothnia is the northward extension of the Baltic Sea that separates the Scandinavian Peninsula from Finland. The much smaller and narrower Gulf of Finland is a second indentation stretching eastward, separating Finland from Estonia. The link between the Baltic Sea and the Atlantic Ocean is rather complex. The Jutland Peninsula of Denmark protrudes northward off the main body of the European landmass. To the east are many moderate size islands that comprise much of Denmark, including Zealand, the home island to Copenhagen. There are narrow channels between these islands, most of them too small or shallow for large cruise ships to navigate. The major channel between the most easterly Danish islands on which the city of Copenhagen is located faces the southeastern portion of the Scandinavian Peninsula in Sweden at the city of Malmö. This deep channel is known as the Øresund, and it is the main outlet for the Baltic Sea. The Øresund widens into the Kattegat, which in turn widens into the Skagerrak that opens into the North Sea

The Baltic Sea is approximately 1,600 kilometers or 1,000 miles long and 200 kilometers or 125 miles wide. It is not a deep body of water, its average depth being 54 meters or 180 feet with a maximum depth of just over 157 meters or 1,500 feet in a trench off the coast of Sweden. The surface area of the Baltic Sea is just over 255,545 square kilometers or 145,000 square miles, about the size of the American state of Montana. Because it is almost landlocked, the waters of the Baltic Sea are not exposed to the massive winter storms of the North Sea.

Land's End at the top of Denmark's Jutland Peninsula where the Skagerrak meets the North Sea

The Baltic Sea is a young body of water, its basin having been carved during the last glacial advance. As glacial ice began its retreat, melt water filled the basin and created the sea. This process occurred around 11,700 years ago. The present shape of the sea was completed around 10,000 years ago.

Given its nearly landlocked position with the only mixing occurring where the waters of the Baltic Sea mingle with the Atlantic Ocean through Denmark, the sea is not nearly as saline as the open ocean. There are so many fresh water rivers draining into the Baltic Sea from the Scandinavian Peninsula and the rest of mainland Europe, thus diluting the normal oceanic saline content. The lower salinity impacts the types of plant and animal communities that live in its waters.

SCANDINAVIAN PENINSULA: The land surrounding the Baltic Sea is generally flat to gently rolling with localized outcrops of hills. The nearest mountains are those of the Scandinavian Peninsula along the border between Norway and Sweden. They separate the river drainage between those flowing directly to the Atlantic Ocean and those flowing across Sweden to the Gulf of Bothnia. Sweden was heavily scoured by glacial ice, and this exhibits a pattern of thousands of lakes with a very complex interlocking of small rivers and streams that ultimately reach the sea. The Swedish coast is deeply indented by the sea and is lined with many thousands of rocky islands. The land is covered by a mix of thick forest composed of both broadleaf deciduous trees and conifers interspersed with farmland. Farther north the forest ultimately gives way to the bleak landscape of the tundra, but such environments are much farther north than Stockholm, and these regions are not visited by the majority of cruise ships except those few that do a circle around the Gulf of Bothnia.

Southern Sweden's gentle countryside

On the western side of the Scandinavian Peninsula the mountainous rib was heavily glaciated with tongues of glacial ice extending westward to the Atlantic Ocean. During the great ice ages, the river channels were scoured and deepened so that after the last major glacial advance, rising sea levels flooded these channels creating the present day magnificent fjords of Norway. The fjords are among the most beautiful sights on earth and are visited by tens of thousands of tourists each year aboard numerous cruise ships during the summer months.

THE MAINLAND LANDSCAPES: Finland is very similar to Sweden in that it contains thousands of lakes, mixed forests but only has limited farmland in its far southern margins. Most of Finland is quite flat to gently rolling and composed of hard granitic rock left over after the top layers of sediment were scraped clean by glacial ice.

The same landscape as Finland extends into Russia. There are several major lakes of glacial origin, Lake Ladoga being the largest. Saint Petersburg is built on marshes formed where the great Neva River drains from glacially created Lake Ladoga, Europe's largest body of fresh water, into the Gulf of Finland.

The shores of Russia's Lake Ladoga – largest lake in Europe

The southern margins of the Baltic Sea extending from Poland all the way around to Denmark are part of the North European Plain. Here the land is quite different in that the glaciers deposited fine sediments in what is now a gently rolling landscape rich in nutrients and given over primarily to farmland. There are heavier populations per square kilometer or mile in Poland, Germany and Denmark, thus little forest cover has survived over the centuries. The landscape is still very beautiful but has more of a manicured manmade appearance than in the lands along the northern shores of the Baltic Sea.

Climatically the entire Baltic Sea region experiences mild to warm summers with periods of rainfall that help nourish the land. Daytime temperatures are normally in the 20's Celsius or 70's Fahrenheit. Autumn is brilliant wherever there are broadleaf deciduous trees that bring rich pockets of gold, orange and red to the landscape. Winter in the Baltic Sea region is notoriously cold and damp. Closer to the Atlantic Ocean in Denmark and far southern Sweden the amounts of snow are far lower, but gray skies and drizzly rain typify the maritime influences. As one goes farther inland or north, the winters become far colder and snow dominates. If you remember the Hollywood movie "Doctor Zhivago," it was filmed in Finland and was supposed to represent Siberia. The scenes of a frosted landscape characterize these lands around much of the Baltic Sea. However, in the last 50 years, global warming has started to moderate the severity of the winters in the Baltic Sea region, but winter is still a long and cold season despite the ongoing moderation. At one time the Baltic Sea would freeze over and navigation would come to a standstill. Today the ice is thinner and the period of deep freeze is of shorter duration than it was half a century ago. Only on rare occasions will the sea freeze over the way it did in mid 20th century. At one time it was possible to drive a car from the Swedish coast to Finland during the winter, saving over 2,00 kilometers in the auto route between Stockholm and Helsinki.

The northern European plains seen in Poland

A BRIEF BALTIC SEA HISTORY

A medieval church in Sweden from the late Viking period

To best understand the culture and the landscape of any region visited, it is important to know something of the history of the region. It is the course of history that molds the culture, creates the visual landscape with regard to both the physical and human elements seen. Architecture, transportation networks, farming patterns and the amount of natural forest or grassland are all impacted by the succession of events that took place in the past. And for this reason, history plays a major role in what the visitor encounters. This is why I place a lot of emphasis in each chapter on the history of the port of call, and of course on its parent country. You are in effect looking at layers of history and can only interpret the visual landscape through its past history. So many of the famous sites you will be visiting are vestiges of the past history of each port of call you visit. In reading this book I ask that you do pay close attention to the history of each country or port of call, as so much of what you see will have far more meaning when you understand its place in the timeline of the events that have shaped each venue.

At the time of ancient Rome, the Baltic Sea region was inhabited by a variety of tribal groups, none having formed what we would recognize as nations. Paramount among the tribes was the Norse, better known as Viking that inhabited Denmark,

Norway and Sweden. They were divided into small chiefdoms each with a hereditary leader. To the south were numerous other tribal groups, the best known being the Germanic peoples who were initially small tribal groups that ultimately grew into small nation states, most ruled over by hereditary princes.

A northern German village from the days before Germany was a single nation

These many groups would eventually become the nations that comprise the Baltic Region of today. A mix of hunting, fishing, gathering and limited farming occupied these people, providing for their needs at what today would be recognized as a primitive level. Ultimately, they accepted Christianity and began to emulate the more settled and advanced peoples living to the south of the Baltic shores.

The middle ages saw the Vikings expand outward through a combination of trade, colonization and raiding. Eventually their seed would be spread west into the British Isles and eastward deep into European Russia. The very name Russia comes from a Slavic adaptation to the name of Rurik, a Viking leader in the east, who became recognized as "Rus." And his seed led to the creation of Rossia or what in English is known as Russia. Viking influences can still be seen physically in the people with blonde hair and blue eyes found from the Ukraine all the way over to the British Isles.

It was also the Vikings who began to call the Baltic Sea the Eastern Sea, in recognition of it being apart from the open waters of the Atlantic. Today in Germanic tongues that is how it is recognized.

By the 13th century, most Baltic Sea peoples had converted to Christianity. Numerous groups spread the Gospel, often by the sword. And with conversion came an end to the dread of Viking raids, as even these fierce warriors began to look more inward and consolidated into kingdoms, ultimately accepting Christian teachings.

Helsingborg, Sweden guards the entrance to the Øresund along with Helsingor, Denmark, which is just across the strait

Baltic Sea history from the time of the Middle Ages includes many conflicts, as trade in wood, flax, amber, furs, salt and other local products brought potential wealth. And with riches came war. During the 13th and 14th centuries, a trade federation known as the Hanseatic League dominated both the North Sea and much of the Baltic region with the Dutch in Amsterdam and Germans in Hamburg at the heart of this trade. But by the 16th century, the powers that emerged were Denmark and Sweden in the west and a united Poland-Lithuania in the east. By the start of the 18th century, Russia began to open its window on the west through Saint Petersburg, emerging as still another major power. At the same time Prussia also consolidated its hold over much of the territory that would later become modern Germany. From the time of Peter the Great in the early 18th century onward through the reign of Catherine the Great and later Tsars, Russia came to be the great Baltic Sea power. The Russians also pushed south into the Black Sea region to challenge the Islamic Ottoman Empire. The Crimean War of the mid 19th century saw the involvement of the British and French with a spillover of hostilities into the eastern Baltic when the French attacked Russian garrisons in Helsinki and Saint Petersburg.

The Swedish fortress of Summonlena in Helsinki, Finland ultimately falling to Russia after years of Swedish rule

The late 19th century saw the unification of Germany in 1871. And with militant Prussia at the focal hub of this new nation, the ultimate end result was Germany's role in World War I. This war ended the German Empire, and a weak German Republic could not counter the League of Nations in their creation of the Polish Corridor that split eastern Prussia from the rest of Germany. It made a relatively weak Poland a target for future aggression.

Russia saw the overthrow of the Tsar in 1917, the Communist insurgency led it into a long civil war that lasted until 1922 when the Soviet Union emerged. Soviet rule extended over eastern Europe with the imposition of the Communist system that lasted until 1991 when the system literally collapsed from within.

In the 1930's, the Nazi Party gained control of Germany and built up a massive war machine that it launched against Poland in 1939, plunging Europe and ultimately many global powers into World War II. This was the most brutal war in all of European history. During the war, only Sweden, Switzerland and Portugal managed to remain neutral and not impacted directly. It ended with Germany being divided, as the Soviet sphere of influence cast a wide net over eastern Europe. Today a modern and united Germany has become the economic and political focus of the European Union.

The magnificent World War II memorial in Gdansk, Poland

. The Soviet city of Leningrad (formerly and again today Saint Petersburg) managed to hold out against a German blockade for over 900 days, but Poland, the Baltic States, Denmark and Norway all fell under the boot of Nazi forces. Both in the Nazi expansion and finally retreat from the Baltic Sea, thousands of ships and planes were lost in the various engagements, essentially turning the sea floor into a military graveyard.

The modern Baltic Sea region since the fall of the Soviet Union has seen the emergence of Estonia, Latvia and Lithuania, the reunification of post-World War II Germany and most of the nations becoming members of the European Union and the North Atlantic Treaty Organization. Today trade and tourism are a major source of income for the Baltic ports in an era of peaceful coexistence unprecedented in past history.

There is a rich architecture throughout the Baltic Sea region, partly influenced by each of the historic periods and the various cultural forces that have shaped the region. Walled cities, storybook castles, magnificent cathedrals and glittering palaces have become tourist attractions. Likewise modern urban centers have developed, and they are exceptionally clean and well ordered, as a result of the high degree of cultural sophistication and prosperity of the various Baltic peoples. There is heavy industry but with careful national planning in such countries as Germany and Poland, it does not mar the landscape. Baltic cities are also important centers of commerce, banking and manufacturing.

The Baltic Sea region is known for its summer fruits and berries, and the season is celebrated all across the region

ENTERING THE BALTIC SEA VIA THE KIEL CANAL

Map of the Kiel Canal route(© OpenStreetMap contributors)

A transit through the Kiel Canal is a beautiful experience, especially if the weather is nice. This transit, which can take six to eight hours, enables ships to cross the far northwestern countryside of Germany, saving hundreds of kilometers or miles and hours of travel time between the North Sea and the Baltic Sea. For those Baltic Sea cruises that begin or terminate in ports such as Amsterdam, Dover, London or Southampton, a transit through the Kiel Canal saves at least one full 24-hour day of travel time. But it also enables the passengers to enjoy a relaxing journey through the north German countryside of Schleswig-Holstein.

THE LANDSCAPE: The canal is 100 kilometers or 61 miles long and it links the estuary of the Elbe River just inland slightly from the North Sea with the Baltic Sea at the German city of Kiel. The savings by using the canal is 451 kilometers or 287 miles around Jutland, the primary landmass of Denmark. It also precludes the prospect of rough North Sea weather, especially when storm fronts move across from the British Isles, carried by the prevailing westerly winds. The North Sea has a reputation for treacherous storms, which is not what cruise passengers are expecting when booking a pleasure cruise. However, the mega cruise ships on itineraries out of England or The Netherlands are not able to transit the canal because their dimensions are greater than the draught and height will permit. They must proceed around Jutland, which at times can be a bit uncomfortable.

Entering the Kiel Canal from the Elbe River traveling into the Baltic Sea

The landscape of Schleswig-Holstein is very beautiful in a pastoral way. It is relatively level to just slightly rolling, having been created by glacial deposition at the end of the last ice age. The land is quite fertile and has always been considered as a prize, contested over in the past by Germans and Danes. From the upper decks of the ship you look out across verdant fields and pastures interspersed with small groves of broadleaf deciduous trees. The farms are prosperous, as are the villages that have developed along the canal. Neatly maintained brick houses with red slate roofs clustered together, often so close to the water's edge that you can easily call greetings to people on shore. There are footpaths used by both pedestrians and bicycles all along the route of the canal. And there are numerous small ferry crossings where once again locals are eager to greet cruise ship passengers. As you sit out on deck or in the observation lounges of your ship sipping a refreshing drink, your ship is essentially taking you on a tour through the northern German countryside.

Northern Germany is under a maritime influence. Summers are generally quite cool and humid. Frequent rain showers are what keep the landscape so lush. During autumn the trees turn yellow and gold, providing a different mood. And in winter the landscape can appear very bleak with bare trees, gray skies and drizzly rain. Snowfall is not unknown, but the snow melts within a few days unless there is exceptionally cold air behind the storm front that brought the snow. But as you proceed east into the country, snow becomes more of a regular occurrence

The idyllic landscape of Schleswig-Holstein seen from the can

THE CANAL'S HISTORY: The concept of a canal to link the Baltic and North Seas dates back to medieval times, but of course the technology was not existent. In 1784, the Danish Kingdom built the Eider Canal, utilizing sections of the Eider River, thus necessitating only 43 kilometers or 27 miles of actual canal. This was not a wide or deep canal, used primarily for barges, as ocean-going vessels even of the day could not navigate its shallow draught.

By 1864, the region of Schleswig-Holstein had come under Prussian control after war with Denmark. The Danes had hoped for British support during their second war with Germany because the Prince of Wales was married to a daughter of King Christian IX. But the British royal house was also tied to Germany through the marriage of Queen Victoria's eldest daughter to the Kaiser. So in the end, Denmark lost this territory. The German navy was adamant about its need to link its naval forces in both the Baltic and North Seas without going around Jutland.

Construction on the Kiel Canal began in 1887. The work was done primarily by hand, as steam equipment was in its infancy. Over 9,000 workers labored for eight years to dig the sea level canal, and this time the entire length had to be created rather than using any major river. By the time of the opening, Kaiser Wilhelm II was on the German throne, the grandson of Queen Victoria through her eldest daughter. The Kaiser dedicated the waterway as the Kaiser Wilhelm Kanal, presumably after his father, but some historians say it was a degree of personal glorification.

The canal was widened between 1907 and 1914, completed in time for the outbreak of the First World War. The German Navy had developed large battleships that needed the extra width and depth to maintain the canal's military capability.

When the war ended, the Treaty of Versailles subjected Germany to harsh and punitive actions, one of those provisions was that the canal be open to both commercial and military vessels of all nations. But in 1936, Adolf Hitler revoked the international status. It was not until after World War II that the canal was once again internationalized, but left under German administration.

Beautiful Rendsburg is the major city midway along the Kiel Canal route

CANAL OPERATIONS: The canal was briefly closed in 2013 as a result of neglect of the lock gates on the western end of the canal. The canal does not have locks that lift or lower ships due to changes in elevation of the land being traversed because it is a sea level route. But at both ends there are lock gates that act as surge protectors, especially at the western Elbe River end, because of possible storms sweeping in from the North Sea, and to a lesser extent the Baltic Sea. Thus depending upon tidal effect or storm surges, there is a small amount of lift or lowering, never more than a handful of meters or feet. Under normal conditions the lifting or lowering of a vessel by a few meters or feet is based upon the tide in the Baltic Sea or Elbe River at the time the ship is entering or leaving the canal.

The canal is wide enough for two-way traffic, and ships are each classified by size and displacement into categories. The largest ships must have German pilots and helmsmen on board to provide for absolute safety in navigating the waterway. Normally only the largest vessels are required to tie up at special bollards and wait for the passage of smaller ships so as to avoid the risk of collision.

Local small ferries cross the canal all along its route

Those who have transited the Panama Canal should not expect the drama of that crossing. Since there is little need for raising or lowering vessels, the Kiel Canal crossing is rather tranquil. The ship will enter the first surge protector and wait until the gates close. There may be a slight raising or lowering of the level of the water depending upon the tide or in the event of the remains of a storm surge. The forward gates will open and then for the next six or eight hours the ship will cruise at a very slow speed through the canal, as the beauty of the countryside glides by. But despite the lack of drama and excitement that one finds in the Panama Canal, this crossing is still very pleasurable. The true beauty of a transit through the Kiel Canal is in the scenic countryside. If you sit on one of your ship's upper decks, preferably in the forward observation lounge or aft on one of the outer decks you will be treated to passing farm fields, orchards, woodlands, small villages and medium size towns. It is almost like being on a slow train or bus crossing the northern German countryside. I have made the transit over a dozen times and always enjoy the serenity and beauty of the countryside seen from this high vantage point and so close up.

The main railway bridge connecting Germany to Denmark crossing the canal

The bridge crew prepares for the exit of the canal

PORTS CLOCKWISE AROUND THE BALTIC SEA

There are so many potential ports of call in the Baltic Sea that I had to consider how to organize this book. Most cruises of the Baltic Sea begin or end in Copenhagen, Denmark or Stockholm, Sweden, traveling either clockwise or counterclockwise around the shore. Thus I thought it would make more geographic sense to start with Copenhagen, which is the westernmost of the Baltic ports and then travel eastward along the northern shore, excluding the Gulf of Bothnia because it is so rare that a cruise itinerary includes this part of the sea. Then from Saint. Petersburg, Russia it made sense to continue along the southern shore, traveling westward toward Copenhagen. The Gulf of Bothnia is treated afterwards since these waters do not contain any major ports, and are seldom included in standard itineraries. It is normally the more upmarket cruise lines utilizing smaller ships that on occasion have an itinerary that includes a traverse of the Gulf of Bothnia.

Each chapter covers a single port, presenting geographic and historic background plus providing you with a guide to what to see and do. I recommend the major sights and give you opening and closing hours where necessary. The venues I offer include alternatives to the standard ship tours for those of you who want to have a greater degree of independence and an opportunity to see more than just the basics. I also offer limited restaurant recommendations because as a cruise passenger, you will only be in port during the day and for a few hours. The restaurants I recommend are ones open for lunch and serving traditional local cuisine. I also offer choice shopping recommendations, again simply because your time is limited.

Please remember that this is not an all-inclusive tour guide, as those mass-market books are aimed at people traveling on their own and needing all the minute details that cruise passengers do not require. You are living on board a floating hotel and do not need accommodation recommendations except for the two ports where most itineraries either commence or terminate, thus when in port you want the information that will maximize your visit and make it memorable. But for those who are traveling alone and not by cruise ship, this book still contains valuable information on the overall nature of each country and port that is far more detailed and valuable than what you will find in the mass market tour books.

COPENHAGEN, DENMARK

The location of Copenhagen (© OpenStreetMap contributors)

Starting a clockwise look at the ports of call around the Baltic begins in the west with Copenhagen, the capital and largest city of Denmark, which happens to be the smallest of the Scandinavian countries. Denmark is made up of the Jutland Peninsula, extending north from Germany, separating the Baltic Sea on the east from the North Sea on the west. In addition to Jutland, the remainder of the country is comprised of numerous islands, many interconnected by road and rail bridges. At its narrow point, the Øresund is a slender strait separating Denmark from Sweden and it is the main transport route into the Baltic Sea and it is here that you find Copenhagen. The location is and has been strategic, as it has controlled the flow of traffic in and out of the Baltic Sea in the days when control of a waterway gave a city or country great power.

THE LANDSCAPE: Denmark covers a land area of 42,895 square kilometers or 16,562 square miles about the ¾ the size of the American state of South Carolina. Its population is just over 5,600,000 people. Demark is considered to be the gateway to the Baltic Sea. Geographically Denmark is classed as a fragmented country because its lands are not contiguous. At the Øresund where Denmark and Sweden almost meet all of the international shipping in and out of the Baltic Sea could be blocked in time of war, giving both countries a strategic advantage in controlling this major inland sea.

Beyond the Øresund lies the Kattegat and Skagerrak Straits, often-stormy bodies of water that separates Jutland from Norway. Almost all of Denmark except Bornholm Island is low-lying and somewhat rocky as the result of having been created by glacial debris at the end of the last ice age. There are many fertile areas, and the country is known for its fine dairy herds, sugar beets, barley and wheat crops along with fruit orchards. Much of the land is still covered in a mix of broadleaf and needle leaf woodlands, presenting a rather idyllic landscape, especially with its neat and tidy villages, each dominated over by a church steeple. There is an almost fairy tale quality to the Danish countryside.

An idyllic Danish country house in Skagen

Many Danish villages are located along the margins of Jutland and the islands where boats can be sheltered, as fishing is also an important part of the Danish economy, as the Danes have always looked to sea for its bounty.

The country is highly industrialized, producing fine quality manufactured goods, especially furniture and clothing. With few natural resources, Denmark must import most of its raw material needs. Danish craftsmanship is noted worldwide for its high degree of quality.

Denmark has a maritime climate, one that is essentially very wet, blustery and cold during the winter, as storms are propelled across its tiny landmass by the prevailing westerly winds. Snowfall does occur, but it does not remain on the ground for lengthy periods of time. Summers are very mild because of the maritime influence of the country being so intricately interwoven with the sea. But there are more sunny days during the summer months, actually at times giving the country a pleasant time for outdoor pursuits. And of course all this moisture means that Denmark is a very green country.

The green islands of Denmark

When flying west between London and the western United States on a non-stop flight, it is possible to see the frozen wasteland that is Greenland, which is a Danish self-governing territory, the largest island on earth. It is quite a spectacle. Today the degree of melting of the Greenland ice cap is controversial. Those who are strong proponents of global warming claim that the melt is at a near catastrophic level. Yet historic evidence shows that when the Viking Leif Erickson and his colonists lived on the shores of Greenland over 1,000 years ago, the climate was milder and the ice was farther back from the shore than it is today enabling limited agriculture not seen today. And then the climate grew colder and the Vikings had to abandon their settlements. And someday if the earth's climate should continue to warm, many coastal margins of Denmark could become flooded, and perhaps they were at the time the Vikings were living on Greenland since it was warmer than it is at present. Food for thought as to the way in which the earth's climates have changed in the past, even before man made greenhouse gasses.

Seeing Greenland from high above on a Transatlantic flight

THE NATURAL SETTING OF COPENHAGEN: Copenhagen is a city of the sea and of course by the sea. There are also canals that tie the various dock and wharf facilities together to create a massive harbor devoted to major shipping, fishing and pleasure craft. And the harbor of Copenhagen is exceptionally clean.

The city developed at the eastern end of the island of Zealand, facing the Øresund, which gave it a strategic advantage in being able to control traffic through the narrow strait that connects the North and Baltic Seas. The island is relatively flat, being composed of glacial deposits making it quite fertile. The natural vegetation cover was one of mixed broadleaf deciduous woodland, but most of it is today relegated to small patches because of the density of settlement.

The climatic regime for Copenhagen is that of a maritime regime with more than adequate rainfall, blustery winters and mild summers. Snow does not generally stick for long in winter, and cold, icy rain is more the norm. While in summer, gray skies and occasional fog outnumber the days when the sky is blue.

The city is built in somewhat of a concentric set of rings that spread westward from the small channels separating it from the eastern small island of Amager. The Christianborg Palace, which is home to the Danish Parliament, is essentially the heart of the city, separated from the rest of Zealand by a semicircular man-made canal. Across the channel separating Zealand from Amager, the suburban community of Christianhaven is also broken into smaller islands by the further construction of man-made channels (see maps at the end of the chapter).

Suburban Copenhagen seen from the air

A BRIEF LOCAL HISTORY: Although a tiny country, the history of Denmark is intimately bound up with the history of much of late 19th and 20th centuries in Europe. The Danish Royal House under King Christian IX married its children into more royal families across Europe than any other. It is often said that no European royal is without Danish blood, thus it makes looking at this miniscule nation's history a must to appreciate its importance. Just to emphasize this point, in the late 19th century one of King Christian IX's daughters was married to the future king of the United Kingdom while her sister was married to the Tsar of Russia. One brother became king of Norway and another became king of Greece.

The Danish tribes are originally of Viking origin just as are the Norwegian and Swedish. There is evidence of their presence in Denmark as far back as 500 BC. From Denmark the Vikings raided and established colonies as far away as England and the Normandy Coast of France. By 950 AD, there was a Viking kingdom in Denmark, and its rule extended into what is now southern Sweden. The Danish Vikings set out across the Atlantic, settling Iceland in the 10th century, and from there the illustrious Leif Erickson continued west to colonize Greenland, and for a brief time the northern coast of Newfoundland, long before Columbus was even born. At one time Iceland and Greenland were united under the Danish Crown. But Iceland gained its full independence in 1944. Although it has home rule, Greenland is still Danish territory, making it the largest colonial territory remaining in the world relative to its physical size. And it is about 45 times the size of its parent country.

The very history of Copenhagen relates to its strategic site. It was founded about

1,000 years ago by Viking warrior Sweyn I Forkbeard and his son Canute the Great. But for the almost two hundred it remained simply a small fishing village until it was fortified in the year 1167 because of its excellent harbor. It immediately became a trade center, initially attacked by the Hanseatic League, but it never fell into League domination. It was during the period of the early 1400's that the city became the royal and military capital of the nation, initially existing as a walled city. Some of the old ramparts can still be seen in modern Copenhagen. What gave the city and Denmark added prosperity was the navy's ability to collect tolls from shipping passing through the Øresund, and it is this prosperity that brought about much of the magnificent architecture seen in the city today.

During the early 11th century the famous King Canute actually united Denmark and England for a period of nearly 30 years. In 1397, the Kalmar Union united Denmark and Sweden and Norway until 1523, Denmark unilaterally laid claim to Norway and its possessions of Iceland, Greenland and the Faroe Islands.

The city lost about one third of its residents during the Black Plague, suffered a major fire in 1728 and again in 1795, but each event only strengthened the resolve of its people to make their city even greater. Much of Copenhagen's classical architecture, including the Frederikstaden and Amalienborg Palace owe their existence to this time period.

In 1814, after the Napoleonic Wars, Denmark was forced to cede Norway to Sweden, which it held until 1905. This was the result of the Congress of Vienna punishing the Danes for having supported Napoleon during his attempt to conquer Europe. But the Danish crown maintained control over Iceland, Greenland and the Faroe Islands, the last two still belonging to Denmark today, but with home rule for each.

For the next hundred years, not much is heard from Denmark, as the nation keeps essentially to itself. However in 1849, the country followed the British example and became a constitutional monarchy. During the Victorian Era in England, King Christian IX of Denmark married most of his children into the royal houses of Europe, making him the 'father-in-law of European royalty. The two best-known examples, as previously noted, are his two daughters, one of whom married the future Tsar of Russia, Alexander III and the other the future King of the United Kingdom, Edward VII. And King Christian's younger son became the King of Norway when that country had no heir to its throne and another son became the king of Greece when that country declared its independence from the Ottoman Empire. The list of descendants of King Christian IX is long and extends into almost every major royal house on the continent. He is referred to by historians as the "Father-in-law of Europe."

Denmark has a parliamentary government, similar in nature to that of Norway and Sweden. The monarchy, one Europe's most prestigious, still exists, but in constitutional form with Her Majesty Queen Margrethe II having only limited powers. Unlike the United Kingdom, the Queen and her family are often seen in public without the benefit of pomp and ceremony, making Her Majesty more accessible to ordinary people, again similar to what is seen in Norway and Sweden

Christianborg Palace is the seat of the Danish Parliament

If anyone wonders why the text did not mention King Hamlet during the discussion of Danish history, it is because he never existed. Although William Shakespeare used Kronborg Castle north of Copenhagen as the setting, the character is purely fictitious. Yet today everyone knows the site as Hamlet's Castle, showing the impact of a work of literature on the reality of tourism. Many tourists visit the castle believing that Hamlet was rea.

One Dane who was quite real, however, was Hans Christian Anderson. His great stories are exemplary of Danish life, the most famous being *The Emperor's New Clothes* and *The Little Mermaid*. Anderson is considered as a national treasure of Denmark. The bronze statue of the Little Mermaid that sits along the Copenhagen waterfront is one of the most visited sites by tourists. It has become the iconic symbol of the city .

British forces liberated the country in 1945, and Denmark became one of the original signatory members of the North Atlantic Treaty Organization. Despite German persecution and eventual extermination of the city's Jewish population, many Danes helped a significant number of Jews escape across the strait to Sweden.

THE PHYSICAL LAYOUT OF COPENHAGEN: The city of Copenhagen is quite compact because most of its residents live in apartment blocks or condominiums. Rather than masses of high-rises, the majority of the buildings in Copenhagen are less than six or seven stories, primarily constructed out of red brick, although some are stone or concrete. There is an overall darker quality to the skyline than other Baltic cities where pastel painted concrete gives the residential areas more overall color. Single-family brick houses are found in the outer suburbs to a greater degree than in most other Scandinavian cities.

The city center is bounded on the west by a string of water storage reservoirs, each having a rectangular shape and surrounded by parkland. There are also numerous beautiful parks throughout the city, some replete with small lakes to lend a more natural looking landscape.

Parking for bicycles at Central Railway Station in Copenhagen

The major streets tend to form a somewhat concentric pattern around the old city core, and east to west streets also tend to branch outward, but not quite in a radial pattern. Major streets are wide enough for multiple lanes, but on all main routes there are designated bicycle lanes since this is a city in which bicycle ownership dominates over automobiles. There are even specific bicycle parking lots almost everywhere. The only other major European city so oriented toward the bicycle is Amsterdam, but it does not quite compare to Copenhagen in the number of bicycles per capita. More will be said about the bicycle and Copenhagen further on in this chapter.

Central Copenhagen has a somewhat regular street pattern, but not quite a grid. And most commercial buildings are also rather unassuming, generally less than 10 stories. There are only a handful of true high-rises scattered across the city, with no major concentration in the city center. Church steeples and a few clock towers tend to break the horizon rather than clusters of high-rise buildings. This lack of a 21st century skyline of modernity gives Copenhagen a greater degree of visual charm,

There are manufacturing districts dotted about the city, but essentially Copenhagen is not a primary industrial center. The city does, however, possess extensive dock facilities, which cruise passengers notice when entering the harbor. Copenhagen is a major seaport because of its strategic location at the head of the Baltic Sea.

The skyline of Copenhagen northeast from the tower in the Christianborg Palace.

CRUISE SHIP DOCKS: There are various docks used by cruise ships in Copenhagen, therefore I cannot be specific as to where you will be docked. Much depends upon the size of your vessel and its itinerary. The three docking locations are:

* **Nordhavn Quay** consists of four docks, each with its own terminal and is capable of handling the largest cruise ships. It is located close to the entrance into Copenhagen Harbor from the Øresund, a distance of approximately 12 kilometers or seven miles from the city center. Taxi or charter bus service is essential for cruises starting or terminating here because of its somewhat isolated location.

* **Langeline** is capable of handling two large or three medium size vessels. It is quite close to the city center, actually a walkable distance for anyone in good condition. I have walked from Langeline into the downtown area on many occasions. This dock is faced by a string of outlet shops but has no terminal facilities. It is approximately four kilometers or 2.4 miles from the city center. Taxi and charter bus service is available for people transferring between the ship and the city with luggage.

* **Nordre Tolbod** is a dock capable of handling one medium to small size cruise ship. It has no terminal but there is a restaurant and gourmet market alongside. This is considered to be a choice location as it is approximately two kilometers or 1.2 miles from the city center. It is also just steps away from the famous Little Mermaid statue. Taxi and charter bus service is available for people transferring between the ship and the city with luggage.

* **Malmö** is Copenhagen's sister city located across the Øresund Strait, actually in Sweden. It is a popular cruise port of call on more upmarket cruise itineraries, and generally not a turnaround port. Train service does exist from the main railway station into Copenhagen for those who wish to visit the city center, although on many cruises stopping in Malmö, Copenhagen is normally part of the itinerary.

SIGHTSEEING IN COPENHAGEN: For the majority of cruises Copenhagen is either the starting or terminating port of call. If your cruise begins in Copenhagen I highly recommend arriving at least two days prior to embarkation. This is one of the great historic cities of Scandinavia and you will find it a captivating and energetic city that you do not want to miss.

If your cruise terminates in Copenhagen you should allow yourself a minimum of two days in which to enjoy this great city. However, many people simply take the guided coach tour of the city while en route to the airport and simply catch a glimpse at what is a city to be savored and enjoyed. Other guests take a guided tour en route to one of the major hotels where the cruise line has contracted to bring departing guests. In this case the tour en route to the hotel is a good way to be introduced to Copenhagen before you establish your own touring schedule. If you have chosen not to spend a day or more in the city, you are missing one of Scandinavia's two great urban centers. The other great Scandinavian city where cruises often either begin or terminate is Stockholm.

* **SIGHTSEEING OPTIONS:** If you are planning on spending time in Copenhagen there are a few options as to getting around to enjoy the many sights of this grand city. These include, but are not limited to one:

** **Ship sponsored tours** – If your ship is simply stopping in Copenhagen as part of a more extended itinerary or in the event that it arrives one day prior to disembarkation then the cruise line will offer a variety of tours within the city. As with all ship sponsored tours you will be part of a group of 20 to 30 or more participants and will be led around at each stop by a tour guide. There are those who like this type of touring, as there is no responsibility in planning on your part. I personally feel that these tours are too superficial and you are removed from more direct contact with the port you are visiting.

** **Private car and driver** – This is my preferred option, but it is of course going to be more costly when booked through the cruise line. The advantage of having a private car and driver is that you have total flexibility to see what interests you the most and linger at each destination as long as you wish. The driver/guide is at your disposal. You may wish to go on line and visit Blacklane at *www.blacklane.com./Private-car/Copenhagen* or 8Rental at *www.8rentsal.com* and enter Copenhagen. You may also wish to check with Tours by Locals at *www.toursbylocals.com* and enter Copenhagen.

** **Rental car** - I do not recommend this option because of the fact that all traffic signs and directions are written only in Danish. And there are very few parking areas adjacent to major attractions. And if you park in a restricted area not knowing so because of the language barrier, your car could be towed. You are better off with a car and driver/guide. A private car is not advantageous in Copenhagen because of the limitations noted in this paragraph.

** **Hop on hop off bus** – A very popular means of getting around is the hop on hop off bus service, which does offer you some degree of flexibility in seeing the city. Check their web page at *www.hop-on-hop-off-bus.com/Copenhagen* for detailed information. Also check out Hop-on-Hop-off Tours for both bus and boat options at their web page, which is *www.getyourguide.com* . Also check out Red Sightseeing at *www.redsightseeing.com* for their options.

** **Taxi service** is available from numerous companies, but it can be rather costly for sightseeing purposes. There are always taxis waiting at the pier if your ship is not disembarking passengers at the end of a cruise, but rather for sightseeing. You can negotiate a tour for several hours or the whole day, as most drivers are fluent in English. If you are staying in a hotel for those whose cruise ends in Copenhagen or has not yet begun, as your concierge about taxi touring.

Touring by taxi is often veery enjoyable and less expensive than having a private car and driver if you find a driver who will give you an hourly rate. Most do speak English or other major European languages in addition to Danish. One company known as Taxa does offer touring by taxi. Check out their web page at *www.taxa.dk* for information on their sightseeing services.

** **Public transportation** – It is easy to get around Copenhagen utilizing the city Metro and commuter rail services providing you are not daunted by the language difference. There are always personnel available to help you in using the automated ticket machines if you find you cannot manage it on your own. The best web page to check is Visit Copenhagen at www.visitcopenhagen.com where bus, Metro and train services are all explained. You will also get information on the Copenhagen Card and Citypass, which will enable you to save on your sightseeing.

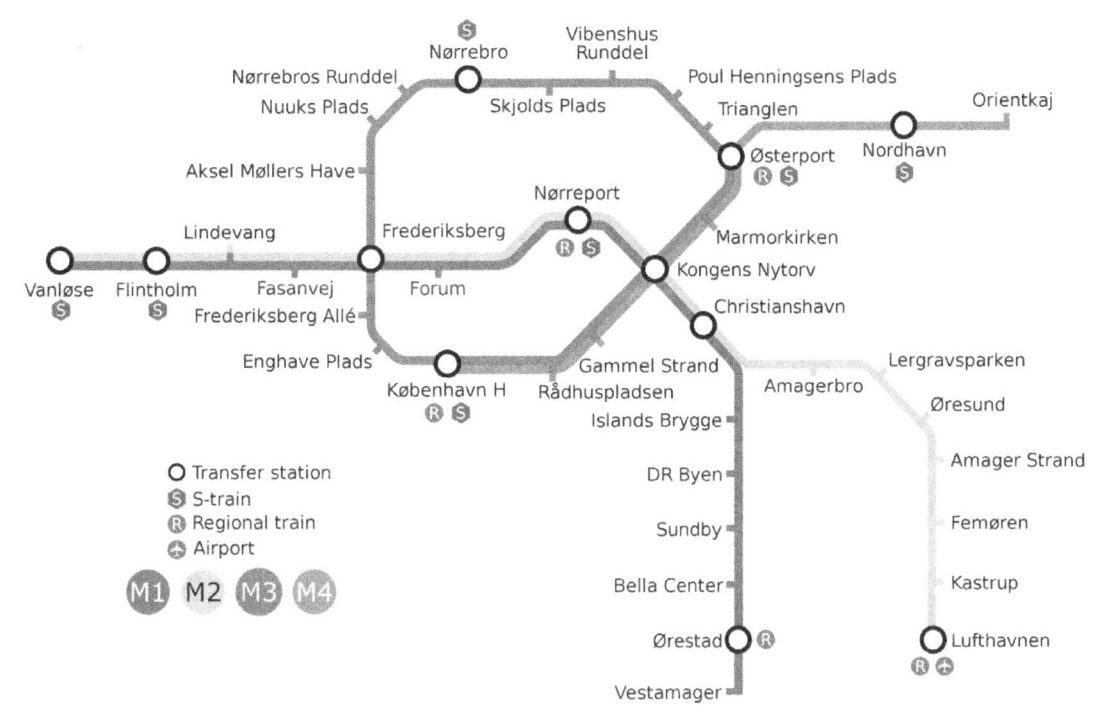

Current map of thee Copenhagen Metro, (Per Wikimedia.org)

** Øresundtåg – This is the high speed train between Helsingør in the north and Malmö, Sweden across the water. You can use this train that runs every half hour to visit Kronborg Castle or go across the bridge to Sweden and spend a few hours visiting Malmö, which is sister city to Copenhagen. Visit for full details at www.oresundtag.se and be sure to engage translation to English.

** Bicycle rental – One easy way to see Copenhagen is by bicycle, if you are capable. As noted before, Copenhagen is one of the most bicycle-oriented cities in Europe, the other major city with this emphasis upon bicycles is Amsterdam. You can easily rent a bicycle in Copenhagen. There are special traffic lanes and also parking lots, so this is one of the best ways to get around. Thousands of people are out and traveling around Copenhagen by bicycle every day, surprisingly even in the rain. But unless you are experienced in riding a bicycle in an urban setting, I caution against it, as you will be tempted to be paying more attention to the sights rather than to riding in traffic.

It is easier to park a bicycle in Copenhagen than to park a car. Bicycle racks are widespread and there are even special parking lots for bicycles. At the central railway station one will find thousands of bicycles belonging to people who commute in and out of the central city.

Here are three well respected and popular bicycle rental companies to check for rental: Copenhagen Bicycles at _www.copenhagenbicycles.dk_ , Bike Rental Copenhagen at _www.bikerentalcopenhagen.dk_ and Copenhagen Bike Rental at _www.copenhagenbikerental.com_ .

The bicycle rules in Copenhagen, as seen here in front of the city's largest department store in the city center

** **Walking** - This is a great city for walking. There are even pedestrian streets and the city has a rather unhurried atmosphere. This is a very safe city in which to walk day or night, and the vast majority of tourist venues are within easy walking distance of the majority of hotels, which tend to be congregated in the city center. You can also combine walking with use of the Metro.

SIGHTS TO SEE IN COPENHAGEN: The city offers a multiplicity of sights that can occupy you for several days, if you have the time. Copenhagen and Malmö combined have a population of two million and both share in a long and glorious history.

There are two focal points to the city center of Copenhagen. One is the **Christianborg Palace** and the second is **Hedbro Plats**, which is located just across the canal from the palace.

The central tower of the Christianborg Palace is open to the public and on a clear day, it provides sweeping 360-degree views of the entire city. It opens at 11 AM daily. The other and larger square is the open plaza in front of the Radhus, or city hall. Located on this larger and most prominent square, it is the very center of the city's downtown area, which like in most European cities, is a mix of residential and commercial buildings essentially cheek by jowl with one another.

The Radhus is a massive brick building with a large clock tower, but in Copenhagen towers are quite common. There are few high-rise in the city, most being located in suburban areas and serving as apartments or condominiums. The inner city is devoted primarily to buildings that date back to the grand days of the 14th through 19th centuries when the city served as a major European port.

Beyond the central city, the remainder of Copenhagen spreads out into the Danish countryside, essentially forming a crescent around the old city. Shaded streets are home to rows of neat little houses, interspersed with beautiful parks and public gardens. There are distinct neighborhoods, each with its own central shopping district, and some with very distinct ethnic flavors because of the Danish government having accepted many immigrants in recent years, especially from the Middle East. But of course this has caused some degree of friction with the Danish people and has helped to segregate these communities from the majority.

The major highlights not to be missed by visitors, shown here in alphabetical order to avoid any bias include:

Amalienborg Palace - home of the Danish monarchy

* **Amalienborg Palace** – Home to the Royal Family where a changing of the

guard is performed daily just before Noon and there is no charge to watch the ceremony. During summer the changing of the guard can draw a moderate crowd, but nothing like that seen in London or Stockholm. The ceremony here is more low key but still quite colorful. This is a palace complex comprised of four separate linked small palaces around a central plaza. Tours are given daily between 11 AM and 4 PM, but you should buy your tickets the day before.

* **Carlsbad Brewery Museum** – The famous Danish brewery is now a museum and gift shop. Carlsberg's Brewery Museum is just southeast of the city center and is one of the stops on the hop on hop off bus tours. It can also be easily accessed by taxi. The museum is located at Gamle Carlsberg Vej in Vesterbro. It is open daily from 10 AM to 5 PM.

* **Christianborg Palace complex** – The seat of the Danish Parliament where, as noted previously, the central tower offers a sweeping view of the city. The tower is open daily from 11 AM to 9 PM for views of the city. The palace and other government buildings are surrounded by a canal that leads off the main channel that separates Copenhagen from Christianhavn.

A sample of a great view from the Christianborg Palace tower

* **Fredericksborg Palace and Gardens** – Used today by the Danish Navy, the grounds are quite magnificent. It is located in the suburb of Fredericksborg, a short taxi ride from the city center. It is also accessible on the Metro line heading west to

the Fredericksborg Station. The palace is not open to the public, but the gardens are open in summer from 6 AM to 11 PM daily. It is in the garden that you will find the famous statue of the Danish king who during World War 11 wore a Star of David arm band, as was required of Jewish Danes.

* **Kastelette** – This great fortress that once protected Copenhagen and now serving as military headquarters is open to visitors. Surrounded by a moat and high grass covered ramparts, it is a very historic and photogenic venue. The grounds of the Kastelette are open from 6 AM to 10 PM daily and there is no admission fee. One beautiful walk is to follow the path around the outer edge of the moat. Another equally beautiful path is found atop the ramparts where you also get spectacular views of the city skyline. The buildings are all part of the military establishment and are not open to the public.

On the ramparts of the Kastelette

* **Little Mermaid** – The signature statue based upon the story of the same name written by Hans Christian Andersen, defines the essence of Copenhagen is located along the waterfront just opposite the Kastelette. This diminutive statue sitting atop a rock may be disappointing to some because it is so small, but it has become the icon of Copenhagen. It is a major stop on the hop on hop off bus and can also be seen from any of the open top harbor cruise boats. An easy way to visit the Little Mermaid if you are boarding your ship in Copenhagen at either Nordre Tolbod or Langeline is to walk over to see her after settling in on board. If you are fortunate

enough to have your cruise ship dock either directly north or south of the statue, she is easily accessible on foot and you can visit more than once. There is no charge to see the statue. Viewing the statue is not inhibited by any barriers and you can see it 24 hours a day.

The Little Mermaid outside the Kastelette - Pride of the city

* **National Museum of Denmark** - Located at Prince's Mansion, Ny Vestargade # 10 in the central city, this is the premier museum of cultural history in Denmark. Plan several hours for your visit, as the collection is quite extensive. The museum is open from 10 AM to 5 PM daily during summer hours. There is a nice restaurant and gift shop within the museum compound.

* **Nyhavn** – The fishermen's harbor located south of the Amalienborg Palace is a major venue for its colorful buildings and seafood restaurants. The small harbor is one of the city's main sites for visitors and it begins at the main square called Kongens Nytorv, which cannot be missed, as it is in effect the heart of the city.

Nyhavn is one of the signature sights of Copenhagen and it appears on travel posters, calendars and other forms of advertising for the city. In addition to enjoying the architecture of the colorful buildings and seeing the fishing boats unloading their valuable cargo, Nyhavn is one of the most popular places in which to dine on fresh seafood. Most restaurants post their menu outside for your inspection. And in the early morning you may see chefs from the Nyhavn restaurants actually selecting their fresh fish right off of the boats.

There are many flat and open tour boats that begin their harbor tours in Nyhavn, so this is a very popular destination, likewise for its many seafood restaurants.

Nyhaven – the fisherman's harbor lined with seafood restaurants..

* **Øresund Bridge and Tunnel** connecting Denmark and Sweden, easily visited by means of the high-speed train between the two countries. Trains run between Copenhagen and Malmö, Sweden roughly every half hour, giving you the chance to cross the bridge once each way.

You can also cross the bridge by automobile, but there is a toll assessed. The automobile crossing is more spectacular because the roadway occupies the upper deck of the bridge giving you a view of its towers. The bridge and tunnel fulfilled a long awaited permanent link between central Europe and the Scandinavian Peninsula, thus eliminating the need for regular ferry boat service.

Remember to take your passport because Sweden does random checks as a result of the number of potential illegal migrant crossings.

* **Radhus** – The old and beautiful city hall and square at the western end of the Strøget is an imposing and monumental structure. Although it look like it dates back to renaissance times, it was actually constructed between 1892 and 1905, inspired by the city hall of Sienna, Italy. It has a high tower that also offers a commanding view of the city, even better than the Christianborg Palace. The tower is open daily from 11 AM to 2 PM, but on Saturday it opens at Noon. It is one of the highest vantage points within the city and vies with the Christianborg Palace tower for its

commanding view.

The magnificent clock tower of the Rådhus - the city hall of Copenhagen

* **Rosenborg Palace** – Home to the Danish crown jewels. The palace is also surrounded by the beautifully landscaped King's Gardens. The gardens are among the most beautiful in the city, especially the rose gardens when they are in full bloom during late spring and summer. It has always been one of my personal favorite spots in Copenhagen to just sit on a park bench and people watch or to simply enjoy all of the flowers in the springtime.

Inside the palace you will see a display of the Danish crown jewels, which are quite impressive. The palace is open for tours between 10 AM and 3 PM Tuesday thru Sunday. There is a small admission fee.

The Rosenborg Palace is home to the crown jewels of Denmark

* **Strøget** – The main pedestrian street of Copenhagen is home to Illum and Magasin du Nord, the two major downtown department stores. It runs between Kongens Nytorv and the Radhus main square. This is the most visited street in the city. The two major department stores are noted for their selection of fine quality Scandinavian housewares and both men's and women's Scandinavian designer clothing.

There are many other fine stores and small eateries located along this pedestrian only street. In addition to shopping, thee Strøget offers many small cafes and bistros that draw significant crowds.

* **Tivoli Gardens** – The 19th Century amusement park in the heart of the city. Tivoli Gardens is best visited at night during the summer months. Its many bands and fireworks add to the 19th century aura. The gardens are directly opposite Central Railway station. It combines the beauty of neatly landscaped grounds with amusement rides, restaurants and outdoor entertainment, especially on long summer nights.

Tivoli Gardens became one of Europe's premier attractions long before the age of Euro Disney. Even in today's modern computer age, the old fashioned rides of Tivoli delight visitors, taking them back to a grand era. During summer Tivoli Gardens is open from 10 AM to Midnight daily. And the evening hours are considered prime time, so buy your tickets early in the day or on line to avoid standing in a long queue.

In the Japanese Garden at Tivoli Gardens

Apart from the palaces, monuments and elegant old buildings in the city center, Copenhagen is about people. The Danes are very warm and friendly, and most speak some English. Sometimes it is just interesting to get onto the Metro, a commuter train or bus and simply visit a suburban district at random. In this way you see a part of the everyday life of Copenhagen with no preconceptions. This is a safe city to visit, and I cannot think of any part of the city where you as a visitor would not be safe. However, I do recommend that as a visitor you do not venture into the immigrant neighborhoods, especially if you are carrying a camera. It is not a safety issue, but more of a comfort matter.

VENUES OUTSIDE OF THE CITY: There are several interesting and important sites to visit outside of the city, and each can easily be reached using the commuter rail system. They include:

* **Fredericksborg Castle** - A magnificent castle about one hour from Copenhagen in the city of Hilerød. King Christian IV commissioned this massive 17th century castle at a period when Denmark was a major power. It is open from 10 AM to 5 PM daily and can be reached from the city by the S-train Line E and then a local bus. At the railway station you can ask for specific directions to the bus.

* **Kronborg Castle** - This brooding castle overlooking the water separating Denmark from Sweden is located in the small city of Helsingør, which can be reached from Central Station via the northbound Øresundtåg. Shakespeare used this castle as the setting for Hamlet and today it is often spoken of as Hamlet's

Castle. It is open daily from 10 AM to 4 PM thru June and hours are extended to 5:30 PM until the end of September. A local shuttle bus will take you to the castle or if you choose, you can walk within about 20 minutes.

Kronborg Castle better known as Hamlet's Castle

* **Louisiana Museum of Modern Art** - This world-renowned museum has a major collection of modern masters. It is also known for its beautiful gardens. Opening hours are from 11 AM to 10 PM Tuesday thru Friday and only until 6 PM on weekends. You can reach the museum by taking the Øresundtåg train from Central Station to the town of Humlebæk and then either walking or taking a local bus. It makes a wonderful full-day outing if you are one who enjoys modern art.

* **Malmö** - This sister city, located across the water in Sweden is often a stop in its own right on many cruise itineraries. Thus there is a chapter later in this book on Malmö that gives you much information on visiting the city. However, if you are coming from Copenhagen, you will most likely be coming by train from Central Station. The train is called the Øresundtåg and it runs approximately on the half hour. The trip takes about 30 minutes and you will arrive in the main railway station in the heart of Malmö, giving you access to all of its major sights. I have both visited the city and also stayed overnight on many occasions. It is quite a significant urban center with an old town, modern central core and some of the most magnificent urban parks to be found in Scandinavia. And it is also home to several very good restaurants. I highly recommend an outing to Malmö.

CHOICE HOTELS: Since Copenhagen is the port of call where most cruises embark or terminate, I have recommended what I consider to be the two best hotels;

one in the five-star category and the other in the four-star category.

* 71 Nyhavn Hotel - Located along the Nyhavn waterfront at # 71, this fine hotel is very well located in the heart of one of the city's most scenic areas. It offers a fine restaurant, but lacks many services such as a dedicated concierge or room service. It also lacks a fitness center. What it features is a great degree of charm and atmosphere that makes up for the other lacking amenities. Their web page is found at *www.71nyhavnhotel.com* . I GIVE IT *** and rate it as $$$ cost wise.

* Hotel D'Angleterre is the top five-star hotel in Copenhagen. It is located on Kongens Nytorv in the heart of the city. It offers the finest in luxury accommodation, dining and all of the services expected from a top hotel. Their breakfast buffet is superb as is their Michelin star restaurant. The only negative that I can point to at the moment is the ongoing construction across from the hotel in Kongens Nytorv where a new Metro station is being built. But this only occurs during the day and does not impact your nighttime quiet. But it does impact the quality of the view from many rooms and suites. Consider this hotel to be five-star in every way, including the price. But the old expression that says you get what you pay for definitely holds true. It is my top choice. Check out their web page for details at *www.ddangleterre.com* . I GIVE IT ***** and rate it as $$$$$ cost wise.

* Crowne Plaza Copenhagen Towers - This modern hotel is located in suburban Tårnby at Ørestads Boulevard # 114-118 and can be accessed from Central Station by commuter rail through Ørestad Station. The hotel offers quality accommodation, restaurant, buffet breakfast, concierge and all other four-star services. It is close to the airport, but some distance by taxi to the cruise ship dock or central city. Their web page is *www.ihg*.com .I GIVE IT ****

* Marriott Hotel Copenhagen - Located near Tivoli Gardens along the water at Kalvebod Brygge # 5, this high-rise hotel is typical of the Marriott brand, one familiar to American visitors. It meets all the requirements of a full service hotel, but it lacks any real degree of Danish flavor. The rooms are well appointed and the hotel features dining, room service, breakfast buffet, concierge service, business services and exercise facilities. Check their web page for details as to the hotel features at *www.marriott.com/Copenhagen* .I GIVE IT **** and rate it as $$$$ cost wise.

* Radisson Blu Scandinavia Hotel is the largest and best-known four-star hotel in the city. It is located opposite the Central Railway Station at Amager Boulevard # 70. This high-rise hotel offers primarily standard rooms that are smartly decorated. Its top rooms are the ones on each of the four corners of the hotel and the higher the floor the better the view. There is also a club level with buffet breakfast and other club amenities. As a major city center hotel, it offers all services including dining, fitness, lounge, concierge, business center, room service and meeting facilities. Of the major hotels it is the most conveniently located to the city center and also to the cruise ship docks. You can easily walk to most of the major historic and cultural venues, and both Tivoli Gardens and the Central Railway Station are mere steps from the hotel's front door. The web site for this Radisson property is *www.radisson-blu-scandinavia-copenhagen.copenhagen-hotel.net* .I GIVE IT **** and rate it as $$$$.

* **Sankt Petri** - This is a boutique hotel with a fine reputation, located in the central city at Krystalgade # 22. As a smaller hotel its guest rooms are very well appointed and have that extra degree of elegance not found in the mass-market hotels. It has a fine dining room, a breakfast buffet, room service, concierge service, business center and fitness center. Their web site is *www.sktpetri.com* .I GIVE IT ***** and rate it as $$$$$.

DINING OUT: And then there is the food. Danish food is heavily oriented toward the sea. It is a seafood lover's paradise. The Danes claim to have invented the open face sandwich. Whether this is true or not, they are absolute artists with the preparation of these delightful morsels. Meats, cheeses, seafood and eggs are the main ingredients of the Danish open face sandwich. To have an open face sandwich followed is a memorable luncheon experience. They are very filling and satisfying, almost a complete meal.

A traditional bakery in Fredericksborg

The Danes are incredible bakers of more than what outside the country is referred to as Danish pastry, usually served at breakfast. In America the term Danish when referring to baked goods is used to describe rather heavy yeast dough pastries eaten at breakfast. But in Denmark the breakfast pastries are light and tender, with butter used rather than oil, as is typical in American Danish. It is a shame that the term Danish is even used and in a way it is an insult to fine Danish baking.

There are many high-end restaurants in Copenhagen, some requiring reservations well in advance. But I personally find these establishments to be rather trendy and too innovative in their attempt to be different rather than following age old values. Over the years of visiting Copenhagen, I have found a few cafes that serve traditional Danish cuisine without the glitz and attempts at grandeur. Here are my recommended choices shown alphabetically:

* **Cafe at Magasin du Nord** - If you are in the Strøget, a good place for a traditional lunch is the cafe on the top floor of Magasin du Nord Department Store. Served cafeteria style, there is a selection of hot entrees, open face sandwiches, salads and desserts, all with traditional Danish flare. Opening hours are from 10 AM to 8 PM daily. Reservations are not needed.

* **Cafe-Petersborg** - This is my favorite restaurant in Copenhagen, and it is located within walking distance of where the majority of cruise ships dock, located at Bredgade 76. When looking at TripAdvisor, this establishment rates a 4.6 out of 5, showing that it is well recognized. A local resident of some note first made me aware of it. Their specialty is the traditional Danish smorgasbord, which is served in stages at your table rather than you having to go to the traditional buffet. The choices are simply sumptuous - incredibly delicious salads, beautiful smoked fish, pork and cheeses. You come away totally satisfied. They are open Monday and Saturday from 11:30 AM to 4 PM and Tuesday thru Friday from 11:30 AM to 9 PM. You can book a table at +45 33 12 50 16.

* **Husmann's Vinstue** - In the heart of the city at Larsbjørnsstrade # 2, this very popular traditional restaurant is noted for its traditional Danish cuisine, especially its open face sandwiches and seafood dishes. The overall atmosphere is inviting and the service is friendly and attentive. The restaurant is open Monday thru Friday from 11:30 AM to 6 PM and on Saturday from Noon to 5 PM. You can reach them at +45 33 11 58 86 to book a table.

* **Kokkeriet** – Located at Kronprinsessegade 65 near the Rosenborg Palace, this is a superb choice for a fine, elegant dinner. The menu features traditional Danish cuisine and seafood prepared with great flair and elegance, making this a wise choice for a great evening experience. Dinner is served Monday thru Saturday from 5 PM to 1 AM and you need to book a table at +45 33 15 27 77.

* **Marv & Ben** – This superb restaurant is found near the Christianborg Palace at Snaregade 4. Their elegant menu is based upon traditional Scandinavian themes, which of course will include an emphasis upon seafood. The ambiance and service are as fine as the cuisine. Dinner is served nightly from 5 PM to 1 AM 11 PM Monday thru Saturday. Call +45 23 81 02 91 to book a table.

* **Pescatarian (The)** – This is a superb restaurant for dinner located near the Kastelette and the cruise ship docks. It is at Amaliegade 49. This is an elegant restaurant with superb Danish cuisine having an emphasis upon seafood. The service and ambiance are also top notch. Dinner is served Monday thru Saturday from 5 PM to 1 AM. Call to book a table in advance at +45 30 63 82 22.

* **Restaurant Amalie** - Located near the Amalienborg Palace on Amaliegade # 11, this is a very traditional restaurant with an excellent reputation for traditional cuisine. Their staff is very welcoming and the service is outstanding. There is much to choose from including herring, salmon, pork dishes, all beautifully presented. The restaurant is open Monday thru Friday from 11:30 AM to 4 PM closing extended to 5 PM on Saturday. You can call +45 33 12 88 10 to book a table.

* **Restaurant Krebsegaarden** - Located just north of the city hall square at Studiestræde # 17, this is a high-end restaurant with an impeccable reputation. I do suggest a reservation because of the nature of establishment. This is a fine dining restaurant, yet the atmosphere is casual and inviting rather than being pompous. The varied menu includes seafood, meats, poultry and a varied selection of preparation methods. This is Danish haute cuisine. The restaurant is open only for dinner Tuesday thru Saturday from 5 to 11 PM. Have your hotel book a table in advance. Call them at +45 2012 40 15 if you wish to book a table.

* **Restaurant Under Uret** - This central city restaurant is located at Oster Farimagsgade # 4, which is walking distance from most major central city hotels. It is a very traditional restaurant with a heavy emphasis upon seafood and the traditional smorrebrod, which is similar to a Swedish smorgasbrød. I highly recommend it because it offers a variety of tastes in one sitting. They are open daily from 11:30 AM to 4 PM. Call +45 28 35 35 10 if you wish to book a table.

* **Restaurante Amadeus** - Located at Kongensgade 62, this basement cafe is noted for its delicate open face sandwiches and a mouthwatering selection of traditional Danish pastries. It is the perfect stop for a light lunch when in the city center. Or if you are really hungry and order a selection of their open face sandwiches, it constitutes a full meal that is delicious. The opening hours are from 10 AM to 6 PM Monday thru Wednesday and until 11 PM Thursday and Midnight on Friday and Saturday. It is not necessary to book a table.

I also direct you to the chapter on Malmö where I have two favorites that you will find listed in the chapter on that city. This is not to say that Copenhagen lacks fine quality dining establishments for dinner. But during summer I find them to be relatively crowded and overpriced whereas in Malmö there is a more relaxed atmosphere and the cuisine is equal to what you will find in Copenhagen. Taking the train there and back adds to the overall evening, as you are in essence dining in another country.

SHOPPING: Copenhagen is a great city for shopping. The Strøget is the main shopping street where you will find high-end merchandise, much of it being of Scandinavian origin. Men's and women's fashion and housewares are two of the important items produced in Denmark and Sweden, and available along this pedestrian street. There are also many furniture design studios, as Denmark is famous for its modern style of furniture and accessories. Of course any such purchases would necessitate the expense of shipping unless the particular design studio has an outlet in your home country.

There are two major department stores featuring a high end array of clothing, accessories and housewares, much of the merchandise being of Scandinavian origin. I highly recommend visiting each of the following:

* **Fields Shopping Mall** - This is the second largest shopping mall in Denmark and offers a wide selection of shops, dining establishment and entertainment venues. It is open daily from 10 AM to 8 PM with extended hours on Friday from 6 AM to Midnight.

Field's is in suburban Amager West and can be reached on the southbound Metro to Ørestad Station. It is very easy for those who enjoy shopping to spend many hours inside this mall.

* **Fisketorvet Shopping Mall** - This very modern mall is the largest in Denmark and is quite an attraction. It offers shopping, dining and entertainment under one large roof. It is located on the Kalvebrod Brygge waterfront just south of the city center. It has 120 retail establishments and is open daily from 10 AM to 8 PM with extended hours on Friday from 8 AM to Midnight.

It can be reached from Central Railway Station by taking a train to Dybbølsbro Station and walking across the railway overpass. Shoppers from abroad will find this a very enticing mall, as there are many high end brand names that are produced in Scandinavia.

* **Illum** - Located along the Strøget, this is one of the two major department store of Copenhagen. It is a bit more upscale than Magasin du Nord (see listing below), but does carry many of the same Scandinavian brand names. The store is open from 10 AM to 8 PM daily, extended to 11 PM on Thursday.

* **Magasin du Nord** - Located on Kongens Nytorv, the square that is presently being redeveloped for a new Metro station. It is hard to miss this magnificent 19th century building facing the square. Magasin du Nord covers a city block and has many floors of merchandise, including so many famous Scandinavian brand names.

The store is open from 10 AM to 8 PM daily, with extended hours to 10 PM Thursday thru Sunday.

Along the Strøget leading to Illum Department Store

* **Royal Copenhagen China** - The primary showroom for this famous brand of Danish tableware is located along the Strøget. The traditional blue and white fine porcelain is famous worldwide. And the shop will ship your purchases. The main store is located at Amagertorv # 6 and is open Monday thru Friday 10 AM to 7 PM and on Saturday until 8 PM.

FINAL WORDS: There is an old song whose lyrics sings the city's praises, "Wonderful, wonderful Copenhagen, salty old queen of the sea….." This is truly a city built by the sea and one whose entire history has been related to its strategic location. Today Copenhagen has no fears of any military invasion, as it did when Denmark was a major player in European history. Today it simply enjoys its importance as the old grand city of Scandinavia.

And Denmark prides itself as being the gateway to Scandinavia, especially now with its road and rail bridge connection to Sweden. And it surprisingly is also the aviation gateway to all of Scandinavia. There are a few direct flights from North America to Stockholm and fewer to Oslo. Likewise Stockholm receives some flights from Eastern Europe and the Middle East. But the majority of overseas traffic is directed to Copenhagen. Scandinavian Airways System, which is jointly operated by Denmark, Norway and Sweden, is headquartered in Copenhagen. Scandinavian Airways System, better known as SAS, is a global airline with flights between Stockholm and most major cities in Europe, Asia and North America. It was one of the earliest airlines to use great circle routes with polar flights to shorten the distances between cities.

The nexus for travel around Copenhagen and into Sweden is Central Station

The only negative statement that many visitors often have about Copenhagen is that the central city is rather congested and does not have the beautiful panoramic vistas of the waterfront, nor the number or scope of magnificent parks that are found in Oslo, Stockholm and Helsinki. And many of the public buildings and palaces are constructed of dark red brick, lending a rather dark appearance to the landscape rather that the stone or painted plaster seen in the other major Scandinavian cities.

I accept this argument and in many ways agree, but appearances are only a part of the picture. Copenhagen may be the least beautiful of the Scandinavian cities, but makes up for it through the warmth of its people, their joy of living and their excellent gastronomy.

COPENHAGEN CITY MAPS

MAP OF THE CITY OF COPENHAGEN

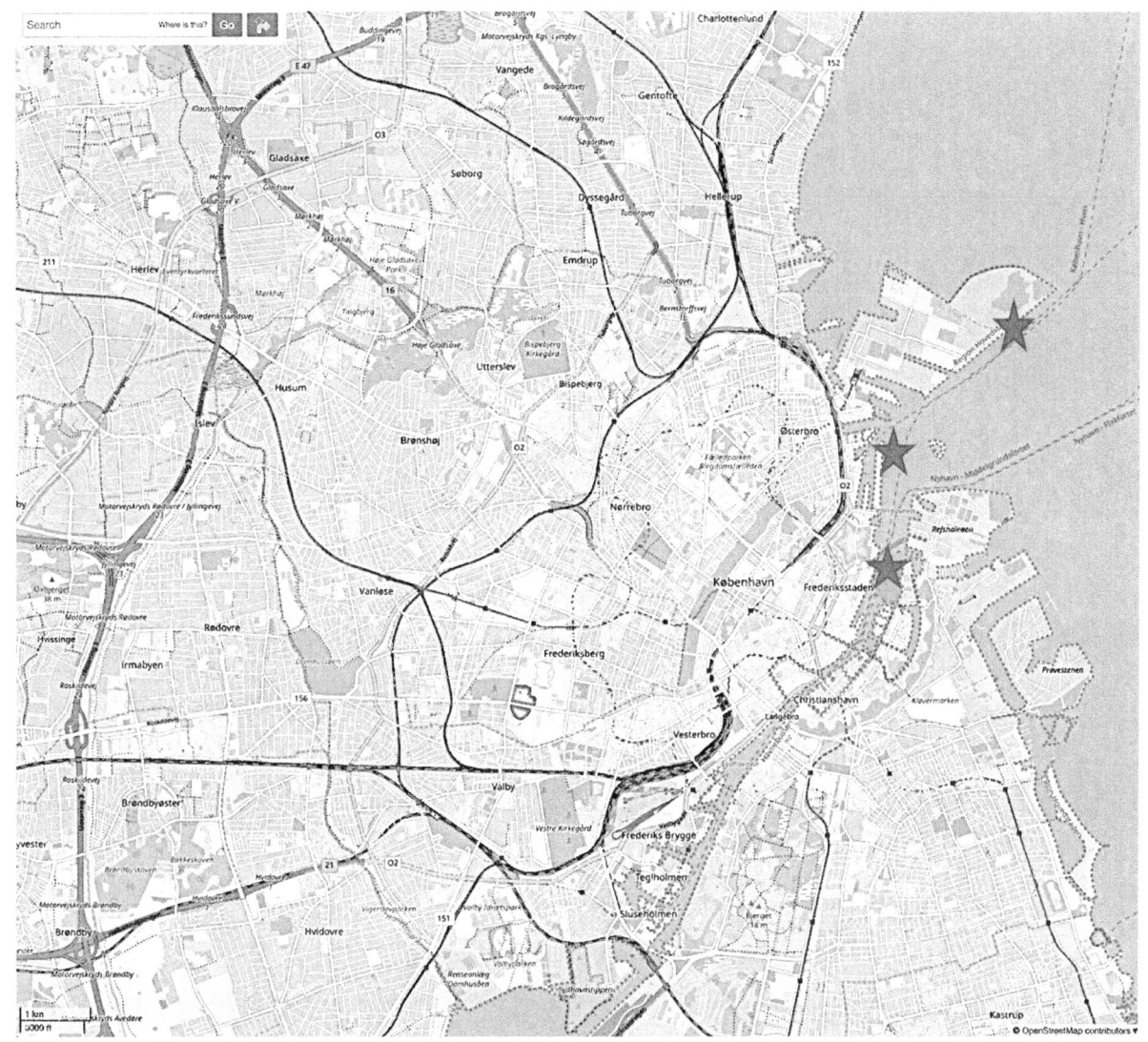

The city of Copenhagen with stars showing cruise ship docks, (© OpenStreetMap contributors)

This map is best viewed directly from OpenStreetMap.com on your personal device where it can be expanded or one specific area can be enlarged. Given the format of this book, it is impossible to display maps with the level of detail you might wish to have while actually out exploring the city. But the OpenStreetMap maps used directly are the tool I always rely upon.

MAP OF CENTRAL COPENHAGEN

Central Copenhagen, (© OpenStreetMap contributors)

This map is best viewed directly from OpenStreetMap.com on your personal device where it can be expanded or one specific area can be enlarged. Given the format of this book, it is impossible to display maps with the level of detail you might wish to have while actually out exploring the city. But the OpenStreetMap maps used directly are the tool I always rely upon.

MAP OF TIVOLI GARDENS AREA

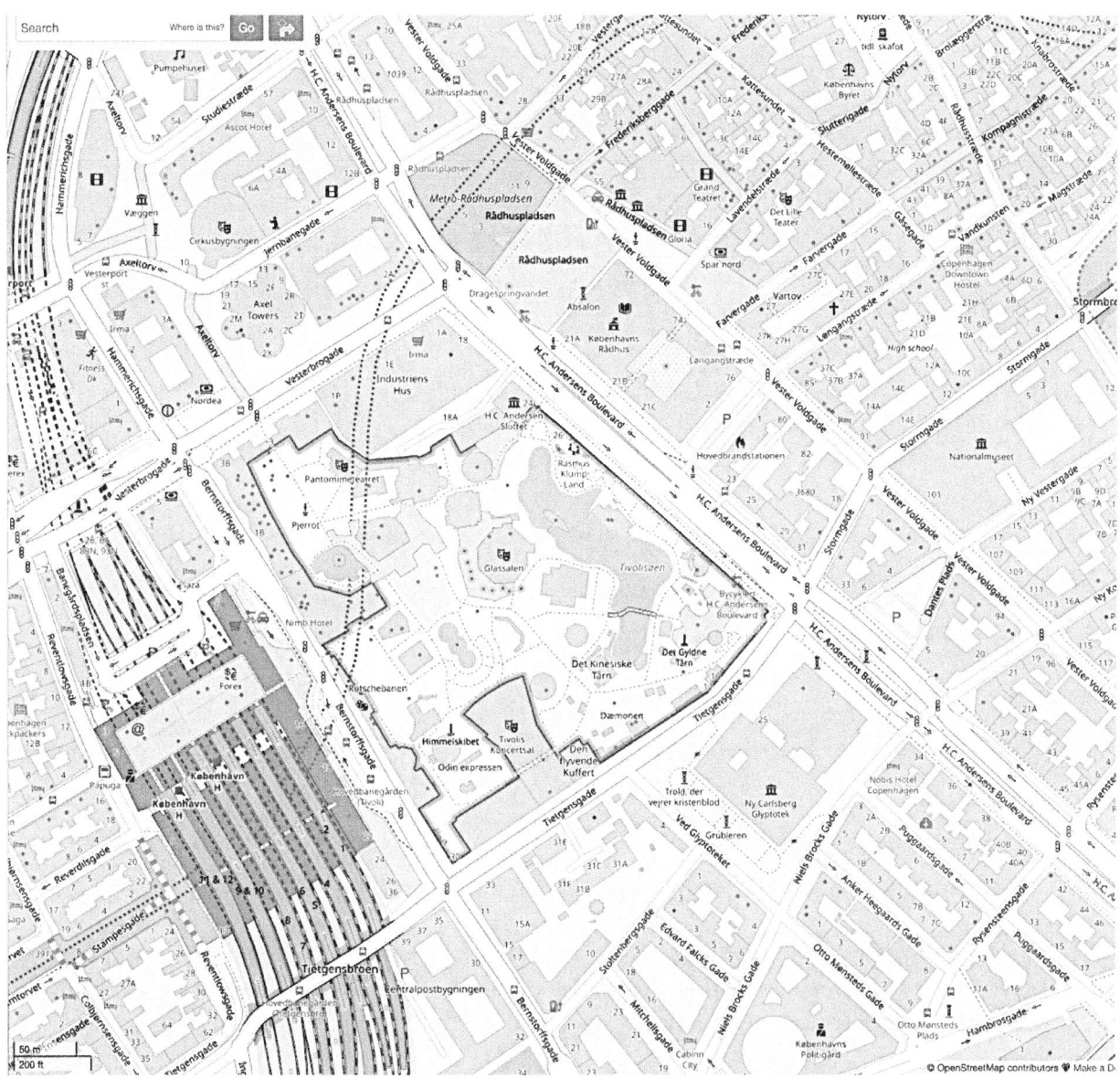

Tivoli Gardens area, (© OpenStreetMap contributors)

This map is best viewed directly from OpenStreetMap.com on your personal device where it can be expanded or one specific area can be enlarged. Given the format of this book, it is impossible to display maps with the level of detail you might wish to have while actually out exploring the city. But the OpenStreetMap maps used directly are the tool I always rely upon.

BORNHOLM ISLAND, DENMARK

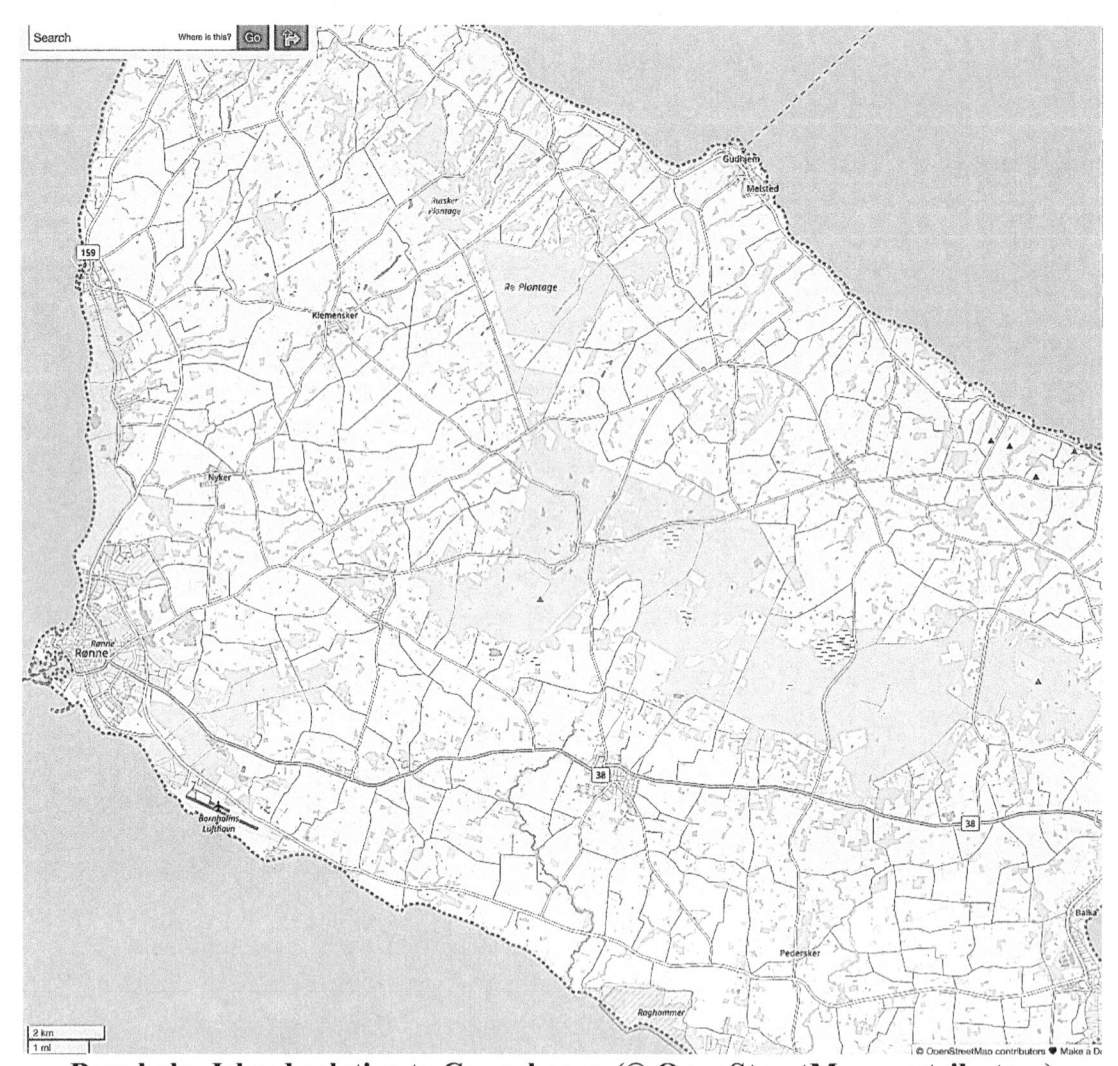

Bornholm Island relative to Copenhagen (© OpenStreetMap contributors)

Very few major cruise itineraries include the island of Bornholm, a part of Denmark. If your cruise includes this rocky island, you will be visiting a destination that few of your friends who have cruised the Baltic can lay claim to having visited.

THE PHYSICAL LANDSCAPE OF BORNHOLM ISLAND: The island of Bornholm occupies a strategic position in the western Baltic Sea, located at a point nearly midway between Denmark, Sweden and Germany. This gave the island a strategic position and therefore made it vulnerable during World War II to Nazi occupation.

Bornholm is the second largest island in the Baltic Sea, covering 588 square kilometers or 227 square miles. By Danish standards it is considered to be one of the country's more rugged areas, its highest elevation reaching 162 meters or 531 feet above sea level. The northern part of the island is relatively rocky, consisting of outcrops of bare continental rock scoured by glaciers during the great ice age. The remainder of the island is relatively low lying and consists of fine sediments giving it a significant agricultural potential. There are nice sandy beaches around the southern margins of the island whereas the northern portion rises quite abruptly from the sea. Bornholm is covered in a mix of pine and broadleaf deciduous trees, but little of the forest cover remains in most areas because of the development of farmland.

Limestone outcrops all over Bornholm, (Work of 7alaskan, CC BY SA 3.0, Wikimedia.org)

The climate is maritime, but more moderate than mainland Denmark, as it is less directly influenced by storms that move across from the North Sea. The island has around a 30 percent rate of possible sunshine and receives an average of nearly 610 millimeters or 24 inches of rain per year.

The main settlement on Bornholm is the island administrative center of Rønne with around 14,000 residents, approximately 35 percent of the nearly 40,000 residents of the island. Ferry and catamaran service exist between Rønne and Copenhagen, Germany, Sweden and Poland. And there is air service to Copenhagen. A few cruise lines, especially those in the high-end market with smaller ships do include Rønne on some of their itineraries. But the majority of cruise lines simply pass by the island. If you are on a cruise that visits Bornholm you will find it a very pleasant experience and a chance to enjoy the rural side of Denmark as opposed to visiting Copenhagen. The island is Denmark's lesser known gem.

A BRIEF LOCAL HISTORY: The name of the island appears as early as the 9th century, and it believed that quite possibly the name Burgundy, a region in France, may result from the settlement of Germanic tribes who took the name from the island. This has yet to become a totally accepted fact, but remains speculative and intriguing.

The fate of Bornholm was contested for two centuries between the Archbishop of Lund and the Danish crown, each building their own fortresses on the island. In 1525, the island came under control from Lübeck, but in 1645, it was attacked and conquered by Sweden. Although Sweden returned the island to Denmark in 1645, it was ceded back in 1658 under the Treaty of Roskilde that had settled the war between the two kingdoms. The people of Bornholm rebelled against Swedish military occupation and then once winning their revolt they gifted the territory to King Frederick III of Denmark, stipulating that the island never again be separated from Denmark. From that time on Bornholm remained an integral part of the Danish kingdom and saw no foreign troops on its soil until World War II.

In 1940, German forces invaded Bornholm, making the island an important base because of its strategic position essentially near the entrance to the Baltic Sea. In the event British or later American submarines would attempt to infiltrate the Baltic, Germany's forces on Bornholm would be a first line of defense. As the war progressed, however, the allies never attempted to penetrate the Baltic Sea. As the war came toward its conclusion, the Soviet Air Force bombed Bornholm because the German commandant refused to surrender to the Soviet Navy. The Germans wanted to surrender to the Western Allies rather than the Soviets, knowing full well how they would be treated if they were taken east. The Soviet bombing of the Island resulted in the destruction of approximately 3,000 homes in the two main communities of Rønne and Nexø, killing many Danish civilians. Soviet forces ultimately landed on Bornholm and captured the German garrison, and then the Soviet forces remained for nearly one year before giving the island back to Denmark since it was the innocent party. The only reason the Soviets gave the island back was to maintain peaceful relations with the West since occupation of Danish territory would have been seen as naked aggression.

Following the war, Denmark became a signatory to the North Atlantic Treaty Alliance, but in keeping with their pledge to the Soviet Union, no NATO forces other than Danish have ever allowed to be stationed on Bornholm. That was a major Soviet stipulation in their return of Bornholm to Denmark. Today with the Soviet Era behind us, there is no threat from Russia with regard to Bornholm.

THE PHYSICAL LAYOUT OF THE CITY: Rønne is a very small city, actually more of a town. There is a small manmade harbor mainly for small craft and the local ferryboat. Small to medium size cruise ships can dock, but only one at a time, thus most large cruise ships do not include it on their itinerary.

Rønne is somewhat hilly, rising up gently from the shoreline. The streets are quite regular, but many of them are either cobbled or paved in stone. This is such a small community that you can walk from the town center to its eastern margins in less than 20 minutes.

Rønne from the air, (Work of Andreas Faessler, CC BY SA 3.0, Wikimedia.org)

The houses, many of which are post WWII because of the bombing, are primarily constructed of brick. Only those older houses that survived the war are constructed of plaster, often with wood trim, representing styles that date back two or more centuries. Both the older houses in Rønne and those built after World War II, tend to have steeply pitched tile roofs, generally red. And many of the older houses are painted yellow, which seems to have some traditional significance across rural Denmark. These older houses have what some architectural students call "gingerbread." This style is seen in many rural Danish villages and is most famous in the northern Danish town of Skagen. Most houses in Rønne are very close to the street and have very small front gardens, if at all.

SHIP TENDER/DOCKING SERVICE: The harbor is quite tiny, but it can accommodate the local ferry or a very small adventure cruise ship. Thus almost all cruise ships that do visit Rønne will anchor offshore and tender guests to the dockside in the harbor. A few of the more upscale cruise lines are capable of docking their smaller ships in Rønne. From there it is a short distance to the town center, but some cruise lines do provide a shuttle. The distance is approximately 1.6 kilometers or one mile to the town center.

The limited dock for small cruise ships in Rønne

The more upmarket cruise lines may offer a shuttle bus into the center of Rønne, but frankly it is really not necessary, as the walk is along the waterfront and should be a part of your enjoyment of the community. The distance from the dock to the center of Rønne is less than two kilometers and is quite enjoyable.

VISITING BORNHOLM: If you are fortunate enough to be on a cruise ship that calls in at Rønne, you will find it a very rewarding experience. Once on shore, tours are offered to explore the island, but Rønne itself is so small that it is best seen on foot.

* SIGHTSEEING OPTIONS ON BORNHOLM: The island is relatively small, but it has a well-developed tourist infrastructure, which offers you several touring options. These are:

** Ship sponsored motor coach or walking tours – Your cruise line will offer several group tours either by motor coach around the island or walking excursions in the small, but distinctive city of Rønne.

If you prefer the privacy of not being part of a group you may also wish to check with Guide Service Denmark at *www.guideservicedanmark.dk* to see what they can offer by way of private touring.

The skyline of Rønne from the harbor

** Private car and driver – This service can be arranged through your cruise line by contacting the shore excursion desk. Private touring is relatively costly but many people, myself included, prefer the freedom of exploring those aspects of a port that most interest them, and without being rushed. You may wish to check on line with www.limos.com/airports/denmark/RNN for local private details.

** Rental cars – There are several rental car services on Bornholm with offices in Rønne. However, I caution against driving yourself, as the roads are relatively narrow and all road sign information is provided in Danish only. Several agencies are found including Hertz, Europcar and Avis. Check on line to see if your preferred agency is listed.

** There are no hop on hop off busses on Bornholm. However, the local bus service does connect the entire island with Rønne. For details send an email to the local tourist office at *info@bornholm.info* telling them what you are seeking.

** Taxi services are available – Check with any taxi driver waiting at the dock to see if you can negotiate a rate for several hours or the entire day. Most speak very good English. The main taxi company is Vognmandsforeningen Dan Taxi, however they do not have a web page. Their phone contact is +45 56 95 23 01.

** Bicycle rental – Danes are very much into riding bicycles. There are bicycle rentals available on Bornholm Island. The best rated company is Sømarkens

Cykeludlejning. Check their web page at *www.somarkenscykeludlejning.dk* for details.

Real Danish pastry

On the main shopping street of Rønne.

Craft market in the town square

Like in Copenhagen, the bicycle is a major means of local transport

** **Walking** – The small city of Rønne is very walkable and pedestrians are totally safe. However, limiting yourself to walking does not give you a wide range to explore.

* **SIGHTS TO SEE IN BORNHOLM:** The major historic sights to see in Rønne shown alphabetically include:

** **Bornholm Museum** - This small museum explores the natural and social history of the island and is worth a visit. It is located on Sankt Mortensgade. It is open on weekdays from 1 to 4 PM and on Saturday from 11 AM to 3 PM.

** **Kastellet** - A round defensive tower was built in 1689 for the protection of the town, but it never saw any military action. It is open to visitors when ships are in port, but no specific hours are given.

** **Rønne Lighthouse** - Built in 1880 and active until 1989, standing near Saint Nicholas Church, it is one of the main features to break the town's skyline. It is built of cast iron and makes quite a statement on the horizon although it is no longer in use. It is open daily but again no specific hours are listed. But when a cruise ship is visiting, it is sure to be open for the duration of the port call.

The Rønne Lighthouse and the Saint Nicholas Church

** Saint Nicholas Church - This is the major church dominating over the Rønne skyline, the oldest part of the building dating to the 13th century. It sits above the harbor at Kirkepladsen #20 and is open daily from 9 AM to 4 PM.

** Town Square - Here in the heart of Rønne you will find a selection of shops and cafes, but do not expect a sophisticated city. This is essentially a large village, but it is colorful and charming and is more typically Danish than the main streets of Copenhagen

A small square in the heart of Rønne.

If you take a tour around the island of Bornholm, usually offered by the cruise line, or it can be private in a local taxi, the main sights will include:

** Ekkodalen - Here is one of the rare spots in all of Denmark where you see a rift in the island's crust, presenting a rugged narrow valley. With Denmark being essentially a flat country, this is an area of rugged landscape that to the Danes is atypical. The valley is also noted for its ability to produce an echo from certain locations.

** Hammershus - A 13th century castle now in ruins since it was abandoned in 1745, but standing as a testament to the medieval history of the island. It is a popular spot with locals for a picnic because of its view out over the sea because of its high promontory location at the northern tip of the island. Normally this is on any trans island coach tour. Opening hours are not currently available, but if you visit on your own you can be sure it will be open on days when a ship is in port.

** Osterlars Rundkirke - Located in the village of Gudhjem, this round church dates back to the 12th century and has been beautifully maintained.
Gudhjem og Norresand Havn Bornholm - Another medieval round church located in the village of Gudhjem. It is open Tuesday thru Saturday from 9 AM to 2:45 PM.

Ronne's gingerbread houses

Various styles of gingerbread

Typical Bornholm style housing

DINING IN RØNNE: There are several nice restaurants around the shores of Bornholm because a small amount of tourism, especially catering to the local Danish visitor, is a very important part of the summertime economy. But unless you take an all day tour around the island, it is not likely you will have lunch included on one of the ship excursions. In the event that you take your own taxi tour around the island, there is a chance to have lunch in a local restaurant.

In Rønne you have a few options for lunch that will give you a chance to experience the rural Danish flavor. I have listed the few restaurants I know in Rønne:

* **Cafe Gustav** - Located at Stor Torv # 8 on the main square, this is a nice restaurant for lunch. The menu is diverse and meals are based upon fresh local ingredients. They serve traditional seafood dishes, especially herring, but for visitors they also make a decent hamburger. The restaurant is open daily from 10 AM to 9 PM Monday thru Thursday closing at 10 PM on Friday and Saturday. Sunday opening is delayed until 11 AM and closing is at 9:30 PM. Reservations are not required.

* **Restaurant Le Port** - Located at Vang #81 in Hasle, just south of Hammershus, this is an outstanding restaurant for lunch. Their traditional Scandinavian dishes with a heavy emphasis upon seafood will delight any visitor. They are open Tuesday thru Sunday from Noon to 3 PM. and in the evening from 6 to 11:30 PM. Reservations are necessary. Call to book at +45 56 96 92 01.

Cafe life on the main square in Rønne

*** Restaurant Skovly** - Located at Nyker Strandvej 40 north of Rønne is an excellent choice for lunch. Their food is freshly made using the finest local ingredients, especially the locally caught seafood. And their breads and desserts are all very traditional. You will need to take a taxi to get here. And you should have the local hospitality rep make a reservation prior to leaving the ship. No specific hours of service are given, but it is sure to be open when a ship is in port. To check on hours or book a table call them at +45 56 95 07 84.

SHOPPING ON BORNHOLM: There are some local handcraft items such as knitted ware or wood carving, but it is difficult to find in most villages, but somewhat available in a few shops in Rønne. There are also numerous potters on the island producing some exquisite pottery, but that is not an easy item to purchase when on a cruise. The most famous product is the long case clock (grandfather clock) that was once handcrafted on the island. But today these are rare and difficult to find.

There is often a local flea market held in the main square of Rønne, and if you are fortunate to be there on one of the days when it is held, you may find some handcraft items.

For a Danish treat while walking or to take back to the ship, remember Denmark is the home of "real" Danish pastry

FINAL WORDS: Bornholm may not be the highlight of your Baltic Sea cruise, but it is a somewhat quaint and charming island to visit. When many travelers book a Baltic Sea cruise, they are looking for the major cities and historic sites, and Bornholm does not meet those expectations. Yet despite its quiet charm, there is a long history of settlement dating to pre Viking times. But give this quiet island a chance and you will come away with an appreciation of rural life in Denmark. And remember that people have been living here for 1,000 years, so there is a sense of history in the more humble architecture that you will see.

The town of Rønne is very typical of many mainland Danish towns and villages. Even though much of it was bombed during World War II and later rebuilt, some of its early architecture did survive or was lovingly rebuilt and it adds a measure of character to the community. There is an inherent charm to Rønne despite not having any great monumental structures or large museums. This is rural Denmark and should be savored for what it is. And the people are welcoming and very polite to visitors, a characteristic that is true of all Denmark.

BORNHOLM MAPS

THE GREATER AREA OF RØNNE

Greater Rønne, (© OpenStreetMap contributors)

This map is best viewed directly from OpenStreetMap.com on your personal device where it can be expanded or one specific area can be enlarged. Given the format of this book, it is impossible to display maps with the level of detail you might wish to have while actually out exploring the city. But the OpenStreetMap maps used directly are the tool I always rely upon.

THE TOWN OF RØNNE

The village of Rønne, (© OpenStreetMap contributors)

This map is best viewed directly from OpenStreetMap.com on your personal device where it can be expanded or one specific area can be enlarged. Given the format of this book, it is impossible to display maps with the level of detail you might wish to have while actually out exploring the city. But the OpenStreetMap maps used directly are the tool I always rely upon.

MALMÖ, SWEDEN

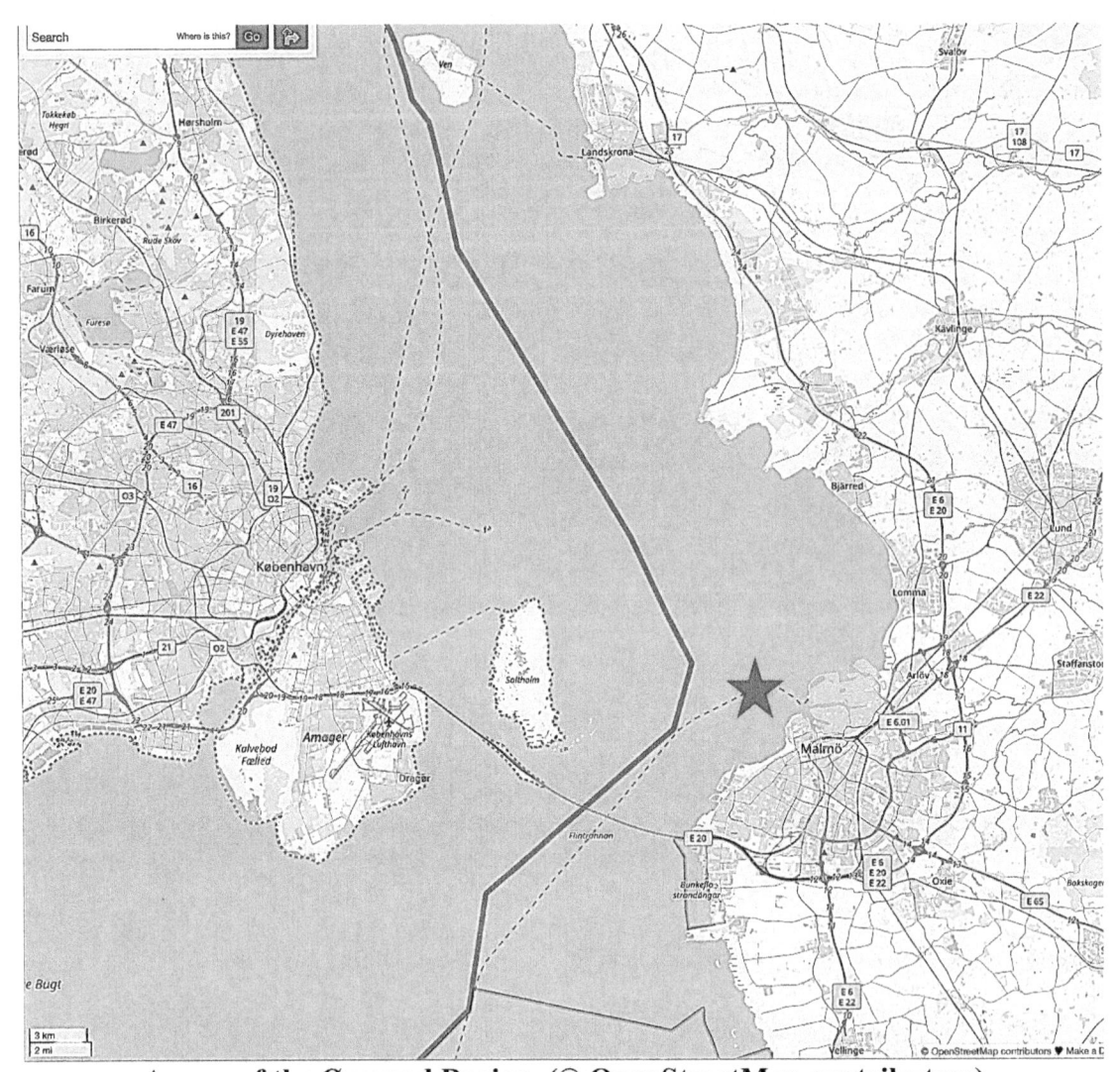

A map of the Øresund Region. (© OpenStreetMap contributors)

Malmö is the third largest city in Sweden with a population of over 680,000, yet it is not well known to visitors from abroad despite being just minutes by train from the center of Copenhagen. The city is essentially part of the Danish-Swedish international urbanized zone called the Øresund Region that includes Copenhagen. For centuries there was a degree of separation between the two cities because it required a ferryboat trip of approximately 24 kilometers or 15 miles between the two harbors of Malmö and Copenhagen, taking 1.5 hours or more to make the crossing. Visionaries had dreamed of a bridge and/or tunnel linking the two cities, and in effect joining both nations. On July 1, 2000, that dream came true with the 17-kilometer or 11-mile long Øresund Bridge and Tunnel. It is now possible for both vehicular and rail traffic to cross freely between the two cities. What has developed is an integrated metropolis, which would then make the combined cities of Malmö and Copenhagen the largest urban area in Scandinavia. Yet the two cities still

maintain their cultural identity and national pride, one being Swedish and the other Danish. With both countries being members of the European Union, passports and border formalities had been eliminated. But in the last five years Sweden has seen an influx of illegal migrants and thus now has a passport check at their end of the bridge for incoming traffic, both by road and rail. On the upper roadway deck a simple sign at the mid-point on the bridge indicates that you are crossing into Sweden or Denmark and prior to Sweden's implementation of passport checks that was the only way to know you had crossed between the two countries.

The border between Sweden and Denmark on the Øresund Bridge

Regular commuter train service connects the center of Malmö with the main railway station in Copenhagen, the journey taking about 30 minutes. Trains continue north on the Danish side to Helsingør where a ferry link connects the city with Helsinborg, Sweden. Many of the trains passing through Malmö are long distance services that link Copenhagen with Stockholm, Göteborg and Oslo. And the local express known as the Øresundtåg begins in Helsingør on the Danish side and many continue on to Helsinborg most terminate in Malmö.

Few cruise line itineraries include Malmö because Copenhagen is often either the embarkation or terminal port for a great number of Baltic Sea cruises. However, there are a few more unique itineraries that link Baltic ports with those along the Norwegian coast, and in these instances Malmö is often included as a port of call.

THE NATURAL SETTING: Modern Sweden is about the size of California, and it has a population of around 9,000,000 people. The country shares a mountainous border with Norway to the west, all of its rivers draining to the Gulf of Bothnia, the northern arm of the Baltic Sea. Southern Sweden contains rich farmland and the country is noted for its fine dairy products. The far north is well into the Arctic tundra and is very sparsely populated. It is primarily the home to the semi-nomadic reindeer herders known as the Sámi, people we call the Laplanders.

The coastal lowlands north of Malmö

Sweden is also a highly industrialized nation, specializing in high tech products. Its industrial role has diminished somewhat, especially in the manufacturing of fine quality automobiles. Saab, once an automotive producer, today is noted for its jet fighters, and the JAS Gripen is said to be every bit as agile and deadly as the American F-16. It is sold to other nations, but Sweden's munitions and aircraft are not sold to countries where hostile intent is evident. Sweden is also noted for its quality furniture and glassware. Two noted Swedish brands are Ikea, the major home furniture and furnishings retailer and Orrefors, a fine Swedish brand of elegant crystal. Most Swedish people live in modern, ultra clean cities and towns, primarily in the southern half of the country.

Sweden is a country that was heavily glaciated during the last ice age. The country is dotted with thousands of lakes, some of them being among the largest lakes in Europe. The coastline is most irregular, containing many deep-water indentations and offshore islands, but given that there are no mountains bordering these beautiful harbors and narrow bays, they are not technically called fjords. All of Sweden is thickly forested, its farmland having been carved from the ancient woodlands. Green and blue are the two colors that describe the natural landscape. The forests that begin in Norway and Sweden pick up again in Finland, across the waters of the Gulf of Bothnia, and then extend clear across Russia to the Pacific Ocean, picking up again in Alaska and extending across Canada to the Atlantic Ocean once again. This vast forest of spruce, fir and larch is called the "taiga," a Russian word for endless forest. The famous Russian author Anton Chekov wrote, "The taiga is so vast that only God and the migrating birds know where it ends." In southern Sweden there is a wide mix of broadleaf deciduous trees that provide brilliant autumn displays of color.

The physical surroundings of Malmö are very similar to those of Copenhagen. The land is relatively flat, much of it devoted to agriculture, but with small clumps of surviving woodland of broadleaf deciduous trees and conifers. There are fewer lakes in the Malmö region because much of the land results from glacial deposition rather than scour. But a short distance to the north, one quickly gets into the part of Sweden where lakes are counted in the thousands. This makes the train journey from Malmö to Stockholm especially pleasant.

The climate of Malmö has a maritime influence, as is true for Copenhagen. The region is exposed to westerly winds that bring copious quantities of moisture from the North Sea, producing an essentially damp, rainy climate. During very cold spells, the rain does turn to snow. Summers are mild, but often there are multiple days of overcast and drizzly rain. Geographers call this a maritime or marine west coast type of climate, essentially that found in the United Kingdom and The Netherlands.

A BRIEF LOCAL HISTORY: The Swedes are descendants of the ancient Vikings, their history rich in tales of warfare and conquest. Vikings are said to be of Germanic origin, but in reality the reverse is true. What are called Germanic peoples today resulted from several migrations into the northern European plain including migrations out of Scandinavia. Yes the languages of Scandinavia are Germanic, but one could easily say the Germans are in part of Viking origin. Many of the myths and legends that German warriors relate to are actually of Viking derivation. Early Vikings explored deep into what is now Russia. The name Russia is taken from Rurik, an early Viking explorer and colonial leader who settled the Valdai Hills around present-day Moscow. In the local dialect, he was known as Rus, and so came Russia, or in Germanic tongues it is called Rusland.

During the 11th century, two Viking kingdoms, Svealand and Gotland united to form what is now Sweden. Between 1157 and 1293, the Swedes conquered Finland, but later between 1397 and 1434, Sweden became vassal to Denmark, gaining its independence in 1435. Later in its history, the Danes once again occupied Sweden between 1517 and 1523. Over the next two centuries, however, Sweden grew in power, eventually occupying parts of what are now northern Germany and the present-day Baltic states of Estonia and Latvia. After being defeated in 1718 in the Nordic War, Sweden lost much of its conquered territory, and in 1809 Sweden lost Finland to Russia, a country with whom it had fought numerous small wars, dating back as far as the 12th century.

In the historic old part of Malmö

In 1810, the Swedish king adopted French Count Bernadotte as his son since he did not have an heir to whom he could pass on his crown. When Count Bernadotte became king, he did not provide support for Napoleon as the French leader had anticipated, but rather joined forces against the French tyrant. After the Napoleonic Wars, Sweden declared itself neutral and has remained so today, not joining NATO or any other military alliances. Today's Swedish Royal House is descended from the House of Bernadotte. Because Sweden aided in the defeat of Napoleon, the Congress of Vienna compensated the country by allowing its crown to merge with that of Norway. Sweden continued to include Norway as part of its territory until 1905. Today each country has its own royal house, which both have blood ties to the Danish royal line, and there is a strong bond of friendship between the three countries.

In 1867, Sweden became a constitutional monarchy and its government has remained so to the present day. King Carl XVI Gustav is the present head of state, but a parliamentary system of government actually rules the nation. Until the late 20th century when parliament amended the law, no woman could inherit the throne of Sweden. In the mid 17th century, Queen Christina refused to marry and ultimately abdicated the throne so as to live in Rome and practice the Catholic faith. Women were thereafter excluded from the succession until the most recent change in Swedish law. As a result Crown Princess Victoria, eldest child of King Carl XVI Gustav, will become the next monarch. And her heir is also a daughter. Thus not since the late 1600's has a queen ruled Sweden, but its future now holds two queens in succession.

There is far less pomp and ceremony associated with the Swedish royal house than in the United Kingdom. It is a far relaxed monarchy, yet people in Sweden have a great love for the Royal Family and take an interest in their lives, but not to the intrusive level as seen in the United Kingdom.

Sweden became a member of the European Union in 1995, but the country, like the United Kingdom, refused to use the Euro, thus the Swedish Kroner is still the national currency. Since the defeat of Napoleon, Sweden has remained a neutral nation. It was this neutrality that was helpful during World War II. A Swedish diplomat named Raoul Wallenberg living in Budapest was instrumental in saving thousands of Hungarian Jews by issuing them Swedish passports. But after the war ended and the Soviet Union entered Budapest, he was never seen again. His disappearance has remained a mystery to this day. The Swedes also gave refuge to many Norwegian freedom fighters and British aviators during the war, thus helping to ultimately oust the Germans from Norway.

Although a neutral nation, the Swedes maintain one of Europe's best-equipped military; a small, but well equipped and trained navy and a formidable air force. Some say that Sweden is among the top ten nations in the world with regard to the potential fighting ability of its air force, the Flygvapnet.

Sweden's most noted citizen of all time, originally a munitions manufacturer, Alfred Nobel, was instrumental in developing a series of prizes to be awarded for major humanitarian and literary accomplishments. Today, both Sweden and Norway are venues for presenting the Nobel Prizes. Each year both the kings of Sweden and Norway present the various Nobel Prizes in ceremonies held in Stockholm and Oslo. There have been many other famous Swedes, especially in the film industry, the two best known having been Greta Garbo and Ingrid Bergman, as well as the director Ingmar Bergman (no relation). And anyone who follows the sport of tennis will recognize the name of Swedish born Bjorn Borg.

The government policy during the last 75 years has been one of combined capitalism and socialism. In Sweden, citizens receive cradle to the grave coverage in health care, education and other social services. The country is always among the top five nations of the world in quality of life when the United Nations publishes its annual report of the best nations in the world. In 2004, Sweden was number one on the list, while in 2005 it was Norway.

By in large Sweden is a very upper middle-income nation, and one will not find any neighborhoods in Stockholm or other major cities that could be classed as a "slum." Sweden and the rest of its Scandinavian neighbors provide a national safety net that is the envy of the rest of the western world. There is essentially very little real poverty, but likewise only a handful are exceptionally wealthy, as the country has a graduated income tax that puts the greater burden on the very rich. For this reason, there is a far smaller range of inequality between those at the top and bottom of the social scale. Sweden also has one of the best educational and health care systems in all of Europe. Swedes are very well educated with a high percentage being university graduates. The national health care program provides for research, and Sweden ranks among the top ten nations of the world in the field of medical breakthroughs.

Malmö still reflects its past centuries of being a major city

The modern Malmö waterfront and downtown seen from the air

Sweden is essentially an idyllic country. Its people know that their lifestyle is considered as being among the five best in the world by the United Nations.

However, there is one less idyllic factor worthy of note. Sweden has allowed a small number of immigrants to come from less developed countries in Europe, Africa and Asia. These people unfortunately are for the most part filling more menial jobs, and their presence is less than welcome by a majority of the population. In turn, some Islamic groups have taken out their anger over Israel on members of the local Jewish community. This has been especially true in Malmö, and it has been a big headache for law enforcement personnel. But look what happened in France when Middle Eastern immigrants have rampaged through several Parisian neighborhoods protesting inequalities. That is not to say this could happen in Sweden, as conditions are far better than in France for immigrants. It is more social than economic here, as Sweden is a somewhat closed society with long standing traditions and cultural values. The only other negative factor has been a minor problem with drug use among many teens, but this seems to be a worldwide universal in the developed nations. Essentially Sweden is about as idyllic a nation as one could find, save for Norway.

Malmö is an old and historic city one unfortunately overlooked by visitors to Copenhagen, yet only 30 minutes away by rail. Malmö dates back to 1275, when it was a dock for the city of Lund, 18 kilometers or 12 miles to the northeast and home to a major cathedral and university. Malmö grew into an important trade center under the Hanseatic League and by the 15th century it was the second largest city in what was then Denmark, which included southern Sweden.

In 1434, a major citadel was built close to the water, and with the existing fortifications, it made Malmö the most heavily protected city in the kingdom. The citadel still stands today, part of a beautiful park complex adjacent to the city center. It is one of the major visitor attractions.

During the 16th century, the Protestant Reformation came to Malmö, making it the first Scandinavian city to accept conversion. And Malmö then had a profound influence upon Copenhagen and other surrounding communities.

By the 17th century, southern Sweden was wrested away from Denmark and became a part of the Swedish kingdom from which that status has never changed. Denmark did attempt to lay siege to Malmö in 1677, but to no avail. Today despite there being strong Danish cultural influences and economic ties, the people definitely are patriotic regarding their Swedish identity.

In 1840, the role of Malmö drastically changed. The Kockums shipyard was opened and within decades it became one of the largest shipbuilding facilities in the Baltic Sea. In addition to shipbuilding, Malmö also became the center for Swedish textile manufacturing. The city became one of the most important industrial centers in Sweden and this role continued into the mid 20th century. The good times were dashed in the 1970's when Swedish industry was thrown into recession, and for a city such as Malmö, which was heavily industrialized, the economy contracted and population shrunk. In 1986, the shipyard closed, and it appeared as it if would plunge Malmö into total depression.

With the building of the Øresund Bridge and the efforts of Malmö leaders to turn the economy around by making the city a center for finance, culture and education, the fortunes began to change. Redevelopment of the old waterfront, increased trade with Copenhagen and the ease of communication that enabled many families to be based in Malmö while the major wage earner worked in Copenhagen all had a positive impact upon the city. The cost of living in Malmö is significantly lower than in Copenhagen, thus anyone with a professional position in the Danish capital, but living on the Swedish side of the water benefits.

Today Malmö offers a picture of historic and modern attributes and its greater regional population has soared to over 680,000. The one darker side to this rapid growth and the development of a new economic outlook has been foreign immigration. Many Islamic communities have been established in Malmö and this created tensions with the long time Jewish community to the point where there have been instances of violence. This is something alien to Swedish culture and the government has taken measures to ensure that this type of behavior does not continue into the future, but unfortunately it is a spillover of the tensions existing in the Middle East between Israel and its Islamic neighbors.

THE PHYSICAL LAYOUT OF MALMÖ: Overall the city is much smaller than Copenhagen, yet it does present a distinct urban landscape. The city occupies the southern shore of a broad bay, and the waterfront actually faces to the northwest. Although close to Copenhagen, on most days it is difficult to see across the water to the Danish capital, but at night the lights of Copenhagen can be seen.

Malmö still retains a significant harbor, but its level of traffic is greatly diminished from when it was a major port. To the west of the harbor, there is a significant beach area where numerous moderate size high-rise apartments are located and much of the waterfront is parkland. From the harbor there are canals that extend to the south and surround the city center, essentially making it an island. And to the west is an extensive park belt from the historic Danish castle extending south and then east around the bottom end of the city center. And even beyond the city center, a large park continues on to the south.

Although not having a grid pattern, most of the major streets in Malmö do tend to follow northwest to southeast and a northeast to southwest pattern with moderate curves and bends. I would not call it a totally irregular pattern, but at the same time it in no way conforms to a grid. But essentially it is relatively easy to find your way around the city. Fortunately for visitors, most of the major sights worthy of your attention are within or immediately adjacent to the city center.

In the city center is Gustav Adolf Torg

SHIP DOCK: If your visit is by cruise ship actually docking in Malmö it will be in the local harbor at Frihamnen located at Grimsbygatan # 21. There are three possible docks for a cruise ship, but no actual terminal facilities. It is not far to the center of the city, no more than a 15 minute walk to the main railway station. Taxis will be waiting. And the more upmarket cruise lines will often provide a free shuttle.

SIGHTSEEING IN MALMÖ: If your cruise itinerary does not include Malmö you can still visit providing your cruise either begins or terminates in Copenhagen and you plan upon spending a few days to do some sightseeing. Assuming Copenhagen is your port of embarkation or termination and you plan two days to visit, you can easily spend three to four hours visiting Malmö just to enable you to capture the entire metropolitan region. I have often stayed in Malmö rather than in Copenhagen either before or following a Baltic Sea cruise, as I find it less crowded and more relaxed than Copenhagen.

There is no need for a car and driver/guide because the central portion of Malmö is very easy to see on foot. If, however, you are arriving by ship with this being a port of call, a shuttle bus is often provided. There are no hop on hop off busses in Malmö because it has not yet developed as a major tourist destination because it is so overshadowed by Copenhagen. But when ships make this a port of call, the cruise line generally offers a city overview tour, which is one good way to at least become familiar with the surroundings.

The main pedestrian only shopping street in Malmö

I routinely visit Malmö because I enjoy its architecture and beautiful parks combined with its less frenetic atmosphere than Copenhagen. On many occasions when I am either starting or ending a lecture tour on board ship in Copenhagen, I stay a few nights in Malmö simply to take advantage of its more peaceful environment. The city of Malmö is quite sophisticated and interesting. It has a rich architectural history with many magnificent old buildings dating back as far as the Hanseatic League. The city also has an outstanding and spacious park system, good museums and very good restaurants. I have spent many enjoyable days in Malmö before or after doing a Baltic Sea cruise. I prefer it to Copenhagen, as it is far less crowded, has a more picturesque setting and offers greater value for the money. Hotels in Copenhagen are outrageously expensive during summer whereas equally good four-star hotels in Malmö are less than half the price. This alone warrants considering Malmö as a base for sightseeing the greater Copenhagen area, especially with the ease of rail connections.

* **TOURING OPTIONS FOR MALMÖ:** Visiting Malmö if your ship is in Copenhagen for a day while en route to or from its final destination will only allow you a single day and there is just too much to see in Copenhagen to attempt a visit to Malmö. If you are either embarking or disembarking in Copenhagen and you are spending extra days, Malmö should be considered worthy of at least a half of a day, easily accomplished via the high speed train service between the two cities.

Some cruise itineraries actually allow a full day port call in Malmö, which then gives you a greater degree of flexibility. The options shown below are based upon a full day with the assumption this is a port of call. However, for those visiting by train or car from Copenhagen, you can ignore some of the options shown.

** **Ship sponsored tours** – The tours offered by your cruise line will only apply to those cruise itineraries including Malmö as a port call. And as in other ports, the tours will be organized for sizeable groups and be accomplished by motor coach, which does not appeal to the more discriminating explorer.

** **Private car and driver** – This is my preferred option, but it is of course going to be more costly when booked through the cruise line. The advantage is that you have total flexibility to see what interests you the most and linger at each destination as long as you wish. The driver/guide is at your disposal. You may wish to go on line and visit South Sweden Limousine at *www.southswedenlimousine.se* to check on their services. I have used them numerous times with great satisfaction. Also check with Limo Group Sweden at *www.limogroup.se* for comparison.

** **Rental car** - I do not recommend this option because of the fact that all traffic signs and directions are written only in Swedish. And there are very few parking areas adjacent to major attractions. And if you park in a restricted area not knowing so because of the language barrier, your car could be towed. All major car rental agencies are available in both Copenhagen and Malmö and there are no special formalities for driving a rental car between the two countries.

** **Hop on hop off bus** – There is a small hop on hop off bus that operates in Malmö, which enables you to explore the city at a reasonable rate. It is a single deck bus with no open top, but still has large picture windows. Check with Travelshop AB at *www.travelshop.se* and then click on hop on hop off Malmö for information.

** **Taxi service** is available from numerous companies, but many of the drivers are not native to Sweden. If you attempt to hire one on the street, be certain of the driver's knowledge of the city and his use of English. The most popular taxi company is Taxi97 Transport Kompaniet. Check their web page for details as to touring. Their address is *www.taxi97.se* and also check Taxi Center Malmö for a comparison. Their address is *www.taxicm.com* .

** **Øresundtåg** – This is the high speed train between Copenhagen and Malmö operating at approximately 30-minute intervals. The journey takes approximately 30 minutes and you do need to take your passport because of the recent checks being made by Swedish immigration officials. Check the railway web site for further details at *www.oresundtax.se* .

** **Bicycle rental** – One easy way to see Malmö is by bicycle, if you are capable. You can easily rent a bicycle. There are some streets with special traffic lanes and also parking lots, so this is one of the best ways to get around. But unless you are experienced in riding a bicycle in an urban setting, I caution against it. Here is the most respected company, Travelshop Malmö at www.travelshop.se . There are also bicycles you can rent from an automated kiosk around town that is called Donkey Republic, but you will not be dealing with a live person.

** **Walking** - This is a great city for walking. There are even pedestrian streets and the city has a rather unhurried atmosphere. This is a very safe city in which to walk day or night, and the vast majority of tourist venues are within easy walking distance of the majority of hotels, which tend to be congregated in the city center.

* **MAJOR SIGHTS TO SEE IN MALMÖ:** Here is my list of local sights within Malmö worthy of your attention shown in alphabetical order:

The HSB Turning Torso, (Work of Ralf Roletschek, CC BY SA 1.0, Wikimedia.org

** **HSB Turning Torso** - This is the tallest building in Scandinavia. It stands close to the Malmö waterfront. The 54-story building was constructed with what is essentially a series of twists, looking like the building is being contorted into a twisted shape. It is the tallest building in all of Sweden. The building serves as a combination residential and office property and the views from each apartment are quite spectacular. It is generally viewed from a distance because the way there is a bit awkward and it is easy to get lost if on foot. There is a visitor's center, but unless there have been changes I am unaware of, there are no tours offered. For the most current information check their website at www.hsb.se/turningtorso .

Lilla Torg is the most popular dining spot in Malmo

** Lilla Torg - In English it is Little Square. This small square just to the south and west of the large square known as the Stortoget is surrounded by a plethora of restaurants that all offer outdoor seating during summer. It is the liveliest place in Malmö on weekend afternoons and evenings. All of the restaurants post their menu choices outside of their entry, making it easier to choose where to dine.

** Lund - This major historic city, home to the University of Lund, which is one of Europe's oldest, is only 20 minutes north from Malmö by train. Lund is a beautiful city and is rich in its medieval and renaissance period architecture. For anyone who is staying a few days in Copenhagen, a visit to Lund is just one more distinct excursion. Total travel time from Central Station in Copenhagen is less than one hour. And for anyone who is actually staying in Malmö the journey by train to Lund is less than 20 minutes, with numerous departures during the day.

** Malmö Town Hall - This elegant building along one side of the Stortoget is a masterpiece of architecture. It was built in 1546 and is still the center of city government. In Swedish it is called the Rådhusset. The building is open for normal business hours, but I have never seen a posting of actual hours or any notification that tours are offered. Most visitors simply enjoy its architecture from the outside, as the plaza in front offers great panoramic views of this historic structure.

The historic Malmö Town Hall reflects Swedish grandeur

** Malmöhus Slott - This is the old castle or citadel dates to 1434 and is surrounded by a moat that was once the cornerstone of Malmö defenses. Today the castle has an extensive historic collection and is in effect a major museum. The citadel is deep within Slottsparken, one of the many beautiful and serene of Malmö's parks. It is just steps away from the Stortoget and a wonderful place in which to relax and simply savor the landscape and small lakes. The castle is open daily from 10 AM to 5 PM.

** Pildardammarna - This is the other large park just blocks south of the city center. It is a magnificently landscaped park with a sizable lake at its center. There is a large lake at the center of this very enjoyable park. This is another beautiful park to enjoy, open during daylight hours, which in summer are very long.

** Ribersborgsstrand - A park that extends for over two miles along the beach that fronts on the Øresund. On a clear day you can walk along the park's main footpath and look across the water to Copenhagen. Unlike Malmö, the waterfront in Copenhagen does not have a beautifully landscaped park backed up by a residential district containing many high-rise apartments.

** Saint Petri Church - This massive early 14th century stone church towers above much of the inner city. It is a beautiful building both outside and inside, having been built initially as a Catholic church before the Reformation. With its tall spire, it is not easily missed when viewed from the Stortoget. The church is open daily from 10 AM to 6 PM and visitors are welcome, but asked to be as quiet as possible since this is an active house of worship.

The interior of Saint Petri Church

** **Slottsparken/Kongsparken** - This is a massive park that lies just to the west of the city center. There are miles of walking trails around the peaceful lakes, and the park is beautifully landscaped. This park offers a sense of tranquility that belies that you are in a city.

There is so much beauty in Kongslotte Park surrounding the old castle

** **Stortoget** - The principal square in the heart of Malmö facing the beautiful and historic town hall is surrounded by a varied array of architectural styles. It is a good place from which to begin any walking tour of the city. If you are coming from Copenhagen by rail, the Stortoget is two short blocks from the railway station.

** **Technology and Maritime Museum** - In the city center at Malmöhusvägen # 7, this museum features exhibits from the days when the city was an important shipbuilding port and industrial center. It also highlights the importance of technology in Sweden's overall growth. It is worth a visit for anyone interested in the history of industry in this region of the world. The museum is open daily from 10 AM to 5 PM.

DINING OUT: Swedish and Danish cuisine are very similar. Both are heavily based upon seafood given that the waters are rich in fish and marine life. In Malmö there are several distinctive restaurants, but as usual I have my favorites that I am listing here, as most of you will be visiting ever so briefly:

* **Café Mäster Hans** - This combination bakery and cafe is legendary for its awesome pastries and good open face sandwiches. There is no table service. You choose want you want and then find a table in what would be similar to cafeteria style. I find it a fantastic place to go simply for dessert even though it is now located well outside of the city center. Their creamy marzipan cake is the best I have ever tasted anywhere. They are located at Karolingatan #1. They are open from 7 AM to 6 PM Monday thru Saturday, but you will need to take a taxi since it is not in the city center. Booking a table is not necessary.

* **Johan P** - This very popular local seafood restaurant is not high on decor, but it definitely is tops for fresh fish and other seafood delicacies. The have excellent gravlax and also fish pate, both being expertly prepared and nicely served. Johan P is located in the city center at Hjulhamnsgatan #5 and they are open from 11:30 AM to 9 PM Monday thru Thursday, remaining open until 11 PM on Friday. Saturday they serve between Noon and 11 PM and Sunday from 1 to 4 PM. I would have to admit that it is my personal favorite seafood restaurant in the entire metropolitan region. To book a table call +46 40 97 18 18.

* **Restaurang Genuin** - Located at Kopenhamnsvagen # 40 just south of the city center, it is best reached by taxi unless you feel like a long walk of approximately 1.5 kilometers from Lilla Torg. This restaurant serves delectable lunch and dinner entrees that will make the trip worthwhile. It is very popular among locals, as it is not in an area frequented by many tourists. So you will have a real genuine Swedish experience. Their hours of service are varied. They are open Wednesday thru Friday from 11:30 AM to 3 PM, reopening Friday from 4 to 8:30 PM. Saturday they serve from 4 to 8:30 PM and Sunday from 1 to 8:30 PM. To book a table call them at +46.

Lilla Torg is home to so many restaurant choices

* Smak Malmö Konsthall - This popular restaurant is located at the art museum, T. Johannesgaten # 7 S, and is noted for its very traditional Swedish cuisine, favoring quite heavily seafood dishes. Its menu is diverse and dishes are artfully presented with a degree of flair. It is definitely high on my list of favorites. They are open Monday thru Saturday from 11:30 AM to 5 PM. Call them to book a table at +46 40 50 50 35.

* Steakhouse Lilla Torg - Although the name indicated steak, this restaurant with its outdoor seating area offers a variety of Swedish dishes. Their Swedish meatballs are very traditional. They also offer a mix of meats, poultry and fish, all well prepared at reasonable prices. They are located at Lille Torg 7 and are open from 11:30 AM to 2 PM Tuesday, from 11:30 to 9 PM Wednesday and Thursday, Friday from 11:30 AM to 1 AM and Saturday from Noon to 1 AM. To book a table call them at +46 40 97 34 97.

SHOPPING: There are no special shopping venues I would recommend for Malmö. They have plenty of shops and one branch of the Swedish Åhlen City Department Store, but it is small and does not have a great variety.

Being so close by train to Copenhagen the city center of Malmö does have extensive shopping, but it is oriented toward local needs and does not cater specifically to visitors.

Fresh local berries being sold on Gustav Adolfs Torg

A visit to Malmö is always delightful, as here in the city's main square

Malmö is so close to Copenhagen and with commuter rail service the majority of residents ride into the Danish capital where shopping is superb.

FINAL WORDS: Most of you reading this book will not have Malmö on your cruise itinerary, as so few cruise ships do stop here. But if your cruise starts or terminates in Copenhagen and you are spending a few days, I do highly recommend visiting Malmö, as it is a worthwhile experience.

I have always found Malmö to offer the same rich historic tapestry that is found in Copenhagen, but the crowds of tourists are nowhere near the level of what is seen in Copenhagen. Malmö is a quiet city, but still offers the same charm as Copenhagen.

One disturbing side note that has reached the international stage is the fact that there have been some increase in neighborhood street crime in Malmö, particularly in the lower income districts where there are large numbers of immigrants from the Middle East and North Africa. It is partly what has precipitated Swedish immigration checks for illegal entrants because Sweden has been overly generous in granting asylum to thousands of arrivals.

MAPS OF MALMÖ

THE CITY CENTER OF MALMÖ

Central Malmö with star showing cruise ship dock, (© OpenStreetMap contributors)

This map is best viewed directly from OpenStreetMap.com on your personal device where it can be expanded or one specific area can be enlarged. Given the format of this book, it is impossible to display maps with the level of detail you might wish to have while actually out exploring the city. But the OpenStreetMap maps used directly are the tool I always rely upon.

THE HEART OF MALMÖ

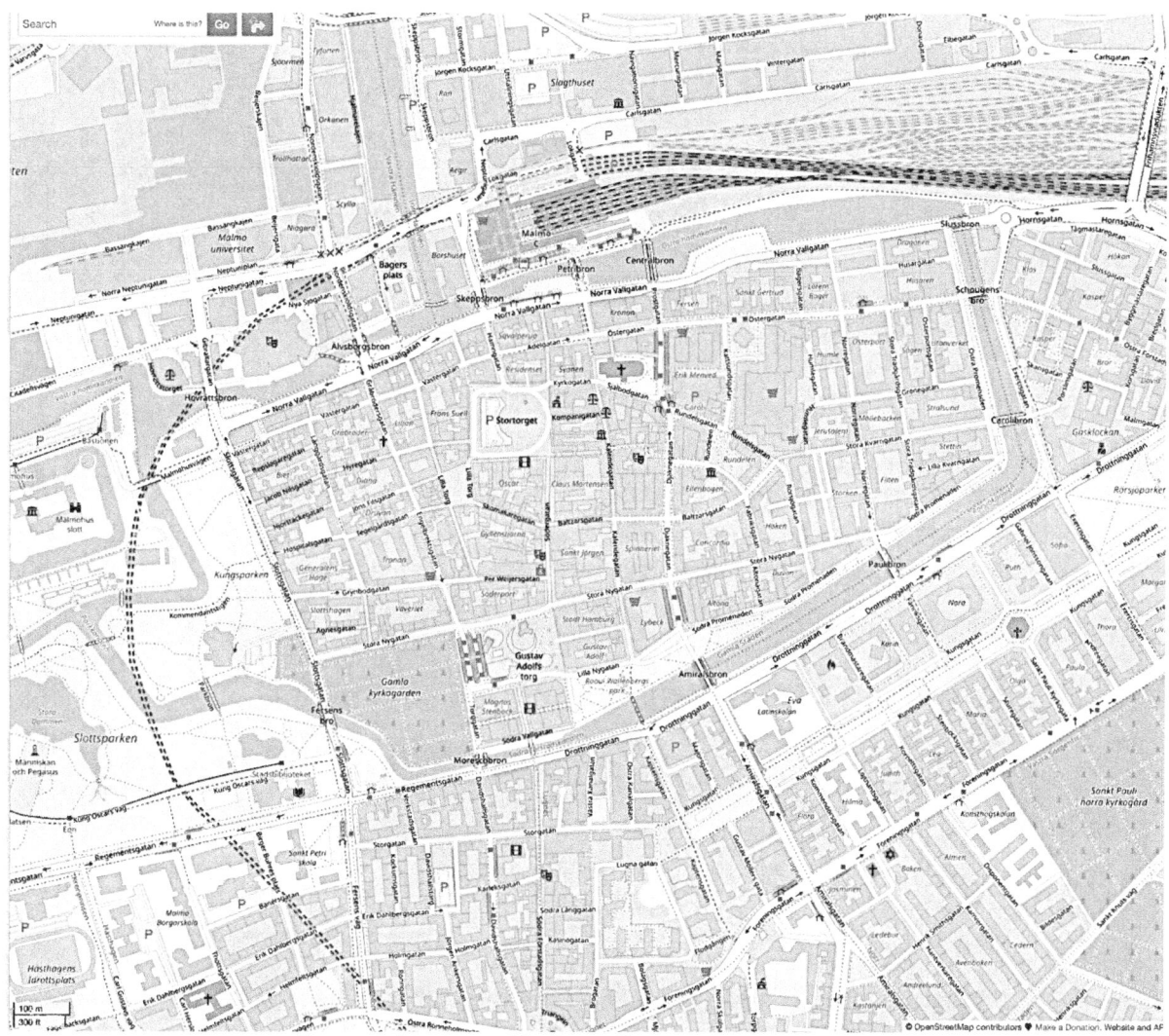

Central Malmö, (© OpenStreetMap contributors)

This map is best viewed directly from OpenStreetMap.com on your personal device where it can be expanded or one specific area can be enlarged. Given the format of this book, it is impossible to display maps with the level of detail you might wish to have while actually out exploring the city. But the OpenStreetMap maps used directly are the tool I always rely upon.

BORGHOLM, ÖLAND, SWEDEN

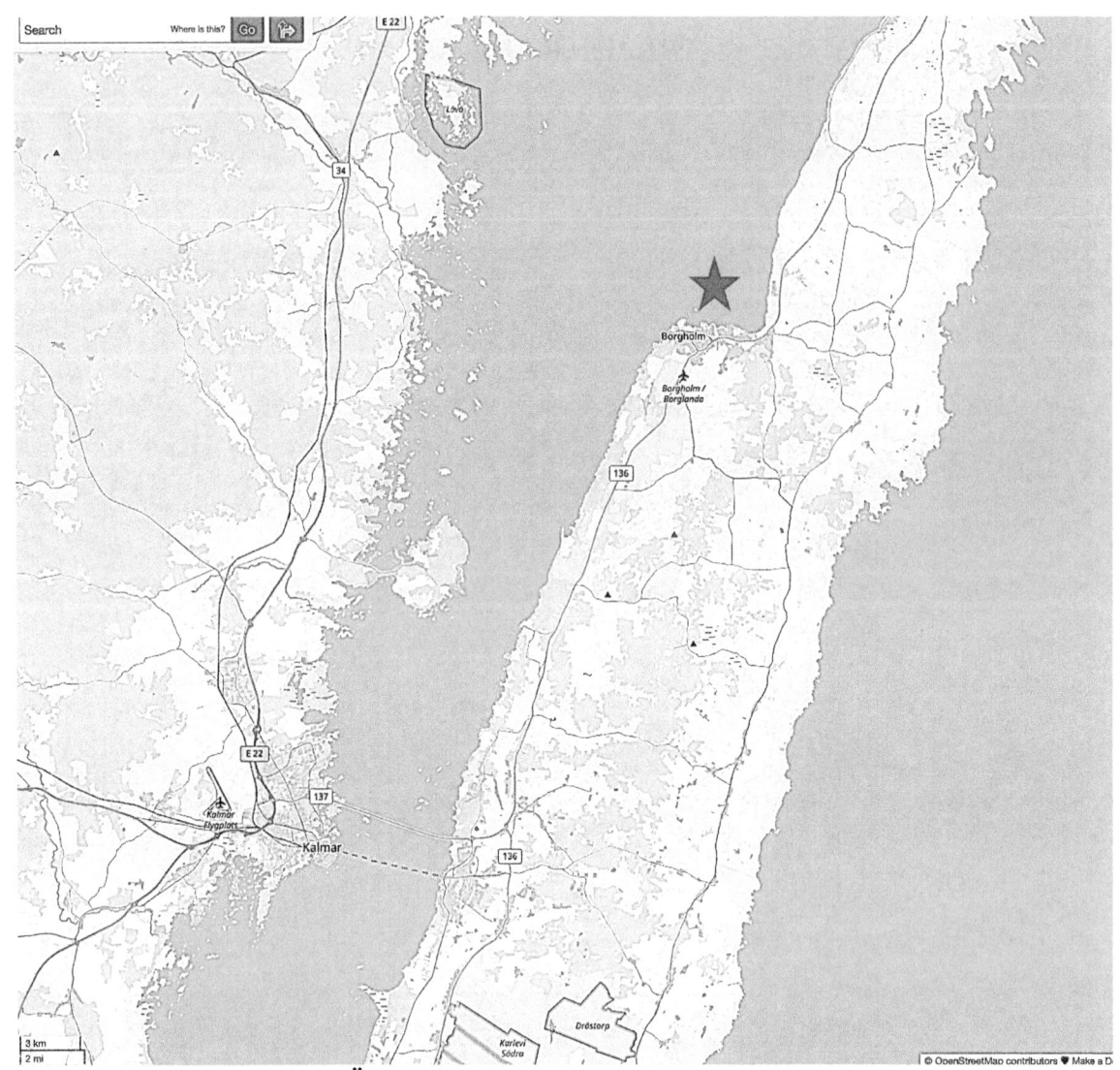

Map of central Öland Island (© OpenStreetMap contributors)

The island of Öland is not well visited by cruise ships, thus if your itinerary includes a stop in Borgholm you should consider it a fortuitous event since you will be seeing a part of Sweden that foreign visitors rarely get to enjoy unless they make a special trip to the island. It has an unspoiled natural beauty and cultural charm worthy of your port call.

THE NATURAL SETTING: Öland is the second largest island in Sweden after Gotland, which is home to the medieval port city of Visby. Öland is located along the southeastern Swedish coast and is a very long and narrow island. Its total land area is 1,342 square kilometers or 418 square miles. Being so close to the mainland the Öland Bridge connects it over a span of only six kilometers. Öland is approximately 136 kilometers or 85 miles long, but it is only 16 kilometers or 10 miles wide. It is a relatively flat island with its highest elevation being 55 meters or 180 feet.

Öland is sparsely populated with approximately 26,000 residents of which only around 5,000 live in the village of Borgholm, the island's major port where your cruise ship will visit. As a small port, there are no facilities to handle cruise ships, thus this is a tender port where your ship will anchor off the cost and you will be taken ashore in the ship's own small boats.

Borgholm shoreline (Work of Kveigrisen, CC BY SA 3.0, Wikimedia.org)

Öland is an island that is primarily composed of sandstone that was deposited hundreds of millions of years ago. There are also areas of limestone that represent marine deposition also having taken place at the dawn of life on earth. These deposits were glaciated, as was all of Sweden. In the case of Öland, glacial scour ground down the island to where today it is essentially flat to gently rolling. But not being composed of exceptionally hard rock like much of the mainland, its fertility does give it the advantage of having an agricultural potential. In recent years, geologists have been exploring the strata for the possibility of discovering pockets of natural gas, a matter considered controversial by island residents.

Likewise the climate of Öland is impacted by being in the Baltic Sea, thus giving it a more temperate climate than interior regions of Sweden. Summers are quite moist and cool, but sufficiently warm for farming. Winters are cold, but not as brutal or long as in the interior of the country.

The island is home to many species of both plants and wildlife, and it was the focus of early study in 1741 by the great naturalist Charles Linnæus from Uppsala, the scientist who gave the world the system of classification of all life forms that we still use today.

A BRIEF LOCAL HISTORY: Öland has a rich prehistory, as studies have shown it to have been inhabited for the past 10,000 years by what would be considered Stone Age hunters and gatherers. Some archaeological sites that represent early encampments are unearthed and available for visits by tourists. But the most important archaeological sites are those of the Vikings who were living on Öland as far back as 1,200 years ago.

The history of Öland prior to its coming under Swedish rule in the late 12the century is rather murky and various historic accounts differ as to its past. Most contemporary historians doubt if it was ever ruled by Denmark, Germanic tribes or was fully independent. If anything, the island was divided among smaller tribes and also saw raids by a variety of foes. A look at the pre Swedish historic period shows that all along the coast there were small fortifications, indicative of the need for protection.

The interior of the old Borgholm castle ruins, (Work of Oregran, CC BY SA 3.0, Wikimedia.org)

Once Sweden took control of Öland, Borgholm Castle became the major defensive fortification by the end of the 13th century, but its original construction dates back to the middle of the 12th century.

In 1310, the king of Sweden divided the kingdom with his two brothers. Öland went to Duke Valdemar, but after his death the island fell to Denmark along with Gotland in 1361.

During the period when Sweden, Denmark and Norway were joined in the Kalmar Union, 1397 to 1523, numerous fortifications were built along the east coast of Öland because of raids from across the Baltic Sea, and Borgholm Castle was enhanced with stronger walls and battlement towers, making it one of the strongest in Sweden. The Swedes left the Union in 1523, and later fought with Denmark, surrendering the castle to Denmark 1611, but Sweden regained control later in the same year, but had to surrender it to Denmark in 1612 under treaty. When the war ended in 1613, Sweden regained the island.

In 1654, King Charles X Gustav undertook a major restoration of the castle, actually creating a royal residence. Construction and improvement of the castle continued until 1709, making Borgholm one of the most magnificent royal residences in Europe.

By 1806, the castle/palace had been neglected and a fire broke out, which turned the structure into the ruin that is today the major attraction when visiting Borgholm. It is a shame that it was never reconstructed at the time or even in the 20th century to serve as a museum of its glorious past.

During the 19th century, the island of Öland saw a decline in its population, with younger people leaving for the mainland. It was not until the Öland Bridge was completed in 1972, that the population stabilized and the tourist industry began to add significantly to the local economy. The bridge also made it possible for locals in Borgholm and its surroundings to seek gainful employment in the city of Kalmar on the mainland.

Borgholm is officially a city despite having less than 5,000 permanent residents, but the status as city dates back to its early historic period. The city is the seat of government for the larger Borgholm Municipality. In addition to being the site of the once great castle, the current Royal Family has its official summer residence at Solliden Palace located on the edge of modern day Borgholm.

THE PHYSICAL LAYOUT OF THE CITY OF BORGHOLM: The main town of Borgholm is quite tiny and in essence is more of a village. It is so easy to cover on foot. Most cruise lines will not offer any tours since the infrastructure makes it difficult to have motor coaches in sufficient number. The harbor is very small and thus all cruise ships must anchor and tender guests on shore. The main core of the city, which remember is really just a town, covers only about one square kilometer or less than a square mile. Extending east along the waterfront are the main residential areas, built in distinct enclaves carved out of the surrounding woodland and farm country. It is a dispersed community consisting of single-family houses rather than apartment blocks. Along the shoreline in the eastern part of town are two massive campground, which in summer is filled with Swedish vacationers living in their mainly white tents.

The Storgata of Borgholm (Work of Bernt Fransson Lindås, CC BY SA 4.0, Wikimedia.org)

Just south of the main core of Borgholm, within easy walking distance, is the Borgholm Slott, or castle ruin, which is the prime attraction of the community. It is unfortunate that this once mighty castle was never restored in the modern age, but the number of tourists visiting Borgholm no doubt does not warrant the expenditure.

SHIP TENDER: There is no dock large enough where even a small cruise ship can tie up in Borgholm. Your ship will anchor offshore and you will be taken to and from the small harbor by ship lifeboats, called tenders. Most cruise lines offer regular service during the port call.

TOURING OPTIONS IN BORGHOLM: Given that as of the time this text is being composed only a single small cruise ship has scheduled a port call for Borgholm on the island of Öland. And it is too early for the 2022 schedules to have been all issued.

In the event that more port calls are planned for 2022, the following information is vital:

* Normally when ships do call in at Borgholm, no tours are offered. The port is small enough that guests can easily walk to most important venues. And there is a local taxi service that will offer hourly touring rates. For information contact Alvar Taxi at +46 485 282 00 for details, as unfortunately they do not have a web page. There are two other taxis in Borgholm, however, they receive very low ratings on line for service and I will not recommend either.

* There are no private car and driver services being offered in Borgholm and there is no hop on hop off trolley service either.

A typical Borgholm residential street (Work of Bernt Fransson, CC BY SA 4.0, Wikimedia.org)

THINGS TO SEE AND DO IN BORGHOLM: Most of what you will want to see in Borgholm is within easy walking distance of where the ship tender will dock. It is very easy to get around the town, as it has a quite unhurried atmosphere. Even Borgholm Slott is close to the town center. There are local island busses, but your time will be limited and therefore it is not recommended that you go off any distance, as you could end up missing the ship's last tender.

These are the important sites to visit while in Borgholm:

* **Borgholms Kyrka** - Located on Torget in Borgholm, this is the main Lutheran church for the community. No tours are offered nor are opening hours posted. If it is open, you will find it rather Spartan inside, as is true for most Swedish Lutheran churches. The exterior is quite beautiful and is one of the more impressive buildings in Borgholm.

* **Borgholm Slott** - This medieval castle that was later turned into a royal palace by the 18th century and then ultimately fell into ruin after a major fire is the number one attraction in Borgholm. It is a short walk south from the main city center and well worth the visit. The castle ruins are open daily from 10 AM to 4 PM.

* **Borgholms Stadsmuseum** - This small museum in an elegant home that once belonged to a wealthy family and shows what life would have been like in the 18th century. It is open briefly on Tuesday, and Thursday thru Saturday from 11 AM until Noon from June 1 through the end of August.

* **Halltorps Hage** - Located adjacent to the Vida Museum, this is a beautiful forest preserve with nature paths that are easy to follow. On a nice summer day it is a very nice place to stroll and simply take in the vegetation and fresh air.

Solliden Palace near Borgholm, summer home to the Swedish Crown, (Work of Annelis, CC BY SA 3.0, Wikimedia.org)

* **Solliden Slott** - This is the official royal residence of King Carl XVI Gustav and his family during the summer. The actual palace is not open to the public, but the magnificent gardens are worthy of a visit. The palace is about three kilometers south of Borgholm and easily reached by taxi, a rented bicycle or a nice walk on a cool, sunny day. The gardens are open daily from 11 AM to 6 PM through the end of August and then only until 4 PM starting September 1 through the fall. For a guided tour of the castle you need to call or email ahead for reservations to sollidenslott@sollidenslott.se. There is also a nice gift shop on site.

* **Vida Museum** - Located south of Borgholm at Halltorp a short taxi ride from the town center, this museum features the glass art of Sweden, which is recognized worldwide for its exceptional beauty. As per the latest information the museum is only open Saturday and Sunday from 10 AM to 3 PM, which may not correspond to most ship itineraries.

As you can see, there are not many highlights in Borgholm, so you may wonder at this point why a cruise itinerary would include this port. Despite there being few specific sights to see, Borgholm is a very pleasant stop and it does give you a glimpse of rural Sweden.

DINING OUT: Borgholm is decidedly a small city, and although it has several cafes and fast food kiosks, the fine dining experience is not forsaken. Here are my few recommendations:

* **Ebbas by the Sea** - This is a pub and restaurant located at Hamntorget with nice views of the water. It serves more of what I would call pub food, including hamburgers, which should satisfy North American tastes. They serve lunch and dinner with opening at 11:30 AM and closing at 10 PM. Booking a table is possible by calling the restaurant at +46 7- 896 41 10 .

* **Evas Kroppkakor** - Located at Hagslættsvægen # 14, this is a traditional Swedish restaurant where the cuisine is prepared according to traditional recipes. This is a bit off the main tourist route north of Borgholm and you will need to take a taxi to get there. Lunch is served only Tuesday thru Saturday between 11:30 AM and 5 PM. Call to book, if necessary, at +46 485 720 15.

* **Hotel Borgholm** - Located in the center of town at Tradgardsgatan # 15, the main dining room serves a very nice lunch with an emphasis upon traditional Swedish cuisine. Their three-course lunch is beautifully served and the dishes are all very tasty. Lunch is served from 11:30 AM to 2 PM daily. Call them to see if you need to book a table at +46 485 770 60.

FINAL NOTE: I have included this chapter just in the event that more than one cruise ship will consider Borgholm as a port call. But from all my research, I was only able to find a single ship, World Voyager visiting on Saturday August 1, 2020. Based upon what I have stated, you may feel that Borgholm will be a wasted day. But trust me, it is a pleasant community and a visit to Borgholm Castle alone will make it a worthy stop. And you would be visiting a place that is so seldom ever graced by a cruise ship. The island of Öland is popular among Swedish visitors, and a chance to be on a cruise stopping here is definitely out of the ordinary.

MAP OF BORGHOLM

BORGHOLM, ÖLAND

Borgholm, Öland, (© OpenStreetMap contributors)

This map is best viewed directly from OpenStreetMap.com on your personal device where it can be expanded or one specific area can be enlarged. Given the format of this book, it is impossible to display maps with the level of detail you might wish to have while actually out exploring the city. But the OpenStreetMap maps used directly are the tool I always rely upon.

VISBY, GOTLAND, SWEDEN

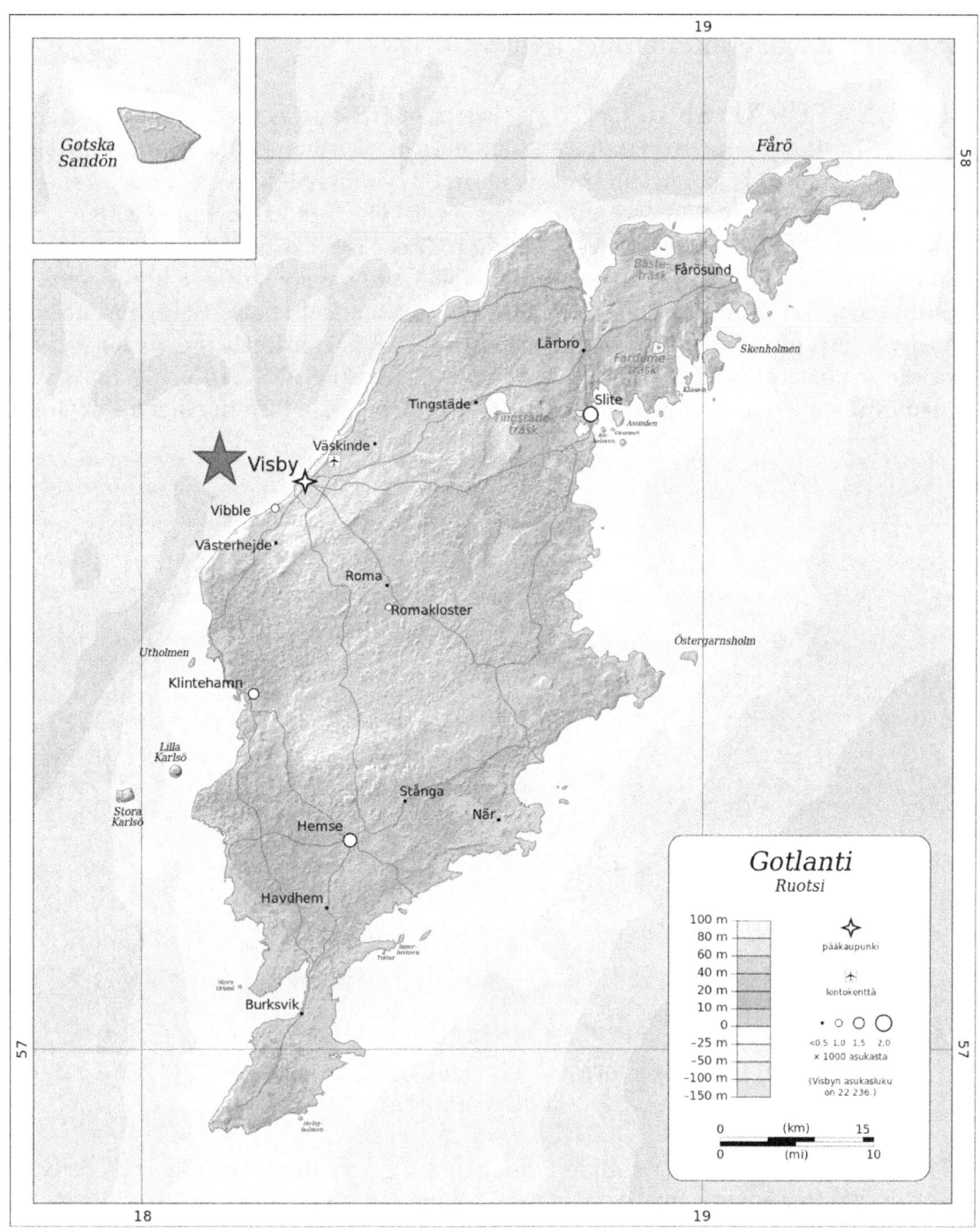

Map of the Island of Gotland (Work of Mysid, CC BY SA 4.0, Wikimedia.org)

The vast majority of Baltic Sea cruises do not stop at Visby on the Swedish island of Gotland. It is a lesser stop, as its port facility is very small and larger cruise vessels would find it necessary to tender their thousands of guests ashore. Most small cruise ship captains have until recently preferred to anchor offshore and use tenders because of the tight quarters of the small harbor. There is a new cruise terminal

close to the narrow entrance to the harbor that is capable of handling small size ships, and several captains do now feel comfortable docking, which facilitates greater ease in passenger transit. Thus a visit to Visby should be considered to be a rare treat if your cruise itinerary includes it.

THE NATURAL SETTING: The island of Gotland is the largest island in the Baltic Sea. It lies approximately 64 kilometers or 40 miles off the southeast coast of Sweden. Gotland is an ancient limestone island with its highest elevations being less than 100 meters or 330 feet above sea level. The island occupies 3,183 square kilometers or 1,229 square miles, making it about the size of the American state of Delaware. The population is just under 60,000 and nearly half live in the main city and provincial capital of Visby. Among the up market cruise lines that do make Visby a port of call, this is a somewhat popular stop. It affords the visitor a chance to see a more provincial side to life in Sweden while also exploring the ancient medieval walled inner town, one of the few such places left in northern Europe.

The beauty of Gotland's forests, (Work of Jacek Lesniowski, CC BY SA 3.0, Wikimedia.org)

The island is flat to gently rolling, but surprisingly as the limestone beds lifted out of the sea, there was some deformation giving Gotland a few rocky outcrops and cliffs rising from the sea. Limestone erodes quickly in a humid climate, and the end result is often very good soil. Gotland is primarily an agricultural island with limited fishing and lumbering. Dairy cattle, hearty grains and root vegetables do well given the blustery climate of the Baltic. There are several low-lying marshlands, especially near the coast. But most of the land is high enough to have good drainage.

The climate, as noted before, is blustery. Gotland has plenty of summer rain and winter snow, but the maritime influence of being an island surrounded by a sizeable mass of water tends to moderate the sharp temperature drops found inland in Sweden during the winter months.

The forests of Gotland present a mix of broadleaf deciduous and conifers. And of course autumn brings a great degree of color to the island. But much of the island's forests are now farm and pasture land.

A BRIEF LOCAL HISTORY: In prehistoric times, the island was home to the Gutes, a hunting and farming people, one tribe among several peoples who came to be known as the Goths that ultimately descendants spread outward across northern Europe. In the 7th century, the Gutes agreed to a nominal relationship with Sweden, paying limited taxes and in exchange receiving a defense agreement and the right to settle on the mainland.

Two local residents in medieval dress for the annual reenactment

Swedish merchants settled on the island, founding Visby in the 12th century. But ultimately clashes with the local Gutes forced the Swedish king to put down a rebellion in 1288.

In 1361, the island was conquered by Denmark and it is told that their capture of Visby was a rather bloody event. By 1398, the Teutonic Knights were the masters of Gotland. They in turn sold the island to the united Sweden, Denmark and Norway in 1409. Since 1645 the island has remained permanently under Swedish control, and today the people are fully integrated into the Swedish nation. However, they do speak a dialect called Gotlandska, which is a mixture of Gutesh and Swedish. And their customs and traditions vary from those of the mainland. Agriculture, fishing and tourism dominate the economy and essentially the island is very prosperous, matching the good life of the mainland.

Every year in early August, the residents of the island hold reenactments of the island's medieval history with most residents dressing in costume. Parades, jousting matches and feasting are all part of the island's celebration of its colorful past. This is one of the best medieval festivals to be found in northern Europe. And if you are fortunate to visit Visby during this period, you will feel like you have been transported back through a time warp. The islanders take their participation in this reenactment quite seriously. This is quite a pageant and it appears as if everyone on the island takes to medieval dress during this time.

Beautiful Almadalen Park

CRUISE SHIP DOCK: Up until 2018 there was a very small dock inside the manmade harbor capable of handling a single cruise ship of under 30,000 tons displacement, but still many captains prefer to tender from outside the harbor wall. Navigating inside the wall is a bit difficult and with only one small dock, the majority of captains found it an exercise in futility. But since 2018, the new but small cruise terminal and dock can accommodate two ships of up to 340 meters or approximately 1,000 feet in length. This has eliminated the need for tender service.

It is a short walk from the new docking location to the town center in Visby and a shuttle is not necessary.

The Visby skyline seen from on an approaching board ship

THE PHYSICAL LAYOUT OF VISBY: Visby's old walled town, today a UNESCO World Heritage Site, is the focus of attention by most who visit by ship. The docks, located in the small harbor inside its narrow breakwater and just south of the old walled city, can accommodate two small or one medium size cruise ship at a time, but many captains prefer to anchor offshore and tender guests to the dock. There is a new cruise terminal facility, but the major problem for captains is the navigation through the narrow breakwater entrance, which some find a bit daunting if there is the least bit of wind or rough sea. From the landing it is a short walk through the wall and into the medieval streets of Visby. Exploring this old city, tasting local cuisine and shopping in the large open-air flea market are the main activities for those who stay in Visby

The old walled city begins at Almadalen Park, a beautifully landscaped garden just outside of the southeastern corner of the wall. The wall then runs completely around the city and includes numerous battlement towers, all in perfect repair. There are several gates that penetrate the wall from both the water's edge and the inland side. But old walled Visby extends eastward over a very sharply edged hill and rises quite dramatically from the sea. The streets within the old town are mostly paved in cobbles or stone and the majority are for pedestrian use only.

Beyond the wall you will find modern Visby where the majority of people live. It is characterized by well-planned residential districts that are either oriented toward apartment blocks or single-family homes. And leading out of the main eastern gate is the principal shopping district of the modern city, very well planned with adjacent parking in typical Swedish manner.

There are also bus or bicycle tours that can be taken outward around the island to enjoy its lush beauty and traditional villages. I do recommend that if you choose an island tour to make certain that it is not an all-day event. It would be a shame to miss the chance to walk around what is without doubt one of the best preserved medieval towns in Europe.

OPTIONS FOR SEEING VISBY: There are several options for sightseeing in Visby and around the island of Gotland. These include:

* **Ship sponsored tours** – Your cruise line will offer a variety of primarily walking tours within the old heart of Visby. And there are a few tour options provided by most cruise lines for seeing the rural portions of the island on either half or full day tours by motor coach.

* **Private car and driver** – This option, may be available through your cruise line. Locally in Visby there are no advertised chauffeur services for hire.

* **Rental car services** – There are cars for rent in Visby, and the major rental agencies such as Hertz and Avis do have local offices. I would not recommend driving yourself. The roads are relatively narrow and all traffic signs are written only in Swedish. In the old heart of Visby the streets are exceptionally narrow and are oriented more toward the pedestrian given that this is a medieval old city. Driving and parking would not serve you well, as you would find few places to park and many streets closed to traffic.

* **There is no hop on hop off bus** in Visby, as the number of tourists visiting and the nature of the infrastructure do not provide adequately to support such a service

* **Taxi touring** – As a small port, there are few taxis available, but if you are intent upon seeing some of the island's countryside but do not wish to do so on a tour bus, then you can negotiate an hourly rate and spend two to three hours touring around the villages and farms of the island. Taxi Gotland offers the best service for touring if you arrange in advance. Check their web page at *www.taxigotland.se* for details.

* **Bicycle rental** – Although there are many steep hills in Visby and around the island, riding a bicycle is an excellent way to enjoy this port if you are physically fit. I recommend Gotlands Cykeluthyrning. Check out their web page for details at *www.gotlandscykeluthyrning.com* . You can also check out Visby Hyrcykel at

www.visbyhyrcykel.se and Gotland by Bike at *www.gotlandbybike.com* for more details as to services.

* **Walking** – This is the best way to see old Visby. Within the old walled city, or to visit the small, but modern new town center a vehicle is totally unnecessary. Despite the steep hillside that Visby climbs, it is not overly difficult for most people to navigate since distances are not great.

MAJOR SIGHTSEEING VENUES: The most important venues not to be missed in Visby are as follows:

* **Adelsgatan** – This is the main shopping or commercial street in the old town portion of Visby. It offers both shopping and dining in a very quaint atmosphere. The street is located near the main inland wall, uphill from the waterfront by approximately three blocks. Most visitors are not aware of this main shopping street, as it is not widely publicized. There are some shops and restaurants close to the waterfront, and this is often as far as a large majority of visitors get because the streets beyond are quite steep.

Adelsgatan is the main shopping street in old Visby

* **Almedalen Park** - located on the southern margin of the town wall adjacent to the harbor, Almedalen Park is a beautiful spot from which to take great pictures of the town skyline. There are many vantage points where you will enjoy the views of the old wall and the skyline. Each summer the members of the Swedish Parliament come to the park and use it as a forum to make speeches regarding the current

political situation. This is a long standing tradition, but not of interest to anyone who does not speak the Swedish language. There is no entry fee and the park is open 24-hours each day. It offers excellent photo opportunities with the wall and skyline of old Visby as a backdrop.

The beauty of Almedalen Park

* **Botaniska Trädgårdens** - Located on the northwestern edge of the town center, these beautiful gardens located just inside the old wall are quite majestic during summer when everything is in bloom. There is no charge to enter the gardens and they are open 24-hours a day. The gardens are small, but very beautiful and worth the slight walking detour to reach.

* **Gotlands Museum** - this museum presents an excellent collection of exhibits and artifacts that help to explain the long and often bloody history of Gotland. Most visitors do not have high expectations, but quickly find that this little museum is an absolute gem. The museum is located at Strandgatan #14 and is open from 11 AM to 4 PM daily.

* **Saint Karin Cathedral Ruins** - The largest Gothic church ruin in Visby located right on the main town square, it was destroyed in 1233. The remaining shell of this Gothic church is quite dramatic and you can see how intricate the original

construction was. The ruins are always open to visitors and there is no admission charge.

Inside the ruins of old St. Catherine (Karin) Cathedral

* **Saint Nicolai Church Ruins** - The largest of the 13th century church ruins found in the town of Visby, Saint Nicolai's walls are still primarily intact and they give you some insight into how churches were built in medieval times. When Valdemar IV of Denmark invaded, much of the city was destroyed in 1361 thus leaving ruins still standing today. The ruins are in the center of Visby and are open 24-hours per day.

* **Santa Maria Domkyrka** - Within the walled city at its northern end is the beautiful Saint Mary's Cathedral, center of Swedish Lutheran worship in the city. Originating in the 12th century, this Gothic style cathedral is beautifully maintained. It is not grand in the manner of large city cathedrals, but given the history of Visby, it is quite striking and beautiful. The cathedral is open during the day to visitors, but please be respectful if a service is being conducted when you visit. Visiting hours are between 9 AM and 5 PM daily.

* **Visby City Walls** - Among the best preserved in all of Europe, these stone walls with most of their battlement towers intact are one of the reasons why UNESCO has declared Visby a World Heritage Site. Most of the wall dates back to the year 1300 and it spans a total circumference of 2.41 miles.

SIGHTS OUTSIDE OF VISBY: Most ship passengers simply spend time walking around Visby, as its old walled portion is very easy to navigate. Touring around the island will show you the beautiful, lush farmland and the few fishing villages, but there are no major sites outside of Visby. The few significant attractions include:

* **Bungemuseet** - A local museum that offers a collection of old buildings to show how people lived in rural Gotland centuries ago. It is located in the small village of Farosund. The museum is open from 11 AM to 6 PM through August 8th and it only remains open until 4 PM daily. It is accessible by taxi unless you take an island tour that includes the museum.

* **Lummelundagrottan** - This is a wet limestone cavern that is still in the process of growing, given the wet climate. It is filled with stalactites and stalagmites in true cave fashion. Located just a few kilometers north of Visby, it can be reached easily by taxi. During summer the cavern is open from 9 AM to 6 PM daily. Guided tours are offered. There is a small cafe on site.

* **Rydal Museum** - Located in the village of Vastra, this museum was once a small textile factory that looks today as it did when it was in production. It is open from 7:30 AM to 4:30 PM Monday thru Thursday, closing at 4 PM on Friday. If it is not on any ship sponsored tour itinerary, you can visit by taxi.

WHERE TO DINE: The cuisine of Gotland is essentially very much like mainland Sweden. However, there is one special treat and that is the saffron infused pancakes served with dewberry jam and whipped cream. This is a very popular dish that should be tried. There are many shops advertising the saffron pancakes and it is very easy to sample with either a cup of Swedish coffee or tea.

Saffron infused pancakes with dewberry jam and whipped cream

Most fine restaurants are not open for lunch, and among those that are, many serve fast food such as pizza, which is not very Swedish. My favorites are recommended for lunch in Visby:

Small restaurants about in the heart of Visby

* **Bakfickan** - Located on Stora Torget #1, this restaurant is especially known for its delicious fish soups and fresh breads. It is a very small and unassuming restaurant, so do not be turned away by its lack of lavish decor. It is a good idea to make a reservation through the local hospitality rep because it accommodates so few people at a time. Hours are from 11 AM to 10 PM weekdays, opening at Noon on weekends and closing at 10 PM. You could also call about booking a table at +46 498 27 17 07.

* **Jessens Saluhall and Bar** - Located at Hæstgatan # 16, this restaurant features grilled fish and meat dishes. The atmosphere is low key, but the service is great and on warm days you can dine al fresco. Their entire menu is based upon what is available fresh each day. They are open from 11 AM to 9 PM daily. You can call to see if they take bookings at +46 498 21 42 14.

* **Lilla Bjers Gårdskrog** - This excellent restaurant with a nice atmosphere in a greenhouse is located just outside central Visby at Lilla Bjers #410. It is open daily for lunch and a reservation is recommended through the local hospitality representative. They are daily from 11:30 AM to 2 PM with Thursday and Sunday opening at 10:30 AM. Dinner is served daily from 5 to 11:30 PM. Call them at +46 498 65 24 40 to see about booking a table.

* **Vardshuset Lindgården** - Located in Visby at Strandgatan #26, this hotel and restaurant offer the finest in traditional Swedish dining. The atmosphere and cuisine are excellent. Be prepared for an unhurried meal, so this is not a place to dine if you are rushed. A reservation is strongly advised and can be made through the local hospitality rep. This is a relatively expensive restaurant, but worth the cost. It is open Wednesday thru Sunday from 3 PM. No set closing is posted. Call +46 598 21 87 00 to book a table.

* **Visby Creperie and Logi** - Located at Wallers plads # 3, this is a popular restaurant with more of a French flair, but also wrapped into a Swedish vibe. Crepes are the main entree, as well as for dessert and it is hard to decide which to choose. It is a popular restaurant with locals, so call +46 73 087 05 06 to book a table . They are open daily from 11 AM to 10 PM.

SHOPPING: I have no specific recommendations with regard to shopping for local crafts. There are numerous shops throughout the old city area, and for sundries or other needs, you need to exit the main east gate into the modern city where you will find a variety of regular shops.

The modern shopping area outside the wall east of the main landward gate

In the main square of the old city there is often a local craft and flea market, especially during their medieval celebrations.

FINAL NOTES: Visby is still relatively unspoiled since the number of foreign tourists is not at a level where it has altered the culture. Tourism is important, but I have always had the feeling that the restaurants and shops cater more to a Swedish audience and therefore the sense is one of a more genuine tourist experience.

I do recommend that when you go ashore you should plan upon spending the whole day. This means treating yourself to lunch at one of the restaurants I have recommended or one that appeals to you on sight. You cannot go wrong, as the food is going to be tasty and you will come away satisfied.

One way of getting to know a community is by just walking its streets, visiting its shops and definitely sampling the local cuisine. Visby definitely possesses atmosphere, and it is a delight to just wander about and soak in the local color.If you wish to tour the island, hire a local taxi, as most drivers speak English. You can go out for an hour or two and simply sample the local countryside. There are no major attractions, but just enjoying the landscape is in itself the attraction.

MAP OF VISBY

CENTRAL VISBY, GOTLAND

Central Visby, Gotland, (© OpenStreetMap contributors)

This map is best viewed directly from OpenStreetMap.com on your personal device where it can be expanded or one specific area can be enlarged. Given the format of this book, it is impossible to display maps with the level of detail you might wish to have while actually out exploring the city. But the OpenStreetMap maps used directly are the tool I always rely upon.

STOCKHOLM, SWEDEN

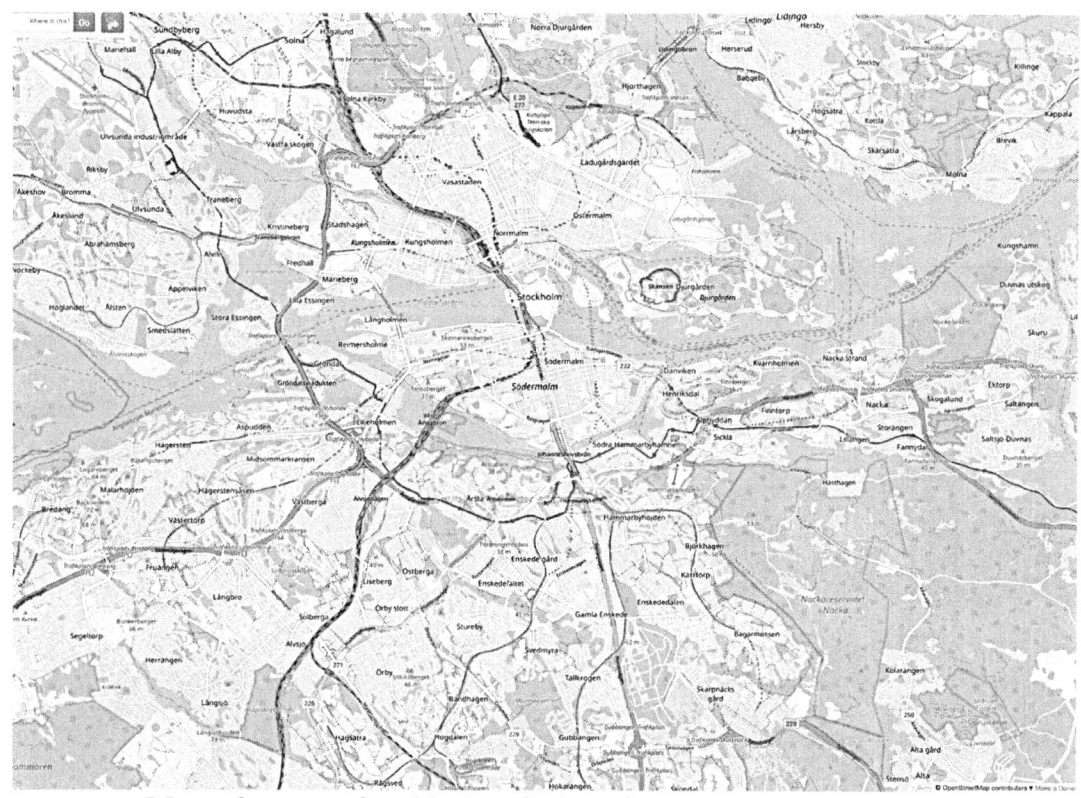

Map of greater Stockholm (© OpenStreetMap contributors)

Everyone has a favorite city including we who are travel writers. When it comes to my favorite European city it is without a doubt Stockholm. There is something about the aura of this elegant city that appeals to my taste, and if I were around 20 years younger, I could easily see myself living here. Stockholm is both the capital city of Sweden and the largest city in Scandinavia, although residents of Copenhagen contest that assertion since both cities are of almost equal size. Often called "The Venice of the North" because of its many waterways and islands, Stockholm is one of the most beautiful of cities on the continent. But I personally do not see the merits of the implication that it is at all like Venice. Stockholm does not have actual canals and its architecture is in no way similar to that of Venice. The many islands and peninsulas are all of natural origin, and the city does not face the open sea, as is true of Venice. Stockholm's green surroundings, its level of cleanliness, its medieval charming Gamla Stan (Old Town) contrasting with its ultra-modern facilities all combine to make Stockholm a city that is world class in both amenities and flavor.

THE NATURAL SETTING: Stockholm is not on the Baltic Sea. The city is located about 100 kilometers or 60 miles west of the Gulf of Bothnia at the upper end of what can only be described as a glacially scoured bay that is filled with approximately 1,000 rocky islands. This island filled channel is called the Archipelago, and it is a playground for Stockholm residents who make good use of

the many forest-covered islands by building vacation homes that range in size from bungalows to mansions. Small ferryboats connect many of the larger villages with the Saltslön, the main harbor in central Stockholm. For cruise ships and long distance ferryboats entering and leaving Stockholm, the transit of the Archipelago takes between three and four hours, as the ships wend their way through this beautiful maze of islands between the city and the Baltic Sea, each required to have a local pilot on board.

Sailing through the Archipelago en route into Stockholm in the early morning

The location of Stockholm resulted in a favored position for the development of a trading outpost because the waters of the large body of freshwater called Lake Mälaren used to cascade over a series of rapids into the Saltslön, thus making it necessary to portage local boats around the rapids. By the 19th century, two small canals with wood locks connected the lake and the waters of the Saltslön, and these small locks are still used today by pleasure craft and barges. The city initially developed on a small island that split the rapids between Lake Mälaren and the Saltslön. Today Gamla Stan is the most historic and tourist oriented part of the city. Several large peninsulas that jut into the upper end of the Archipelago combined with several large islands both in the Saltslön and Lake Mälaren have been built up and compose the central city of Stockholm. But unlike other European cities where the city center and the suburbs merge into a blur of urban development, Stockholm is quite unique. The inner city area is relatively small and is separated from the outer suburbs by zones of natural woodland that are replete with walking trails and public sports venues. And each of the outer suburbs is separated from the next by further parklands. This gives Stockholm a very airy and open feel with plenty of breathing room where people are not living in one continual urbanized zone.

Dozens of small villages on quiet coves in the Archipelago

Elegant homes on Lidingo Island in the Archipelago on the edge of Stockholm

At nearly 60 degrees north latitude, Stockholm experiences long, cold winters with very little daylight. Snow can often accumulate to major depths, lending beauty to the city's many parklands, but of course creating difficulties for automobiles, busses and trains. And until more recently, the waters of the Saltslön would freeze over. However, in recent years, the severity of winter has lessened throughout much of the Scandinavian Peninsula, no doubt tied to global climatic change. This has enabled a longer period for navigation through the Archipelago, but for at least two months, shipping is severely limited.

Summer days are long, the height of summer experiencing just over 20 hours of daylight. Temperatures are mild and there are frequent rain showers. I must say that overall the overall climate is not one of the most endearing attributes of Stockholm, but the people of Sweden are accustomed to their climate and do not find it to be inhospitable. And on a mild sunny day it is exceptionally beautiful.

A BRIEF LOCAL HISTORY: The origin of Stockholm can be traced to what is now Gamla Stan, the old city and it dates back to approximately the year 1000. The meeting of the waters of Lake Mälaren with the waters of the Saltslön was a natural location for people to come together and trade. The Saltslön is part of the greater series of channels and islands that ultimately lead to the waters of the Gulf of Bothnia.

Although the site of Stockholm can be documented from old Viking stories known as the Norse sagas, the use of the modern name is not seen in any written documents until the year 1252. But the exact origin of the city is still shrouded in controversy. Some believe it grew into a small trade center because of nearby iron mining while others say it was developed as a small fortified community to help stave off attacks from tribes coming across from Finland to plunder and other scholars contend that its development was based primarily upon trade.

By the start of the 14th century, Hanseatic League influences can be seen, as German traders were established on Gamla Stan, the architectural remnants still visible today. Trade in furs would have been quite lucrative at this time in Baltic history, and the forests of Sweden were rich in fur bearing animals.

The strength of Denmark in the late 1400's was resisted by the German merchants of Stockholm and ultimately helped propel a move for Swedish independence from the Danish controlled Kalmar Union. Once the union was dissolved in 1523, Sweden began to rise as an important nation with its own royal house firmly led by Gustav Vasa, and Stockholm ultimately became the capital in 1634.

Between 1713 and 1714, Stockholm lost about one third of its population to a major plague, and this loss brought about economic stagnation. No longer was Sweden considered to be a major player in Baltic affairs, and it had to rebuild its economy and reputation. The plague occurred during the period known as The Great Northern War (1700-1721) when Russia rose up initially under Peter the Great and threatened the power of Sweden. Ultimately the country contracted in size and lost is great military and economic supremacy. Stockholm has become a major economic center prior to the war, and after the Northern War its influence waned.

On the historic streets of Gamla Stan

Swedish pride seen at the Changing of the Guard in the Royal Palace

The industrial revolution of the 19th century brought about great changes, as Sweden embraced industrial development and trade. Sweden used its mineral and forest resources to become one of the early industrial giants. And with such people as Alfred Nobel, its lead in scientific development related to the industrial world grew. And as the capital, all trade and finance centered upon Stockholm. It was during this period that much of the elegant architecture seen today was built. As the major economic and governmental center there was a lot of in migration to Stockholm and the city grew outward in size. Unfortunately as growth continued into the early 20th century, many of the more elegant buildings of the 19th century gave way to the more utilitarian architecture of what was sometimes considered to be the period of "Swedish Modern." Today the city skyline does reflect both eras.

There is a high degree of patriotic spirit. The Swedish flag, which consists of a royal blue background atop which there is a yellow cross, is flown everywhere. All of the Scandinavian nations are proud of their heritage and proudly show their flags. This is also a deeply religious nation, the dominant faith being that of the Swedish Lutheran Church. Many old church buildings date back centuries, their spires often being the tallest landmarks in each neighborhood. At one time in past centuries, Swedes were fined and severely ostracized if they did not attend Sunday church services. Today religion is separated from state, and such Draconian laws do not exist. Although the Lutheran faith dominates, there are other religious minorities in the country. Stockholm has a small, but active Jewish community, and recent immigrants from the Middle East have brought Islam to Sweden. Religious minorities have always been accepted since the days of the Protestant Reformation, and persecution has never been a fact of Swedish life.

This country's neutrality protected all of its citizens from Nazi invasion during World War II, as the Germans firstly saw no strategic reason to violate that neutrality and secondly they wanted to have one friendly power that could validate German treatment of captured nations. The Swedish Red Cross was often invited into German concentration camps, shown artificially created settings in which detainees were well treated, this in hopes that the Swedes would spread the word to America that Germany was not abusing Jews and other minorities. At first this ruse had some effect, but the Swedes ultimately saw through German actions.

Today there is great interest in the protection of the aura of the past, and it is of course an important selling point for the growing tourist market. Gamla Stan, heart of old Stockholm, is today the most visited part of the city.

THE PHYSICAL LAYOUT OF STOCKHOLM: Greater Stockholm has a metropolitan population of about 2,5 million people. But few high-rise buildings are seen on the skyline. Rather it is the church spires and old castles and palaces that dominate the city. The Saltslön is the main harbor around which the central city is built, part of Stockholm having been developed on outlying islands (see the maps at the end of this chapter). Most of the central business area consists of buildings from the 17th, 18th and 19th centuries mingled with more modern structures, but most under ten stories. There are many parks and small plazas, and even the major streets are lined with trees. Stockholm is a very green city as well as being so exceptionally clean. Swedes are highly respectful of their public places and litter is something rarely seen.

With numerous islands and peninsulas, there is a strong interplay between land and water. Yet the way in which bridges were restricted to the narrowest channels, most of Lake Mäleran and the channels of the Archipelago are free of spans and give the overall city a very natural appearance in which the urban landscape blends beautifully with the natural one. The main components of Stockholm include:

* **Gamla Stan** - The small island that is the heart of the original city. It contains the oldest buildings in Stockholm and is also home to the Swedish Royal Palace. With its narrow streets and centuries old buildings, this small island is the original heart of Stockholm. It is also the most visited part of the city, especially because of the daily changing of the guard at noon, which culminates in the courtyard of the Royal Palace.

Kungstradgarden in the heart of Normalm

* **Normalm** - The commercial core of modern Stockholm is located just to the north of Gamla Stan and it has a fairly regular street pattern. Normalm shows a mix of architecture from the last three centuries, but tends to be dominated by 20th century buildings. It is here that the true commercial heart, or downtown of Stockholm is found. It is home to the major named stores, small shops and hotels as well as banks and government offices.

* **Blasiholman** – This is a small peninsula on which is located the Grand Hotel, facing to the Royal Palace. Essentially it is an extension of Normalm, the city center.

Aerial view of central Stockholm from over Blasieholmen (Work of Jeppe Wilkström, CC BY SA 3.0, Wikimedia.org)

Strandvagen along the Ostermalm waterfront

* Ostermalm - The trendy up market commercial and residential district that extends along the northern shoreline just east of Normalm is one of the most prestigious parts of the city. The finest shops, boutique hotels and dining establishments are found in Ostermalm. There are also numerous foreign embassies found here as well.

In the heart of fashionable Kungsholmen

* **Kungsholmen** - This is another fashionable district, actually an island just to the west of Normalm. The magnificent Stockholm City Hall, a very palatial structure dominates the lakefront in Kungsholmen. There are also several historic old buildings in this district as well.

* **Sodermalm** - This is a large and very rocky island with steep hills located immediately south of Gamla Stan. Sodermalm shows a mix of architectural styles from the last three centuries. It also has at its core a significant shopping district.

* **Drottningholm** - A large and very beautiful island, Drottningholm sits in Lake Mäleran just to the west of the city center. It is here that the Royal Palace where the monarch is in residence is located. Drottningholm Palace is not to be confused with the main Royal Palace on Gamla Stan where the Crown offices are housed.

* **Lidingo Island** - The largest island in the greater Stockholm area, this is a very elegant residential community with many very upscale mansions combined with numerous high-rise apartments. Lidingo Island is connected to the mainland with both highway and railway bridges.

A Metro that runs underground through the central city and at ground level in the suburbs connects the various component districts together through a single central station under Normalm known as T Centrolan. There is also a commuter rail network out of Central Railway Station in Normalm that links all of the outermost suburbs with the city center.

There are very few residential neighborhoods consisting of single-family houses until you get into the outer suburban areas of the city. Most Stockholm residents live in apartment blocks of various types. In the older part of the city, they crowd together and often front right on the street. In the newer suburbs, the apartment blocks are set into park or garden areas, giving their residents ample room to enjoy the out of doors. Once out of the central city, the various suburban districts are interspersed with parkland that gives the overall city a feeling of spaciousness. Stockholm is not one contiguous city of built up sectors.

Most of the buildings in Stockholm are built either of stone or brick. Many of the older stone buildings are covered in a coating of plaster, which is painted in pastel colors. This gives the city a rather bright and airy look. And when combined with all of its open green spaces and the many bays and coves of both Lake Mälaren and the Saltslön the city has an atmosphere of great airiness. Given the long cold winters, most buildings have rather steeply pitched roofs covered in slate tiles. Thus this city of the far north, where winter nights are long, is colorful with regard to its architecture. During the summer the parks are lush with rich green grass and the flowerbeds are bursting forth with a myriad of blooms, adding to the overall color of the city, while the winter landscape can be rather bleak to those who are not fond of snowy vistas.

CRUISE TERMINALS: There are several places where cruise ships are capable of docking in Stockholm. Where your ship docks is a combination of its size and draught as well as the importance of your cruise line with regard to the payment of docking fees. Smaller ships belonging to the more upmarket cruise lines do seem to have the advantage of being able to dock in the inner city.

For the majority of cruise itineraries in the Baltic Sea, Stockholm is either the embarkation or terminal port. Only a handful of itineraries do not either commence or terminate in Stockholm.

These are the major docking locations for cruise ships in Stockholm:

* **Stadsgården 160** is the most favored docking location by passengers, located under the high cliff on the northern side of Södermalm Island. This location has no terminal, but it is easily accessible to Gamla Stan and Normalm on foot, which is especially convenient if your itinerary calls for a touring day in Stockholm either prior to sailing of or termination of your cruise. It is easy for tour busses, taxis and private cars to literally meet guests right at the ship's gangway. I have walked into the heart of the city from this site many times.

* **Stadsgården Cruise Center** is just to the east of the first location at Stadsgården 160. This is where Viking Cruise Lines along with a few other companies whose ships are of medium size will dock. This location is known as Saltsjön and does have an actual terminal building. Being about 300 meters or 1,000 feet farther away from the ramp leading over to Gamla Stan it is slightly farther to walk into the city center if you have a day of touring before sailing or terminating your cruise.

* **Frihamnsgatan 115** is a major dock where large cruise ships will be moored. This is a part of the significant harbor used by Tallink and Silja Lines for their at ferryboats. It is located at the far eastern edge of Östermalm and is not easily accessible from the city center on foot. However, if you have a day before sailing or the termination of your cruise, it is a bit of a walk to the Gärdet Station on the Stockholm subway, which will take you into the city center in minutes.

* **On days when many ships are in port,** small to medium size vessels can often be moored just north of Frihamnsgatan 115 at an open berth without a terminal building. This is actually advantageous if you have a day of touring, as it is only half the distance from the Gärdet Station.

* **Small cruise ships from the upmarket cruise lines** are often moored in Gamla Stan along Skepsholm when the port is crowded. Although there are no terminal facilities, this is an absolutely choice location for touring, as you are right in the heart of Gamla Stan just steps from the Royal Palace.

SIGHTSEEING IN AND AROUND STOCKHOLM: The majority of cruise itineraries for the Baltic Sea either begin or terminate in Stockholm, as is true in Copenhagen. In those instances the cruise lines do not offer tours of the city or its surroundings other than quick drive through excursions en route to the airport for departing guests or to a major hotel for those staying over in the city. This is true in most cases, but a few itineraries do include a full day and night in Stockholm either before sailing or before you disembark. In either case, I highly recommend that you stay a few days in Stockholm either before or following your cruise if the city is at one end of your itinerary otherwise you will be missing the grand crown jewel of Scandinavian cities. I rank Stockholm second only to Saint Petersburg with regard to being the Baltic city with the most elegant architecture and richness of its culture. This is a city that entices visitors to linger because of its many historic sites and its grand architecture, showing that Stockholm has been the capital of a nation whose roots go back to days when the Swedes were a mighty power.

SIGHTSEEING OPTIONS IN STOCKHOLM: Here are the various options for seeing the sights Stockholm has to offer either on the day in your itinerary or while you are in a hotel prior to or post cruising:

* **Ship sponsored tours** – If your cruise line is offering tours will depend upon the itinerary. If Stockholm is the embarkation or terminal port for your cruise is a critical factor. Normally if you are embarking, there will be no ship sponsored tours unless a full day in port is provided prior to sailing. But if your cruise is terminating in Stockholm, the cruise line may arrive a day prior to the end of the cruise and offer a variety of group motor coach tours.

If your ship is not allowing a day prior to disembarkation, an overview tour offered by the cruise line en route to one or more hotels will simply give you a glimpse of the city more in passing while the tour takes you to one or two venues for photo opportunities. And for departing guests there are often overview tours while en route to the airport for your flight home.

View from Gamla Stan to the Grand Hotel at the upper end of the Saltslön where harbor and lake cruises have their docks

* **Private car and driver option** – For more independent exploration it is necessary to either pre order a car and driver through the ship's shore excursion desk or after leaving the ship you can do so through your hotel concierge. To book a private car and driver/guide on your own, here are my suggestions:

** **Blacklane** is a very well respected operator that offers you private sightseeing at *www.blacklane.com/chauffeur-service-stockholm.*

** Look into Tours by Locals at _www.toursbylocals.com/stockholm-tours_ to see what they offer.

** You may also wish to check with Freys at _www.freys.se_ to view their services.

* **Rental cars** – All major car rental agencies have offices in Stockholm. You can rent a self-driving car but most do not have automatic transmission. And keep in mind that all traffic information signs are written in Swedish only. Parking is another issue, as there are not many places where you can park at major venues.

* **Hop on hop off busses** are found in the central city, most congregating opposite the Opera House on Gustav Adolf Torg. These busses have routes that enable you to visit most of the major scenic venues of the city, and they provide maps and interpretative services on board. Visit on line for full details and route descriptions at _www.hop-on-op-off-bis.com/Stockholm_.

* **Taxi services** – There are numerous licensed taxis in Stockholm and you may be able to negotiate an hourly rate. Be sure that any taxi you use has the yellow rate information sticker in its side window, as this denotes it is a licensed vehicle. The best known company is Taxi Stockholm at _www.taxistockholm.se_ where you can check rates and book on line.

Stockholm's clean and efficient Metro

* **The Metro** is very efficient and fast, and its network makes it possible to visit most major venues. However, within the central part of the city the Metro travels underground so you do miss much of the scenery between stops. But in the suburbs,

the trains do run at ground level. All day visitor passes are available at a nominal rate. The pass can also be used on surface busses and the one tramline in the city center. Visit on line with www.visitstockholm.com/using-the-subway for full details. All routes converge at T-Centrolen in the heart of the city underneath Sergelstorg, which makes it easy to use the system. And at this main station there are maps and multi-lingual information available.

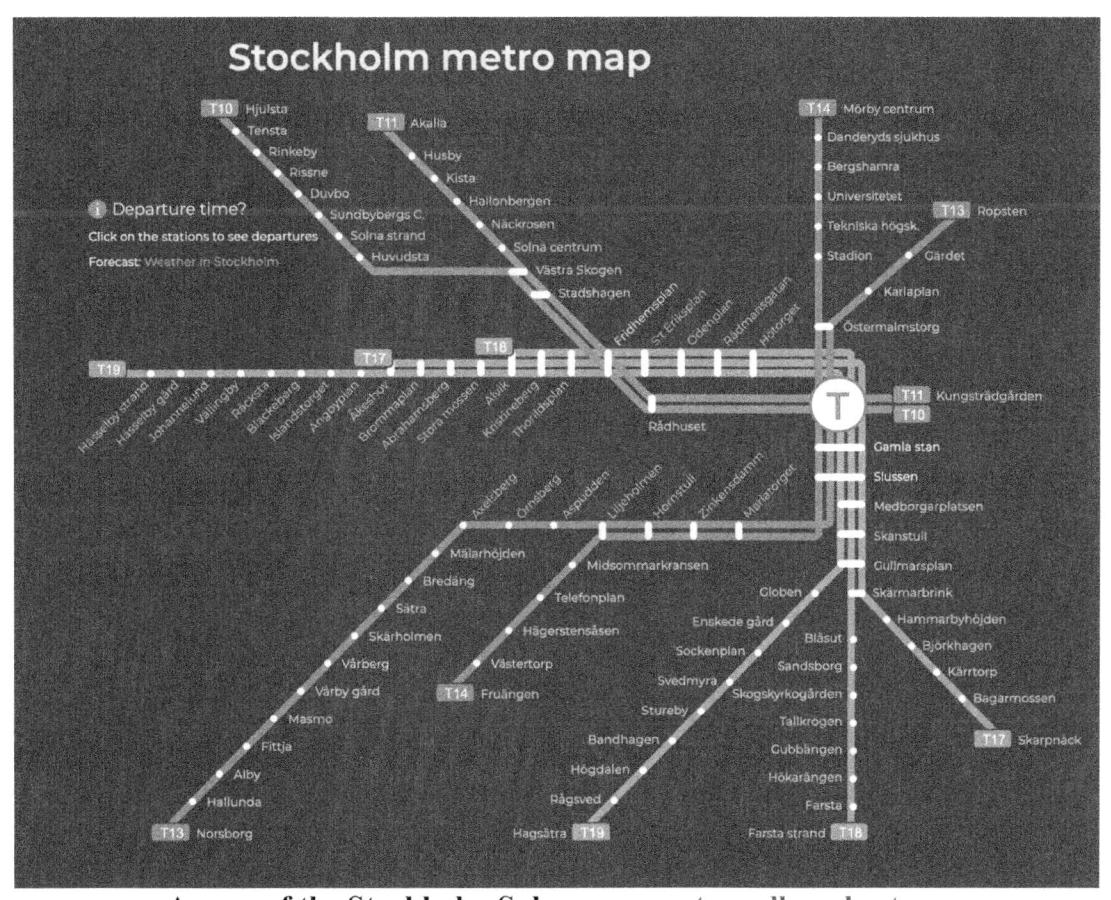

A map of the Stockholm Subway, www.tunnelbanakarta.se

* **Stockholm also offers several boat excursions** through both Lake Mälaren and the Saltslön. These tour boats are a nice way to spend a few hours viewing the city skyline from the water. There are also boats that visit some of the popular nearby island communities in the Archipelago, the most frequented being Vaxholm Island. You will find the majority of the tour boats docked in front of the Grand Hotel and they will post their various offerings.

* **Walking** – With the vast majority of hotels being located in Gamla Stan, Normalm or Ostermalm, walking is still another way to get around Stockholm's inner core where most of the tourist attractions are located. With regard to potential crime, Stockholm is one of the safest cities in Europe, so there is no need for worry. However, some pickpockets are found around tourist venues, as is true almost everywhere today.

SIGHTS TO SEE IN STOCKHOLM. This is a major city with a rich history and a beautiful setting, thus there is plenty to occupy several days when visiting. I recommend that you purchase the Stockholm Pass to save money on entrance fees. Go to www.stockholmpass.com/Official to purchase the pass.

I recommend the following important Stockholm venues to be visited shown here in alphabetical order:

*ABBA Museum - for fans of ABBA, this is a must, as the museum honors the famous music of the 70's and 80's. For those who are ABBA fans, this museum is now a must. The museum, located on Djurgården, is open daily from 10 AM to 7 PM through August and then from 10 AM to 6 PM starting in September for the fall months, but extended to 7 PM on Wednesday. If using public transportation it is easy to reach from Hamngatan in the city center utilizing the light rail line.

* Djurgården – A large wooded peninsula of land right in the heart of the city and home to many museums and recreational venues. From here one will find the best views of the downtown skyline and Gamla Stan. It is easy to reach Djurgården by means of the city's only tramline that runs from the city center and stops at all major venues on the peninsula. The following important venues are located on Djurgården and can be reached on the light rail tram that leaves from Hamngatan adjacent to the main Metro crossing of T-Centrolan.

* Drottningholm – One of the city's most beautiful islands, which also contains Drottningholm Palace, home to the Swedish Royal Family. There are limited tours available to many of the important public rooms in the palace. Tickets must be secured by your hotel or online for tours that are offered between 10 AM and 5 PM through September and then only to 4 PM in October. You can reach Drottningholm via the Metro Blue Line to Brommaplan and then the Drottningholm bus to the palace. The palace web page where you can arrange for tickets is www.kungligaslotten.se and then click on English at the top right.

* Gamla Stan – This small island is home to the oldest buildings in Stockholm lining narrow and twisting streets. It was on Gamla Stan that the city began, and its architecture reflects its long parade of historic events. There are many small cafes, bistros and coffee houses along with very elegant restaurants in Gamla Stan. Gamla Stan is walking distance from most major city center hotels; it is also connected to the Metro with all southbound red and green line trains stopping on the island. There are also many souvenir, craft and gift shops all through the island of Gamla Stan. And it is here that the changing of the guard takes place each day at the royal palace.

* Humlegården – this is a major central city park, but not as crowded as the Kungstradgården. It is not a tourist attraction, but it is rather just a quiet park in

which to sit and watch the locals enjoying the out of doors. It is located in Ostermalm and can be accessed via the Metro Red Line to the Ostermalmstorg Station.

Kungliga Slottet is the Royal Palace in Gamla Stan

* Kungliga Slottet - Sweden's Royal Palace is said to be one of the largest in all of Europe. The king does not live in this massive building, but rather occupies a smaller palace in the suburb of Drottningholm. Kungliga Slottet is used for state occasions. Like at Buckingham Palace in London, there is a ceremonial changing of the guard every day, but the Swedish palace guards wear uniforms more tailored and 21st century looking. Pomp and ceremony is not as much a part of Royal life, as it is in Britain, but the changing of the guard is quite elaborate and a must for every visitor. The palace is located at the northern end of Gamla Stan, just steps from the city center. It is easily accessible on foot, by taxi or the hop on hop off bus. Tours are offered during visiting hours from 10 AM to 4 PM daily. Guided tours are offered in several languages. For more information check the website at *www.kungligaslotten.se* where tickets can also be purchased.

The changing of the guard ceremony attracts a large crowd, but nothing like that seen at Buckingham Palace in London. The guard parade begins in the city center and the guards and their band march west along Hamngatan, the main shopping street. It then turns south to Gamla Stan when it approaches the King's Garden opposite the large NK Department Store. Here along the east side of the park you can get a good close up view of the guards, but then you will not make it to the palace for the actual ceremony.

Changing of the guard at the Royal Palace

Spring flowers in the Kungstradgården

Kungstradgården - the most popular inner city garden, crowded with young workers during the lunch hour. It is one of the prime meeting spots in Stockholm located in the very heart of the city. Also known as King's Gardens, it is in the heart of the commercial district and as noted previously, it is a good place to watch the parade of guards on their way to the royal palace for the changing of the guard ceremony.

* **Lill-Jansskogen** – a massive garden and sports complex that includes academic, sports and recreational facilities, located on the northern end of the island. Much of the park is natural woodland and offers the amenities of being in the country when you are in fact in the city. It is open year around for both summer and winter sports activities.

* **Nordiska Muset** – the museum devoted to Nordic culture will give visitors a good look into the life of the ancient Scandinavian people. The museum also gives you much of the historic detail about the countries of Scandinavia as well. There is an excellent restaurant serving lunch and an incredible dessert selection daily between 121 AM and 3 PM, extended to 4 PM on weekends. It is open from 9 AM to 6 PM through August and then from 10 AM to 5 PM daily with extended time to 8 PM on Wednesdays. The museum is in Djurgården and easily reached on the light rail line.

* **Ostermalm** - the suburban area immediately east of the city center, Ostermalm is home to very high-end shops and great restaurants. It is also a prime residential district with beautiful 18th and 19th century apartment blocks. It is easy to walk to Ostermalm from most hotels in the city center, or via the tramline that goes to Djurgården. Ostermalm is one of the most beautiful urban districts in the city.

* **Riksdag** – This is the Swedish National Parliament is located just north of Gamla Stan on its own tiny island, a beautiful building of 19th century architecture. Sweden's parliament carries on lively debates, as this nation truly understands the concept of democracy, and the Swedish people take a great deal of interest in the running of their nation. There are guided tours offered from late June until late August, guided in English at Noon, 1, 2 and 3 PM on weekdays. Arrangements can be made through your hotel concierge.

* **Skansen Open Air Museum** - This combination amusement park and outdoor village attempts to recreate the setting for rural Swedish life over the past centuries. It is a venue that can be enjoyed by adults and children as well. The grounds are quite extensive and a lot of walking is required to see all of the historic outdoor exhibits. During summer Skansen is open daily from 10 AM to 6 PM. For anyone traveling with children, Skansen is one of the most popular of venues for keeping young ones entertained.

* **Södermalm** – This is a hilly island that contains some of the oldest residential neighborhoods in Stockholm. It is located south of the island of Gamla Stan, connected by a major road and railway bridge. It is also accessible via the southbound red and green Metro lines from the city center.

* **Stockholm Skyview** - The Ericsson Globe is a spherical landmark in the southern part of the city. The Skyview is a series of gondolas attached to a track that wraps around this towering dome, reaching an apex of over 130 meters or 425 feet above street level. The 30-minute ride is quite exciting and the view on a clear day is rather breathtaking. This is a very popular attraction, thus it is important to have your hotel secure tickets in advance. If you happen to be on a cruise that is offering tours in Stockholm because the itinerary does not make this a city of embarkation or debarkation, then guided tours may be offered. It is one of the best ways to get a fantastic overview of the city. Rides are given between 10 AM and 6 PM weekdays, but only to 4 PM on weekends. Your hotel can book tickets via telephone.

The grand exterior of the Stadhuset

* **Stockholm Stadhuset** - the beautiful Italian Renaissance city hall was built in the early 20th century with palatial grandeur. Although it is a working city hall, it has many public rooms that would rival any royal residence. The various public facilities are used for a variety of important events, but most notable in the grand interior court is the annual Nobel Prize banquet. The most magnificent room in the Stadhus is the Gold Hall that contains massive wall murals all done in mosaic tiles, most containing gold leaf. Tours are given hourly in a variety of languages depending upon the makeup of the visitors at the time. You cannot wander around the building on your own. You must be on a guided tour. Guided tours are offered from 9:30 AM to 3 PM daily, but the languages offered vary with the composition of people present. English is the most common foreign language tour offered. Visits to the tower for a fantastic view of the city occur at 40-minute intervals starting at

9:10 AM and continuing thru 3:50 PM. Sorry there is no elevator (lift) and you must be able to climb the stairs to the top of the tower.

The great battleship Vasa

* Vasa Museum – This is a museum built around one of the world's largest 17th century wood warships every constructed. But because it was top heavy, it sunk soon after launching. The Vasa is one of the greatest attractions in Stockholm, often rated highest on the list of venues to be visited. The museum is open from 8:30 AM to 6 PM daily through August and then from 10 AM to 5 PM starting September 1. The Vasa Museum is easily reached in Djurgården via the light rail line from the city center.

DINING OUT IN STOCKHOLM: Cuisine in Stockholm is absolutely one of the best parts of visiting the city. The number and variety of restaurants is quite significant. Restaurants abound in central Stockholm, and Swedes pack into them for both lunch and dinner since this is an affluent country and dining out is almost a national pastime.

Traditional Swedish smörgåsbord is the buffet type lunch that is unlike what most visitors would call a buffet. It is without a doubt the most Swedish of all dining experiences. There is a great variety of both hot and cold dishes, many centering on the sea, as fish of all types are popular in this part of the world. Smörgåsbord is not eaten from a single plate as so many North American buffets present. Waiters will advise you to use as many dishes as you wish, and to eat slowly, sampling one course at a time. Various types of smoked fish, pickled herring and salmon will be served along with boiled potatoes as the first course. This is followed by soup and/or a variety of cold salads. Then one chooses from a variety of meats, including reindeer and a great variety of cheeses and crisp flatbreads. As for desserts, it is hard to beat the Swedish bakers. They produce variety of elegant fruit dishes, all types of crisp and buttery cookies and delectable pastries.

Once again I will recommend only those restaurants that I have found present traditional Swedish cuisine in a warm and inviting atmosphere where service adds to the dining pleasure. And as in Oslo, these dining experiences tend to be rather expensive. But at least you are getting the best that the country has to offer. My choices in Stockholm include:

* **Fem Små Hus** - A restaurant that occupies the basements of five small houses and that is where it gets its name. The traditional Swedish cuisine and service are absolutely elegant. There is a broad menu including a variety of traditional meats, fish and seafood. And for an appetizer, I strongly recommend their herring platter with a good Swedish beer on the side. Fem Sma Hus is in Gamla Stan at Nygrand 10. They open at 5 PM and close at 11 PM Tuesday thru Thursday and close at Midnight Friday and Saturday. Reservations are highly recommended. You can book on line at *www.bookatable.se*

The Veranda at the Grand Hotel

* **Grand Hotel** for smörgåsbord - for those who are willing to pay significantly for lunch, this is a memorable treat. I have been to the Grand Hotel for its unrivaled smörgåsbord several times. And every experience has been memorable. The Grand Hotel is located on the waterfront opposite the Royal Palace and Parliament on Sodra Blasieholmshamnen 8. Smörgåsbord is served from 11:30 AM until 4 PM

weekdays. You can book a table on line at www.grandhotel.se and go to the Veranda Dining Room.

* **Kagges** - At Lilla Nygatan # 21 in Gamla Stan, this is one of the fine dining establishments where you will find traditional Swedish cuisine served in an elegant setting with impeccable service. This is five-star dining without question. Reservations should be made through your hotel, as you do not just walk into this type of restaurant. They are open Wednesday thru Sunday from 5 to 10 PM. Call them at +46 8 796 81 02 to book a table.

* **Kajsas Fisk** - A traditional Swedish fish restaurant located at Hotorgshalle # 3 in Normalm, this is a very popular local restaurant. They are well known for all of their fresh seafood dishes, and in particular for their seafood soups. This is a very casual restaurant and reservations are not needed, but it can be crowded in the evening. Their hours are Monday thru Thursday from 11 AM to 6 PM, closing at 7 PM Friday and 4 PM Saturday. Call them at +46 8 20 72 62 to book a table.

* **Lilla Ego** - Located at Vastermannagatan # 69 in the upper end of Normalm, you will need a taxi to get there. However, after a fine and memorable meal, you may wish to walk it off by strolling back to the central city. This is one of the finest dining establishments in Stockholm with traditional Swedish cuisine served in an elegant setting with gracious waiters. It is necessary to have your hotel make a booking, as this is not the type of restaurant you just walk into. This is haute cuisine Swedish style. Their hours are Tuesday thru Friday from 4 PM to 10:30 PM, Noon to 3 PM and 4 to 10:30 PM on Saturday.. You will remember the evening and may even wish to return. To book a table you can call them at +46 8 27 44 55.

* **Mom's Kitchen** - This traditional restaurant with traditional home cooking Swedish style is located at Nybrogatan # 40 in Ostermalm is very popular with locals. You will find Swedish meatballs, fresh fish, poultry, reindeer and other national delicacies. The surroundings are cozy and the service is great.

I would recommend a reservation just to play safe. They are open weekdays from 11 AM to 3 PM. Call +46 8 661 27 27 to book a table.

* **Operakälleren** - located upstairs in the grand Opera House, this dining room presents an atmosphere that leads you to believe you are in the palace of the king. The cuisine and service are fit for a king. The restaurant is part of the Opera House at Karl XII Torg in the heart of the city and opens at 6 PM for dinner until 1 AM.

The upstairs terrace does serve light lunches outdoors in a casual atmosphere from Noon to 3 PM providing that the weather is amenable to outdoor dining. I have enjoyed this as a change of pace from eating indoors. To book a table call +46 8 676 58 00.

Operakelleren is very elegant

* **Stockholm Gästabud** - At Osterianggatan # 7 in Gamla Stan, this cozy restaurant without any pretenses serves genuine Swedish cuisine from traditional meatballs to a variety of seafood dishes and poultry. Reservations are not accepted, so it is casual and you can relax over excellent food at moderate prices. They are open Monday thru Thursday from 1 to 10 PM Monday, Thursday and Friday and from Noon to 10 PM Saturday and Sunday. To book a table call +46 8 21 99 21.and 12:30 to 10 PM Sunday

* **Wardshuset Ulla Windbladh** - you can have lunch or dinner in this old house or on their breezy terrace set amid the trees of Djurgården. Their seafood dishes are richly prepared and are as fresh as is possible. Every morsel is a delight. Potatoes and vegetables are also prepared to perfection. And once again I recommend their herring appetizer. I must warn everyone that this restaurant uses a lot of butter in its cooking, so take an extra dose of cholesterol medication and enjoy. The address is Rosendalsvagen 8, walking distance from the tramline that runs through Djurgården, alighting at the stop for the Vasa Museum. Hours are from 11:30 AM to 10 PM Monday, 11:30 AM to 11 PM Tuesday thru Friday, 12:30 to 11 PM Saturday, but closing at 10 PM Sunday. To book a table indoors or out on the patio call +46 8 534 897 01.

The architecture of Wardshuset Ulla Windbladh

SHOPPING: Sweden is a country with both a wide variety of manufacturing industries and traditional crafts. IKEA is a name well known in the rest of the world, and their flagship store is located in Stockholm. Swedish home furnishings and glassware are famous throughout the world, as this is country where impeccable taste is a part of the basic culture. In central Stockholm there are three principal large shopping venues, each with its own flavor:

* **Åhlen City** - The main store is located at Sergels Torg and Drottninggatan, is a large multipurpose department store that offers a good variety of moderately priced clothing, accessories and housewares. This is the largest department store in all of Sweden, but it does not have the high end ambiance or merchandise as NK Department Store just down Hamngatan two blocks away. This is their main store and it is open from 10 AM to 9 PM weekdays, 10 AM to 7 PM Saturday and 11 AM to 7 PM Sunday

* **Gallerian** is a large central city shopping arcade located on Hamngatan just to the east of N K Department Store. It offers a mix of clothing, accessories, electronics, toys and also has several distinctive cafes. This is a modern and impressive shopping arcade that has something for everyone. The mall is open daily from 10 AM to 8 PM and on Saturday from 10 AM to 6 PM and Sunday from 11 AM to 6 PM.

* **N K Department Store** - Of the three, NK, which stands for Nordiska Kompaniet, is very upscale and comparable to the American Neiman Marcus or British Selfridges, although not quite as large as Selfridges. It located in the heart

of the city on Hamngatan # 18-20, and carries such Scandinavian labels as Sand, J. Lindblad, Tiger and Johannsen. If you are looking for quality Scandinavian brands then this is the store in which to shop. Even members of the Swedish Royal Family have been seen as customers.

The store opens at 10 AM and is open until 8 PM Monday thru Friday, closing at 6 PM Saturday. Sunday hours are from 11 AM to 5 PM.

The main foyer in NK Department Store

Outside of Normalm, the other major shopping area is Ostermalm, which offers several high-end shops and one large shopping arcade with a great variety of local merchandise of high quality. There are also numerous gourmet food shops and candy stores in Ostermalm along with a few bakeries that are hard to resist.

BEST HOTELS IN STOCKHOLM: As Stockholm is the other major port of call where Baltic Sea cruises either begin or terminate, many of you will be staying over in the city either before or following your cruise. I do strongly recommend at least a minimum of two days in the city, as Stockholm is one of the grand cities of northern Europe. Personally speaking it is my absolute favorite city for both its natural beauty and architecture. In addition to the physical side, Stockholm is a friendly and very personable city, one you will enjoy.

This is a city of many hotels, and your cruise line may have a contractual arrangement with one or two of them to houseguests before or after the cruise. I will recommend what I feel are the best hotels offering true hospitality and luxury.

I do not recommend the old style boutique hotels, especially those in Gamla Stan because I find them to lack the comforts so many of us cruisers want. Many are not air conditioned, some have no elevators (lifts) while others do not have a bellman to help with luggage. I am a firm supporter of four and five-star quality hotels. Yet I know from experience that many cruisers do like these quaint hotels, especially in the older areas of a city, and in Stockholm Gamla Stan appeals to a large number of cruisers.

Here are my recommendations for what I consider to be the best hotels in Stockholm:

* **Elite Eden Park Hotel** - Located in Ostermalm at Sturegatan # 22, this four-star property is a moderate size hotel that offers deluxe rooms and suites with breakfast included. The hotel is air conditioned and offers all the major amenities one would expect from this category of hotel. The best rooms overlook Humlegården Park. I GIVE IT **** and rate it as $$$$ expense wise.

* **Grand Hotel** - Located on the waterfront facing the Royal Palace on Soedra Blasieholmshammen #8, this is the most famous and beloved hotel in Stockholm. It is here that the Nobel laureates are housed each year when being awarded their prizes. This is a very expensive hotel, but it offers all the amenities you expect in a posh and famous establishment. Depending upon the price you are willing to pay, the rooms vary from small to quite large, facing the city or the waterfront. As for dining, the Grand Hotel is also famous for its smorgasbrod. I GIVE IT ***** and rate it as $$$$$ expense wise, but well worth the money spent.

The Grand Hotel is Stockholm's finest

* **Hotel Diplomat** - Located in Ostermalm, a very fashionable part of the city close to the core, this hotel is very popular with those who are seeking five-star luxury but at a lesser price than the Grand Hotel. The hotel faces the water with its most elegant rooms on Strandvagen #7C. It has fine dining and all the major amenities. **I GIVE IT ***** and rate it as $$$$$ expense wise.**

* **Hotel Lydmar** - Located at Soedra Blasieholmshammen #2 almost next door to the Grand Hotel, this five-star property presents a combination of Old World and ultra-modern chic. The building dates back to the early 20th century, but the appointments are rather "hip," in current vernacular. The hotel includes breakfast in its daily rate, which is relatively high, but well worth the price. And they have what has become a very popular restaurant for its innovative cuisine. **I GIVE IT **** and rate it as $$$$ expense wise.**

* **King's Garden Hotel** - Located on the west side of the King's Garden (Kungstrådgården) in the very center of the city at Væstra Tradsgårdsgarden # 11 B, this boutique hotel features modern amenities, but with an Old World twist. The rooms are bright and decorated in a 19th century motif, but yet at the same time modern. Breakfast is included in the tariff. The hotel offers all major four-star services and is air conditioned. **I GIVE IT **** and rate it as $$$$ expense wise.**

* **Sheraton Stockholm** - This hotel is in the four-star category, but if you book on the concierge level, the service is what I would consider almost five-star. The hotel is at Tegelbacken #6 one block from Central Station and facing the water with great views of Gamla Stan and City Hall. This is a commercial hotel, but especially well run at prices that will please any cruiser. And its dining room, though not elegantly appointed, does serve outstanding meals, well above the quality you might expect from a major chain hotel. **I GIVE IT **** and rate it as $$$ expense wise.**

A VISIT TO UPPSALA: If there is one side trip I highly recommend while in Stockholm it is a visit to the city of Uppsala, located about 50 minutes by fast train north of Stockholm. Trains leave from Stockholm Central Station about once every half hour and no reservations are required. Uppsala is the fourth largest city in Sweden and has a metropolitan population of just over 200,000. It is a very old city, and actually the site has been inhabited for thousands of years. Just north of the present day city is Gamla Uppsala, containing mounds that date back approximately 2,000 years and predate even early Viking settlement.

The city of Uppsala dates to medieval times and became a center for the teaching of Christianity to the pagan worshipers who once had a temple in Uppsala dedicated to ancient Norse gods. By 1164, the city became a major Catholic center of worship, but during the Protestant Reformation, its great cathedral was converted from Catholic to Lutheran. The cathedral is constructed of brick and is the second largest Gothic structure in Europe with such construction. It was consecrated in 1435.

Looking out over Uppsala from the castle

Uppsala Castle dominates the skyline

Standing on a hill overlooking the city is Uppsala Castle, built in 1549 by King Erik XVI. It was from this castle that the government announced the abdication of Queen

Christina in 1654. But after the fire of 1702 it lost its prominence as the seat of Swedish government. Today the castle is host to many banquets, conferences and other important events, but it still dominates the skyline of the city.

Uppsala is best known for Uppsala University, which was founded in 1477. It is still one of Europe's most venerable institutions of higher learning and has been home to several Nobel laureates in a number of academic fields of study. One of its most famous scholars was Carolus Linneaus who was in residence at the university when he developed his taxonomical classification system for plants and animals, the one still in use today. Anybody who has studied the biological sciences is familiar with the classification of plants and animals by phylum, class, order genus and species. This is the work of Linneaus.

HOW TO VISIT UPPSALA: To visit Uppsala, simply go to the Stockholm Central Station and buy a ticket either from an automated machine or a ticket seller. There is a train to Uppsala approximately every 30 minutes and the journey takes less than one hour. The railway station in Uppsala is right in the center of town.

Arriving in Uppsala on the fast train from Stockholm

You can also arrange through your hotel for a car and driver or utilize one of the recommendations I noted earlier to spend a day in Uppsala. However, private car and driver service will be exceptionally expensive and not really necessary.

Once in Uppsala it is very easy to walk around the city center and explore all the major sights. However, if you wish to have an introductory tour just ask one of the taxi drivers outside the railway station. Most speak fluent English and will be very pleased to show you around the city for an hour or two at a nominal charge. But be sure to agree on a price at the start.

Uppsala does not have a hop on hop off bus or trolley for visitors. This is a university oriented city and casual visitors are not that numerous, which is a shame, as it is one of the most delightful of smaller Swedish cities.

THE MAJOR SIGHTS TO SEE IN UPPSALA: Here are the highlights of what are the major sights you want to see when visiting Uppsala, shown alphabetically:

* **Carolus Linnæus Museum** – The noted scientist Carolus Linnæus is the father of our whole system for assigning scientific names to plants and animals. He was a professor at Uppsala University and this museum is dedicated to him. The museum is located at Svartbäcksgatan 27 and is open during summer on weekdays from 9 AM to 4:30 PM.

Kungsangsgatan in the heart of Uppsala

* **Central Uppsala** – Explore this delightful city center that borders the fast flowing Fyris River with the Uppsala University campus on the opposite side. There are beautiful parks with walking paths following the river. The main shopping street known as Kungsangsgatan in the city center is pedestrian oriented and reflects the youthful population of this important university city.

* Gamla Uppsala – This is an ancient prehistoric site dating to before the Vikings and is quite fascinating with its burial mounds. You can easily visit for an hour or two by taxi, having the driver wait. The onsite museum is open from 10 AM to 4 PM daily.

The ancient burial mounds in Gamla Uppsala

* Uppsala Castle – Standing above the city this was once a royal residence for the Swedish crown. Today it is used primarily as a hall for major banquets and gatherings.

The castle is open for visitors to explore on a guided tour Tuesday thru Sunday from 1 to 3 PM and the art gallery within the castle is open from Noon to 4 PM daily. And the view from either upper floor windows within the castle or from the grounds at its rear give you a good look at the city of Uppsala.

* Uppsala Cathedral – This is a massive brick cathedral of gothic origin that was initially built in 1272 and has been added on to and modified since with the last developments in 1893. There are very few brick gothic cathedrals in Europe with Uppsala Cathedral and St. Mary's in Gdansk, Poland being the two best known. The castle towers dominate the skyline and is a most impressive structure. Today it serves as a Swedish Lutheran house of worship but was initially Roman Catholic until the Reformation. . Visitors are welcome daily between 8 AM and 6 PM and there is a brief welcoming service held at Noon. The north tower is open daily between 10 AM and 4 PM for dramatic views of the city.

Uppsala Cathedral

DINING OUT: There are many small cafes in the city center of Uppsala where you can have refreshment or lunch. Most are located along the small river that runs through the city center, separating the Old Town and university campus from the main shopping area. My four favorite restaurants are:

* **Domtrappkällaren** – Located at Saint Eriks Grand 15, this has been one of my favorite places for lunch in Uppsala for many years. It is a small restaurant and in good weather does offer limited outdoor seating.

The cuisine is Swedish and they start off your meal with a self-service salad selection that is quite traditional. The cuisine is excellent and the service is great if you go during off hours. At lunch time they are packed because it is very popular with local business personnel and university faculty, so I always go at around 2 PM. They serve Monday 11 AM to 9 PM, from 11 AM to 10 PM Tuesday thru Friday and Noon to 10 PM Saturday. Booking is not necessary.

* **Guntherska Hovkonditori & Schweizeri** – Located at 31 Östra Åagatan along the river, this is an incredible sweet shop serving up the most incredible pastries and cakes you will find anywhere. They also serve delicious light meals, but are best known for their awesome baked goods. They are open Monday thru Friday from 9 AM to 7 PM and on Saturday and Sunday from 10 AM to 6 PM. Booking a table for lunch is not necessary.

Awesome pastries at Guntherska Hovkonditori & Schweizeri

Fresh and smoked salmon on display at Hambergs Fisk

* **Hambergs Fisk** - A superb small restaurant where you can choose your fresh fish still in the refrigerated case. It is then prepared for you in the manner you wish.

This is one of the best places for delicious fish at lunch or dinner. Located at Fryistorg number 8. They are open weekdays from 11:30 AM to 10 PM. You do not need to book a table.

*Stationen - This rather distinctive restaurant is located in the old railway station building adjacent to the modern terminal. You can sit and watch the trains coming and going while dining on a variety of entrees, salads or simply have coffee and an elegant, decadent dessert.

Their closing hours are somewhat complex, as noted here. They open every day at 11 AM and close at 11 PM Monday, Midnight Tuesday, 1 AM Wednesday and Thursday, 2 AM Friday and Saturday and 11 PM Sunday. Reservations are taken, but the best time to dine is after 1:30 PM when the local lunch crowd is diminished and you do not need a booking. To book you can call +46 18 15 35 00.

A few hours in Uppsala will be quite memorable and it will give you the feel of life in a city rich in history, steeped in academic tradition and still vital in the 21st century.

FINAL WORDS ON STOCKHOLM: There is so much more to the overall flavor of Stockholm than just the city center. Residential Stockholm is divided into numerous districts separated from one another by waterways and parklands. Thus the city lacks the contiguous feeling of a large metropolis and gives each part of the city a feeling of being a town in its own right. The entire city is linked by an extensive Metro, or subway system, which is clean and efficient.

As noted previously, most Swedish cities are heavily dominated by apartment and condominium developments with single -family homes found in the outermost suburban areas. Most visitors never bother to check out local neighborhoods, but I highly recommend that if you have the time, you should just choose one or two suburbs at random and take the Metro to visit. You will find that Swedish planners have been very careful to design suburban communities to where they have a nucleus of shops and services adjacent to the Metro station and then apartment blocks or single family homes radiate out from this core. Sweden is noted for its careful development of urban satellite communities.

The people of Sweden consider themselves fortunate to live in a country where life is essentially without want. The country's overall standard of living places it among the ten highest in the world, and the quality of life is, along with Norway, considered to be one of the best in the world. But as previously noted, immigration has brought about some social tensions within the nation. Although the Swedish people are generous and receptive to including those less fortunate, they do worry about an erosion of their lifestyle if immigration is carried to extremes. Fortunately the leaders of the nation have been able to temper their desire to help people in other countries with a need to maintain the integrity of their way of life at home. And Stockholm truly represents all that is good about the Swedish way of life. It is a city

of elegance, sophistication, and historic charm and above all it is a city of graceful living.

MAPS OF STOCKHOLM

GAMLA STAN AND NORMALM

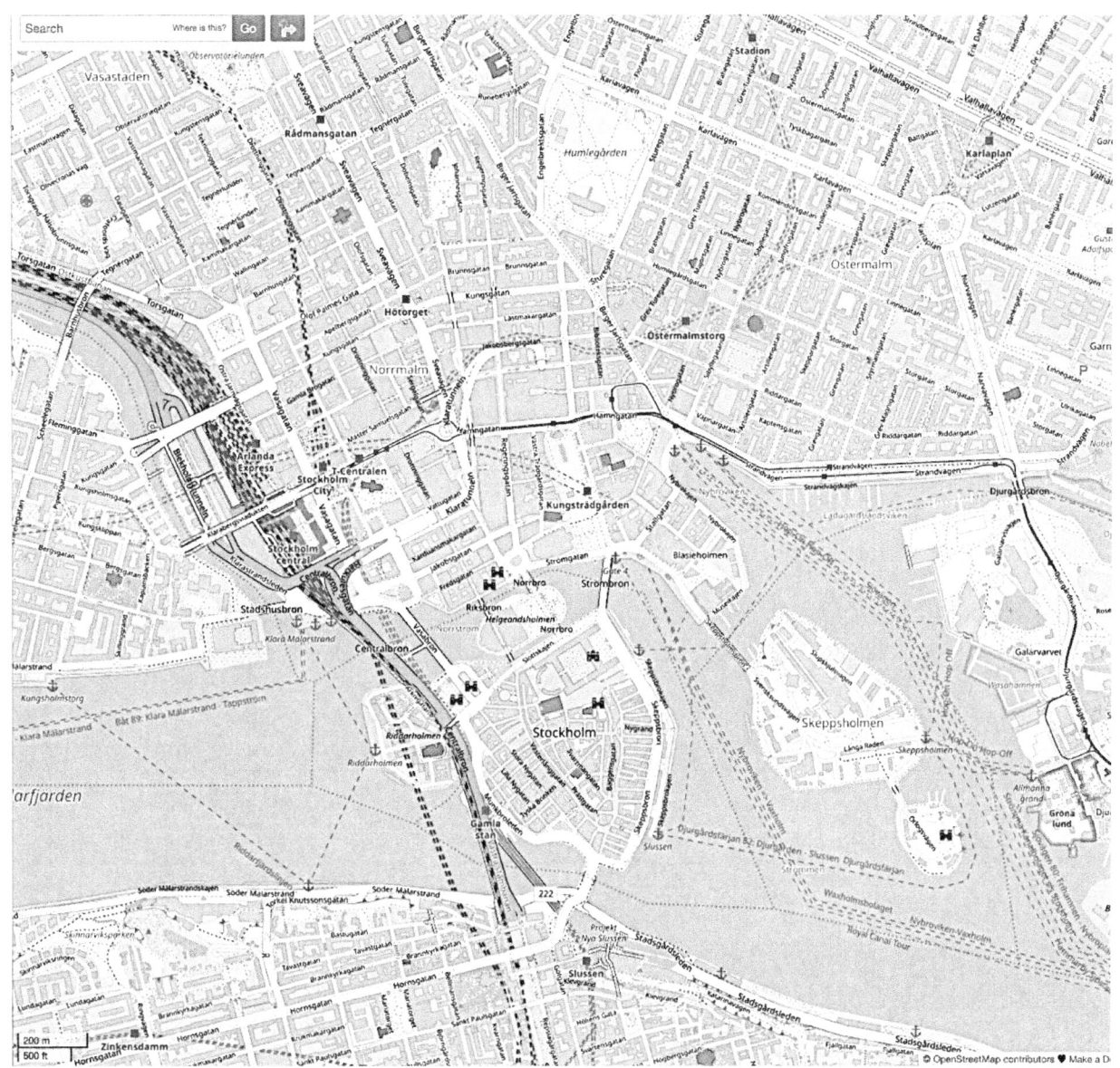

Old Town and Downtown Stockholm with star showing cruise ship docks, (© OpenStreetMap contributors)

This map is best viewed directly from OpenStreetMap.com on your personal device where it can be expanded or one specific area can be enlarged. Given the format of this book, it is impossible to display maps with the level of detail you might wish to have while actually out exploring the city. But the OpenStreetMap maps used directly are the tool I always rely upon.

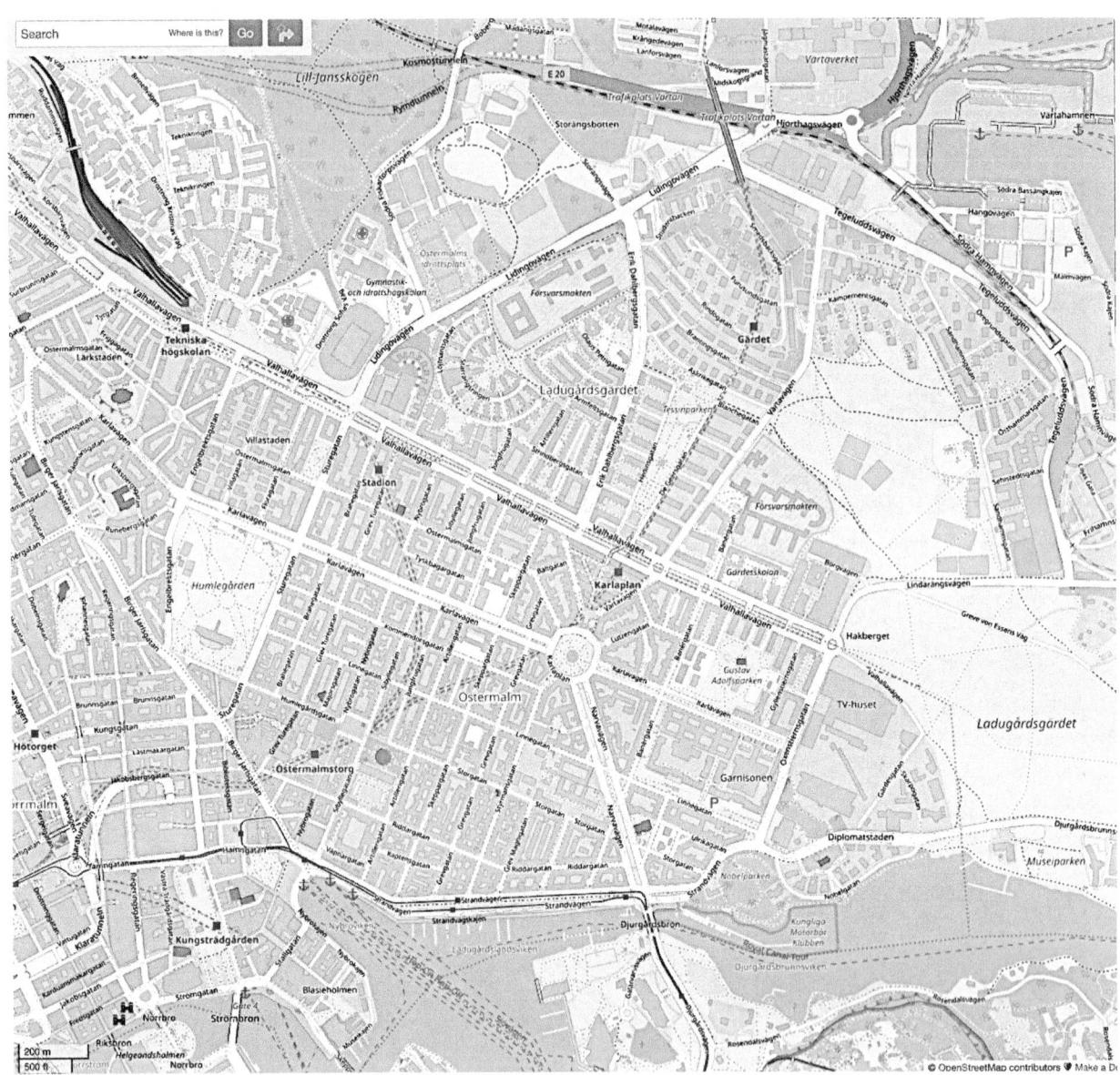

OSTERMALM

Ostermalm

This map is best viewed directly from OpenStreetMap.com on your personal device where it can be expanded or one specific area can be enlarged. Given the format of this book, it is impossible to display maps with the level of detail you might wish to have while actually out exploring the city. But the OpenStreetMap maps used directly are the tool I always rely upon.

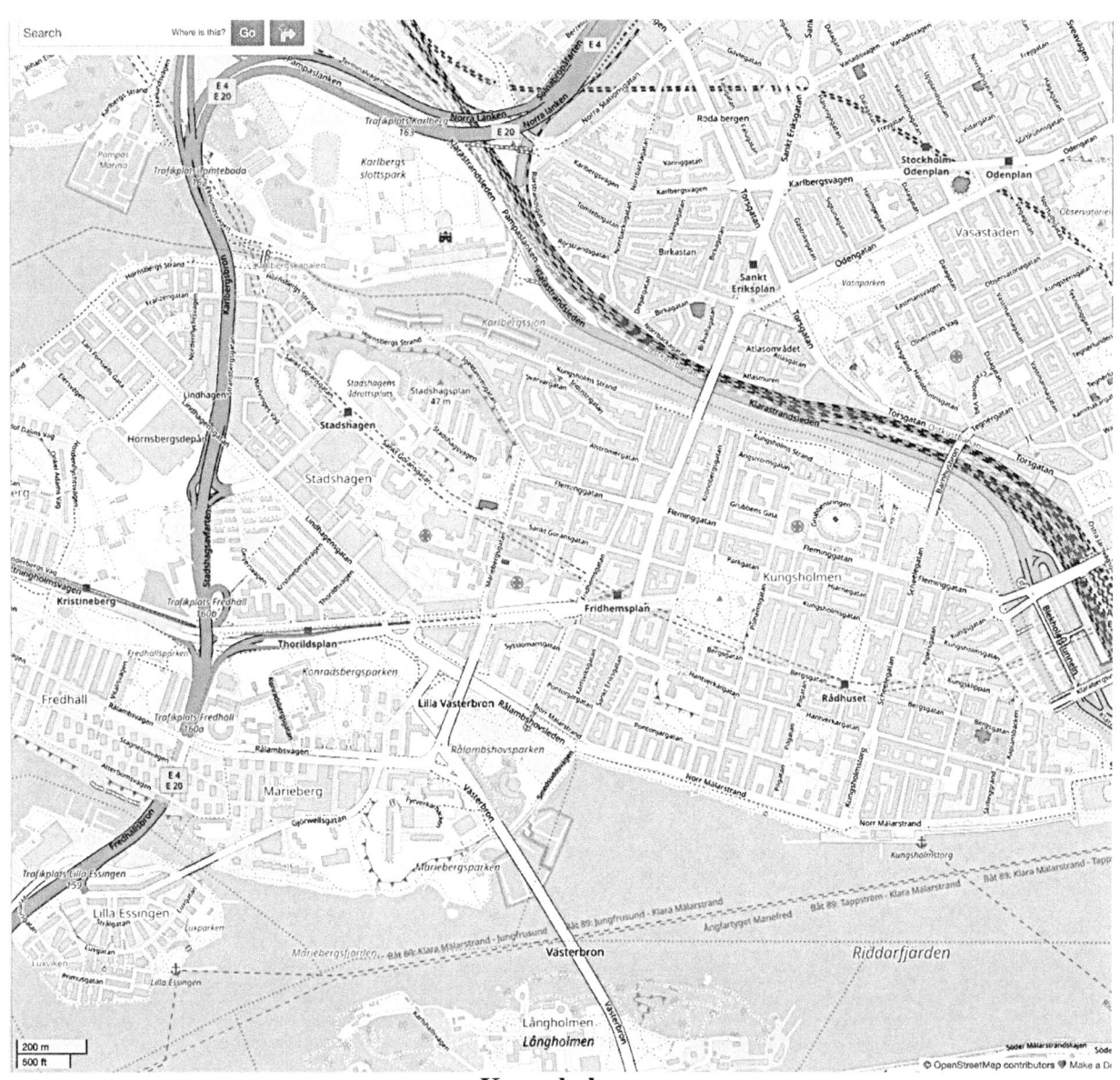

KUNGSHOLMEN

Kungsholmen

This map is best viewed directly from OpenStreetMap.com on your personal device where it can be expanded or one specific area can be enlarged. Given the format of this book, it is impossible to display maps with the level of detail you might wish to have while actually out exploring the city. But the OpenStreetMap maps used directly are the tool I always rely upon.

CENTRAL UPPSALA

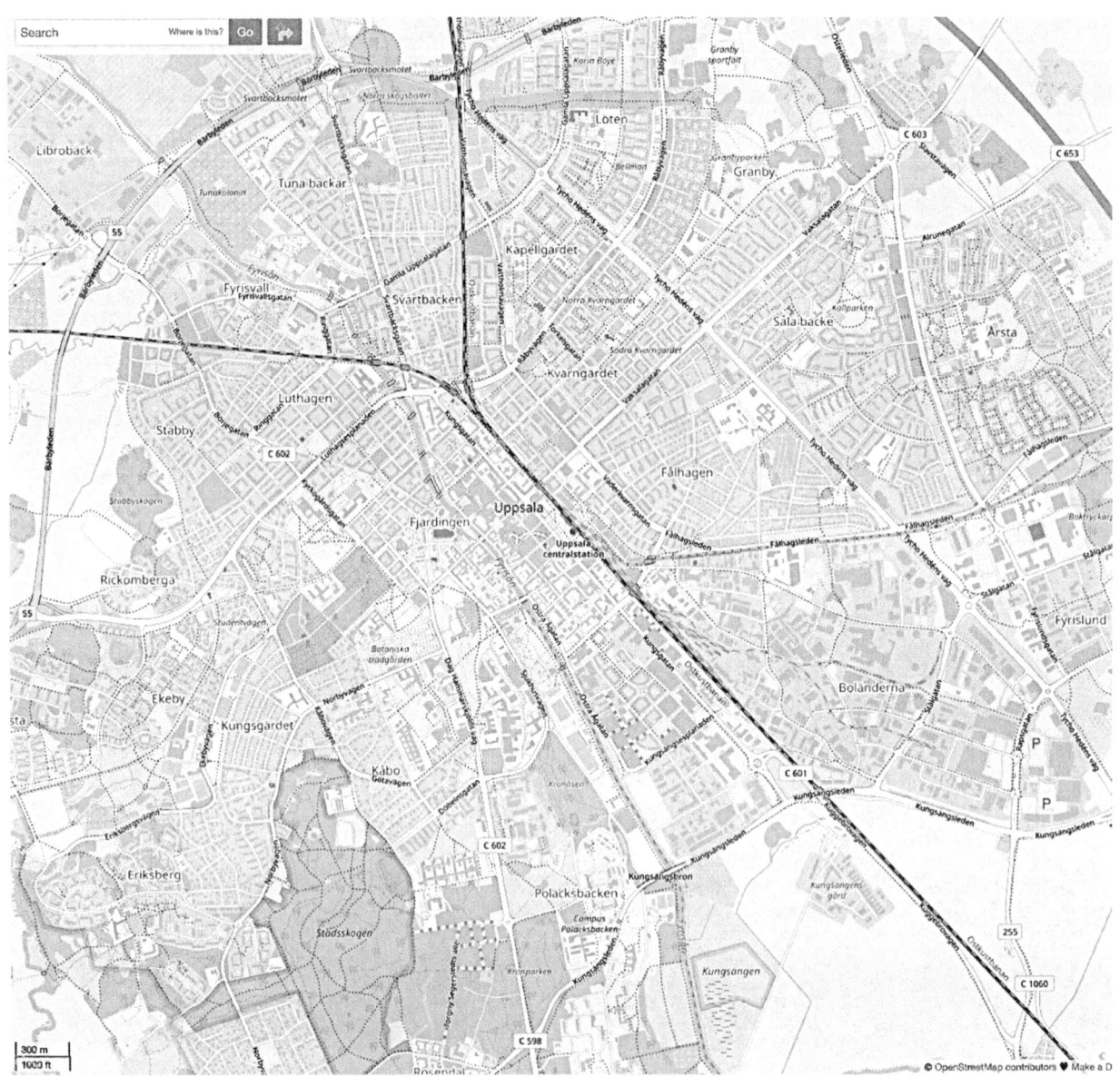

Central heart of Uppsala, (© OpenStreetMap contributors)

This map is best viewed directly from OpenStreetMap.com on your personal device where it can be expanded or one specific area can be enlarged. Given the format of this book, it is impossible to display maps with the level of detail you might wish to have while actually out exploring the city. But the OpenStreetMap maps used directly are the tool I always rely upon.

HELSINKI, FINLAND

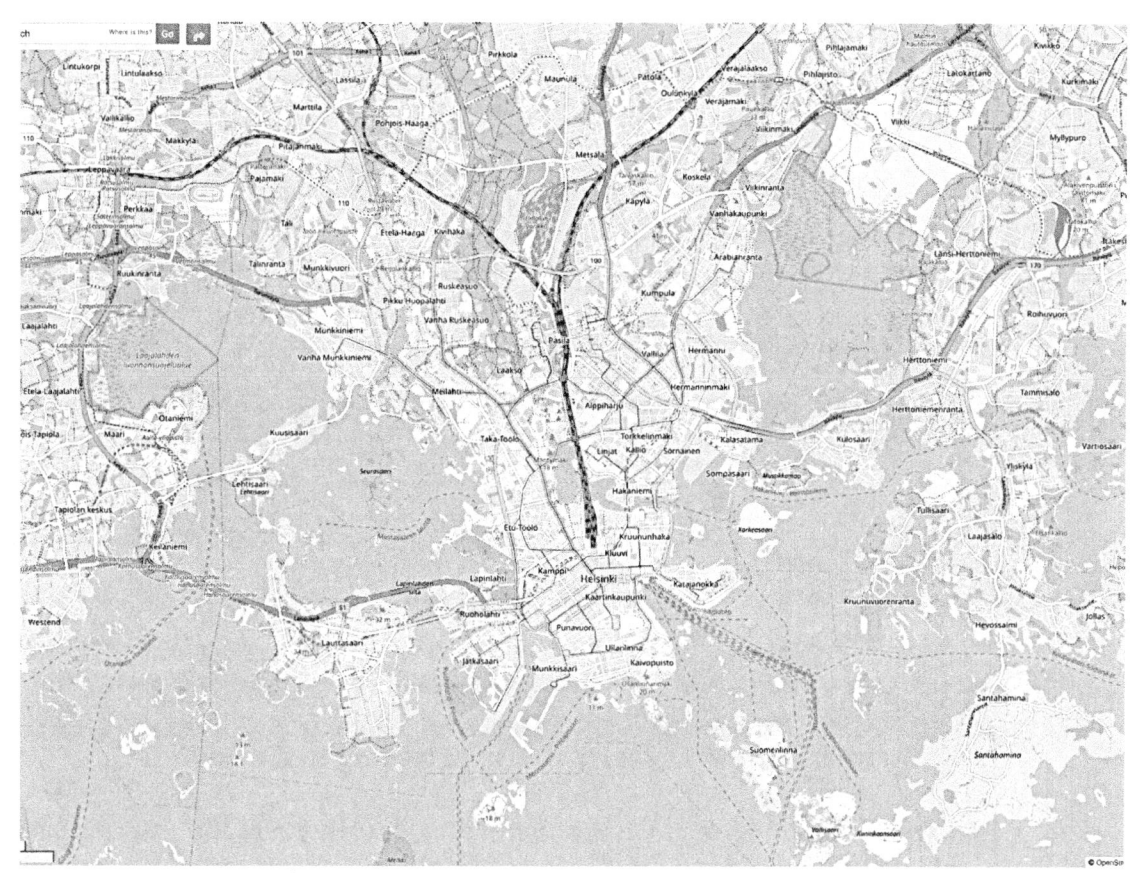

A map of greater Helsinki (© OpenStreetMap contributors)

I have visited Helsinki, Finland 51 times and find it to be one of the most charming and relaxing cities in the Baltic Sea area, second only to my favorite, which is Stockholm. It is not as grand or elegant as Stockholm, but it has a very warm and welcoming atmosphere. Finland has one of the five highest standards of living in the world, and this is obviously reflected by the character of its largest city. I had noted that Stockholm was my favorite city, one in which I would choose to live if I were younger. I would clearly place Helsinki as my second favorite city if I were to consider moving to Europe. I hope this tells you something about how the city impresses me simply as a great place to live.

When most North Americans think of Finland, unfortunately not much comes to mind. A few, however, will tell you that the sauna is of Finnish origin, and that is indeed correct. Most homes in Finland have a sauna. But they use it quite differently than most other cultures that have adopted the sauna do, especially during winter. The Finns dash out of the sauna and roll in the snow during winter, or plunge into an icy river or lake, if accessible, during summer. Those in the city use a cold shower to bring their body temperature down after steeping in the sauna.

An aerial view over central Helsinki looking to the south

Foreigners who know modern classical music, recognize the great Finnish composer Sibelius. His symphony "Finlandia" is a magnificent work widely known by classical aficionados. But for the most part, that would be the extent of basic knowledge of Finnish culture and custom.

And some foreigners recognize that Nokia is a Finnish company, showing that Finland is a player in the high tech market.

Anyone who shops for fine quality homewares will also recognize the brand name of Marimekko for its fine quality products. And once again, Marimekko is a Finnish company of note.

THE NATURAL SETTING: Finland occupies the eastern shoreline of the Gulf of Bothnia, that northern arm of the Baltic Sea. Its southern shoreline fronts on the Gulf of Finland, which is the eastern arm of the Baltic Sea. And it shares a border in the far northwest with both Norway and Sweden while its long eastern border is with Russia.

Finland shares a common landscape with the rest of Scandinavia, one of glaciated land, dotted with lakes and covered in dense forests. As glacial ice scraped much of what is now Finland, there were numerous depressions created that later filled with water when the glaciers later melted. Finland is thus covered by a high percentage of freshwater lakes, they actually number over 60,000 in a nation that is approximately the size of the American state of Montana. In the south there were some pockets of glacial deposition, but most of the country is composed of the hard basement rock that was scraped clean by the advancing ice. In most Finnish cities and towns there are large outcrops of hard granitic rock that cannot be built upon, thus being left as rugged natural parkland.

This landscape of beautiful spruce forest is just on the edge of Helsinki

About 75 percent of the country can be classed as taiga or what is better known as boreal forest, with the very far north falling into the tundra zone. Remember the Russian term taiga refers to the great forests of conifers with some mix of broadleaf deciduous trees, especially the birch that is so venerated in Finland. In late 2018 after the devastating fires in the American state of California, the American president pointed to Finland as an example of how to manage the forests to prevent fires. What he did not realize is that the climate of Finland provides for a very cool and wet summer combined with frigid winters. Thus although the forests around urban areas are groomed, it is not for fire protection but rather for recreational use. Drought, which can cause a spruce forest such as those in Finland to burn, is very rare in the type of climate found in the northern Baltic Sea region. California is in a Mediterranean climatic zone where periodic droughts and dry summers create a very high fire danger. And pine trees exude a lot of resin, which makes them highly flammable when they dry out.

The tundra of Finland, mainly above the Arctic Circle is that bleak and cold land where trees cannot grow. And of course in a land this far north, winter is the dominant season. The tundra is home to the reindeer herders known as the Sami who roam from northern Norway all the way into the western Arctic of Russia.

Anybody who remembers those magnificent snow scenes in the famous Hollywood movie *"Doctor Zhivago,"* they were all filmed in Finland, not in what was then the Soviet Union. The landscape is so much like that of Siberia where the story of Doctor Zhivago's exile was supposed to have taken place.

Despite its harsh environment, Finland possesses some agricultural land in the far south that is sufficient to provide all of the basic needs except for those foodstuffs that are from warmer climates. The country's population is only a bit over 5,000,000, so it is not in any way a crowded land. Thus the land can more than supply the basic needs. And the timber of the taiga is a great natural resource.

A BRIEF LOCAL HISTORY: The Finnish people are not of Germanic or Slavic origin despite being considered culturally as Scandinavian. Over the centuries their culture has been greatly influenced by both Sweden and Russia, but most heavily by the Swedish culture. Essentially the country is considered to be Scandinavian based upon cultural affinity, not linguistic. The Finnish people originally come from the Ural Mountains of what is now Russia, having migrated into their present home thousands of years ago. Their language is classified as Uralic or Finno Ugric, and it is related only to Hungarian and Estonian, but culturally all three countries are distinctly different. It is said to be a difficult language to learn because of its distinctive grammar that has nearly one dozen endings to nouns and pronouns.

From 1581 to 1809, Sweden controlled Finland as a province of their empire. To this day, Swedish is the second language of the country, and there is a large Swedish population living around Finland's second largest city of Turku, west of Helsinki. For over a century, the Swedes feared that Russia would try to take Finland from them, and they even built a massive fortress guarding the deep-water entrance to their port of Helsinki.

The Russians gained control over the Finnish people in 1809. The Finns resented being under Tsarist rule for over a century until they rebelled in 1917, taking advantage of the turmoil of the Russian Revolution. Lenin recognized Finland's independence concurrent with the establishment of the new Soviet Union. The Soviet leader recognized that there was a sizeable political wing sympathetic to the Communists in Russia, but few in Finland. Internal civil conflict in Finland lasted less than a year, and the Communist forces were defeated. But in the process, Finland becomes a republic and no royal line was established, as had been originally planned. Under Swedish rule, there was a Finnish noble class, but subservient to the Swedish kings.

Culturally there are many similarities with Sweden, in part due to the many centuries during which Finland was a part of the Swedish Empire. There are still large enclaves of Swedish settlers, descendants of those who populated parts of Finland during Swedish occupation. But Finland also shows architectural remnants and some cultural traits resulting from its occupation by Russia. In the country's cuisine there are also strong Swedish and Russian influences, as will be noted later.

Much of central Helsinki shows the Imperial Russian style of architecture

During World War II, the Soviet Union under the leadership of Joseph Stalin decides to take back Finland for strategic reasons, but the Finns put up a mighty resistance, beating back the Red Army in a brutal series of battles from 1939 to 1940. However in 1941, the Soviets attacked again, but this time Finland accepts help from Nazi Germany with reluctance. The war again ends in a standoff, but the Soviet Union manages to keep the territory it won, the region of Karelia, which to this day is still part of Russia. Primarily the Russians wanted a greater buffer zone around Saint Petersburg, or what was then called Leningrad, because the old border put Finland within less than 160 kilometers or 100 miles of the city. When Saint Petersburg was founded, the proximity of then Swedish dominated Finland was a source of irritation. And this is the one reason that in 1809 the Russians went to war and took Finland from Sweden, making it a duchy of the Russian Empire.

Because of Finland having invited Nazi forces into their country, they were left with an imposing war reparation debt to the allies at the end of World War II. It was not a fair burden because the Finns never supported Nazi principles, nor did they participate in military activities against any nation except the Soviet Union. Despite the harshness of the debt, Finland repaid every penny of the reparation.

After World War II and its loss of territory, Finland walked a tightrope being right on the Iron Curtain border with the Soviet Union. The country's various political parties were careful never to offend the USSR during this long Cold War period, remaining essentially a neutral nation. Since the fall of Communism, Finland has felt free to ally itself with the rest of Scandinavia, and in 1995, the Finns joined the European Union. Unlike Sweden and the United Kingdom, Finland has embraced the use of the Euro. The greatest hope of the Finnish people apart from continued economic prosperity is to someday be able to negotiate with Russia for the return of all or a part of the region known as Karelia. The people of that region are Finns, but forced to live under Russian domination as a minority in their own homeland. But given the rather nationalistic fervor in Russian political circles, Finland has not yet broached the subject of a return of Karelia. Thus around 1,000,000 Karelian Finns live in Russia, a fact of life they do not enjoy.

Finland maintains a federal parliamentary system of government. Finnish nobility has not been a part of the country for several centuries. Although once a part of the Russian Empire, the Finnish people understand and deeply value the concepts of democracy. And they take an active interest in politics, as do the Swedes. There are numerous political parties and coalitions. National and regional elections are important and people actively participate in Finnish democracy.

A BRIEF HELSINKI HISTORY: The city of Helsinki owes its founding to King Gustav I of Sweden who had it established under the Swedish name of Helsingfors to be a rival trade center to the Hanseatic League port of Tallinn, Estonia located just across the Gulf of Finland. But Helsinki never grew into a major port, and it languished in poverty. In 1710, a plague nearly wiped out most of its meager population. To help advance the development of Helsingfors, in 1748, the Swedish began construction of an island fortress at the entrance to the harbor. Although a mighty deterrent to Russian intervention, the fortress was captured by the Russians in 1809, ending Swedish control of Finland. This mighty fortress is today a UNESCO World Heritage Site, recognized by its Finnish name of Suomenlinna. It will be discussed further as one of the city's major attractions.

The Russians created the Grand Duchy of Finland, moving the former Swedish capital from Turku to Helsingfors, which ultimately became accepted by the Finnish name of Helsinki. As the administrative center of a Russian duchy, Helsinki grew into a significant city with much of its public architecture reflecting a Russian style rather than Swedish.

The 20th century saw the Finnish revolt against Russian rule, the later attempts at Soviet invasion and finally culminated in 1952, with the city being the first continental European city to host the post-World War II summer Olympic games. Since the mid 20th century, Finland has risen to prominence in high tech activities; the manufacturing of quality and well-designed household furnishings and furniture, thus making Helsinki an important city in these areas. Nokia, a company that gained much worldwide recognition for many of its innovations in telecommunications, and it is headquartered in Espoo, a suburb of Helsinki.

THE PHYSICAL LAYOUT OF HELSINKI: Helsinki is the capital and largest city of Finland. Its metropolitan population is just over 1,000,000, and it is a city spread out into the surrounding forests. Central Helsinki occupies a small peninsula of land bounded on the east and west by indented and scalloped natural bays (see maps at the end of the chapter). The peninsula is composed of hard granite rock that was exposed by glacial action and there are many rocky outcrops all through the central city that cannot be built upon, and they add character to the landscape. The peninsula is relatively hilly and this does provide for a greater degree of urban character in the same was as in San Francisco. But the basic street pattern adheres essentially to a basic grid within the central city. Beyond the peninsula, Helsinki is made up of distinct neighborhood nodes with centralized shopping and public services in one small core surrounded by apartment blocks and single-family homes on streets that do not adhere to any regularized pattern. Major boulevards and expressways interconnect these districts, which are interspersed with parkland and natural woodland similar to that of Stockholm. Thus there is no sense of one contiguous city without natural breaks. This pattern makes Helsinki a very beautiful city encompassing much natural woodland into the urban matrix.

A typical planned Helsinki suburb on the west side of the city

Modern suburban Helsinki enclaves have both apartment blocks and single-family homes, all impeccably landscaped and each tucked into the woods. There are many similarities in the newer sections of the city with the architecture and land use patterns of Stockholm. There is a feeling of openness and an unhurried atmosphere to Helsinki that belies the fact that this is the economic and cultural heart of the nation. Like Sweden, the Finns have practiced excellent urban planning and design, making their cities exceptionally livable. Helsinki is noted for some striking modern pieces of architecture, as Finnish architects are highly creative. A Finnish architect designed the magnificent city hall in Toronto, Canada. One of the most celebrated architects in the United States has been Arlo Sarinen, a man of Finnish ancestry.

The central part of the city is ringed by an active port facility, the largest in the country. Finland produces a wide array of manufactured goods, and it is known for its paper products, wood and wood pulp, with much of the exporting through Helsinki. The city also serves as the country's hub for its relatively extensive railway network, thus goods are easily brought to Helsinki for shipment abroad.

Central Helsinki's peninsula is relatively compact, and it does not offer such an intense array of historic sites. Within the central district are the important landmarks that represent the multi layered Swedish and Russian influences. There are also many residential streets in central Helsinki, dominated over by rows of apartment blocks. Like Stockholm, single-family homes are relegated to the city's outer suburban districts. But even in the suburbs there is a strong emphasis upon apartment blocks, which of course take up less space than single-family homes.

Brunnsparken is just one of many harborside parks

Like all major cities in Scandinavia, Helsinki is heavily dominated over by parks and open green belts. Although parts of the waterfront are devoted to docks and commercial facilities, many areas are still left as parkland. At the southern end of the central city peninsula is Brunnsparken, which overlooks several small islands also devoted to parks and historic buildings. Just north of the Olympic Stadium, in the suburb of Laakso-Dal is a massive open green area known as Mansasparken that essentially separates the residential areas into east and west sectors. In this massive park, much of which is actual forestland, there are numerous roads and trails, offering a lush and inviting respite from urban life. During winter it is used for cross-country skiing and its small ponds freeze over and are used for ice-skating.

Helsinki's outer suburban districts appear to merge into the surrounding forest and lake country, which is so much a part of the Finnish landscape. These are modern areas primarily consisting of single-family homes on large tree covered lots. Shopping malls and a network of good traffic arteries connect these suburban districts to the central city.

CRUISE SHIP DOCKS: Where your ship will dock in Helsinki is determined by the ship's size or displacement and draught. The larger cruise ships must dock in the commercial port area while smaller and medium size ships, especially those of the more upmarket lines are given berth close to or directly in the city center. These are the docking areas in Helsinki:

* **Helsinki West Harbor Cruise Terminal** is where the large size cruise ships will dock. It is unfortunately not immediately adjacent to the city center, but the distance is walkable for those physically fit. The distance to the Esplanadi in the city center is approximately three kilometers or two miles through interesting residential neighborhoods once leaving the dock area, but the terrain is a bit hilly, as is true for most of Helsinki.

* **South Harbor** area has four different berths that are located within very easy walking distance of the Esplanadi in the center of the city. And the walk is through very attractive neighborhoods. There are, however, no terminal facilities, but there is plenty of parking for tour busses, taxis and private vehicles. The closest of the docks is immediately adjacent to public transportation via the Number Four tram, which stops one block away. And it is also adjacent to ferryboat access to Suomenlinna Ferryboats that take visitors to one of the city's most historic sites.

SIGHTSEEING IN HELSINKI: The city of Helsinki is visited by hundreds of cruise ships of all sizes during the summer Baltic Sea season. Depending upon the itinerary, Helsinki either precedes or follows a visit to Saint Petersburg. Most visits are for approximately eight to ten hours, but on some itineraries among the smaller up market cruise lines, an overnight visit may occur. As with most ports, the cruise lines offer a variety of tours oriented primarily to the urban area, including the usual overview bus tour to point out the major highlights in a three to four hour excursion. But there are many local venues or sites that are not included in many of the ship offerings.

* **SIGHTSEEING OPTIONS IN HELSINKI**: Large cruise ships dock in the commercial port area and it is essential that the cruise line provides a shuttle bus into the city center for guests not going on group tours or for guests who have returned from their tours. The smaller up market cruise lines dock in a small cove where the Baltic Sea ferryboats dock. This is adjacent to the large waterfront

marketplace, which is in the very heart of the city. Guests can then walk from the ship right into the major scenic and historic venues.

If you choose to strike out on your own, there are several ways in which to maximize your sightseeing of Helsinki. If you plan to not have a private car or rental vehicle, I suggest you get the Helsinki Card, which gives you many benefits. Visit on line at *www.helsinkicard.com* .Options for sightseeing include:

** **Ship sponsored tours** – All cruise lines visiting Helsinki offer a variety of tours for groups, the size of each group depending upon the cruise line. But these are motor coach tours with only a few venues actually visited or given a photo stop. For those interested in more personal freedom, these tours do not offer that convenience.

** **Private car and driver** – This is always my favorite option because of the freedom it gives you to see those sights that most interest you and to have a timetable that is to your taste. The shore excursion desk on most ships can order a private car and driver, but the cost is far higher than you can arrange yourself. In Helsinki I recommend:

*** **Blacklane**, which is a well-respected chauffeur service. Their web page is *www.blacklane.com/Helsinki* .

*** You may also wish to look at Tours by Locals found at *www.toursbylocals.cp./Helsinki-Tours* .

*** Also check 8Rental, which can be found at *www.8rental.co,/chauffeur-service.helsinki* .

** **Rental car** – All major global and European auto rental agencies will be found in the city center. However, before renting a car and driving on your own, consider that most vehicles have manual transmission and all signs and directions are written in both Finnish and Swedish, but none are in English. And keep in mind that the city is quite spread out and its street pattern is not the easiest to follow.

** **Hop on hop off busses** are available – This is a popular option and often a bus will come to the dock area where the larger cruise ships berth. Smaller up market cruise ships generally dock in the small harbor alongside the Katajanokka Peninsula, which is right next to the large outdoor public market. The hop on hop off busses congregates at the fountain where the Esplanadi Park begins, just beyond the marketplace and also in front of the large Finnish Lutheran Cathedral. To learn more about the services offered visit on line at *www.citytour.fi* or you can also check out *www.hop-on-hop-off-bus.com/Helsinki* for details and route maps.

** **Taxi service** – Hiring a local taxi on the dock offers an alternative, and most of the drivers are competent in explaining the sights you are seeing. Taxi drivers in Helsinki for the most part do speak English. But most are not generally accustomed to being guides, thus you must do your homework and know what you want to see and have some prior knowledge as to the significance of each venue.

*** You may wish to check on line with Taksi Helsinki Oy, which receives moderate reviews, at *www.taksihelsinki.fi*

*** I also recommend Kovanen, which is more of a multiple option transport service. Their web site is *www.kovanen.com* .

** **Helsinki Metro** – The Metro does not cover many parts of the city, but you can use it to visit suburban areas in both the east and west ends of the city. It is quite convenient, fast and safe.

The green trams ply most major Helsinki streets

** **Local public transport** is easy to use, and all day passes can be purchased. Helsinki has a major network of trams (streetcars) that ply up and down all the major streets in the central city. Bus routes then interconnect to offer easy access to sights beyond the tram network. If you are planning on using public transport, I always recommend as an introduction to the city a one-hour ride on Tram number 2 or 3. These trams each make a large figure eight loop through the city center, starting and ending at the fountain opposite the public marketplace. Although there is no narration, there is a pamphlet available at the local tourist office or often brought on board ship by local representatives. This pamphlet contains a map and description of all major sights of interest along the route. For a cost of around three Euro, it is a good way to initialize your sightseeing in Helsinki. However, if you are coming into the city center by shuttle bus from one of the large cruise ships docked in the port area, you will have to make your way to the fountain at the foot of the Esplanadi to begin the route.

** **Walking** is one easy way to see many of the venues in the heart of the city, and Helsinki is a graceful city in which there is no frenetic sense of hurry, and walking is especially enjoyable. But given the hills in the central peninsula, a day spent walking will give you more than sufficient exercise and it should include a bountiful lunch in which you try Finnish cuisine.

* **MAJOR SIGHTS TO SEE IN HELSINKI**: The most important venues that I recommend as must see sights in Helsinki include the following shown here in alphabetical order:

** **Edustkuntatalo** – The Finnish National Parliament buildings. Its white stone architecture shows strong Russian overtones, somewhat resembling government buildings of the Soviet Era. It is not overly attractive, but rather has a utilitarian appearance. Located on Mannerheim Boulevard, it can be seen by walking north from the upper end of the Esplanadi Park. It can also be reached by means of the number four tram, which can be boarded on Aleksanteringatu, the main shopping street. Visit on line at *www.lyyti.fi* to arrange a tour of the parliament.

Lunch hour on the Esplanadi in the city center

** **Esplanadi** - the main park in the center of the city, the Esplanadi is a place where Finns enjoy catching some sun and resting on park benches or the rich lawns, especially workers during the lunch hour. And there is often entertainment. There are also two popular teahouses located in the park that serve light refreshment and full meals.

* **Finlandia Hall** - Opposite the parliament, Finlandia Hall is the city's ultra-modern convention center. The visitor's gallery and cafe are open on weekdays from 9 AM to 7 PM. Guided tours can be arranged on site, but they are not given on a daily basis.

** **Finnish National Art Gallery** - this gallery features the national collection of art, both from abroad and works of art created by Finnish artists and sculptors. The gallery is located across from the national parliament building on Mannerheim Boulevard. The gallery is open from 10 AM to 6 PM Monday thru Friday with extended opening until 8 PM Wednesday. Saturday the museum closes at 5 PM and is not open Sunday.

The Hakaniemi Market

** **Hakaniemi Market** - on the northeast side of the city center, this is one of the oldest and most venerated outdoor markets that also sell a variety of fresh produce, seafood and meats. It can be reached by means of the number three tram by simply asking the driver to notify you of the stop. The market opens at 8 AM and remains open until 6 PM daily, but closes at 4 PM Sunday.

* **Helsinki Opera House** - This new opera house is also an ultra-modern example of Finnish architecture and is to be found just north of Finlandia Hall. It can be reached by continuing north along Mannerheim Boulevard beyond the parliament building either on foot or on any one of the trams that ply this major boulevard.

To my knowledge the Opera House does not offer tours, but tickets can be purchased for performances at the box office or on line at www.oopperaballeti.fi prior to performances.

** Kaisaniemi - The Botanical Garden is one of the least known places of interest in Helsinki. It is located adjacent to the Railway Station and can be reached via the number two or three tram by asking the driver to notify you of the stop.

The garden is not very large, but it features the local flora of this northern land, both trees and flowers. For anyone interested in gardening or in natural landscapes, this should be a place to visit. It is open daily from 10 AM to 4 PM. It is a very restful and beautiful spot in the middle of the city where you can enjoy seeing the natural landscape carefully preserved.

The peaceful Botanical Garden

* Lutheran Cathedral - a very striking white building with a sweeping staircase that rises up from Senate Square. The statues atop the outer facade are the result of a demand by Russian Tsar Alexander II that the building be decorated, in keeping with Russian Orthodox tradition. The story is that while on a visit to Helsinki, the Tsar was offended by the simplicity of the building, being of course accustomed to the lavish decoration of Russian Orthodox churches. You can visit the cathedral between 9 AM and 6 PM except when services are being conducted.

The Lutheran Cathedral in Senate Square

* **National Museum of Finland** - Located north of the parliament building along Mannerheim Boulevard, this is the primary museum for the entire nation and it features both natural and historic exhibits in a rather large, but old building. Again it can be reached by means of the number four tram. The museum is open to the public Tuesday thru Sunday from 11 AM to 8 PM.

* **Olympic Stadium** - in 1952, Helsinki was the first city to host the post-World War II summer Olympic games. The stadium is used for sports activities today, but it represents the resumption of Olympic competition after the war. At present you can only see the stadium from the outside as a result of an extensive remodeling that will not be completed until 2019.

* **Senate Square** – The primary city square, which is the very heart of central Helsinki. This is the place where most Helsinki residents will arrange to meet if they are coming into the central city. During summer it is quite crowded with tour busses from the various cruise ships, and it is also a major location for boarding the hop on hop off busses. Dramatic steps lead up from the square into the Lutheran Cathedral, which is the most dominant building in the entire city.

* **Seurasaaren National Park** - An historic park that depicts Finnish life as it was centuries past. Recreated structures along with genuine old buildings have been assembled from all over the country. Visitors walk the country lanes and experience old Finland complete with locals who dress in costume and perform various tasks just as their ancestors did. This site is popular with both locals and visitors alike.

One of the hop on hop off bus route will take you to Seurasaaren National Park, or you can also get there by taxi. This is not a venue that the cruise lines appear to have much knowledge of, and that is a shame because it is one of the most interesting of cultural experiences. The park is open from 11 AM to 5 PM daily.

An old farmstead in Seurasaaren National Park

* **Sibelius Park and Monument** – Dedicated to the world famous Finnish composer whose epic work "Finlandia" portrays the very soul of the nation. Finns have a great love for Sibelius and this is a special monument. The monument is always one of the photo stops on the highlight excursion offered by most cruise lines. If on your own, it can be accessed by the hop on hop off bus or the number four tram from stop for the Olympic Stadium. There are no posted hours, as the monument sits in an open park.

* **Suomenlinna Fortress** – One of the city's most historic sites, this old fortress and its many walls are at the heart of the Swedish attempt to protect their territory from Russia. It occupies a group of small islands that once protected the entrance to what was then the main harbor in the city center. To reach Suomenlinna you must either take one of the local ferry boats from the Waterfront Marketplace, or you can take a guided tour offered by most cruise lines since this is an important national venue. You can visit the fortress on your own, go as part of a guided tour or through your cruise line's special guided tours. Guided tours on site are given in a variety of languages, and you must first check with their web page at *www.suomenlinna.fi* for details. The web site claims to show opening hours, but

apparently there is some trick to getting the hours to appear. I do know that by 9 AM the fortress is open and I have seen ferryboats returning as late as 8 PM during the summer.

The great fortress of Suomenlinna

* **Temppeliaukio Church** – An example of modern Finnish architecture, this church is carved out of rock and topped with a copper dome. It is in no way like a Gothic or Renaissance church you expect to see in a European city. The church is located in a residential neighborhood just northwest of the city center and can be reached on the number two or three tram by asking the driver to alert you to the stop. The church is open Monday and Tuesday from 10 AM to 5 PM, Wednesday from 10 AM to 3:30 PM, Thursday from 10 AM to 5 PM, Friday from 10 AM to 11:30 AM and again from 3 to 5 PM. Weekend hours will vary with the season and the services being held.

* **Uspenski Cathedral** – An example of the Russian Orthodox influence that is still found in Helsinki. The city was a provincial capital under Tsarist rule for a period of just over a century. This massive red brick cathedral sits atop a granite outcrop of rock located just above and visible from the outdoor Waterfront Marketplace. You can visit the cathedral between 9 AM and 6 PM daily, and between 10 AM and 3 PM Saturday and from Noon to 3 PM Sunday except when services are being conducted.

* **Waterfront Market and Old Market Hall** - at the foot of the Esplanadi, this is the large public market area where fresh produce, fish and prepared foods are available along with handcraft items. Inside the market hall there are many stalls serving ready to eat delicacies that offer a taste of Finland. The outdoor stalls with white awnings generally sell handcrafts and souvenirs while those with red or orange awnings are selling fresh produce, fish, baked goods or ready to eat take away foods. And there are tables and benches where you can sit and partake of the foods purchased. Sunday is the only day in which the waterfront market sees fewer vendors opening and it is not as active the rest of the week. The hours of the main market hall are from 8 AM to 6 Pm daily except Sunday when it is open from 10 AM to 5 PM.

DINING IN HELSINKI: Like the rest of Scandinavia, excellent seafood, cheeses and rich desserts characterize its cuisine. Helsinki is a city where one can enjoy the blending of Swedish and Russian cuisines through their marriage into Finnish gastronomy. The Finns do an excellent presentation with open face sandwiches at lunch despite this being a Danish tradition. Milk soup with fish and potato is a genuine Finnish tradition and you must taste it to appreciate it. And like in Norway and Sweden, reindeer is also a popular main dish.

During the summer dining out of doors is popular, especially during the "white nights" when the sun does not set in Helsinki until nearly midnight. And along with the meal, the Finns enjoy either vodka or beer, and alcohol consumption is rather high.
Once again I will only be recommending a handful of dining establishments based upon my own personal experience. Very few ships will stay overnight for you to enjoy dinner ashore, thus my recommendations are all based upon having the best lunch possible and include:

* **Finlandia Caviar** - This unique small restaurant is reminiscent of Russia in that the menu features caviar, both red and black, expensive to moderate, but a taste treat for anyone who loves caviar. And to go with it you have your choice of the finest champagnes or vodka. Despite the high cost, you will not be having a meal. I consider this more of an afternoon snack or appetizer. It is located at Elelaranta # 20, opposite the old market hall at the waterfront market square. They are open Monday thru Thursday from Noon to 9 PM, Friday and Saturday from Noon to 10 PM. Only consider coming if you truly love caviar. To book a table, call them at +358 10 5817850.

* **Karl Fazer Cafe** - A venerable cafe located on Kluuvikatu between the Esplanadi Park and Aleksanterinkatu. Open seven days a week from 7:30 AM to 10 PM, Karl Fazer Cafe is famous for its delectable open face sandwiches and rich delicious pastries. This is a self-service restaurant where you select the items you wish to eat from servers behind the line. Then you must find a table, which during much of the day can be daunting, but people are often willing to share if they are

sitting alone and have empty chairs. But the quality of the sandwiches and desserts make it all worthwhile. In addition to light meal service, they have a bakery and candy shop worthy of note. I never leave without buying some of their incredible dark chocolate to take home. Bookings are not accepted, but if you go at off hours it will not be as crowded. All of the restaurants inside Stockmann Department Store are operated by Karl Fazer and there is a small Karl Fazer Café inside The Forum. None of their locations require reservations. Their main café hours are Monday thru Friday from 8 AM to 10 PM, Saturday from 10 AM to 10 PM and Sunday from 10 AM to 6 PM.

Dining al fresco at the main Karl Fazer Café

* **Nokka** - At the yacht harbor just steps from the lower end of the Esplanadi - Kanavaranta # 7 F, this is a truly Finnish restaurant of the high-end type. Their authentic menu features Finland in an excellent light with fresh seafood, meats and poultry dishes expertly prepared and served. And leave room for one of their elegant desserts. They serve Wednesday thru Saturday from 4 to 11 PM. Have your ship's concierge book a table if coming for dinner or call them at +368 9 61285600..

* **Olo Ravintola** - Next to the Helsinki City Hall at Pohjoisesplanadi # 5, this is a true gourmet lover's dream of a restaurant. The menu is diverse, but true to contemporary Scandinavian standards as well as being vegetarian friendly. Their menu features actual meals where all of the component dishes are paired to provide you with the best taste treats of Scandinavia, using the freshest ingredients. Have your ship's shore concierge book a table, as this is not the type of restaurant where you simply arrive unexpected. They are open Wednesday and Thursday from 6 PM to Midnight and Friday and Saturday from 4 PM to Midnight. You can book a table on line at www.dinnerbooking.com.

* **Ravintola Kappeli** - This traditional orangerie is located at the bottom end of the Esplanadi and has both a quick cafe and a sit down restaurant. This is a great place for lunch or dinner and features a great variety of Finnish delicacies. At lunch hour it can get rather crowded, so go at off hours. This is a true Helsinki institution. Open from 9 AM to Midnight Wednesday thru Saturday and from 11 AM to Midnight Sunday thru Tuesday. Call to book at +358 10 7663880 to see if they will accept a booking.

* **Ravintola Kuu** - Located near the Opera House and accessible from the city center on foot or by taking the # 4 Tram, this is a superb restaurant that is highly acclaimed by locals. The menu features Scandinavian and Finnish cuisine with fresh seafood, reindeer, poultry and vegan dishes in a warm and friendly atmosphere. Hours of service are Tuesday thru Friday from 4 to 11 PM, Saturday from 1 to 11 PM and Sunday from 1 to 9 PM. Call +358 9 270909973 to book a table.

* **Ravintola Teatteri** - Located at the upper end of the Esplanadi, this teahouse is famous for its lunch, dinner and midnight snacks. They offer a great variety of Finnish and other European dishes including soups, salads, entrees and desserts. You can also find traditional open face sandwiches at lunch. They are open from 10 AM to Midnight on Monday, 10 AM to 1 AM Tuesday thru Friday, and from 11 AM to 1 AM Saturday.. To book a table call +358 9 61285000.

* **Restaurant Savotta** - Located at Aleksanterinkatu number 22, opposite Senate Square, this small indoor-outdoor restaurant features traditional Finnish cuisine served in a friendly and casual atmosphere. Their menu includes traditional milk and salmon soup, fresh fish, wild game and tempting fruit desserts, all prepared in the manner of a traditional farm, utilizing fresh ingredients. I have eaten at Savotta at least once every summer during visits to Helsinki and I have never had anything less than a superb meal. Savotta is open from 4 to 11 PM Tuesday thru Saturday. Reservations are advised, but not necessary during off hours between 2 and 5 PM. This is a popular restaurant with tourists, as it is often highly recommended when visitors ask. To book call +358 9 74255588.

***Restaurant Savu** - Located on a tiny island, but connected by a road and foot causeway, this country style restaurant is a true delight. It is a bit difficult to reach by public transport, but the closest would be the number seven tram from Aleksanderinkatu to Liisankatu and then walking east about one mile. Otherwise it is best to take a taxi from any of the city center venues such as Senate Square or Stockmann Department Store. Owned by the same people who operate Savotta, this restaurant features a smaller menu, but one devoted to traditional Finnish soups, seafood and game with a more limited, but excellent dessert. I highly recommend it as a place where you will rarely find tourists since its following is local. Savu is open from 5 PM to Midnight Wednesday thru Saturday. Reservations are advised by calling +358 9 74255574.

* **Stockmann Department Store** - The three main restaurants on the top floor of Stockmann Department Store are all run by the famous Karl Fazer Cafe, which is noted above in a separate listing. But for a quick meal in surroundings that are not overly crowded either before or after the regular lunch hour, I highly recommend this as your lunch stop. There is a main restaurant with menu service, and it features the national soup - a creamy salmon and potato soup. There is a cafeteria serving a variety of hot entrees and the servers will explain the daily choices. The third option is their open face sandwich and dessert cafe. This self-service section offers a variety of cold, open face sandwiches featuring beef, salmon and shrimp that are each a work of art. There are also slices of hot quiche. And the highlight is the cake and pastry section offering exquisite flavors. The restaurants are open concurrent with the store's hours, with lunch starting at Noon daily. No reservations are taken.

* **Vinkkeli** - Located at Pieni Roobertinkatu # 8, a few blocks south of the Esplanadi, this highly acclaimed restaurant serves traditional Scandinavian and Finnish cuisine in a relaxed and friendly atmosphere with impeccable service. They use the freshest ingredients and the menu is quite varied, but of course fresh seafood ranks high on their list of entrees. They serve lunch Monday thru Friday from 11:30 AM to 2 PM and dinner Tuesday thru Saturday from 5 PM to Midnight. You should call to book a table at +358 29 1800222.

Guidebooks will list hundreds of restaurants in Helsinki and I am sure that I have missed some great eateries, but the ones I have listed are outstanding.

To satisfy that sweet tooth try any of the pastry counters inside Stockmann Department Store for the best selection

SHOPPING IN HELSINKI: Even though I am not a shopper, I do find that when it comes to good Scandinavian design in clothing and housewares, Helsinki is a good place to shop. Much of the men's and women's clothing is of Scandinavian origin, primarily from Danish and Swedish manufacturers. But when it comes to household design, the Finnish brand of Marimekko has become world famous. Here are my choices for shopping venues:

Busy Aleksanterinkatu

* **Aleksanterinkatu**, which is the main shopping street. It lies one block to the east of the Esplanadi Park. This street is lined on both sides with the major and lesser stores and boutiques.

* **Forum** - Located on Mannerheim Boulevard opposite Stockmann, Forum is a city block size shopping arcade filled with 120 stores offering a great variety of merchandise spread over five floors. Sokos is open from 9 AM to 9 PM weekdays, 9 AM to 7 PM Saturday and 11 AM to 6 PM Sunday.

* **Marimekko** - This famous Finnish brand known for its innovative designs in clothing and housewares is available in the major department stores, and at their main showroom located at Puusepankatu 4. The main showroom can be reached via the Metro to Herttoniemen Metroasema. There is also a small showroom on the Esplanadi. Showrooms are open from 9 AM to 6 PM daily

* **North side of the Esplanadi Park** is lined with numerous boutique shops from the fountain to Stockmann Department Store.

* **Sokos Helsinki** – This is a second major department store, Sokos is located on Mannerheim Boulevard at Kaivokatu. Though smaller than Stockmann, Sokos is also a full service department store offering many of the same quality brand names as Stockmann but with smaller selections. It is open Monday thru Friday from 9 AM to 9 PM, Saturday from 9 AM to 8 PM and Sunday from 11 AM to 6 PM.

The massive size of Stockmann Department Store

* **Stockmann Department Store** - this is the largest retail store in all of the Baltic Sea. Stockmann occupies a large triangular shaped block where Aleksanterinkatu and Mannerheim Boulevard meet. This is a household name in Helsinki. Founded by a German merchant in the late 19th century, Stockmann has grown into a major institution. With eight floors and two basements worth of merchandise, you can buy just about everything except an automobile. Clothing, shoes, accessories, housewares, furniture, appliances gourmet groceries, books, magazines, children's toys and optical goods can be found inside Stockmann. The food hall in the lower basement has some of the flavor of Harrod's in London for its quality and displays. Fresh and prepared foods are mouthwatering and will build up your appetite simply by looking. Stockmann is open from 9 AM to 8 PM daily, Saturday from 9 AM to 7 PM and Sunday from 11 AM to 6 PM.

FINAL WORDS: Helsinki is a city that mixes Old World style with crisp modern architecture with its dominant Swedish and Russian flavors. The city is spotlessly clean, as is true of all Scandinavia, and it is one of the safest cities for foreign visitors. Fortunately for American, British, Irish, Australian and Canadian visitors, English is widely spoken throughout the city. I never tire of visiting Helsinki. Yet I often hear from shipboard passengers that they found the city to be rather uninteresting, so it is impossible to please everyone.

And like both Norway and Sweden, the standard of living in Finland is very high. The tax base is also high, but the government provides excellent health care and universal education. In 2014, UNESCO did a survey of public education in the major countries of the world. Overall the Finnish public school system was rated as being the best in producing a well-rounded education and preparatory program for students attending university.

Finland is a country that embraces both an active participation in the European Union at the same time fostering its own identity with a great sense of national pride. It also has found a close trade and social partner in Estonia, located a short distance across the Gulf of Finland. These two nations were separated from one another during the long period of Soviet domination of Estonia. Their closeness is based upon the fact that both countries are Finno Ugric speaking nations. And Estonia's lower tax base means that many products are less expensive than in Finland. There are fast ferries that shorten the crossing time to approximately one hour thus making it possible to visit Tallinn for just the day.

HELSINKI MAPS

THE CENTRAL PENINSULA

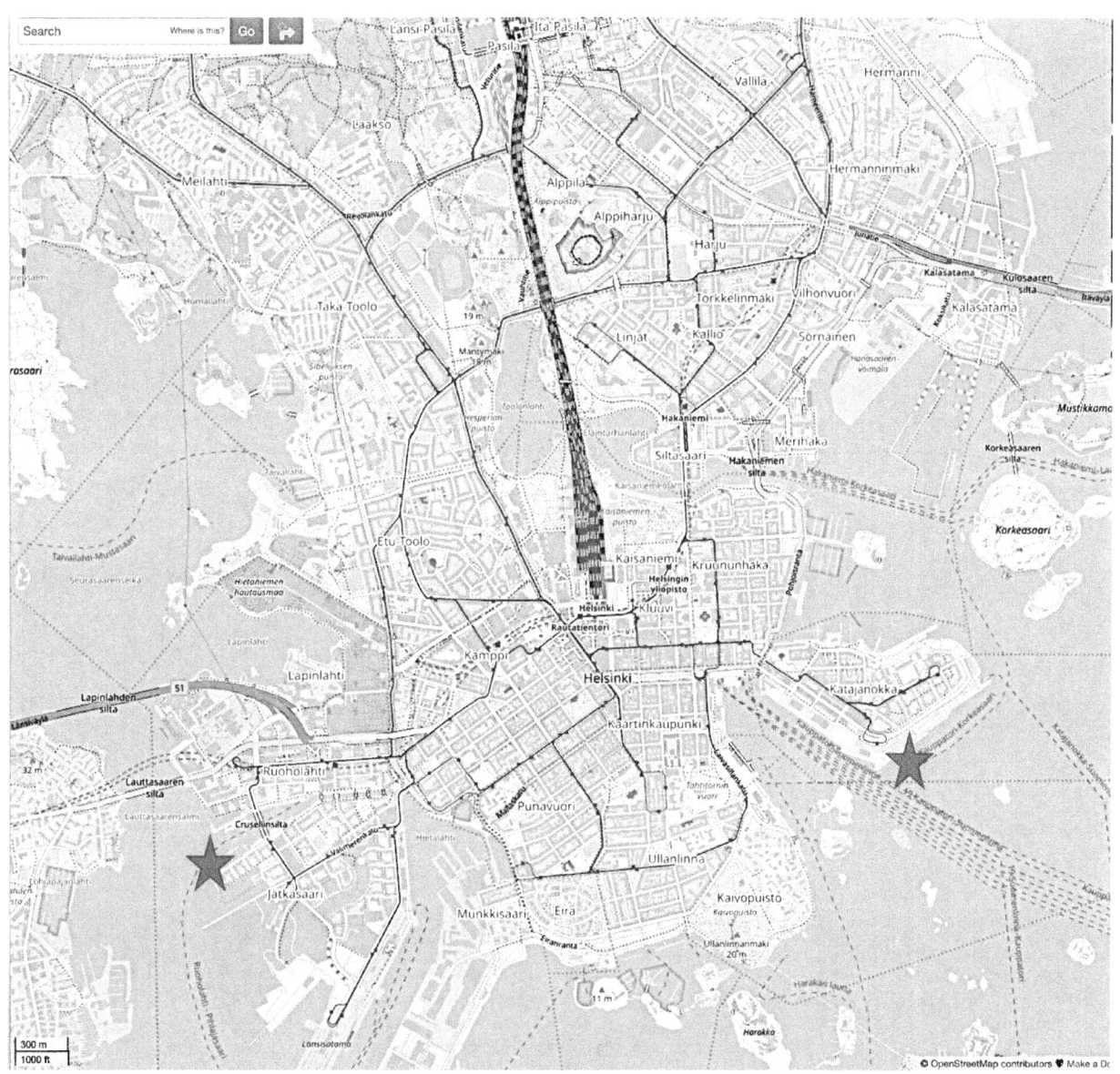

The central peninsula with stars showing cruise ship docks, (© OpenStreetMap contributors)

This map is best viewed directly from OpenStreetMap.com on your personal device where it can be expanded or one specific area can be enlarged. Given the format of this book, it is impossible to display maps with the level of detail you might wish to have while actually out exploring the city. But the OpenStreetMap maps used directly are the tool I always rely upon.

HELSINKI'S CITY CENTER

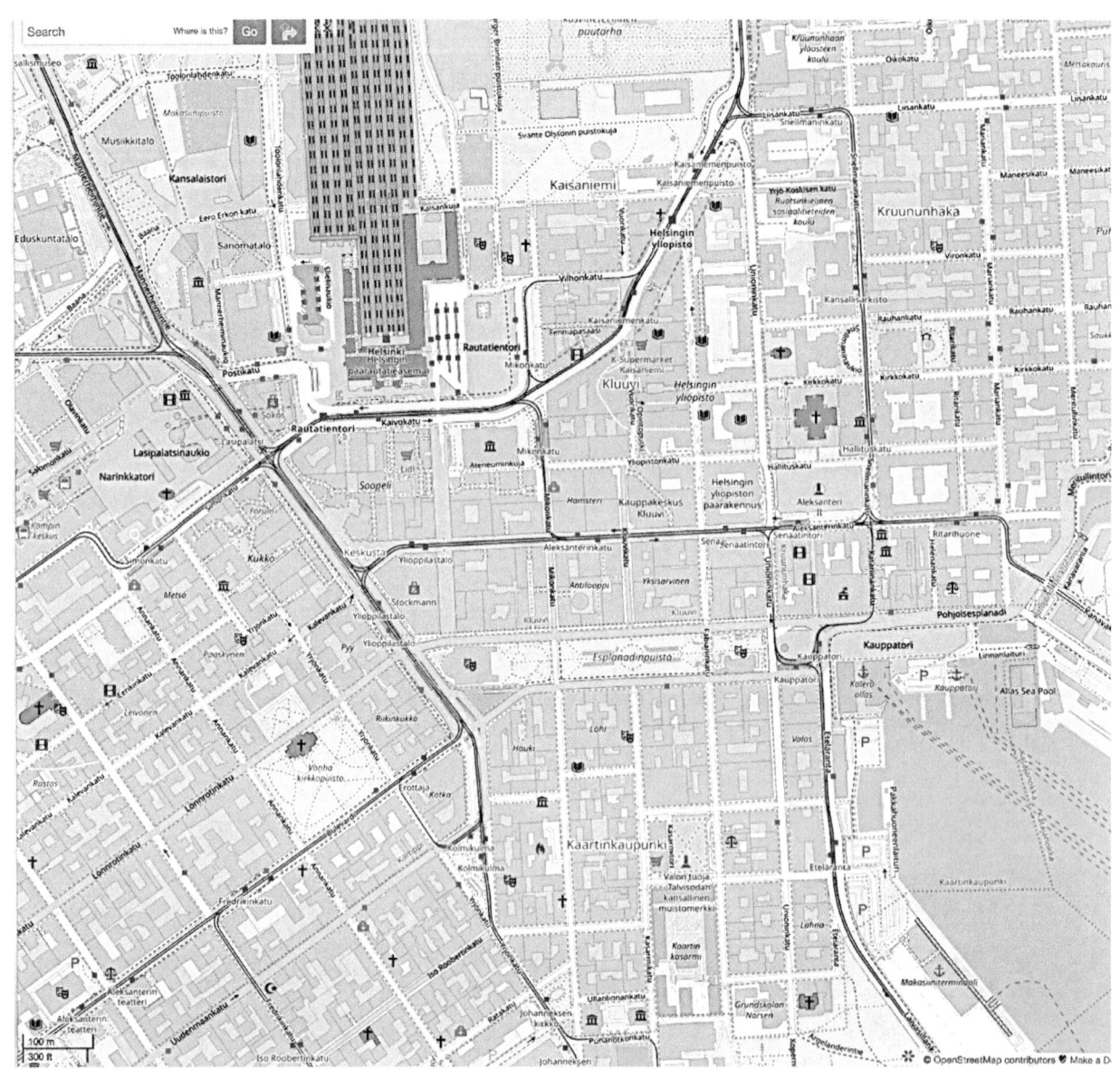

City Center of Helsinki

This map is best viewed directly from OpenStreetMap.com on your personal device where it can be expanded or one specific area can be enlarged. Given the format of this book, it is impossible to display maps with the level of detail you might wish to have while actually out exploring the city. But the OpenStreetMap maps used directly are the tool I always rely upon.

SAINT PETERSBURG, RUSSIA
САНКТ ПЕТЕРБУРГ, РОССИЯ

A map of the Russian Federation

VISITING RUSSIA - VISA OR NO VISA: On every major Baltic Sea itinerary the crown jewel port is Saint Petersburg, the old imperial capital of the Russian Empire. The city is rich in monumental architecture representative of the power of Tsarist Russia. But after the Communist Revolution of 1917 and the civil war that followed, the emerging Soviet Union turned its back on this grand city, relegating it to becoming an industrial giant. The old buildings deteriorated and what became Leningrad was dull and drab. But since 1991 and the emergence of the new Russia, Saint Petersburg has become the country's showplace, and today attracts millions of visitors. Many cruise lines spend up to three days docked in Saint Petersburg while some only spend two days. Either way, it is insufficient time that allows one to simply see the major highlights of this amazing city. I have been to Saint Petersburg 51 times, spending three days each visit. I still find new neighborhoods, small museums and elegant old buildings tucked away in places that are off the main tourist routes. This is a city to be savored, but at least you will be introduced to its grandeur in either a two or three-day visit.

Most cruise visitors from North America and Western Europe do not obtain Russian visas in advance of their visit. Without a visa you are limited to leaving the ship only with a valid excursion ticket from the cruise line or from a licensed tour operator. You may be ashore only for the duration of the tour and you cannot go off on your own to explore. Contrary to what many people believe, going off on your own is as safe as in any large city of Western Europe. What is daunting for most is the lack of many English-speaking locals combined with the use of the Cyrillic alphabet, which renders reading signs next to impossible unless you have studied the language. There are a few signs written in Roman alphabet at major tourist sites and in some of the internationally recognized stores. You can easily download the Cyrillic alphabet with explanatory notes from the Internet and this will make it possible to at least read a street sign or the name of a store. I have taught people to be able to basically read the Cyrillic alphabet within an hour or two.

If you have a sense of adventure and are the type of person that wants to experience new things on your own without being spoon fed by a guide, I strongly urge you to go through the process and expense of obtaining a Russian visa. This enables you to come and go at will. If you are visiting on one of the large size cruise ships, you will be docked in the main cruise port, which is on the outer edge of the city center. To go off on your own does require a very long walk or a ride on the local trolley bus and Metro to get to the city center. There are also what are called Comfort Taxis that can be ordered via the telephone. They are a cut above the regular taxis in that they are quite clean, comfortable and very safe. The driver will be waiting at a specific time at the location provided. You can also pre book the return trip in advance. Thus going ashore from the major cruise port is not as daunting as it sounds.

If you are visiting on one of the deluxe cruise lines utilizing smaller ships, you will dock along the Neva River and be within one or two kilometers from the heart of the city. It is a great advantage not only for private exploration, but even the group tours spend far less time in traffic to reach major venues. Cruise lines such as Silversea, Seabourn and Regent have ships small enough to utilize one or the other of two docks along the Neva River.

The Russian Visa affixed inside your passport

Having the freedom of a visa enables you to sample the delectable Russian cuisine, as there are many restaurants that do not host large tour groups. The visa enables you to get out at night for dinner - a real taste treat. And yes the city is very safe to get around Saint Petersburg at night. Remember that during summer it does not get dark until almost midnight. Fortunately I happen to speak and both read and write Russian, and this enables me to travel around with great ease, but there are tens of thousands of visitors who come on their own without knowing the language and they still find it a memorable experience if they have planned ahead and secured a Russian visa.

There are a handful of countries that do not require a visa for a short cruise visit to Russia, and their citizens can come and go freely without the need for a tour ticket. Nationals from Argentina, Brazil, Chile, China, Hong Kong, Israel, Kazakhstan and several others are among those not needing visas.

INTERACTING WITH RUSSIANS: Russians tend to be reserve with visitors because they for the most part cannot converse with us, but if you learn just a few words of Russian it will open so many doors for you when you do venture out on your own. Russian people are so appreciative of our efforts to attempt to converse with them. And contrary to what many of us believe, they are quite welcoming in their own quiet way. Once you do make a friend in Russia, you find that they are warm, loving and very loyal. They do like those of us from the West even though our governments may not always be on the best of terms. It is always best when visiting among Russians to not talk of political matters unless you have come to know the person quite well, or in cases where they bring up the topic and want to hear what you have to say.

Over the many years I have been visiting I have bonded with several Russian citizens. We are capable of speaking quite openly about sensitive political matters. But I am always very much aware of the need to remember that even though we are now good friends, I am a visitor in their country. So when I want to be critical of the Russian government, I always do so in a polite and diplomatic manner.

THE NATURAL SETTING: Welcome to Russia. An old Tsarist saying notes that, "Russia is not a country, it's a world." Ever since the expansions brought about by Tsar Peter the Great in the early 1700's, Russia has been the world's largest nation in physical size. When in 1991 the former Soviet Union split into 15 individual nations, Russia itself still remained as the world's largest country in land area. It is hard to imagine Russia's scope. Modern Russia contains 17, 098,296 square kilometers or 6,601,670 square miles, making it nearly the size of the total United States and most of Canada combined. To imagine the magnitude of the country, picture yourself getting on a train in San Francisco and going to New York and then staying on the train while crossing the Atlantic Ocean, eventually reaching Paris, France. That gives you an idea of the east to west distance across Russia that one can travel by rail, from Moscow to Vladivostok. In actuality, the country is even wider as there are still well over 1,600 kilometers or 1,000 miles in longitude between Vladivostok and the far eastern edge of Siberia, where Russia meets Alaska. Yes Alaska, because Russia is America's neighbor as hard as that may be to believe. American readers may remember that vice presidential candidate Sarah Palin in 2000 said, "I can see Russia from my front porch." She as an Alaskan meant that in a figurative manner, as Alaska is a neighbor to Russia. There are two islands in the Bering Straits that are less than three kilometers or two miles apart. One belongs to the United States and the other to Russia. During the Cold War years, soldiers stationed on these two islands would supposedly exchange visits during long, dark winter nights, crossing over the frozen waters via snowmobile, sharing beer, vodka and cards, of course in secret. Whether this is true or not, neither military will confirm.

In May 2015, I was visiting Petropavlovsk on the Kamchatka Peninsula in far eastern Siberia as part of a Trans Pacific cruise. I was being escorted around by the ship's local tour representative and when we were having lunch, I asked, "If there were roads connecting Petropavlovsk with Saint Petersburg, approximately how long a journey would it be?" He thought for a moment and then answered, "If there were roads, which there are not, it would be approximately 16,000 kilometers (10,000 miles) between the two cities." This example should further impress you with the immensity of Russia as the world's largest nation. Yet its population is only 144,500,000, less than half that of the United States.

Only a miniscule piece of this great nation fronts on the Baltic Sea, but it contains a city that has embodied the grand era of the Tsars as its window to the west. The city of Saint Petersburg is located in the western end of the country, actually along a narrow strip of coastline on the Gulf of Finland. With loss of former territory, the city is only about 112 kilometers or 70 miles from the Estonian border to the southwest and 90 miles northwest to the Finnish border. The city occupies what was once swampy ground along the banks of the Neva River where it enters the Gulf of Finland. Behind the city, about 46 kilometers or 30 miles distance is the massive Lake Ladoga, the largest lake in Europe. Lake Ladoga is the result of glacial scour during the last ice age and it is a major body of water covering 17,611 square kilometers or 6,800 square miles. The Neva River empties from this massive lake into the Gulf of Finland, carrying a tremendous volume of water right through Saint Petersburg.

The entire area around Saint Petersburg is thickly forested in spruce, larch and birch, what is referred to as taiga, that great boreal forest that stretches across Eurasia and North America. There are hundreds of small lakes and ponds dotting the region, and it is essentially quite beautiful in a panoramic manner rather than a spectacular one. It is a shame that few cruise visitors ever arrange for tours out into the countryside because there is so much to see in the city. And the cruise lines concentrate their efforts on offering excursions to the most important of the cultural and historic sites. Only those cruise lines that offer a one-day sightseeing excursion by fast train to Moscow provide an opportunity to see the countryside of northwestern Russia, but only in passing while journeying to and from the national capital.

Saint Petersburg has very long and cold winters with a minimum of daylight hours. Temperatures can drop well below freezing for weeks on end. Summer may be a short season, but days can warm up to where one does not need a jacket. And the most beautiful part of summer is what Russians call the "White Nights." From the middle of June to late July there are over 21 hours of daylight, and the evening light casts a golden hue across the city. It is on such golden evenings that many shipboard guests wish they had a visa so as to be able to take a walk and enjoy such evenings.

The countryside just east of Saint Petersburg

RUSSIA'S DYNAMIC HISTORY: A visit to Saint Petersburg is all about history. No other city encompasses its history into the venues that visitors come to see in the same way as does Saint Petersburg. To understand the nature of the city of Saint Petersburg, it is first necessary to know something about Russian history. Consider this section of the chapter essential to developing an appreciation for the sights you will see when visiting.

The city was born out of the desire of one Tsar to change the face of Russia, which he certainly did. Brutal would be an understatement for the whole of Russian history. Russians have known not only a harsh and unforgiving environment that has limited the country's ability to adequately provide for its raw material needs, but also their history has been one of bloodshed, depravities committed by the Tsars and wars fought both internally and externally. And from 1918 until 1991, the country was ruled over by the Communist ideology that opposed individualism and material wealth. It is often stated that the reason why there appears to be a somber quality to the people stems from the hardships that have been endured by the masses over many centuries. This may be an over simplification, but it is food for thought. The other factor you must accept is that in traditional Russian culture it is actually considered to be impolite to smile at strangers you do not know, so this gives the illusion that Russians are unfriendly.

It was during the ninth century that Slavonic tribes began to settle in the Ukraine, Belarus and in the Valdai Hills around what is now Moscow. Previously, Scythians inhabited the land, dating back to the third century BC, later having been overrun by the Germanic Goths, ancient enemies of Rome. The Slavonic people are believed to have originated in the rugged mountains of the Balkans, slowly migrating out onto the Steppes of the Ukraine. The first actual Russian state does not occur until around 850, its name being the Grand Principality of Rus, the name taken from the ancient Viking colonial leader Rurik who established settlements in the area between present day Moscow and Kiev. When the Principality collapsed in 1132, central Russia was divided into small city-states that often warred with one another. In the middle of the 13th century, much of Russia fell under the domination of the Mongol hordes. By 1462, the Grand Principality of Muscovy emerged, given its commanding position over the headwaters of the Volga River. The first leader of the Principality to forcibly unite all of the various fiefdoms into one large nation was Ivan IV, known as Ivan the Terrible, who proclaimed himself Tsar of all the Russias. The term Tsar was taken from Caesar, a reference to the grand rulers of ancient Rome. From 1533 to 1584, he consolidated his power in a brutal reign that was filled with murders and intrigues. During a rage, the Tsar clubbed his own son and heir to death, just one example of what occurred during his time on the throne.

Following the death of Ivan, Russia was plunged into a series of court intrigues, a Polish invasion and finally it emerged still unified under the first of the Romanoff Tsars, Mikhail in 1613. But it was under the reign of Mikhail's grandson, Peter I, ultimately known as Peter the Great, that Russia became a world power. Tsar Peter ruled from 1696 to 1725. During his reign, he decreed that the Boyars or court nobles must wear more western style dress, shave off their beards and become more accustomed to the ways of the outside world.

Once Tsar Peter had solidified his hold on the throne, the Tsar set off on a journey of several years, visiting the Netherlands to learn about shipbuilding and trade, and then to England and France where he saw grand and elegant lifestyles while discovering the latest trends in the sciences. He came to realize just how backward and isolated his country was. And he knew that Russia had to be opened up to the ideas and customs of the West if it was to ever take its place as a modern European nation. But how to achieve this was the question that Tsar Peter had to ponder.

Upon returning to Russia, Tsar Peter decided that the capital must be moved from its inland location in Moscow to a window on the Gulf of Finland from which it would be possible to travel by sea to the western nations of Europe, at least during the summer months. Peter pressed into service thousands of craftsmen to drain the swampy ground and began erecting a new capital, but one whose architecture would be patterned after that of Paris. And thus began the development of the city of Saint Petersburg. The Tsar forced the nobility to move to the new city, and he commanded them to build palatial homes. At the same time that he was developing his new city, he also oversaw the expansion of his empire into the reaches of Siberia and down into the steppe and desert lands of Central Asia.

Tsar Peter the Great, founder of Saint Petersburg

The city of Saint Petersburg got its greatest boost in terms of architectural construction and grandeur under the Empress Catherine, known as Catherine the Great. Apart from Peter, she became the most famous of all Russian rulers, and she was not even Russian. She was born a German princess in a rather obscure backwater principality, but she was sent to Russia to marry the nephew and heir of the Empress Elizabeth, daughter of Peter the Great. Catherine was baptized into the Orthodox Church and quickly learned the court intrigues in the palace. Her husband was not a willing partner, and to this day it is unclear if the son she bore was truly his. After her husband came to the throne upon the death of Elizabeth, in 1762, a palace coup deposed her feeble husband, and with the support of the military, she was proclaimed Empress of Russia, not just the regent for her son Paul. She ruled in autocratic fashion until her death in 1796. She was responsible for many cultural reforms, the development of the arts and she expanded the empire to the Black Sea and deep into Siberia.

But Catherine's greatest accomplishments were in Saint Petersburg. She expanded the Winter Palace into its present state of glory, adding a great art collection, which is today second only to the Louvre in Paris. She also expanded what was a small summer palace south of the city into one of the world's most splendid palaces – Tsarskoye Selo. Catherine brought a grand European elegance to the city, and this curried great favor among the nobility. However, her palace love affairs with military officers and politicians meant that nobody in government was on solid ground. By the time of her death, Saint Petersburg was considered to be one of the glittering capitals of Europe. But of course all this grandeur was at the expense of the poor peasants whose labors built the fabulous palaces and churches that made the city grand. Russia at the time of Catherine was a nation of two classes. There was the nobility and its retainers along with wealthy merchants. These people, a minority of the total population, lived in luxury. Many actually lived lives of splendor, surrounded by the most elegant of furnishings and dressed in the utmost of high fashion clothing. Then there were the masses, or peasants. The majority lived on the land, but not as independent farmers. Most were consigned as serfs to the landed estates of the nobility, essentially one step above slave labor. In the cities, the urban poor were those who tended to the most menial of jobs or worked in the small factories and craft shops.

The Hermitage or Winter Palace was primarily the result of the efforts of Catherine the Great

Following Catherine's death, the next succession of Tsars varied from totally autocratic to somewhat benevolent. In 1812, the forces of Tsar Alexander I combined with an unusually brutal winter defeated Napoleon, ending the greatest threat of its day to the Russian Empire. In 1861, Tsar Alexander II freed millions of peasant serfs from their indentured service to the landed nobility. This ultimately led to his assassination and to a terribly autocratic rule by his son, Tsar Alexander III. His rule was the first of many underlying factors that would lead to the eventual downfall of the House of Romanoff.

Tsar Nicholas II and his beautiful wife Tsarina Alexandra were to be the last of the Romanoff line and the end of an era for Russia. His uncle, King Edward VII of the United Kingdom, had warned him that he needed to establish a parliamentary system of government and end autocratic rule. The Tsar tried the concept, but when the Duma (parliament) appeared to show a degree of independence, he closed it down. The Tsar embroiled Russia in a war with Japan that American President Theodore Roosevelt had to negotiate a peace treaty to conclude in 1905, and this made the Tsar quite unpopular. It also angered Japan's leaders because it kept them from what would have been a victory over Russia in far eastern Siberia.

The golden splendor of icons inside Saint Isaac's Cathedral

There was the issue regarding the young heir who suffered from hemophilia. A Siberian monk by the name of Rasputin was able to convince the Tsarina that he had mystical powers to heal. At times Rasputin appeared to be able to help the young Tsarevich, but in so doing, he wheedled his way into the inner circle, and there were fears among the nobility that he had a profound influence upon both the Tsar and the Tsarina. It was decided among a group of nobles that Rasputin had to die. He was invited one night to the Usupov Palace, served poisoned sweets and wine, which he survived. He was later shot and finally thrown into the one of the canals of the Neva River. Ultimately, he died, and nobody was ever apprehended for the crime.

In 1914, Russia entered the war against Germany and the Austro-Hungarian Empire because of their longstanding pledge to defend Serbia. The war was a disaster and the Tsar was unable to muster sufficient loyalty to keep troops from deserting the front. In February 1917, he was forced to abdicate, and a provisional government was established. A Bolshevik leader named Vladimir Ilich Ulyanov, later to call himself Vladimir Lenin, inspired riots in Saint Petersburg and Moscow. In October 1917, the

Bolshevik forces stormed the Winter Palace and the provisional government collapsed. The Tsar and his family were exiled to Siberia, and in 1918, they were all grouped together for what was supposedly an official photograph before being moved to another location. But they were brutally executed by firing squad and their bodies were then soaked in acid, burned and buried. Thus the Communists felt assured that there would be no turning back.

The bodies of the Tsar and his family were discovered in the early 1990's, identified through DNA, matching them to Prince Phillip of the United Kingdom because of their bloodline connection through the Danish royal house. They were then returned to Saint Petersburg and given a formal state burial in the Peter and Paul Cathedral, as was befitting a Tsar, thus bringing full circle the history of tsarist Russia.

Lenin's victory was followed by years of bloody civil war, which ended in 1922 with the creation of the Union of Soviet Socialists Republics. The capital was moved back to the Kremlin in Moscow, leaving Saint Petersburg as a second-class city. Lenin thought that Saint Petersburg expressed the height of decadence and as the leader of a Communist state, the capital needed to be located in the nation's heartland. When Vladimir Lenin died in 1924, the city of Saint Petersburg was renamed Leningrad in his honor, and that name lasted until 1991. And the city became a major industrial center, leaving the grand palaces and churches to deteriorate, as they were inconsequential to Communist doctrine.

The old Leningrad City Hall, a monument to Soviet Era style

This dictatorial and monolithic state would last until the end of 1990. The Soviet Union became a powerful state, but at the expense of its people. Freedoms were highly limited, especially after Lenin died in 1924 and Joseph Stalin came to power. It is now known that his various purges and incarcerations in the notorious gulags of Siberia cost the lives of over 20,000,000 Russians. Only during World War II, when Nazi Germany invaded Russia, did Stalin find that there was true support among the masses. He did engender a certain fatherly image that the Russians seemed to need to aid in their victory over the Germans. Russia did receive massive foreign aid from the United States and the United Kingdom. Red Army determination once again combined with a brutal winter helped to defeat Germany and ultimately turn the tide of the war, but at a cost of another 20,000,000 lives.

During the war, the Nazi forces attempted to take the city of Leningrad, but were held at bay by a tenacious people and detachments of the Red Army. The Germans surrounded the city and for 900 days they attempted to starve it into submission. The city was bombarded and shelled on a regular basis and people died of not only explosions, but also of starvation and cold. Only during winter could the Red Army supply the city by driving convoys of trucks over the frozen Lake Ladoga to the east, a perilous journey both because of the dangers of thin ice toward late winter and the harassment by Nazi forces that led to several major battles along the southern margins of the lake. This was one of the most terrible of sieges in modern history. There are many monuments in Saint Petersburg to commemorate this terrible event and Russia's victories over the German forces. However, most group tours never include these monuments because the tour operators focus primarily upon the glories of Tsarist Russia before 1917. But if the Siege of Leningrad is of significant interest, you can have the ship's shore concierge staff arrange private excursions for you that will focus on this theme.

The Soviet Union became the Cold War enemy of the United States and Western Europe, especially after it too developed nuclear weapons during the 1950's. Several dictatorial leaders ruled after Stalin's death in 1953, the two most famous being Nikita Khrushchev and Leonid Brezhnev. During the 1980's, a new and moderate leader came to power. His name of course was Mikhail Gorbachev, the man who began to open the doors through his policies of glasnost and perestroika, openness and restructuring. But it was too late to restructure the system, as the Soviet Union was over extended and starting to crumble. The end came on December 31, 1990, when Mr. Gorbachev dissolved the Union of Soviet Socialist Republics. The Russian Federation emerged, and it has had its problems, scandals and is only now becoming far more stable economically.

The people of Russia have known bitter hardship throughout their long history. Yes there are many glories, and Saint Petersburg displays the opulence and elegance of a romantic era of tsarist life. But for the average Russian, just earning enough to survive has always been the primary goal. It is true that Russians love to sing and dance, and there is an exuberance to their style of folk dancing that pierces the soul. But these expressions were reserved for weddings and special occasions. Most of the music that one hears is melancholy and tugs at the heartstrings. It is a deep and moving part of the Russian soul.

A small part of the 900-day Siege Monument

In 1991, as Russia emerged out of the former Soviet Union, it quickly set about to restore old place names, bring back the role of the Orthodox Church and restore many of its monuments to the past. One of the most memorable of events was the final internment of the remains of Tsar Nicholas II and his family, brutally murdered by the Bolsheviks. Even the President of Russia attended the ceremony, marking a reestablishment of ties between the new Russia and its illustrious, if not sometimes brutal, past history. Today Saint Petersburg is the showplace of how Russia adapted itself to western ways. Its elegant palaces and churches again glitter with the aura of the old empire.

Once again people enjoy taking a stroll along Nevsky Prospekt, the grand main boulevard of the city. Looking at the glorious architecture, it is not hard to imagine being back in the days of the Tsar when this street was the place to be seen among the city's royal and noble classes. There are still many cafes that serve light meals or evening refreshments. And during the summer when the sun only dips below the horizon for a couple of hours, the buildings take on a distinct golden glow, which the Russians also refer to as the "White Nights." But in today's reality, Nevsky Prospekt is no longer just a street that caters to the rich nobility and royalty of Russia, as it once did.

The grandeur of Saint Isaac's Cathedral

THE PRESENT POLITICAL REALITY: To fully understand the nature of life in Russia when you visit Saint Petersburg, it is essential to understand the current state of foreign relations between Russia and the West. This is a sensitive topic, yet it is bound to come up during one of the excursions sponsored by the cruise line or during a private tour or when meeting Russians if you explore on your own. The vast majority of the people of Russia support the foreign doctrines of their current government led by President Vladimir Putin. In the West he has become somewhat vilified and compared to the former hard line Soviet leaders of the past. In Russia, he has a strong measure of public support, but there are those who quietly are critical of his policies. The Putin government does not readily tolerate much open criticism or hostility. The opposition has grown in recent years, but it is still very small compared to the support the president has from the majority of Russians. But being in the minority, most people are often reluctant to speak about their president, however, you will find those who do speak quite openly and reflect some of the attitudes expressed by western media. To best understand the current government, it is important to recognize the following facts:

* Government in Russia is somewhat autocratic, but this is written into the national constitution. The bulk of real power is not vested in the Duma (parliament) but rather rests with the office of the president.

* The president may serve for two consecutive six-year terms, and following an absence of one term, he may serve again for a maximum of two more consecutive terms. This leads to the potential for a strong man leader to emerge, one who can hold he reins of power for a lengthy period. President Putin has served for eight years under the old four-year term, then served as the prime minister for one term and is now back in the second six-year term of office. Some critics claim he will attempt to change the constitution to enable him to serve a third consecutive six-year term. That remains to be seen and there is little point in speculating at this time.

"Papa" Lenin is a reminder of the long autocratic history of Russia

* The main political party that has been in power since 1991, the United Russia party holds 341 seats out of the 450 seats in the Duma. And President Putin is the party leader. This vast majority means that the Duma is fully supportive of the President's decisions.

* The United Russia party has been quite forceful in suppressing outward opposition to its policies. Many westerners believe that the President and key party officials have used intimidation and bribery to achieve an ongoing role as the preeminent force in the country

* President Putin has appealed to national pride by exerting pressure on western leaders to recognize Russia as a major political player in world affairs. His outward actions have unfortunately brought western condemnation of many political actions, sanctions against the economic sector and in the end has entrenched the Russian leadership into an adversarial relationship with the West.

Misunderstanding of Russian political processes and the sentiment of a vast segment of the American populace created this current atmosphere of confrontation with Russian leaders becoming more intransigent in flexing their political and military muscle. This has become quite evident in the recent campaign of Russian military actions in support of the Syrian president contrary to the position of the majority of western leaders.

When Russia took control of the Crimean Peninsula in 2014, western leaders and media condemned the action without any attempt to understand the underlying factors involved. This immediately started a rapid deterioration in relations between Russia and the West. Yes it was an aggressive act on Russia's part, and it was a total contravention of international relations. But President Putin, with a vast majority of Russians behind him, saw it differently. From their collective point of view, Crimea had been a part of Russia since Tsarist times when it was taken away from the Ottoman Empire. The population of the peninsula was and had always been predominantly Russian. During the 1950's, Soviet leader Nikita Khrushchev transferred the territory to the Ukrainian Soviet Socialist Republic to quell their insistence that they needed more coastal access. It was an inconsequential matter because Ukraine was a part of the Soviet Union. The population of Crimea was still Russian and Moscow still controlled the whole of the nation.

When the Soviet Union dissolved in 1991, the Ukraine leaders chose independence, and Crimea thus was lost to Russia since it had been acknowledged as part of the Ukraine. A treaty was signed enabling the large Russian naval base in Sevastopol to be leased, and therefore the Russian military maintained a strong position in the region and contributed heavily to the economic base.

In 2012 when the Ukrainian people began to pressure their government for closer economic and social ties with the European Union, the Ukrainian leader who was very closely allied to Russia's President Putin, resisted. This ultimately led to massive protests that became somewhat violent and led to the president fleeing the country. Elections were held and a very pro-western president was elected. This in turn angered the Russian minority in Crimea and also in the industrialized eastern portion of Ukraine where there have been close economic and trade links with Russia dating back to the Soviet Era.

Russian leadership saw an opportunity to win back the Crimean Peninsula and this helped stir up feelings that led to a 2014 referendum in which over 90 percent of the populace voted for a reunification with Russia. And the Russian military presence made it impossible for the government of the Ukraine to counter the momentum that swept the region. Thus Crimea was officially annexed by Russia, a move that was not in accordance with international law because of the rapidity in which it occurred, especially without any concurrence by the Ukrainian government. Although Russia had sufficient grounds to make a case before the United Nations, they chose immediate military action and this has cost them dearly with regard to relations with the West.

Navy Day on the Neva River celebrates Russian military might

The events of Crimea stimulated rebellion among those of Russian cultural origin and those sympathetic to maintaining ties with Russia in the eastern Ukraine. And ultimately this has led to what is essentially a civil war in that part of the country. And clearly there has been Russian assistance to the rebel forces, a matter that has further angered western leaders. At the moment in early 2020, the situation is essentially a stalemate.

It is within the context of the events herein described that visitors are still cruising to Saint Petersburg. I felt it important to help clarify what underlies the current tensions between Russia and the West. But as a scholar of Russian history and as a traveler who has been traveling and cruising to Russia numerous times each summer since 2010 while presenting my lectures on board ship, I can offer full assurance that you will be safe when visiting Russia. Tourism is a major source of income to the country, especially to Saint Petersburg. Russian people on a non-governmental level do not hold it against the West that our governments and theirs are not in agreement over the issues of Ukraine, ISIS and the Middle East in general. But despite these political divisions, we are welcomed and respected. I do caution you to be circumspect in the way in which you answer any questions of a political nature. Remember that you are a guest in their country. Russians are essentially proud of their nation and its present accomplishments and they do not want to be "lectured to" or spoken down to by westerners. The Soviet Era is over, and they do not want us to cast them in that light. Likewise, we are treated overall with respect so long as we show a mutual level of respect despite whatever feelings to the contrary any of us may have. You are in Saint Petersburg to view the historical marvels of its past glory, so enjoy it.

Greater Saint Petersburg written in the Cyrillic alphabet, (@OpenStreetMap.org)

THE PHYSICAL LAYOUT OF THE CITY OF SAINT PETERSBURG:
Saint Petersburg occupies very low-lying ground along both shores of the Neva River along with several large islands within the river's massive delta (see maps at the end of the chapter). The Neva is a short, but wide river that empties from Lake Ladoga 46 kilometers or 30 miles to the east of the city into the Gulf of Finland, the easternmost arm of the Baltic Sea.

With the potential for storm surges brought on by passing weather systems now combined with rising sea levels, a massive dike has been built across the Gulf of Finland connecting the southern shore with the northern and carrying atop it an expressway that links Kronstadt Island with the mainland. The island has been and continues to be Russia's naval base for the Baltic and North Atlantic fleet. To enable ships to enter and leave Saint Petersburg, there is a large opening in the dike that can be closed by two great gates. The expressway is carried under the opening in a deep water tunnel. This is a very impressive project and Kronstadt is a fascinating place to visit now that it is open to the public for the first time since the Bolshevik Revolution of 1917.

When the city was founded, it was necessary to dig canals to help drain the land so that building foundations could be stabilized in the soft alluvial soil. Today these canals serve primarily as routes for small pleasure and tourist boats to navigate among some of the oldest of the city's neighborhoods. Beyond the river delta and its low-lying bottom land the countryside rises slightly into a gently rolling landscape, but there are few hills and no mountains anywhere in sight. The countryside is covered in coniferous taiga forest interspersed with groves of birch trees. And there are numerous small lakes and ponds, many of them today being surrounded by dachas (country homes) for weekend use. There is only a small amount of agriculture around Saint Petersburg because of the length and severity of the winter. Dairy cattle, root vegetables, apple orchards and some rye, barley and oats can be raised in the local area.

A great high altitude aerial view of Saint Petersburg, (Work of Solundir, CC BY SA 4.0, Wikimedia.org)

The heart of the city occupies the land south of the main branch of the river known as the Bolshaya Neva. Suburbs extend well to the south where the land begins to rise up out of the bottomland. The two largest islands, Vasilevsky and Petrogradsky, are both heavily urbanized and each one houses several hundred thousand residents. The smaller northern islands of the delta provide recreational space for sports venues along with large dachas for the wealthy on Krestovsky Island.

The focal hub of St. Petersburg lies immediately south of the Bolshaya Neva and its grand boulevard known as Nevsky Prospekt radiates out to the southeast from Palace Square that fronts on The Hermitage. A great many of the important monuments of the Old City are clustered around Palace Square. If you are on a small, upmarket cruise ship you most likely will be docked on either the south or north side of the Bolshaya Neva and within easy walking distance of the heart of the city.

Aerial view along the south bank of the Bolshaya Neva toward Palace Square, (Work of A. Savin, Wikimedia Commons)

Vasilevsky Island and Petrogradsky Island also contain many important monumental sites that technically are still considered to be in the central city. In this case, if you are on a larger cruise ship docked in the main cruise terminal, you will be able to walk throughout Vasilevsky Island and also to Palace Square. Petrogradsky Island and the major venues along and adjacent to Nevsky Prospekt will be too far for you to walk. And it is doubtful your cruise ship will provide a shuttle since the majority of guests do not have visas and will be touring by means of the ship sponsored tours.

I do advise you to obtain a Russian Visa despite it being an arduous process, as otherwise you miss the opportunity to any independent exploring other than that which can be arranged by private licensed operators. And the cost factor is quite a problem for most visitors.

The north shore of the Neva's northern branch is known as the Primorsky District. It is one of the new and expanding areas of the city. Both here in Primorsky and in the suburbs south of the old central city, massive high-rise apartment complexes have

developed. In these outer regions the building crane is often said to be the most common bird. There are cranes everywhere, as new apartment buildings rise. They vary in quality from large blocks housing thousands of working-class residents to narrower, elegant blocks that can cost the equivalent of many hundreds of thousands of Euro.

East of the Neva River after it bends into a north to south axis, the area has seen far less development. This area, known as the Nevsky District, has the potential for great urban growth because it is close to the city center, but it has been more industrialized in past decades and is only now starting to see more residential and commercial growth.

The modern Primorsky District from the air in winter, showing the new Gasprom skyscraper, tallest in Russia, (Work of Красный, (CC BY SA 4.0, Wikimedia.org)

Fortunately for Russia, the Germans were never able to destroy Saint Petersburg during World War II, despite their great siege of the city. They cut off the city by forming a blockade across the land between the Gulf of Finland and Lake Ladoga. During winter, the Red Army was able to bring in limited supplies by truck convoys across the frozen lake and then down a well-protected road that became known as "Doroga Zhizny," meaning the Road of Life. There were many battles fought in the marshes and lowlands across this zone, but ultimately the Soviet forces prevailed. But during that siege there was tremendous loss of life.

Many of the city's landmarks and especially the two summer palaces south of the city were destroyed, but lovingly rebuilt after the war. Even under Communist rule, there was a strong appreciation for the classical and elegant architecture, thus the building of modern structures was forbidden in the city center even though initially many old buildings were allowed to languish. As Communism was replaced by free enterprise, and as Russians began to value the importance of tourism, the heart of Saint. Petersburg became an attraction that could become a major selling point for visitors. And it has worked. This is a must see city for people visiting the Baltic Sea region. In fact, it is the highlight of the region. In 1990, the historic heart of Saint Petersburg and many of the outlying palaces became a UNESCO World Heritage Site, assuring the protection of the integrity of this incredible city.

Church of the Spilled Blood in the historic city center

New construction is relegated the second and third rings of development surrounding the old city. The second ring consists of buildings from the Communist Era – mostly gray blocks of apartments and massive government buildings. But those built in the Stalin Era are considered to have architectural merit. Many have been renovated and restored while their exteriors remain in the Stalinist style. These buildings are also valued for residential use because of the apartments having larger rooms and high ceilings. But in many parts of the middle or second ring of the city are thousands of buildings built in Khrushchev and Brezhnev Eras. These are rather unadorned blocks, many of the having been hastily built with inferior materials. Today, most of these buildings are eyesores and they are hard to modernize and make attractive. But as the city continues to grow, contractors find it more advantageous to tear them down in favor of modern 21st century high-rise housing.

In the third ring one finds the glitzy new high-rise condos and apartments that are highly sought after by Russia's new middle and upper classes. And with the newly found prosperity that has come to Russia, there are magnificent apartment blocks and condos in the city's outer ring that would resemble the finest of such buildings found in North American cities, but of course these are for the wealthy class.

Some of the new apartment blocks being built in the outer suburban areas, especially in the southwest of the city, are massive. Many are up to 30 stories in height and stretch for several blocks in length as one contiguous building. These blocks are definitely impressive and they do reflect the demand for new housing. The suburban landscape should be seen by cruise passengers other than just in passing while traveling to either Peterhoff or Catherine's Palace. They represent the progress being made in modern Russia and these suburbs are very impressive.

Moskovsky Prospekt is the grand southern boulevard

Several major boulevards sweep inward to the old city center, in some ways like the spokes of a wheel. Two of the most notable are Kammennostrovsky Prospekt in the north, crossing Petrogradsky Island en route to the Field of Mars. In the south, Moskovsky Prospekt is another major urban boulevard. Both are lined with older apartment blocks mixed with new construction.

What is most impressive is the development of the city's expressway system. There is one outer ring expressway that begins in Petrogradsky District and encircles the city, coming into the far southern portion of the city along the edge of the Kirovsky and Krasnoselsky Districts. The Western High Speed Diameter is a new partly elevated expressway that runs south in the northwestern part of the city, feeding in from the Finnish border. This amazing piece of construction crosses the three branches of the Neva River in its massive delta and then traverses above the major commercial docks before it joins the A118 belt expressway in the far southwest near the international airport. This route, which opened in late 2016, cuts off over one hour of travel time for people living in Petrogradsky or on Vasilevsky Island when en route to the airport or the southern suburbs.

You will be surprised if one of your tours utilizes this expressway just how much traffic you will see. It appears on the surface that almost everyone in Saint Petersburg has a car, and most of them are quite new, just a sign of an economy that surprises those of us from the West.

The ultra-modern Western High Speed Diameter

CRUISE SHIP DOCKING: Depending upon the size and draught of your cruise ship you will most likely dock in the new and modern Marine Façade, which fronts on the Gulf of Finland at the far western edge of Vasilevsky Island. This modern terminal accommodates more than five or six cruise ships at one time and can be quite overwhelming, but for most visitors who are on group excursions it is not that daunting a place to navigate. Each time you leave your ship and each time you return, you will go through an immigration lane and have your passport inspected. You must have a valid tour ticket from your cruise ship, a valid tour voucher from a recognized tour company if you made your own arrangements or a Russian Visa or hold a passport from a country not requiring a visa to be able to leave the terminal and enter the city. This is a time consuming problem, but is one you must endure.

If you are on board a small luxury cruise ship you will be very fortunate in docking along the Neva River in the heart of the city. Only small ships of less than 30,000 tons are capable of sailing up the ship channel into the lower Neva River and docking at either the English Embankment or the Lieutenant Schmidt Embankment where small cruise terminals are located. The English Embankment is the absolute choice dock because it is on the south side of the Neva River and only a few blocks west from Palace Square, which is the heart of the city. The Lieutenant Schmidt Embankment is across the river on the north bank, which is a part of Vasilevsky Island. It is still very close to Palace Square, but separated from it by approximately two kilometers or just over one mile and one river crossing.

For those few guests who have a Russian Visa or hold a passport not requiring a visa it is possible to get around the city on your own. But without a knowledge of the Russian language and/or an ability to read the Cyrillic Alphabet, it still can be daunting. From Marine Façade it is simply too far to walk into the city center, requiring a private car and driver/guide, a prearrange Comfort Taxi or utilizing a trolley bus and then the Metro. From the English Embankment it is possible to walk into the heart of the city and from the Lieutenant Schmidt Embankment a short trolley bus ride is usually required.

GETTING AROUND SAINT PETERSBURG IF ON YOUR OWN: Without question, Saint Petersburg will be the highlight of any Baltic Sea cruise. No other city in the region is as large or offers as many palaces, churches and museums to the visitor. Remember that this was the capital of the entire Russian Empire for just over 200 years, especially at the peak of the era of grandeur that Russia copied from the western courts. Although visitors come to see the historic architecture from Tsarist times, modern Saint Petersburg will surprise visitors with its massive high-rise construction, large shopping malls and well-designed urban parks. Saint Petersburg is presently the third largest city in Europe with a population of over 6,000,000. It is only exceeded by Moscow and London in population.

* ORGANIZED TOURS – Most ship passengers will be visiting Saint Petersburg on organized excursions operated by the cruise line rather than going exploring on their own. The reason for this, as noted previously, is based upon the strictness of the Russian immigration laws. Only passengers from a country not required to have a visa or passengers who have secured a visa are allowed off the ship at will. Unfortunately thee majority of visitors, especially from Western nations simply balk at the potential trauma in obtaining a visa for Russia. In the end, they miss out on so much.

* PRIVATE TOURS – There are several private tour operators that provide excursions either in groups or privately, and they will arrange the necessary documents to enable visitors to leave the ship. But just like the cruise-organized tours, visitors are only allowed off the ship for the duration of the private or small group tour.

There are numerous private tour operators licensed by the government to handle the proper documentation for private tours in the event you do not have a visa. The company that I trust exclusively is Baltic Travel for all my private car and driver arrangements. You can contact them via e-mail at welcome@baltic.spb.ru for details and prices. Another option is to have the cruise line arrange private cars and driver/guides, but once again visitors are only allowed out for the duration of the tour unless they have a visa or are from an exempt country. The private car option through the cruise lines, however, is very expensive.

The best way to explore on one's own is to hire a guide either with an automobile or one who will escort you via public transportation. So long as the tour operator is licensed by the government they can issue temporary visas good for the duration of each tour in the same way as the cruise line tours. And here I again highly recommend Baltic Travel. I am in no way soliciting business for them, but as a travel author and professional geographer I have come to rely upon their services exclusively. They are a company that services many of the major cruise lines, but if you book directly through them you will save on the higher cost the cruise lines pass on to passengers for private cars and drivers and/or guides. For most guests I recommend having both a driver and a guide since few of the drivers speak English. However, keep in mind that you are in control of what you want to see. If you have specific interests that go outside of the so called box of what the guides are accustomed to there may be some resistance on their part to accommodate you unless you are very insistent. Remember that you are paying for their services. And in today's Russia there are very few places that are off limits to visitors.

* **UTILZING THE METRO OR TROLLEY BUSSES** – To utilize the Metro you must either be in the company of a guide from a licensed company that issued you a temporary visa for your tour, a licensed guide escorting a tour sponsored by the cruise line, have a passport from a country that does not require a visa or have a Russian entry visa. The Metro with its elegant and ornate stations is a fast and efficient way to get around the city.

There is one shortcoming in that the Metro does not have any line that encircles the city, thus if going in a particular direction to visit a venue, one then must retrace steps back into the city center and then change to another line to head in a different direction. There are many trolley busses and regular busses that run every few minutes. But once again it is essential to know the language or have a guide, otherwise getting around will be somewhat difficult, but not impossible.

** **From the Marine Façade** – If you are traveling on board one of the large mega cruise ships it will dock at the major cruise terminal, which is located at the far end of Vasilevsky Island, requiring utilizing public transportation to reach the city center. Ship shuttle busses are not provided because so few guests have visas where they can take advantage of the opportunity to get around on their own. There is a public shuttle bus number 158 that runs every 30 minutes from Terminal Three to the Primorskaya

Metro Station. From there you can take the Metro to Gostini Dvor in the heart of Nevsky Prospekt. The cost for the shuttle is 25 Rubles and for the Metro it is 28 Rubles, and you must have Russian currency since no exchange service is possible outside of the terminal.

Map of the Saint Petersburg Metro, (Work of St. Petersburg Metro by L.m.K., CC BY SA 3.0, Wikimedia.org)

** From English Embankment or Lieutenant Schmidt Embankment – If you are cruising with Silversea, Regent or Seaborne, you will be docking along the Bolshaya Neva River in the city center or across the river on Vasilevsky Island. From either location you can walk to many good restaurants. Do not rely upon taxis because they often do not frequent these riverside quays, or if they do, most drivers are not versed in English. Likewise you may easily be overcharged since no meters are generally used. From the English Embankment on the city center side of the river, walk to the corner of Ploshchad Truda, cross over and then walk two blocks south to Konnogvardeysky Boulevard, which has a green strip down the middle. Walk east two blocks to the bus stop for trolley bus number 22. This bus will take you to Nevsky Prospekt for a cost of 25 Rubles. It saves you a walk of around 1.5 miles. If your ship is docked across the river on Vasilevsky Island, you simply need to walk out to the Lieutenant Schmidt Embankment, walk to the traffic light, cross over and then walk one very long block north to Bolshoi Prospekt where you will find a trolley bus stop number ten or 11. This bus will also take you to Nevsky Prospekt.

The Saint Petersburg Metro can only be described as grand, (Work of Florstein , CC BY SA 3.0, Wikimedia.org)

MAJOR LANDMARKS OF SAINT PETERSBURG: Most visitors coming by cruise ship will see many of the highlights of Saint Petersburg by means of being part of a variety of ship sponsored coach tours. Despite the variety of tours, they all share one element in common - conformity. You are part of a selected itinerary that gives you essentially no choice but to follow your guide and be lectured to about whatever it is you are seeing.

For those willing to spend a bit more money, there is a better way to explore Saint Petersburg, one that gives you more freedom and flexibility. This is the private tour where you have a car or van with a driver and a licensed guide. I do, however, offer this warning; if you just select from various venues to visit, but without specifying your tastes or preferences, you will receive the same prepared guided lecture in each venue that you would receive on a group tour. The advantage that most people do not take is to customize what you want to see. With a car, driver and guide, you are NOT limited to the major venues that the group tours are visiting. You can explore neighborhoods, see how people live, work and shop. You can visit lesser known churches, palaces, museums or go out simply shopping. You can dine in local restaurants. You can take a tour into the countryside. You can visit a school, ride on the Metro, go to a sporting event or a folk performance. Essentially it is your choice as to what to see or do. Many tour operators will discourage such individualized activity because their guides are pre-programed to simply mirror the group tours. There are times you must simply insist that you want to do something not on the normal list of activities. There are no laws preventing you from seeing more of Russia. Over the years, I have been places and seen things that no tourist has probably ever experienced. True I always have a visa, but in the case of using a private car, that is irrelevant.

In my list of sight to see, I will be including many lesser known attractions or venues that most visitors are not even aware of. This is for the purpose of alerting you to what is available if you choose the private car option. Street addresses are not provided, as these major landmarks are so recognized visually and are identified on city maps to the point that an address written in Cyrillic would have no literal reference. I cannot possibly list every site in the city, as the majority of you who read this book are only be able to visit on guided tours without a visa or a passport from a country not in need of one. And even if you have the freedom to explore on your own, there is no way in two or three days that you will even be able to see all that I do note in this book. I have tried to make this list as broad and comprehensive as possible, broken down into major sight, lesser venues and those located outside of the city such as the summer palaces.

* MY MAJOR RECOMMENDATIONS IN THE CITY – These are the most significant venues that you should try and see. But most ship itineraries give you two to three days in Saint Petersburg, hardly enough time to see everything you would like to explore. My suggested venues are listed alphabetically for want of a better way to present them:

** Alexander Column, commemorating Russia's victory against Napoleon in 1812 stands in the middle of Palace Square. The angel atop the column symbolizes peace following the Napoleonic Wars.

** Battleship Aurora – This historic vessel is found from the academy, tied up along the bank of the river is the old battleship Aurora, which fired the opening shot of the October Revolution in 1917, and it can be visited It is open from 11 AM to 6 PM daily except Monday and Friday.

** **Church of the Savior on Blood** (better known as the Church of the Spilled Blood) was built to memorialize Tsar Alexander II, who was assassinated in 1881. Tsar Alexander III, who ordered the church, wanted it to make a statement that would speak to the true Russia. Thus the building is more characteristic of the famous Saint Basil's Cathedral, which stands just outside of the Kremlin walls in Moscow. It has become the most iconic landmark in the city because of its true Russian flavor. During summer the church is open from 10:30 AM until 10:30 PM through the end of September. The church is closed on Wednesday. Tickets must be purchased prior to entry.

Domes of the Church of Spilled Blood seen from the Field of Mars

** **Hermitage (The)** – Said to be the second greatest art gallery in the world after the Louvre in Paris. This is the most important part of the Winter Palace. The overall palace has more than 1,000 rooms as 117 separate staircases. Catherine the Great is credited with having brought the palace to its full grandeur through lavish spending on the building and its interior furnishings as well as its great art collection. The Hermitage was fortunately spared being destroyed or turned into government offices. Even the Communists recognized that it represented not only tsarist oppression, but also the grand history of the nation, and it was a valuable treasure for its artistic beauty. All through the Soviet Era, the building was maintained and open to the limited number of visitors that came to Leningrad. Since the fall of the Soviet Union, the Hermitage has undergone much restoration, some of it continuing to the present. It is considered to be the country's second greatest showcase after the Kremlin in Moscow. Yet visitors are surprised to find that on a warm to hot summer day, windows are open in the Hermitage. There is no air conditioning system and the valuable treasures are exposed to the outside air and humidity, something most museums containing priceless art would never permit. Because the building itself is also an architectural treasure, it would be exceptionally costly to literally rebuild the interior after installing a proper air conditioning and dehumidifying system. Apart from the cost, it would take a large labor force several years to totally rebuild the palace. Therefore no work has been done, and thankfully summer is a short season in Saint Petersburg. Opening hours are from 10:30 to 6 PM, Tuesday, Thursday, Saturday and Sunday. On Wednesday and Friday the museum keeps open until 9 PM. The museum is closed on Monday. Tickets can be purchased for early opening, but this must be done in advance and some cruise lines even offer an early opening tour, which gives you one hour before the full crowd arrives. Frankly even if you have a visa, attempting to visit on your own without prior ticket purchase can be exhausting, as you will wait several hours before gaining entry. It is best to visit the Hermitage as part of a group tour.

The grand Ambassador's Staircase inside the Hermitage

** Lady of Kazan Cathedral - This is another major working church in which services are held throughout the day. Located on Nevsky Prospekt, this massive cathedral has a Romanesque exterior, but the interior is pure Russian Orthodox. Visitors are welcome, but are asked to be respectful of worshipers. The cathedral is open to the public daily from 9 AM to 8 PM.

Along Nevsky Prospekt, the great boulevard

** **Nevsky Prospekt** - Extending southeast from Palace Square is Nevsky Prospekt, the main street of Saint Petersburg, a once fashionable boulevard that is today reclaiming some of its former grandeur. During tsarist times, Nevsky Prospekt was home to the finest and most elegant shops in Saint Petersburg, as this boulevard catered to the rich. Today the buildings lining the street have been restored and many serve once again as shops and restaurants. One of the old building complexes has been modernized on its interior and turned into an upscale shopping center that includes a branch of Stockmann Department Store from Helsinki, showing that old and new can blend together without sacrificing the external appearance. Some cruise lines do offer what they call a "shopping tour," which in essence is a way to get you to be able to spend some free time in the city center that is focused upon Nevsky Prospekt. If you do not have access to a private car, driver and guide, this is a good option, as it enables you to spend a bit of free time in the heart of the city. If of course you have a visa and feel comfortable using local transport, I highly recommend visiting this grand boulevard to be able to gain a feel for the commercial heart of Saint Petersburg.

** Palace Administrative Building stands on the south side of Palace Square. It was here that the civil servants of the Russian Empire did their work to run the government. Today this fully restored building serves as an office complex and has residential units and shops. Most tourists just see and photograph its massive façade from Palace Square

Palace Square looking to The Hermitage

** Palace Square – The most striking feature of the old city center is Palace Square along the Neva River. The grandest building on the square is the Tsar's Winter Palace known as the Hermitage, a magnificent example of Russian baroque architecture. It was from Palace Square in October 1917 that the Bolsheviks stormed into the palace itself, bringing an end to the provisional government and setting into motion the era of Communist domination.

** **Peter and Paul Fortress** - Across the Neva River from the Winter Palace, occupying its own island stands the formidable Peter and Paul Fortress. It was built by Tsar Peter the Great in 1703, but was later used primarily as a prison by later Tsars. Initially the fortress was built to protect the city, since Russia and Sweden had been at odds over many Baltic territories. Within the fortress stands the imposing Peter and Paul Cathedral, where most of the Tsars and other royals since Peter the Great have been laid to rest. The most recent burial was in 2000 for Tsar Nicholas II and his entire family in a special room at the rear of the cathedral. Tickets must be purchased prior to entry, and the fortress is open from 8 AM to 5:40 PM daily except Wednesday.

The Peter and Paul Fortress

** **Petrogradsky Island** is also a large residential district of the city that contains more upper and middle income apartment blocks. Its main boulevard is Kammennostrovsky Prospekt, which is home to many fine examples of Art Nouveau architecture from the late 19th century. The Imperial Naval Academy is to be found on Petrogradsky Island.

** **Russian State Museum** - Located inside the Mikhailovsky Palace, this museum features a massive collection of Russian fine art, crafts and sculpture. Unlike the Hermitage, it is seldom a focus of attention for foreign visitors and therefore is not nearly as crowded. Russian art, especially late 19th century impressionism, is superb and the finest works are exhibited in the state museum. It is open from 10 AM to 6 PM daily except Tuesday, with extended hours until 8 PM on Monday and 9 PM on

Thursday. Tickets are purchased upon entering the building. The palace gardens are open with no charge from 10 AM until 10 PM daily. The gardens offer beautiful views of the domes of the Church of the Savior on Blood, which is adjacent.

Walking to Saint Isaac's Cathedral

** **Saint Isaac's Cathedral** - Saint Petersburg possesses many glorious Russian Orthodox cathedrals, the two most noted being Saint Isaac's and the Church of the Savior on Blood. Saint Isaac's is the city's largest cathedral with its golden dome making the third largest in the world, but its architectural pattern speaks more to Western Europe than it does to the Russian tradition, but with its lavish use of gold and its icons covering the walls the interior is truly Russian Orthodox. The cathedral is open from 10:30 to 6 PM daily except it is closed Wednesday. Evening hours are 6 until 10:30 PM during summer, lasting through September, but Wednesday. Tickets must be purchased prior to entry.

** **Saint Nicholas Naval Cathedral** - This is still a working church in which services are held throughout the day. It is one of the most beautiful buildings in the city with its white and blue walls and golden domes. Visitors may enter most days unless a special ceremony is taking place. There is no charge and you are asked to be respectful and keep outside of the roped off area for worshipers. The cathedral is open daily from 7 AM to 7 PM.

The grand façade of Saint Nicholas Cathedral

** **Vasilevsky Island** - The two large islands north of the old city center are called Vasilevsky and Petrogradsky Islands. Each dates back to the 19th century and is home to a wide range of architectural styles for large apartment blocks that were built for both working class and merchant class families. The major cruise terminal where larger vessels dock is located on Vasilevsky Island, and you will be driving through it en route to various venues and in returning to the ship. Some smaller cruise ships will be docked along the Lieutenant Schmidt Embankment of the Great (Bolshaya) Neva River, which is on the southern edge of the island. The best known photo stop on Vasilevsky Island is the Strelka or split where the second branching of the Neva River occurs. The two Rostral Columns depict the rivers of Russia and served as lighthouses. The view to the Peter and Paul Fortress as well as the Hermitage makes this one of the most important photo stops in the city. And it is always congested with traffic since there are no designated parking areas. The Russian Institute of Art and Saint Petersburg University are housed on the eastern end of Vasilevsky Island leading to the Strelka. The Russian Institute of Art does have a student gallery open to the public for a nominal charge every day except Tuesday.

* **MY RECOMMENDATIONS FOR MINOR VENUES IN THE CITY** – These recommendations are harder to see as part of a group tour. If you are on your own with either a visa or pre-arranged car and driver you stand a better chance of visiting these lesser known, but equally fascinating venues:

** Alexandrinsky Theater - On Nevsky Prospekt, this is the city's other major performing arts center, built to resemble the famous Bolshoi Theater of Moscow. Many cruise lines will offer an evening performance here or at the Marinsky Theater, and it is a worthwhile experience.

Incredible edibles at the Eleseevsky Gastronom

** Eleseevsky Gastronom - This is one of the most elegant food shops in the world, and it dates back to tsarist times. During the Communist period it was allowed to remain open and serviced the high level party officials and their families. It is located on Nevsky Prospekt across the street from the Alexandrinsky Theater and easy to find because of its distinct Art Deco style. This incredible food shop is never seen on any ship sponsored guided excursion, but should be on your list if you are doing a private tour or going out on your own. You will be dazzled by its displays of fine quality food and it is hard to walk out without having made a purchase. It is open every day of the week from 10 AM to 11 PM.

** Engineer's Castle, also known as Saint Michael's Castle - This is a rather massive building set adjacent to the Summer Gardens. It was built for Tsar Paul I, but the tsar spent very little time here because he was assassinated 40 nights after occupying the castle. The story of this horrific event after so much went into the building of the castle is what is so fascinating to visitors. It is open daily from 10 AM to 6 PM but closed on Tuesday. Hours are extended until 9 PM on Thursday.

** Fabergé Museum - Located along the Fontanka Canal Embankment in the central city, this museum was once the home to the illustrious jeweler Karl Fabergé who is world famous for his masterful creations for the Russian Royal Family. During the height of tsarist rule, Saint Petersburg was considered to be the most opulent of European capitals, despite the fact that its masses lived in poverty. At one time, the French jeweler Fabergé had his studio and showroom on Nevsky Prospekt. He became world famous for his masterpiece jewel encrusted golden Easter eggs commissioned by the Tsars for their family. They were generally given as Easter gifts. These eggs were decorated in precious stones, and most opened up to reveal miniature scenes within. The home of Faberge has been recently opened as a museum, but to date none of the cruise lines have included it on their itineraries. Today many of them survive and are part of the 19th century treasures on display both in Saint Petersburg and Moscow. A few of the eggs have reached the art market, and when one on rare occasions comes up for auction, it generally fetches a price in the millions of dollars. You may visit the museum as part of a group tour or on your own. Unguided visits are allowed from 10 AM to 8:45PM daily while guided tours are conducted only until 6 PM.

** Field of Mars - This great open park or parade ground dates back to the earliest years of the city as a place for military maneuvers. It affords a splendid view of the domes of the Church of the Savior on Blood. It also is home to a monument and eternal flame honoring the October Revolution. There is no charge to visit.

Nighttime at Gostiny Dvor, the city's grand shopping arcade, (Work of Andrew Zorin, CC BY SA 3.0, Wikimedia.org)

** **Gostini Dvor** - One of the city's oldest shopping arcades, it is not tourist oriented but it gives you a chance to become a part of everyday life. It is located on Nevsky Prospekt at Ulitsa Sadovaya and is a crossroads of several major Metro lines. Inside the arcade are small shops that are individually owned and sell just about everything imaginable. Its interior is like a gigantic maze, but it is fascinating and you can often find some good bargains on Russian made objects, including clothing, jewelry, household goods and a variety of vodkas, chocolates and other local snack foods. It is open daily from 10 AM to 10 PM and should not be missed.

** **Marinsky Theater** - The home of one of Russia's two great ballet companies, this 19th century theater is an architectural gem. Next door is the new and controversial modern theater of the same name. There are performances of opera and ballet during the summer and most cruise ships do offer an evening performance at the new or old Marinsky. It is a treat, as Russian ballet in particular is hard to match.

** **Nine Hundred Day Siege Monument** - Located at the far end of Moskovsky Prospekt in Victory Square, this breathtaking monument is a tribute to the million people who died during the Nazi siege of Leningrad and to the soldiers who protected the city from capture.

Visiting is a very emotional experience, as it makes you ponder the great suffering of the people during World War II, and also the great loss of life. The exterior consists of a massive obelisk and many heroic bronze statues. Inside the amphitheater shaped bowl are eternal flames and plaques to the heroic defenders of the city, and finally underground is the actual museum for which there is a small entry fee. It is open from 11 AM to 6 PM Thursday to Monday, and from 11 AM to 5 PM on Tuesday. The monument is closed on Wednesday and the last Tuesday of each month. This is a very somber place and it is quite inspirational. It helps you appreciate the tremendous suffering of the residents of Leningrad during the war. Unfortunately most tour coaches do not stop and the guides never mention it even when passing by. This is a shame, as it would give visitors a totally new perspective regarding the people of Russia and their past suffering during World War II.

** **Old Leningrad City Hall and Lenin Statue** - Here you have a chance to see one of the largest statues of Lenin, set amid beautiful fountains. It will make you feel like you are back in the Soviet Era. It is located along Moskovsky Prospekt where Leninsky Prospekt begins. This is in the southern part of the city. Saint Petersburg is a city that revels in its grandeur, but this statue and old city hall complex is also a reminder of the country's Soviet history, as it was the birthplace of Vladimir Lenin and the Communist revolution. Because of Lenin's prominence, the great statue of him still stands in front of the former Leningrad City Hall, a building that was constructed during the Soviet Era. There are no opening hours since the great statue is outdoors. But the fountains are not always operational.

Today "Pappa" Lenin is an anachronism

** Park Pobedy - A large park dedicated to honoring the great military heroes of the former Soviet Union, Park Pobedy's victory avenue lined with statues of the Soviet military heroes of World War II. Apart from walking the row of Soviet heroes, the park itself is quite large and has many paths that wind around its lakes. It is a nice respite from the busy city. The park is open daily in summer from 10 AM to 6 PM.

** Piskarovskoye Memorial Cemetery - Here is one of the most moving and somber of all monuments in Saint Petersburg. It is located in the northeastern part of the city in the Kalininsky District along Prospekt Nepokoronnykh. This memorial park, which is kept in an immaculate conditions, is the resting place for 0ver 400,000 Leningrad residents who lost their lives during the 900-Day Siege during World War II. With soft classical music playing and a massive bronze statue of Mother Russia looking down upon the grounds, you cannot help but be touched by the incredible sorrow that befell the city during the war.

The memorial is open daily during summer from 9 AM to 9 PM. A visit here is in essence a way of paying respect to the sacrifices made by the residents of this city. It is hard to leave this monument without having tears in your eyes. It is a very moving experience. Again it is unfortunate that this somber memorial is not on any of the organized group coach tours around the city.

Piskarovskoye is rarely visited by foreigners because so few know about it

** Summer Garden - These beautiful gardens also contain the very small palace that was home to Tsar Peter the Great during the early years of building Saint Petersburg. The gardens offer a very shady and cool respite from the city center, especially on a warm and humid day. The gardens are open from 10 AM to 9 PM daily during the summer months.

* Yusupov Palace - This is one of many palaces that belonged to a noble family. But the Yusupov Palace, located along the Moika River Canal is most famous because it was here that in 1917, Prince Yusupov arranged to murder the Siberian Monk named Rasputen who was supposedly treating the Tsar's son for hemophilia and had the Tsarina under his influence. Many in court feared his influence and they detested is lecherous ways, so the Prince arranged to do him in.

The grizzly story is told to visitors to the palace in every gory detail and this is a very popular venue for those who love a good mystery. It has become an exceptionally popular tour for all who visit St. Petersburg, and the palace can get quite crowded.

The palace is open from 11 AM to 5 PM daily, but large tour groups mainly from the cruise lines crowd into the building all day long. It is difficult for anyone alone to be able to gain easy entry.

A model of Rasputen having poisoned pastries in the Yusupov Palace

* RECOMMENDED MAJOR SITES OUTSIDE OF THE CITY – Many of the summer palaces and several other significant venues are found outside of the city, some as far as 30 kilometers or 18 miles distant. Thus you will need to either participate in a group tour or have private arrangements. I show them in alphabetical order:

** Catherine's Palace or Tsarskoye Selo (the proper Russian name) - This is a grand summer palace commissioned by Catherine the Great, located outside of the city by some 45 kilometers or 30 miles in the city of Pushkin. This lavish palace is a massive blue, white and gold building with equally magnificent gardens.

The palace was totally destroyed during World War II, yet it was fully restored under the Communist regime because of its monumental importance. It is difficult to reach the palace without being on a group tour or having a car, driver and guide. And it is not practical to attempt to go without an escort guide because preference on entry is given to groups or those with individual guides.

During summer the early opening is reserved only for tour groups. Individual hours are from Noon to 6:45 PM daily except Tuesday. The palace also has an excellent restaurant and entertainment is provided for group lunches.

A visit to Catherine's Palace is an absolute must

The grand ornate Kronstadt Island Cathedral

** Kronstadt Island – This island in the middle of the Gulf of Finland is very historic, as it has served the role of being the naval base protecting the city from seaward invasion since shortly after its founding in 1704. The island became the modern naval base for the Baltic and North Sea fleet and after the Communist takeover and the creation of the Soviet Union, its significance increased. During the Cold War, it was off limits to foreign visitors. Kronstadt Island will not be seen on any itinerary despite its historic importance and interest. If you have a car and driver/guide you can visit Kronstadt. You would need to spend half a day to visit. You would traverse the great dam that protects the city, then visit the great cathedral, see the various World War II monuments and memorials and also be able to take close up pictures of any of the Russian Navy ships that happen to be in port at the time.

** Lake Ladoga and Doroga Zhisny - During World War II, the Red Army managed to get some supplies into the city during winter by maintaining at great effort a supply line across frozen Lake Ladoga. This massive lake, the largest in Europe, is just east of the city. Supplies were brought to help in the suffering during the 900-Day Siege. Today the road is marked every kilometer with a monument and there is a memorial arch at the lakeshore where the convoy reached land. Apart from its historic significance, the drive there and back is also quite scenic and gives a visitor a chance to see some of the Russian countryside, but you will need a car and driver for this venue.

The magnificent grounds of Pavlovsk Palace

** Pavlovsk Palace - The palace of Prince Paul, son of Catherine the Great is located close to Catherine's Palace. It was given to Prince Paul by the Empress to celebrate the birth of his first son, the future Alexander I. The actual building is nowhere near as grand as Catherine's Palace, but thought smaller, it is no less elegant. However, the massive grounds offer one of the largest and most beautiful park settings in all of greater Saint Petersburg. It is open from 10 AM to 6 PM daily except the first Monday of each month. There is a separate admission for those who want to visit only the park.

The golden fountains of Peterhoff Palace

** Peterhoff Palace or Petrodevoretz (the proper Russian name) - Built by Peter the Great, this smaller summer palace is no less magnificent on its interior. But it is best known for its incredibly designed exterior gardens. The palace is situated on a hill overlooking the Gulf of Finland. With the forces of gravity, Tsar Peter designed the elaborate water cascades and fountains that are graced by over 160 gold statues, making this the Russian Versailles in every way. If you only have time to visit one of the two great palaces, my recommendation is for Peterhoff without hesitation. It is open during summer from 10:30 AM to 7 PM every day except Monday. The gardens are open under separate admission unless you buy a combined ticket. Garden hours are from 9 AM to 8 PM. The fountains are turned on at 11 AM with a musical fanfare that is quite spectacular and not to be missed. You can arrive by private car or on a motor coach tour. Priority entry into the palace is given to group tours. It is also possible to arrive or depart via a hydrofoil with direct access back to the docks along the Neva

River near the Hermitage. Some group tours include this means of transport for one way.

Traveling to either of the three palatial estates or to Lake Ladoga enables visitors to get out into the countryside and sample a taste of rural Russia. Here small, unpainted wood farmhouses encircled by vegetable gardens stand as they once did in tsarist times. And in the small towns there are miniature versions of the great cathedrals, but built out of wood rather than stone or brick.

DINING OUT AND SAMPLING RUSSIAN CUISINE: Russian cuisine is based upon simple ingredients, as the peasants had little, partly out of poverty and partly because the land offers a limited bounty. But there was a creative spirit among Russian housewives, and the cuisine is surprisingly rich in variety. Root vegetables like beets and carrots are important, along with potatoes and cabbage and bits of meat when people could afford such a luxury. Fish is also a major element in the summer diet, especially sturgeon and salmon. And Russians love fish eggs that are salted and preserved - what we know as caviar. The finest quality is sturgeon roe from the Caspian Sea. But a less expensive red salmon caviar is also very popular.

Russian cooks were able to develop quite a varied and even elegant menu. In today's good restaurants such dishes as blini (filled crepes), perogi (stuffed dumplings), ukha (sturgeon, salmon and potato soup) and borsch (beet soup) are served to visitors as standard Russian fare. And to start of a great meal, one must sample Caspian Sea caviar along with traditional Russian vodka, which is quite strong. On most full day tours, especially out to the two summer palaces, lunch is generally included. And it is most often a traditional Russian lunch. But for those of you who have a visa or out on private tours, there are many fine restaurants from which to choose for lunch or dinner.

For those who will be sightseeing with a private car and driver/guide or those who have a visa and can go off on their own. I make the following restaurant recommendations, which are based upon my many years of enjoying the flavors of Russia. Booking a table is essential, but given the prominent language barrier it is best to have your driver or a Russian speaker on the ship's staff make your booking, thus I am not providing telephone numbers. My recommendations are shown here in alphabetical order:

* **Dom Restaurant** – Located at Moika River Embankment # 72, this elegant Russian restaurant is just across the canal and south of St. Isaac' Cathedral. The extensive menu features a variety of traditional Russian dishes such as pelmeni, blini, borsch and many seafood and meat entrees. The hours of service are between Noon and 11:30 PM Monday thru Friday and 1 to 11:30 PM on weekends. Have your driver call ahead for a reservation to +7 8122 930 72 72.

* **Eliseevsky Gastronom** - This is one of the most sumptuous food halls you have ever visited. It features breads, lunch meats, cheeses, caviar, smoked fish, glace fruits and nuts along with absolutely artistic pastries that are beyond description. It was opened in 1903 and during the Communist era it served the elite party members. You

can have light sandwiches and desserts at the few tables in the center of the hall, but this is primarily a food emporium where you take home the goodies. It is an irresistible establishment located on Nevsky Prospekt one block south of Ulitsa Sadovaya. It is open daily from 10 AM to 11 PM and no reservations are taken.

A display of edible shoes made of chocolate at the Eliseevsky Gastronom

* **Grand Europe Hotel Caviar Bar** – If you truly love genuine caviar and are willing to pay for it, this is where you should come. Every variety of quality Russian caviar is available and served in numerous ways with either fine champagne or vodka. The Caviar Bar is open daily from 5 to 11 PM and the hotel is one of the cornerstone buildings in the city center at the corner of Nevsky Prospekt and Mikhailovskaya Ulitsa. It is open daily from 5 to 11 PM and reservations are a must. Have the ship's concierge call +7 812 329 60 00 to book a table.

* **Grand Europe Hotel** main dining room called **L'Europe** is a very elegant and favored place to dine for those who want the finest quality and service possible. The menu is very grand, as the name implies, featuring continental and Russian dishes served with impeccable style and grace. Dinner by reservation is from 7 to 11 PM on Friday and Saturday. Have the ship concierge call +7 812 328 6630 to book a table. The hotel is one of the cornerstone buildings in the city center at the corner of Nevsky Prospekt and Mikhailovskaya Ulitsa.

* **Katyusha Restaurant** – Located on Nevsky Prospekt # 24 in the city center, this very popular restaurant features an extensive menu filled with Russian favorites, European dishes and also vegetarian friendly cuisine. Both the food and atmosphere are very conducive to developing a strong sense of feeling for Russian culture. And the service is also excellent. The restaurant is open daily from Noon to 11 PM with extended closing at Midnight Friday and Saturday, and reservations are recommended, true to most good Russian restaurants. Have your ship concierge call +7 812 640 16 16 to book a table.

* **Podvore** – This is one of the best known restaurants among visitors who journey to the city of Pushkin and visit Catherine's Palace. Many tour operators who service the cruise industry use this restaurant for their lunch included tours. Podvorye is designed to resemble a Russian hunting lodge and to add to the atmosphere, they provide traditional entertainment. If you go on your own (reservations a must) you will choose from a very extensive traditional menu. But if you are part of a group tour, the meal will already have been predetermined. I have been told that when he is in Saint Petersburg, this is one of President Putin's favorite restaurants. I can personally say that the quality here is worthy of serving the president. The hours of service are between Noon and 11 PM daily. Have your ship's concierge call +7 812 454 54 64 to book a table at least a day in advance, as this is very popular with visitors.

Podvore looks like an old traditional hunting lodge

* **Restoran Tsar** - This is a must if you want a combination of an elegant Russian atmosphere combined with great traditional food. The atmosphere is like that of a private dining room in the tsar's palace. And the menu selections cover almost all aspects of great Russian dishes. If I had to name one favorite restaurant in Saint Petersburg it would be Tsar. The quality, menu selection and level of service are all absolutely outstanding. It is located in the city center on Ulitsa Sadovaya 12, and open from Noon until 11 PM daily. Reservations are essential. Have your ship's concierge call them at +7 812 640 16 16 to book a table.

Salmon served with mashed potato and creamy dill sauce at Restoran Tsar

* **Russian Vodka Museum and Restaurant** - Although the name sounds touristy, this is a popular venue with locals in Saint Petersburg. Yes there is a vodka museum, but it is the restaurant that is to me the primary feature. The decor is very simple, almost 19th century in its austerity. But the menu is extensive and the food is genuine Russian fare, well prepared and served by waiters who do speak good English. It is located near St. Isaak's Cathedral, great for those of you on smaller ships that will dock along the Neva River just a few blocks away. It is open from Noon to 7 PM daily. And reservations are recommended, a basic trait in Russia. You receive a warmer welcome if you can say that you already have a reservation. The address is Konnogvardeyskiy Boulevard. Have your ship's concierge call +7 812 570 64 22 to book a table.

* **Sadko** - One of my favorite genuine Russian restaurants that although some tourists find with their guides, it is primarily a local favorite. The menu at Sadko is quite extensive and everything is prepared just as if you were eating in someone's

grandmother's kitchen. Located opposite the Marinsky Theater on Ulitsa Glinka 2, and open from Sunday thru Wednesday from Noon to 10 PM and from Noon to Midnight Thursday thru Saturday. Have your ship's concierge call +7 812 903 23 70 to book a table.

* **Singer Cafe** - This venerable cafe is found upstairs in the House of Books, which in Russian is Dom Knigi. Singer Cafe dates to the 19th century and has been a hangout for writers and artists even during the Soviet Era. It does get rather crowded during the lunch hour, but the sandwiches, blini and other traditional lunch dishes are superb, as are their amazing pastries. It is located on Nevsky Prospekt 28 on the second floor of Dom Knigi. Singer Cafe is open from daily from 9 AM to 11 PM and they do not accept reservations.

* **Stolle** – This popular Russian "fast food" restaurant has several locations across the city. Its most recognized restaurant is at Nevsky Prospekt # 11. Stolle is famous for its varied baked goods, among them are the meat and other savory pies, which are quite filling. My favorite, and a beloved dish in Russia is the savory cabbage pie. The mushroom pie is also another classic as are their sweet fruit pies. They also offer take away service. The restaurants open at 9 AM and close at 9 PM. They do not take reservations.

There are many other restaurants in the city that specifically cater to visitors, but the ones I have listed above are quite genuine and will give you a great Russian experience. I am sure that there are dozens, if not hundreds, of quality restaurants I have not visited despite my 51 trips to Saint Petersburg. If nothing on my list appeals to you, ask your driver/guide for their recommendation.

SHOPPING: Unless you have a visa, it will be difficult to shop other than for souvenir items at shops or vendors where your tour operator chooses to stop. Among the souvenir items are the nested matrushka dolls and lacquer boxes. But be observant. Most are mass-produced and will sell anywhere from $20 to $200 depending upon size. However, if you want a genuine matruskha or box, it must be hand signed by the artist either on the bottom or for the box at one corner of the painted image. Genuine handmade dolls or boxes can cost anywhere from $100 for a very small one up into the thousands of dollars for the larger and more ornate dolls or boxes.

Amber jewelry is another gift item that many visitors purchase, but one must be careful, as fake amber is difficult to tell from the genuine article. Purchases should be made in a quality shop where some form of written guarantee is provided. But even then it is still a gamble. I would recommend that if you wish to purchase amber jewelry, wait until your ship visits Tallinn, Estonia, as the selection is much larger and the quality is higher.

Today visitors can buy small replicas of the famous Faberge eggs, or the hand painted wood eggs that were given among the peasant class. These are very traditional items that make nice moderately priced gifts. A real Faberge egg is beyond the reach of visitors, as they are so highly prized that if one does come up for auction, it sells for millions of Euro or dollars.

And one item of note is the widespread sale of Soviet military medals; hats and other non-lethal souvenirs of the former military might from the Communist Era. Many are genuine, but there are also a lot of reproductions, so once again buyer beware. When you buy from a street vendor you have no guarantee of authenticity.

Museum quality lacquer boxes can run into the thousands of dollars

There are several shops for both the souvenir merchandise as well as for clothing, accessories and decorative objects d'art that I feel comfortable in noting in this book. My recommendations include:

* **Bolshoi Gostiny Dvor** - The main shopping arcade on Nevsky Prospekt 35, with its own Metro stop underneath, this is a virtual maze of arcades lined with individual shops that sell just about everything from food to cosmetics, food items, housewares, gifts and even souvenirs. It dates to the late 19th century and is very typically Russian. It is open from 10 AM to 10 PM daily. It is very easy to spend hours in this emporium that has almost everything you might want to buy as a visitor, and then some. This is the largest single shopping emporium in Saint Petersburg.

* **Galeria Shopping Mall** - Across from Stockmann you will find a very modern yet traditionally Russian shopping mall with over 290 shops and restaurants. This is quite a massive establishment and worthy of your visit. It is located on Ligovsky Prospekt 30A,. It is open daily from 10 AM to 11 PM, but restaurants inside the mall close at 8 PM daily.

* **Kuznechny Market** - This is one of the largest public food markets in Saint Petersburg, and some cruise lines actually bring guests here for a look and to sample some of the take out foods. The market offers produce, meat, fish, cheese, honey, dried fruits and nuts as well as baked goods. It is a fascinating place to visit. Located at Dostoyevskaya Ploschtad and can be reached on the Metro through Vladimirskaya Station. It is open from 8 AM to 8 PM daily, but closes at 7 PM on Sunday.

In the Kuznechny Market you will see a great abundance of fresh food

* **Red October** - This is a highly reputable and extensive gift shop that sells Russian arts and crafts from the low priced matrushka dolls all the way up to one of a kind original dolls and lacquer boxes along with very high-quality amber jewelry. They also have a free vodka bar, but be careful as a few vodka shots and you may buy more than you desired. They also have a large selection of caviar. Located at Konnogvardeiskiy Boulevard 6, just up the street from the Russian Vodka Museum.

* **Stockmann Department Store** - The well-known Helsinki mercantile has opened a beautiful new store at Nevsky Prospekt 114-116,. This five-story store is not as large

as the main store in Helsinki, but it carries a wide variety of merchandise including some Russian brands. The store is open from 10 AM to 11 PM daily.

FINAL WORDS: Whether you have a visa or are required to participate in ship's tours, you will come away from Saint Petersburg with a new understanding of Russia. You will also bring away memories of a grand city that saw its share of turmoil and war, but one that has now risen again to recapture some of its old imperial glory. In my years of cruising and lecturing on the Baltic ports of call, I have never met a ship's guest who was not enchanted with Saint Petersburg. Some guests found that they were not comfortable being in Russia and felt that they were either being watched by government minders while the majority found the people to be surprisingly friendly and warm. It is a matter of whether you are fully open to a new experience without any preconceived perceptions. Given a chance, the Russian people will show you that we are not all that different.

Saint Petersburg is a great city, historic, vibrant and expanding as part of its role as a great cultural center for the new Russia. A visit to Saint Petersburg should be viewed as a great treat and as a chance to see what life in Russia is really like. You will find it most revealing.

You will be dazzled by the historic architecture of Saint Petersburg

SAINT PETERSBURG MAPS

THE CENTRAL CITY

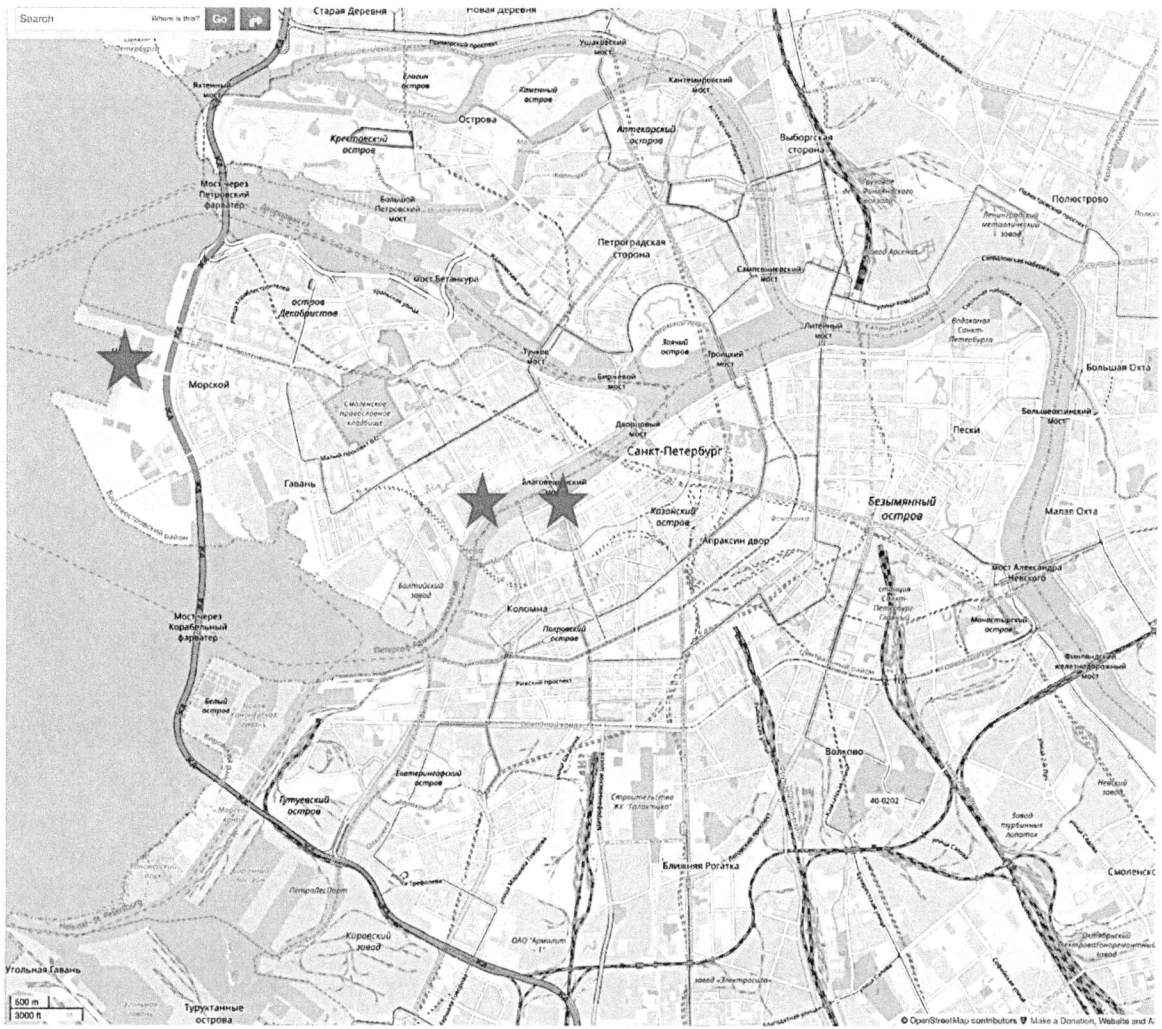

Central Saint Petersburg in Cyrillic with stars showing cruise ship docks, (@OpenStreetMap.org)

This map is best viewed directly from OpenStreetMap.com on your personal device where it can be expanded or one specific area can be enlarged. Given the format of this book, it is impossible to display maps with the level of detail you might wish to have while actually out exploring the city. But the OpenStreetMap maps used directly are the tool I always rely upon.

INNER SAINT PETERSBURG

The inner heart of Saint Petersburg, (@OpenStreetMap.org)

This map is best viewed directly from OpenStreetMap.com on your personal device where it can be expanded or one specific area can be enlarged. Given the format of this book, it is impossible to display maps with the level of detail you might wish to have while actually out exploring the city. But the OpenStreetMap maps used directly are the tool I always rely upon.

THE NEVA RIVER IN THE CITY CENTER

Along the main channel of the Neva River. (@OpenStreetMap.org)

This map is best viewed directly from OpenStreetMap.com on your personal device where it can be expanded or one specific area can be enlarged. Given the format of this book, it is impossible to display maps with the level of detail you might wish to have while actually out exploring the city. But the OpenStreetMap maps used directly are the tool I always rely upon.

THE SOUTHERN SUBURBS

Along Moskovsky Prospekt, (@OpenStreetMap.org)

This map is best viewed directly from OpenStreetMap.com on your personal device where it can be expanded or one specific area can be enlarged. Given the format of this book, it is impossible to display maps with the level of detail you might wish to have while actually out exploring the city. But the OpenStreetMap maps used directly are the tool I always rely upon.

THE NORTHERN SUBURBS

The newly developing Primorsky District, (@OpenStreetMap.org)

This map is best viewed directly from OpenStreetMap.com on your personal device where it can be expanded or one specific area can be enlarged. Given the format of this book, it is impossible to display maps with the level of detail you might wish to have while actually out exploring the city. But the OpenStreetMap maps used directly are the tool I always rely upon.

PETRODEVORTEZ AND PETERHOFF PALACE

The Peterhoff Palace area, (@OpenStreetMap.org)

This map is best viewed directly from OpenStreetMap.com on your personal device where it can be expanded or one specific area can be enlarged. Given the format of this book, it is impossible to display maps with the level of detail you might wish to have while actually out exploring the city. But the OpenStreetMap maps used directly are the tool I always rely upon.

PUSHKIN AND CATHERINE'S PALACE

Tsarskoye-Selo, Catherine's Palace, (@OpenStreetMap.org)

This map is best viewed directly from OpenStreetMap.com on your personal device where it can be expanded or one specific area can be enlarged. Given the format of this book, it is impossible to display maps with the level of detail you might wish to have while actually out exploring the city. But the OpenStreetMap maps used directly are the tool I always rely upon.

TALLINN, ESTONIA

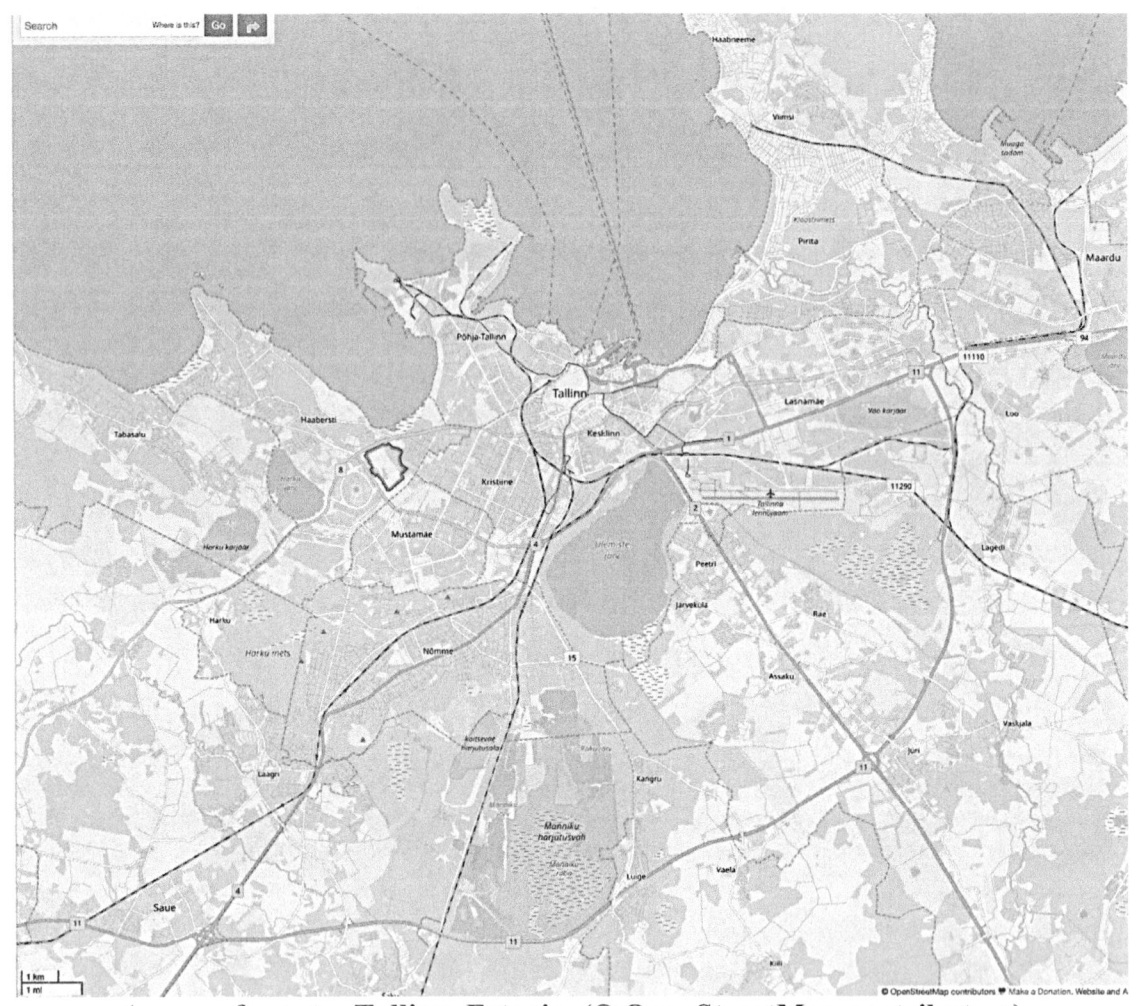

A map of greater Tallinn, Estonia. (© OpenStreetMap contributors)

At the start of the century if you would have told someone you were going on a cruise and the ship was visiting Tallinn, most people would have asked you where it was. Today it is one of the most popular Baltic Sea ports of call.

ABOUT ESTONIA: Estonia is a very small country, covering 45,099 square kilometers or 17,413 square miles. It is about the size of Denmark, but it only has a population of 1,400,000 people. The flag of Estonia, which has three horizontal stripes, blue, black and white in that order, symbolizes the physical geography of the nation. The blue represents the Baltic Sea on which Estonia borders, the black is symbolic of the dark soil that nourishes the people and some say the white stands for the snows of winter, others say for purity. This small country emerged out of the former Soviet Union in 1991 and is doing quite well economically despite its small population. And its capital city of Tallinn is one of the most visited ports on the Baltic Sea apart from Saint Petersburg, Russia.

THE NATURAL SETTING: Estonia is the product of the last ice age. As glaciers retreated, they deposited small areas of fine till, which became Estonia's deep, rich soil, but many parts of the nation are rather rocky and bare, as the glaciers stripped the land to bedrock. The glacial ice also pockmarked the land, leaving behind over 1,500 small lakes. Likewise, as sea level rose, many shoreline areas were flooded, giving Estonia over 800 islands.

Suburban Tallinn spreads into the surrounding forest

The land is thickly forested in a mix of broadleaf deciduous and coniferous trees, presenting a verdant landscape. It is essentially the same landscape surrounding Helsinki and Saint Petersburg, what the Russians call taiga. A significant portion of the forest has been cleared over the centuries for agricultural people would have asked, "where's that?" As Baltic Sea cruises have gained popularity in the past 15 years, Tallinn has become one of highlights after Saint Petersburg, its story book Old Town being the major feature that visitors find so captivating.

The Estonian climate is identical to that of southern Finland and the region that surrounds Saint Petersburg. Summers are cool and very mild, punctuated by rain showers. Winters are long with more darkness than daylight, and cold with plenty of snowfall. This is definitely a harsh climate, but one that has in some way helped to shape the rugged Estonian personality.

A BRIEF LOCAL HISTORY: The history of Estonia is linked to that of its other two Baltic Sea neighbors, Latvia and Lithuania. All three have spent the greater part of their existence dominated over by the larger powers surrounding them, in particular by Imperial Russia and of late the Soviet Union. Modern Estonia only dates back to 1991 with the breakup of the Soviet Union.

The people of Estonia have lived in their homeland for at least 5,000 years. Their ancestors are related to those of Finland, as this is one of the other two Baltic nations that speak a Uralic or Finno Ugric language. The Estonian and Finnish tongues are very closely related, and given their close proximity, they have exceptionally close socio-economic ties. High-speed hydrofoil service enables one to travel between the two capital cities in approximately one hour. Car and passenger ferryboats also ply back and forth on a frequent schedule that takes a bit longer. Many Finns cross over to Tallinn to shop, especially for beer or vodka because the prices are so much lower in Estonia as a result of lower taxation. And now there is no currency exchange issue since Estonia did join the Eurozone.

The old walls and towers of Tallinn date to medieval times

Early Estonian history saw the country as a part of the Danish Empire from 1219 until it was literally sold to the Teutonic Knights in 1346. The Swedish Empire conquered the territory in 1561 and held it until Russia under Peter the Great began to expand its Baltic coastline in 1721. Russian domination lasted for two centuries until the country broke free during the Russian Revolution of 1917. To the present day, the Russian language is widely spoken and one still sees signs written in the Cyrillic script. This is primarily due to Estonia having seen forced movement of Russians to dominate the country's industries when it was a part of the Soviet Union. Estonia's population is 30 percent Russian thanks to that forced migration during the Soviet Era. This has presented problems since independence, as the Estonian majority still feels a degree of enmity toward Russians because of the years of Soviet domination. And some worry that this could prompt Russia to someday invade to protect their brethren, as was the case with Crimea and is still simmering between Russia and the Ukraine. I personally do not believe their worries are valid, especially with Estonia being a member of both the European Union and NATO. Any military action against Estonia would have to be met by NATO force otherwise the alliance would crumble.

After the Russian Revolution, all three of the Baltic States declared their independence. But the Germans occupied the country in 1918, uniting it with Latvia. With the end of World War I, Estonian independence was restored in 1919. The country's political scene was not very stable, going through 11 changes of government between 1921 and 1931. However, Soviet occupation in 1940, ended independence, the Russians taking the country at a time when the German forces were occupying France, thus the West paid no heed to Estonia. When Hitler abruptly terminated his peace pact with Russia in 1941, Nazi forces rolled through the Baltic States on their march toward Leningrad, thus putting Estonia under harsh German rule until the Soviet Union pushed them out in 1944. From then on, the country remains a part of the Soviet Union and experienced renewed ethnic subjugation despite having been declared the Estonian Soviet Socialist Republic. This condition was true in the two other Baltic States. They existed in name only but their governments were dominated by loyal Communist Party leaders most of who were Russian.

The Russian Grand Duke's palace is now the Estonian Parliament

Since gaining its independence in 1991 with the collapse of the Soviet Union, Estonia has shown a remarkable ability to thrive. The country's economy is a mix of agriculture, timber and textile manufacturing. Agriculture is limited by the lack of sizeable areas with good soil. The country is known for its fine dairy products and summer fruit orchards. The only significant grains that Estonia is capable of growing are oats and rye, thus the national breads are of a rather heavy and coarse texture, as is true in much of Russia. Trade with the western nations of Europe and increasing tourism, especially from the cruise industry have given the economy a significant boost. And financial services and electronics also play a major role. Estonia has little foreign debt and its government generally operates on a balanced budget. The ratio of public debt to the gross domestic product is the lowest within the European Union, which it joined in 2004 thus making it a member of the Eurozone. The country is also a member of the North Atlantic Treaty Organization, one of the first remnants of former Soviet domination to join.

THE PHYSICAL LAYOUT OF THE CITY OF TALLINN: The national capital is Tallinn, a city whose greater area population of 500,000 makes it the largest city in the country, containing nearly 35 percent of the national total. Tallinn occupies relatively level ground that wraps around a wide bay extending in from the Gulf of Finland. There are a few small glacial lakes around Tallinn, the largest being just to the southeast of the main city core. And on the margins of the city the land does show some degree of undulation with moderate size hills.

A view from Upper Old Town out across Old Tallinn with the cruise port in the background

The most impressive feature is the hill close to the shoreline upon which the original town started to develop in medieval times. This is what is today called Old Tallinn, an almost totally walled in city with two distinct sections. Most of it is just very slightly above the level of the surrounding land and is called Lower Old Town. Then there is an abrupt scarp that causes a small knob to rise up about 30 meters or 100 feet above the rest of its surroundings. This has become known as Upper Old Town and is where once the aristocracy lived. The major portion of the wall system has remained intact, but a portion was destroyed during World War II and not rebuilt. But it is still safe to call Old Tallinn a walled city.

The main gate into the Lower Old Town

New Tallinn spreads both east and west of Old Tallinn and has fairly regular streets that do not twist and turn too greatly, although it cannot be called a grid pattern. And then to the south the city stretches for several kilometers along a few arterial streets. There are no major expressways and essentially traffic is light and there is more the feel of an overgrown town than that of a large city.

On several of the streets there are trams that provide the only major form of public transit apart from busses. The trams add an extra layer of color to the city and are actually enjoyable to ride as a visitor. Despite the language barrier, people will show a visitor how to time stamp the ticket while onboard.

In modern New Tallinn outside the old wall where the hop on hop off busses congregate

The city shows all the signs of being a part of the dynamic lifestyle of modern Europe with Internet cafes, people carrying cell phones and an array of beautiful new shops in its downtown. But Old Tallinn, largely unchanged with its cobblestone streets and buildings dating to medieval times, is the gem that visitors come to see. Many buildings also represent post medieval development during the Hanseatic League, when Estonia served as a major trading center between the east and west. The city of Tallinn, as the focal hub of Estonian culture, was under alternate domination of Denmark and Sweden during much of its medieval history. By the early 1700's, Estonia fell under the domination of Russia, and despite its brief sojourn into the realm of independent states during the 1919 to 1941 period; the influence of Russia has been the strongest of any outside factors. Surprisingly though there is little architectural influence in Old Tallinn given that Estonia always traded with the West. The architecture of the older parts of Tallinn show more Germanic or Scandinavian influences than Russian. Because of the strong ties to Denmark and Sweden prior to being absorbed into the Russian Empire, Old Town Tallinn's buildings look more like those you would find in Copenhagen or Stockholm, with steeply pitched roofs tiled in slate, multi-pane windows and richly adorned facades plastered over and painted in muted pastel colors. The Old Town constitutes the heart of Tallinn, and today it can often be so crowded with tourists when four to five cruise ships descend upon its port at the same time. This may be profitable for the local merchants, but it can be a bit maddening for the visitor. If you are exceptionally lucky, your ship will be the only one in port. I have experienced this on several occasions.

Most of the time during summer there can be three to as many as five mid to large size cruise ships in port at the same time. And you can well how congested the Old Town becomes.

CRUISE SHIP DOCKS: Cruise ships dock in Tallinn at one of three piers all located together in the main harbor adjacent to where the many Tallink Ferryboats dock. There are no terminal facilities, but there is a long tent that houses many vendors selling souvenirs and handcraft items. The majority of cruise lines offer shuttle bus service from the parking area where the three piers have their tour busses and private cars waiting. By shuttle it is approximately a five to six minute drive to the front of the Russian Cultural Center, which is then two blocks from the main gate into the Old City.

SEEING THE SIGHTS IN TALLINN: In today's cruise market, Tallinn has become one of the most popular Baltic Sea ports of call. The docks are within easy walking distance from the main gate into the Old Town, yet most cruise lines provide a shuttle bus, which for the majority of passengers is not really that advantageous. The Old Town is highly walkable and is the main focus of the majority of visitors. But for those who want to explore the entire city or even get out into the countryside, there are several viable options.

* **SIGHTSEEING OPTIONS IN TALLINN:** There are numerous ways to explore Tallinn, and for the vast majority of guests on board ship no visa is required to visit Estonia, as it is a member of the European Union. Thus you can come and go from the ship with no formalities, as is true in Saint Petersburg. Here are the various options open to you:

** **Ship sponsored tours** – The cruise lines all offer a variety of tours in Tallinn, most by motor coach, but covering different aspects of the city or the Estonian countryside. And there are also group walking tours of the Old Town.

** **Private car and driver** – This is always my favorite means of sightseeing, but as a geographer I often prefer to get away from the main tourist venues. If a more thorough tour is what you are looking for, this should be your option. You can arrange for a car and driver through the onboard tour desk.

You may also wish to check out the following companies offering private cars for sightseeing:

*** Amber Transfers at www.amber-transfers.com and click on Estonia to view their services.

*** Private Transfer at www.privatetransfer.ee to view their services.

In all honesty, having a private car and driver for the day is an extravagant expense because the city is compact and by walking or using the local streetcar or hop on hop off bus, you can visit all of the major venues. For me to say this is significant, as I normally favor the use of a private car and driver/guide

** **Rental cars** – I do not recommend renting a car and driving yourself in Estonia. Almost all rental cars have manual transmission and all road signs are written in Estonian and/or Russian, making it very difficult for foreign drivers if they do not know one or the other language.

** **Hop on hop off bus tours** – There are numerous hop on hop off busses in Tallinn and their main stop is where the ship's shuttle bus will deposit you on the edge of the Old Town in front of the Russian Cultural Center. This is also the exact location where cruise ship shuttle busses drop off and pick up their respective guests.

*** Red Sightseeing is the main operator and you can check their offerings at *www.redsightseeing.com* and then click on Tallinn.

*** You can also check with *www.getyourguide.com/Tallinn/HopOnHopOff* to link with the bus tours.

** **Taxis** – There will be numerous taxis waiting at the dock. You can hire a taxi for several hours or the whole day, but be certain to come to an agreement on price before starting out. And make sure that you will be comfortable with the driver's command of your language. The best rated company is Tallink Takso. Check out their web page at *www.tallinktakso.ee* where you can book directly.

** **Walking** – This is a great way to explore both the Old Town and New Town areas because Tallinn is so small, the old and new cities are side-by-side. Walking is the best way to see both the Old Town and the adjacent newer shopping area. The weather is most often cool, and there are plenty of cafes where one can take a rest. But always take with an umbrella, as it can rain with little warning during the summer months.

* **MAJOR SITES TO VISIT:** The Lower Old Town occupies the small hill overlooking the harbor, and it is accessible from the ship on foot although most cruise lines provide shuttle bus service for those who do not elect to go on a tour. In 1944, when the Red Army advanced on Tallinn to drive out the Germans, there was significant shelling and many buildings were badly damaged or destroyed. Since the war, ongoing restoration has removed those scars, as the people rebuilt Old Town with loving care, because to the Estonians, this small section of the city was their pride and joy.

** **Palaces** – The city has two palaces but only one is accessible to visitors. These palaces are:

*** **Kadriorg Palace** - Built by Peter the Great for his wife's summer enjoyment, today this is a classic example of Russian imperial architecture. Today the palace is part museum and part home to the President of Estonia. The park and gardens are now open to the public where once they were reserved for the Tsarina. This is the only major venue not within walking distance of where the ship's shuttle busses drop off guests. It is necessary to take a taxi to visit the Kadriorg Palace, and numerous taxis will be found throughout the city center. The hop on hop off busses also start their routes where the ship shuttle busses drop off passengers, and Kadriorg Palace is on their circuit. Tickets are available at the palace. Opening hours are from 10 AM to 6 PM Tuesday, Thursday thru Sunday and Wednesday has extended hours until 8 PM. The palace is closed on Monday.

The Kadriorg Palace commissioned by Peter the Great

*** Toompea Castle – The castle is today the seat of government and tours are given daily Monday thru Thursday from 10 AM to 4 PM for groups of up to 35 people. Tours are offered in English, Estonian and Russian. They are not part of any ship sponsored walking tour and must be sought out on your own. Generally most visitors are not interested in such a specific tour.

** Churches – There are numerous magnificent Lutheran churches and the dominant Russian Orthodox Cathedral.

*** Alexander Nevsky Cathedral (Orthodox) is located in the Upper Old Town opposite the Grand Duke's Palace. This cathedral looks very old but only dates back to the 19th century when the Russian Tsar ordered it be built as part of the show of domination over this province of the Russian Empire. Russian Orthodox cathedrals in Russia are more ornate, but Alexander Nevsky is still quite well decorated and worth of a brief visit.It is generally open to the public unless special services are being held.

Alexander Nevsky Cathedral (Orthodox)

*** **The Saint Mary's Cathedral (Lutheran)**, also called the **Toompea Cathedral**, is a beautiful structure with its tall bell tower. It is always visited as part of the walking tours of Old Town. This 13th century cathedral was established during a period of Danish rule and is the oldest of the churches in all of Estonia.

Tours are offered in a variety of languages on Monday thru Thursday from 10 AM to 4 PM and on Friday from 10 AM to 3 PM. The most specific time for an English language tour is on Friday at 11 AM>

** **Secular landmarks** – There are numerous landmarks in the Old Town of Tallinn that are part of any walking tour. These include (alphabetically):

*** **Kiek in de Kök** - This giant round tower built in 1475 was the main battlement tower for the defense of Old Tallinn. Today it and the museum offer a look at the ancient history of the city.

The museum is open from 10 AM to 5:30 PM daily. It is located very close to the shuttle bus drop off and can be visited with only a slight detour.

A view from the Upper Old Town wall showing the part of the new city skyline

*** **Market Square** – In the heart of Lower Old Town is the former market center, now a popular gathering spot filled with restaurants, all serving outdoors during summer. And facing the square is the historic old Town Hall dating back to medieval times.

This is a very busy spot when ships are in port, as so many of the most popular restaurants are clustered around the square. Depending upon how many ships are in port, there are often song and dance performances at the lunch hour.

*** **Town Hall** – This stone building with it tall and thin spire sits on the market square and is still used for a variety of public functions. It is one of the oldest public buildings in Tallinn and dates back to the year 1404.

This is the oldest town hall in the entire Baltic Sea region. Most often the building is open for the public between the hours of 11 AM and 4 PM.

Today the market square in front of the Town Hall is the site for many festivals and dance performances where once it was a true market square back in medieval times.

The Tallinn Town Hall and Market Square

A portion of the Old Tallinn City Wall

*** **Old Tallinn City Wall** – Built from the 10th century onward, the wall surrounds most of the Lower Old Town with a separate wall around the Upper Old Town. There was some damage during World War II, but the wall with its battlements is still for the most part intact, however, the mighty wood gates no longer are present.

The wall around the Upper Old Town does offer three vantage points for spectacular views out over the Lower Old Town with the modern downtown skyline impinging upon the view. Tallinn has been growing with such dynamic speed since 1991 and its downtown core reflects the productivity and prosperity with a string of very modern high rise buildings not commonly seen in the city center of most European capitals. The modern skyline of new Tallinn is quite dynamic considering the small population of the city. It is more reminiscent of the skylines of small cities in Canada.

In the heart of modern downtown Tallinn

** **Modern Tallinn** – It has only been since 1991 that the country has seen the rapid economic development resulting from becoming an integrated member of the Baltic community. Tallinn has experienced significant growth, yet still retains the flavor of a small city because that is what it truly is. The city center of modern Tallinn is sprouting beautiful ultra-modern high-rise office towers that are very reminiscent of North American cities, reminding me somewhat of Halifax, Nova Scotia in eastern Canada. No other Baltic Sea city possesses a downtown skyline that is as modern and has as many tall buildings as found in Tallinn. Likewise, the city center has two major department stores, one of which is linked to a large shopping mall. Within the central portion of the city, there is a lot of remodeling of older buildings, demolition of those unworthy of restoration, and there is a lot of new construction, showing that Tallinn is a city going places economically.

*** **Opera House and Concert Hall** - Located in the new downtown area, opposite the main square that is just across from the main entry gate into the Old Town, these two beautiful buildings date back to the late Russian imperial period. These facilities are only open when performances are being held and therefore during most days can only be viewed from the outside. They are side by side and face the main entry gate into the Lower Old Town opposite the park.

*** **Tallinn Song Festival Grounds** - This outdoor musical venue was where the Estonians expressed their desire for freedom from Soviet domination through song and not violence. If on your own, the song festival grounds can be reached on the hop on hop off bus or via a short taxi ride. The grounds are on the eastern side of the waterfront from the downtown area. Opening hours are from 9 AM to 5 PM daily.

*** **Tallinn TV Tower** - This tall broadcasting tower has both an observation deck and restaurant. It is 314 meters tall, which is approximately 1,000 feet, making it the tallest structure in Estonia. People come for the views on a clear day, as it is possible to look across the Gulf of Finland and with binoculars you can see the skyline of Helsinki, Finland. The tower is well to the east of the city center, and it is rarely included on ship tours. The TV tower is on the hop on hop off bus route to the eastern suburbs. It is open daily from 10 AM to 7 PM, but should only be visited on a clear day otherwise you waste time and money. When it is clear, the view is incredible.

The residential areas reflect both the Soviet Era with rather grim apartment blocks, but not of the magnitude seen in larger cities in Russia. And today many of those reminders of the Soviet Era are either being remodeled or replaced. There were always private family residences, and today that trend can be seen in the leafy suburbs of Tallinn along with modern glass fronted apartment blocks that would be considered upmarket.

Tallinn has distinct neighborhoods that represent different eras in its growth. In the far southern suburb of Nomme, one can see beautiful houses that date back to the interwar years when Estonia briefly flourished. In Kadriorg, the tree-lined streets reflect the grand era of the Tsars, when Estonian and Russian aristocrats held the power of the country in their hands. But the Lasnamäe district reflects the drab block-like apartment complexes built during the Soviet era. Despite the ugliness of the Soviet influenced architecture, people in Estonia today have allowed their negative feelings regarding Communist rule to diminish, and the country maintains an active trade with its giant neighbor Russia.

The only way to visit any of these neighborhoods, for those who are interested in residential architecture, would be through having a private car or hiring a taxi, as the tour busses do not generally include purely suburban districts as part of a tour. However, keep in mind that few taxi drivers speak much English, if any. A few city tours will include a visit to the Kadriorg Palace, thus the route you will take shows some of the beautiful wood villas that were built by Russian aristocrats.

The outdoor public market in suburban Nomme

ESTONIAN CUISINE: The cuisine of Estonia is worth sampling. Like all Baltic Sea countries, it is heavily oriented toward fish and seafood along with fresh vegetables. The breads are very dark, as in Russia and Finland, but the Estonian version is softer and sweeter. It is delicious with fresh butter. Vegetable and fish soups are also very popular, as are many varieties of fish generally baked. There are numerous restaurants in the Old City and they are especially busy on days when multiple ships are in port. Over the years I have found one Lower Old Town restaurant located on the town square to be consistently good. And I also have a favorite that is not in the historic old town area. I hereby recommend the following restaurants (shown in alphabetical order):

* **Finlandia Caviar Tallinn** – This unique caviar and oyster restaurant is located in the Lower Old Town at Vaike Karja # 1 not far from the main gate. This restaurant is devoted to the finest quality Russian and Scandinavian caviar and fresh oysters served in a variety of ways. They also have tasting plates where you can sample various types of caviar and oysters. The prices are high, but if you love either genuine caviar or high-quality oysters, it is well worthwhile paying the price. They are open Monday thru Thursday Noon to 9 PM, Friday and Saturday Noon to 10 PM and Sunday Noon to 6 PM. Why not treat yourself if this is something you crave. This is the part of the world where it is at its best. It is a good idea to call ahead for a table at +372 5383 8959.

* **Kaerajaan** - Located on the old town square at Raekoja plats 17, this is a superb restaurant that offers modern versions of traditional Estonian cuisine. Surprisingly it is not as highly rated on Trip Advisor as many other Old City restaurants, but I have always found it consistently good year after year and everyone I have suggested it many guests have always come back and told me how much they enjoyed it. You can dine indoors or outdoors depending upon the weather. They are open from 10 AM to 11 PM. They do not accept bookings for a table and can get quite busy at lunch hour so either go early or late.

* **Kohvik Komeet** - Located in the ultra-modern Solaris Mall, this restaurant with its wrap around windows offers a great view of the Old City and the Opera House. It is on the fourth floor of the mall, reached by elevator. The food is superb and their pastries are beyond belief. They have a variety of delicious soups, hot and cold entrees, good salads and of course you must save room for dessert. The restaurant is open for breakfast, lunch and dinner and you can always come just for their incredible pastries. It is open daily from Noon to 11 PM, but closing Sunday at 9 PM. Few, if any tourists ever venture here on their own and they are missing one of the best dining experiences in Tallinn. It is not necessary to book a table.

* **Lido** - Also located in the Solaris Mall, this restaurant is part of a chain found in Scandinavia and the Baltic States. Lido is a buffet style restaurant that offers an incredible variety of dishes with local flavor. And in true Estonian fashion, they also offer outstanding, decadent desserts. It is open daily from 11 AM to 9 PM, but closes at 9 PM on Sunday. Again this is a restaurant that few tourists will ever discover on their own. They do not accept bookings for a table.

* **Vaike Rataskaevu 16** – Located in the Lower Old Town just a block west of the Old Town Hall at Rataskaevu # 16, this is one of the most popular restaurants among visitors to the walled city. The menu is quite diverse and features Estonian, Russian and Scandinavian dishes served in a very historic setting. The quality of the cuisine and the service are both excellent. Because of its fine reputation, it is recommended that you have your cruise ship travel desk book a table in advance. Their hours of service are Noon to 11 PM daily, remaining open until Midnight Friday and Saturday. To book a table call them at +372 601 1311.

SHOPPING: Finnish visitors love to come and shop for clothing, accessories and household goods because of lower taxes that translate to lower prices. You will find Scandinavian and German brands of high quality, so if you are interested in adding to your wardrobe or looking for gift items for the home, then Tallinn is a good place to shop. There are two major malls and two major department stores in the city center of Tallinn:

* **Kaubamaja Department Store** - This is an Estonian department store located in the heart of the city, attached to the Viru Shopping Mall. The layout of the store is a bit complicated to understand. On the ground floor part of the store is open to the Viru Shopping Mall and part is across a major boulevard. Yet on the upper floors it is all together as one level.

This store offers a wide variety of clothing, accessories, toiletries and housewares that are all of high quality. And in clothing and household linens it features some very high style with a unique local sense of design. Kaubamaja does represent what I would consider higher end shopping with a unique Estonian sense of style. The store is open seven days a week from 9 AM to 9 PM.

* **Solaris Mall** - Located across from the main entrance to the Opera House, this mall offers a variety of excellent shops featuring clothing, footwear, health and beauty aids, jewelry, books and a full-service supermarket. There are also numerous restaurants and a multiplex cinema inside the mall. The mall is open from 9 AM to 11 PM daily, but shops are only open from 10 AM to 9 PM, but restaurants stay open until 11 PM as does the grocery store.

Inside the modern Solaris Mall

* **Stockmann Department Store** - This is a branch of the famous Stockmann of Helsinki. It is much smaller and does not have the great selection you will find in Helsinki, but it still is a major store with plenty to choose from. It has a complete line of clothing, accessories, household goods and a grocery department. Stockmann is a few blocks from the Viru Shopping Mall, next to the Swissotel. The store is open from 9 AM to 9 PM daily, but on Sunday it does not open until 10 AM.

* **Viru Shopping Mall** - located across the park from the main gate into the Lower Old

City. The mall is the largest in the city center and it is attached to the high-rise Viru Hotel. And Kaubamaja Department Store is a part of the mall. The mall also includes 109 shops, a major bookseller that has a large selection of English language books and a full service supermarket, The mall is open daily from 9 AM to 9 PM.

FINAL WORDS: The people of Tallinn are gracious and friendly, and among the younger generation English is widely spoken. This is a very safe and clean city where you will feel comfortable venturing out on you own.

Today the city of Tallinn is experiencing a summertime invasion by the cruise industry. In the last few years, a new wharf had to be added to accommodate the mega cruise ships, as all of the major lines bring visitors to Tallinn. There are times when as many as five ships can be in port on a given day, with most guests intent upon visiting the old town. Such crowds do take away from the enjoyment of the port, but are welcomed by the merchants and restaurants because of the revenue being generated. It is recommended that after spending a couple of hours in the Old Town that one is better off taking a taxi or hop on hop off bus to the Kadriorg Palace and Gardens and then exploring the adjacent neighborhood of 18th and 19th century Russian homes of former nobles. And then a visit to the city center can be quite rewarding because it affords a look at everyday commercial life. For those who wish to venture afar, bicycle rentals or the use of taxis will enable you to visit more of the city than just its core area. I also recommend spending an hour walking around the modern downtown core of Tallinn to see how prosperous and progressive it is. The modern downtown reflects the new role of Estonia within the European Union as a progressive country that is on the cutting edge architecturally.

TALLINN MAPS

THE CENTRAL CITY

Central Tallinn with star showing cruise ship docks, (© OpenStreetMap contributors)

This map is best viewed directly from OpenStreetMap.com on your personal device where it can be expanded or one specific area can be enlarged. Given the format of this book, it is impossible to display maps with the level of detail you might wish to have while actually out exploring the city. But the OpenStreetMap maps used directly are the tool I always rely upon.

THE HEART OF TALLINN

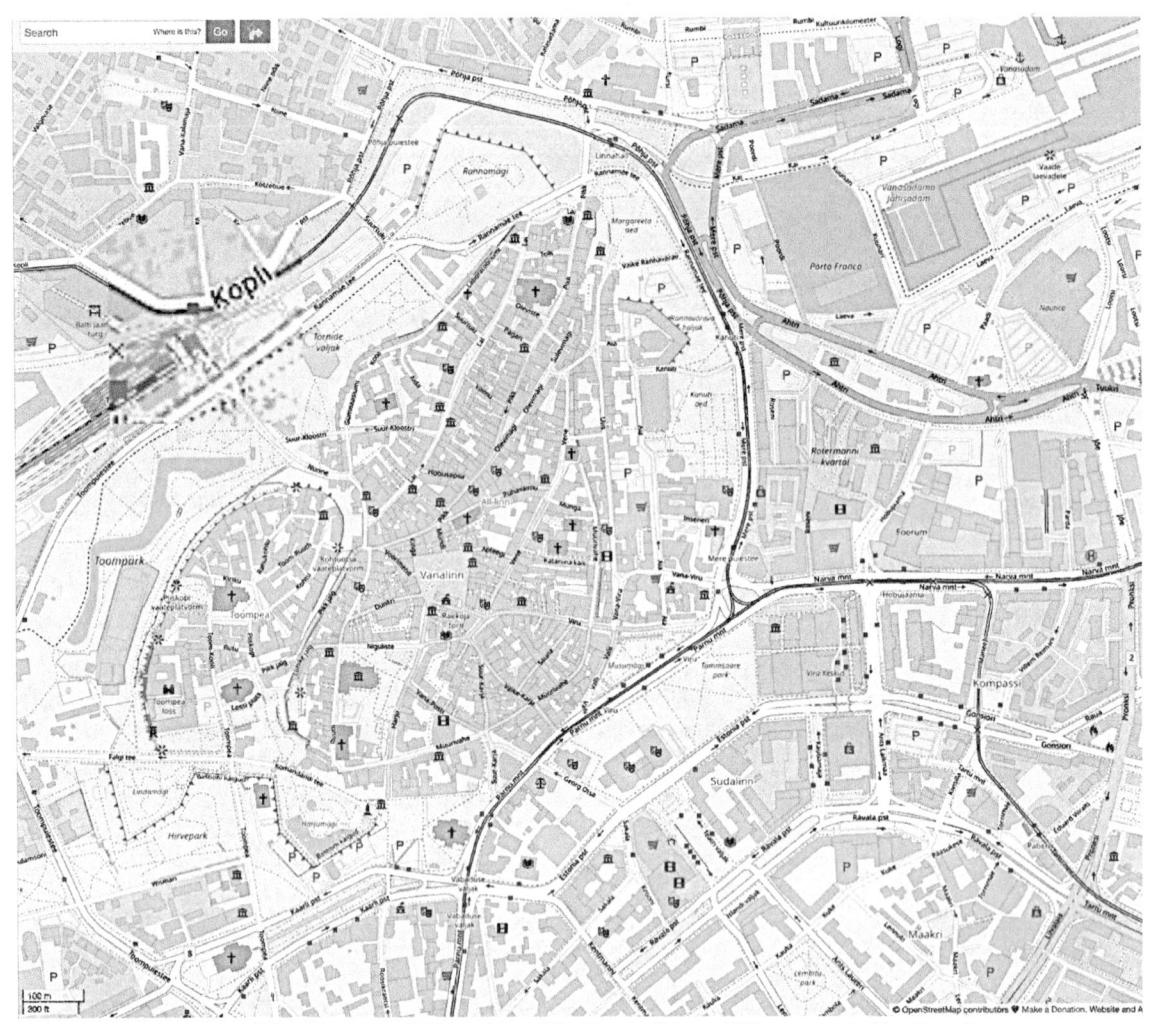

The heart of the city, (© OpenStreetMap contributors)

This map is best viewed directly from OpenStreetMap.com on your personal device where it can be expanded or one specific area can be enlarged. Given the format of this book, it is impossible to display maps with the level of detail you might wish to have while actually out exploring the city. But the OpenStreetMap maps used directly are the tool I always rely upon.

THE HISTORIC OLD TOWN

Old Town and part of the downtown, (© OpenStreetMap contributors)

This map is best viewed directly from OpenStreetMap.com on your personal device where it can be expanded or one specific area can be enlarged. Given the format of this book, it is impossible to display maps with the level of detail you might wish to have while actually out exploring the city. But the OpenStreetMap maps used directly are the tool I always rely upon.

RIGA, LATVIA

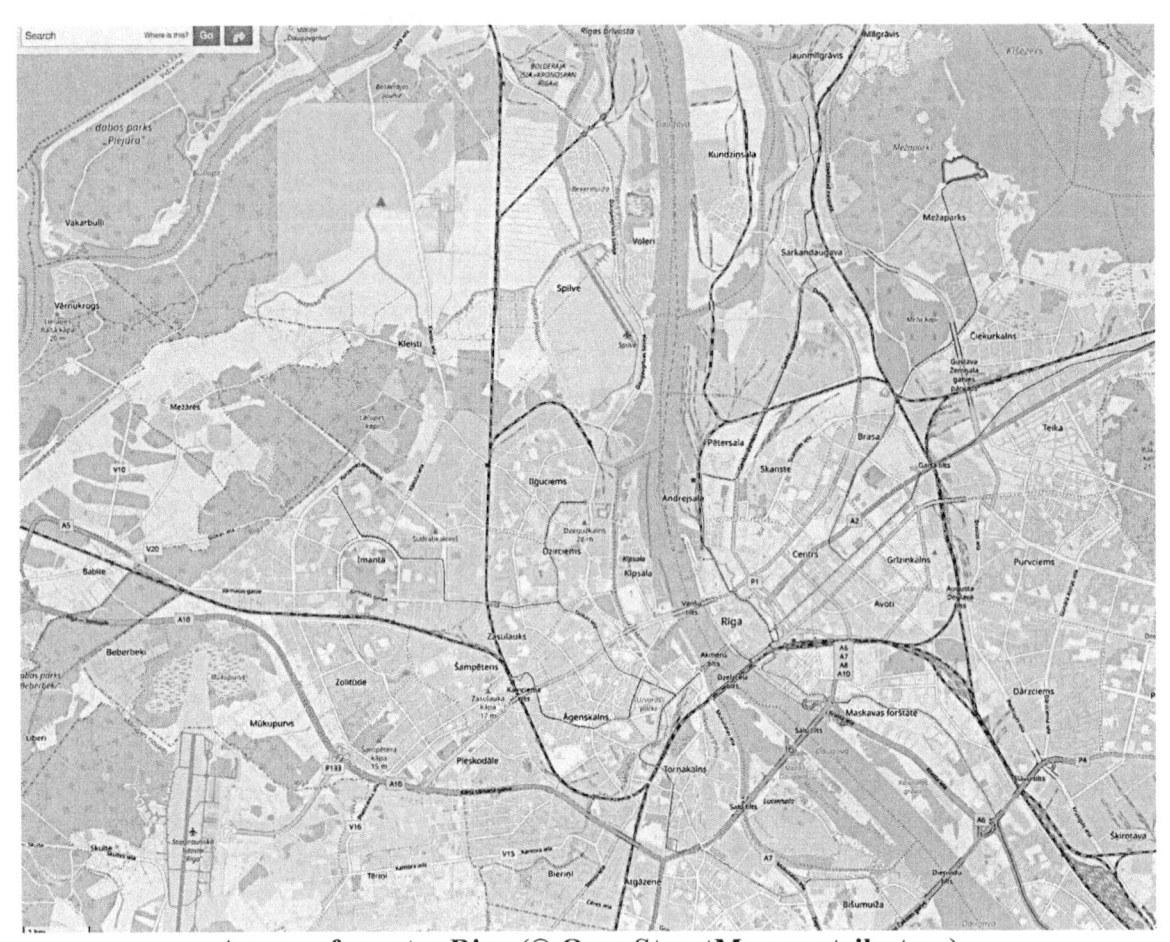

A map of greater Riga (© OpenStreetMap contributors)

Visits to Riga by cruise ships are becoming more frequent. For several years, the Latvian government imposed such high fees for docking that most cruise lines chose to avoid the port. Now the fee schedule is more in line with other Baltic ports and the city of Riga is deriving benefits. Like Tallinn, the city of Riga was also not well known among North American or Western European visitors unless they had ancestry from this region.

At one time Riga was the home to a large Jewish population and many of those Jews migrated to Canada or the United States. Americans or Canadians of Jewish ancestry from Latvia would have been aware of the city's existence. World War II decimated the remaining Jewish population in Latvia, just as had been the case in Poland.

Today Riga is becoming better known for its beautiful architecture and parks, and rightly so, as it is the largest city in the three Baltic States with a metropolitan population of 1,018,000, yet it has the feel of a small and unhurried city with very little traffic congestion. Once cruise ship passengers have a chance to spend a day in Riga, they come away with a whole new level of understanding of Latvia and its people.

THE NATURAL SETTING: Latvia is the middle of the three states referred to as the Baltic Republics. It occupies 64,589 square kilometers or 24,938 square miles, making it approximately the size of the American state of South Carolina. Estonia lies to the north and Lithuania is situated to the south

Typical Latvian countryside, (Work of alnico_fan, CC BY SA 3.0, Wikimedia.org)

The landscape of Latvia is one of lush green countryside, dominated by low hills and flat plains. There are many lakes and marshes of glacial origin. The Baltic Sea indents itself deeply into the country in what is called the Gulf of Riga. Latvia is covered in the same mixed broadleaf deciduous and coniferous forest as Estonia, but much land has been cleared for agriculture over many centuries. There is more fine glacial sediment found in Latvia, providing for a healthy agricultural base

Summers are short, but warm and moist thus enabling limited agricultural production of grains, fruits and vegetables. Being just farther south than Estonia by a about a degree or so of latitude, the country has a slightly longer summer with just about a degree Celsius of more summer warmth. Winters are long and cold with heavy snowfall, but in the last decade winters have tended to be milder, as is true throughout the Baltic region.

A BRIEF LOCAL HISTORY: Latvian prehistory can be traced back to ancient hunting peoples over 9,000 years before the modern calendar. But it was not until the

13th century AD that Germanic armies conquered the country and forced its ways, including Christianity, upon the tribal peoples.

The city of Riga began to develop as a trade center during the early part of the middle ages with strong Viking influences because they found that the Daugava River gave access to the interior and they were interested in spreading their trade network far and wide.

The old Hanseatic Era Town Hall of Riga

Christianity came to the city by decree when the Pope ordered an armed contingent to land in 1200 to forcibly convert the people. And by 1282, the city of Riga was a member of the Hanseatic League and fully involved in economic interaction with the entire Baltic region. Because of its location, it served as a gateway to the interior of Russia before the establishment of Saint Petersburg in the early 18th century.

Because Riga was an important center in the Hanseatic League, this period accounts for much of the Old Town's architecture. During the period 1558 to 1583, the country fell under combined Lithuanian and Polish Rule, and by 1600 much of the territory came under the control of Sweden. The Swedes brought many schools to the common people and eased the impact of rural serfdom, so to this day it is remembered as a peaceful period in Latvian history.

Because of the split of the country between Swedish and Germanic/Polish influences, the northern part of the country accepted the Lutheran faith while southern Latvia was drawn into the Catholic Church. There was also a large Jewish population in Latvia, which remained an important spiritual and cultural force impacting the entire nation until World War II when most Latvian Jews were decimated during the Holocaust.

During the 18th century, Russia became the dominant political influence and many of the Swedish reforms were erased, leaving the peasants once again under the control of wealthy land barons. Rural freedoms would not be seen again until the 19th century when reforms allowed free farmers to claim pieces of land.

In Riga and the few other cities, industrialization brought about a more enlightened work force whose views were anti tsarist, sparking unrest among the people. This ultimately led to an explosion of nationalism not only in Latvia, but also in the other two Baltic states. It erupted in violence along with the 1905 uprisings within Russia proper and can now be looked at as one of the preludes to the Russian Revolution.

The three Baltic States had a brief period of independence following World War I because of a weakened Germany and Russia's civil war and the start of the Communist Era. This period of independence was short lived. At the start of Nazi hostilities, the Soviet Union infiltrated Latvia in 1940, and incorporated it into their nation. In less than a year, the Germans invaded the Baltic States on their march toward Saint Petersburg, which was at that time known as Leningrad. More than 200,000 Latvians and 70,000 Latvian Jews were exterminated during this period of occupation. After the Soviet Union re took the Baltic region, there were many harsh measures placed upon the people, as part of the overall system of collectivization of agriculture and industry. Thousands were either deported to Siberia or executed. This stands in sharp contrast with the original plan for the Soviet Union in which each ethnic republic was to govern its own internal affairs.

Under Mikhail Gorbachev, a relaxation of restrictions on the Baltic peoples ultimately led to the full independence of each by 1991. And by 1994, all Russian military troops were withdrawn. Like in Estonia, there are those in Latvia who fear that today's Russian nationalism and the outspoken pledges to protect the interests of Russian speakers in bordering states could lead to a possible invasion. Canada has sent a small contingent to demonstrate NATO's concern over the future of the Baltic States since Latvia is a member of NATO as well as the European Union. I personally believe that such perceived military threats are minimized by the umbrella of both the European Union and NATO. These Baltic countries are not the Ukraine where Russia's justification for invasion or infiltration is based upon a past common history dating back centuries.

Like its neighbors to the north and south, Latvia is now an independent parliamentary democracy, a member of the European Union and NATO. And it recently joined the Eurozone. It is enjoying new freedoms and economic prosperity along with a newly found tourist trade given that for so long it was a rather drab and dreary place to visit under the Soviet system. Like Estonia, the Latvian nation became heavily dominated over by the Soviet Union after World War II, with many Russian factory workers having been moved into the country by the Communist government. However, the percentage of Russian descendants is not as high as it is in Estonia and thus there is not as much of a feeling of tension between the two ethnic groups today.

Latvian Heroes Monument in central Riga

The people of Latvia share many cultural traits in common with the other two Baltic nations, but each is distinct despite the many similarities that they share with one another. The Latvian language is totally unique and is distantly related to the language of Lithuania, its southern neighbor. The cuisine, music and traditional costumes are similar to both of its Baltic neighbors despite the linguistic and cultural differences.

THE PHYSICAL LAYOUT OF THE CITY OF RIGA: Being a small country, the capital city of Riga is the largest city and cultural hearth of the nation. The city is situated along the Daugava River just a few miles inland from the Gulf of Riga. Dredging has made the river navigable to large oceangoing vessels, and Riga is the most important seaport of the three Baltic nations. Since the start of recorded history, the Daugava River valley has been seen as a transit route for merchants and the spreading of cultural ideas between the coast and the interior of west central Russia.

Because of the tide of invaders throughout its history, the city of Riga reflects influences from Poland, Sweden, Germany and Russia in both its architecture and its overall cultural flavor. But because of immigrants from Germany coming to dominate the city's commerce, the German population at one point came to over 40 percent of the city with German being the second language of the streets. However, later Russian domination, especially during the Soviet Era, made Russian the official language in both written and spoken forms. Only now has the Latvian language once again taken center stage as the official language of the country. However, many people still regularly speak Russian and German in their daily activities.

A view over the heart of central Riga

The city of Riga did suffer damage and great loss of life during both World Wars I and II. It is estimated that over 30 percent of the population perished during World War II alone, especially the city's large and important Jewish population. As in Estonia, the Russians forcibly transferred thousands of their own citizens into Latvia to help justify their takeover of the country. Most of these people settled in Riga and many of their descendants remain today, a potential source of friction existing with the Latvian majority.

The main part of the city of Riga is situated on the eastern bank of the Daugava River and it spreads out from the Old Town core. Here the streets encircle the original main square where the House of Blackheads, which is the old Town Hall, exhibits the excesses of Hanseatic design. Across the square is the new town hall, which actually dates to the early 19th century. Old Town was once surrounded by a wall, but today the beautiful Kronvalda Park through which runs a small chain of lakes indicates where the wall once stood backed up by a moat. Within this confine is a collection of buildings dating as far back as the late middle ages lining narrow streets that are mainly pedestrian oriented. But unlike Tallinn, motor vehicles are permitted on many of the streets, and there have been permits issued for the construction of modern buildings.

On the streets of historic Old Town Riga, which today are vibrant

Beyond the park is the newer city of Riga. The main street of Brivibas Ilea begins at the Kronvalda Park and extends in a straight line northeastward, essentially dividing the new city in half. The central core revolves around this street with essentially regular blocks and extends outward for several kilometers. Other major streets radiate out from Kronvalda Park and the various districts of the city have formed around these major boulevards. In the northern end of the park, along and to the north of Elizabetes Ilea is a late 19th century area of Art Nouveau architecture that has no equal anywhere else in Europe. For those who appreciate this style of architecture the district has become very much of a tourist attraction.

As one gets farther out from the modern city core, there are still many areas that show the rather regularized and non-descript apartment blocks built during the Soviet Era after World War II. These same apartment buildings are seen in almost every city of the former Soviet Union. Today with the economic prosperity in Latvia, many of these buildings are either being modernized or replaced.

Architecturally Riga is more Germanic and Polish in flavor with many large and imposing old churches, palatial homes and a massive castle. Unlike Tallinn, which appears more like a Scandinavian city, Riga tends to bear a stronger physical resemblance to cities in Germany or Poland. The city's Old Town has been declared a

World Heritage Site by UNESCO and is today the focus of tourism, just as is true in Tallinn. In the city's central core there are very few modern high-rise buildings. Old Riga developed along the eastern bank of the Daugava River. Its architecture shows the impact of the city having been a major trade center during the 18th and 19th centuries, as unlike Tallinn, the buildings in Riga are more commodious and show a greater degree of affluence. The few medieval buildings that survive, especially the old Town Hall, known as the House of Blackheads, are far more ornate and elegant in style than any seen in the other two Baltic States. The two great cathedrals are also built of brick and stone and present magnificent facades and towers, again displaying the city's great position of influence. The Russian Orthodox Cathedral is late 19th century in origin and built just beyond where the wall of the Old Town once stood, which today is a beautiful crescent shaped park that bounds the Old Town. Unlike Tallinn, the wall that once surrounded the landward side of Riga has long since disappeared, save for a small segment. It is now the park that delineates the Old Town from the modern city center to the north.

West of the Daugava River is the newer part of Riga that has only more recently seen development. The most modern office and residential towers in the city are found lining the western bank of the river and stand in quite a degree of contrast to the church spires of Old Riga on the eastern bank. There is a growing number of very modern high-rise towers being constructed along the west bank of the Daugava River along with some notable pieces of public architecture such as the city's dramatic library. But beyond the riparian zone, the western part of the city consists of distinct small districts some of which are of 19th century vintage with beautiful private homes while others contain the grim apartment blocks of the Soviet period. And still other newer districts represent modern 21st century residential development. They are stitched together by several major boulevards that radiate out from the three major bridges that cross the river. The western bank is difficult for visitors to reach, as it is too far to walk from where cruise ships dock. Local bus or trolley bus service is available, but the Riga tourist offices have not publicized the use of public transport for visitors. Riga still is developing its tourist infrastructure.

CRUISE SHIP DOCK: There is a long embankment just opposite the Old Town where cruise ships are able to dock. There is a small cruise terminal, but most passengers simply leave their ship and either board a motor coach or their private car. And some may negotiate for a taxi. The Old Town is an easy walk from the dock so a large percentage simply take off on their own since they will be capable of seeing most of the major sites on foot.

SIGHTSEEING IN RIGA: Visas are not needed for most ship guests and thus you will have easy access to the city. There is no Metro but a mass transit system of busses and electric trolleys can be accessed easily if you are adventurous and are not frustrated by the language barrier..

* SIGHTSEEING OPTIONS: There will be numerous tours offered, but for those who do not enjoy group motor coach tours you will have freedom to explore Riga in a variety of other ways The best options for getting around are:

** Ship sponsored tours** – For many guests taking the half day ship-sponsored overview tour, which generally involves driving around the city and having the major highlights pointed out while a guide provides narration provides a good introduction. There are also ship sponsored walking tours of the Old Town district, providing the narration you do not get on your own.

** Private car and driver/guide** can be arranged by the shore concierge, but their charges are often quite high. I would recommend contacting one of the following services:

*** Limousine Services at *www.limousine-service.lv* can provide information regarding private touring availability and prices. This is the largest limousine company in the city and is very reliable.

*** Also visit the web page for Riga Limo Service at *www.rigalimo.com* to compare their rates and services.

** Rental cars are available**, but I highly recommend against driving on your own. There are few cars available with automatic transmission. Parking in the central city is very difficult to find and you could inadvertently park illegally resulting in your car being towed. All traffic signs are written in Latvian and some older signs are bilingual, but the second language being Russian using the Cyrillic alphabet.

** Hop on hop off bus** service in Riga – Utilizing the hop on hop off bus as both a means of overview, but also to enable you to visit more venues with less walking is one less expensive approach than a private car. And you have the benefit of narration, giving you a better comprehension of the city. Visit the Red Sightseeing web page at *www.redsightseeing.com* and click on Riga to see what is offered.

** Taxi service** is available – Normally there are few taxis at the cruise ship dock because it is so close to the Old Town center. Most drivers speak little to no English, which can be limiting for the majority of guests. If you wish to book a taxi for sightseeing, visit on line with either of the two major companies below:

*** Baltic Taxi at *www.baltictaxi.com*.

*** Red Cab found at *www.redcab.lv* to explore the taxi tour option. Again language may be a barrier.

** There is no mass transit system** in Riga. There are busses and a couple of tram lines, but given the language barrier, it would be very difficult for a visitor to attempt to navigate.

** **Walking** is a great option, as cruise ships dock alongside the Old Town and you can explore much of this historic district and into the modern city on foot if you are capable. There are many cafes, bistros and coffee shops where you can have a respite during the day and if the weather is nice, this is a good way to enjoy the historic district. And the Art Nouveau streets are also within walking distance to the northwest of the Old Town.

* **MAJOR SIGHTS TO SEE:** In my many visits to Riga, I did an overview tour the first time, and in successive visits I have simply concentrated upon walking in one or two areas at a time. But I do have the advantage of visiting on multiple occasions, which most cruise passengers do not have. By combining an overview with your own or a ship-sponsored walking tour, you will be able to come away with a distinct feel for Riga.

My recommendations for the sights to be seen in Riga include the following (listed in alphabetical order):

** **Alberta Ilea** - Located in the northwest part of the central new city, this street dates to the early 20th century and is lined with an assortment of Art Nouveau apartment blocks. The architecture is quite unique in that so many Art Nouveau structures are grouped together in one street. The local tourist representative who comes on board ship will show you how to walk to this street not far from the ship's dock. It is also clearly marked on tourist maps. If you go there first from the ship it is only six blocks walk along beautifully shaded streets

The distinctive Art Nouveau of Alberta Ilea

** **Central Market** - Located just east of the Old Town area, this is one of the largest and most elaborate public markets in the Baltic States. The displays of meats, seafood, cheese, breads, condiments, fruits, vegetables and baked goods will make your mouth water. It will also give you a better understanding of Latvian cuisine. The market is open seven days a week from 7 AM to 6 PM, but individual shops or stalls may not adhere to these basic hours.

The colorful Central Market of Riga brimming with good food and caviar is in high demand by foreign visitors

** **House of Blackheads** - This is the most iconic building in Riga seen earlier in this chapter. The meeting hall was built in 1334, during the height of the Hanseatic League's role in the city, and it is an exceptionally ornate and distinctive building. The original building was bombed during World War II, but has been faithfully reconstructed. It is open from 11 AM to 6 PM daily, but closed on Mondays.

** **Jugenda Stila Nami** - A collection of distinctive three-dimensional Art Nouveau buildings of the Jugenstil style that is not seen in other cities, this is still another pride of the city. The buildings are located on Elizabetes and Strelnieku Streets, which meets with Alberta Ilea. Any tourist bureau map will show this district. If you are already planning to visit Alberta Ilea, this collection is just a continuation of the Art Nouveau style.

** **Kronvalda Park** - This large park encircles the landward side of the Old Town. It is beautifully landscaped, has small lakes and fountains along with flower beds to provide an overall quiet green space between the old and new cities. There are beautiful fountains, vibrant flower beds and portions of the former moat that reflect the sky and trees on a bright sunny day. The park is an excellent place to rest, especially on a warm day. It is also a great place to simply people watch. It is also a great place to just relax and enjoy the fresh air.

The beauty and serenity of Kronvalda Park

** **Latvian Ethnographic Open Air Museum** - Located not too far from the city center, this museum provides a look into the past centuries of Latvian life, especially that of the rural lifestyle. It is located at the far northeastern edge of the city and can be reached easily by taxi. The address is Brīvības gatve 440, Vidzemes priekšpilsēta and it is open from 10 AM to 5 PM daily.

** **Museé Art Nouveau** - Located on Alberta Ilea, this museum provides those who are devotees of Art Nouveau even more upon which to feast the eyes. The museum is open daily except Monday from 10 AM to 6 PM.

** **Museum of the Occupation of Latvia** - This is a venue for true history buffs, as it presents in vivid detail the Imperial, Nazi and Soviet occupation of Latvia. It is located at Raiņa bulvāris 7 in the heart of the Old Town. It is open daily from 11 AM to 6 PM. The subject matter is rather disturbing and the museum definitely points to the hardships of the Latvian people during so much of the 20th century.

** Old Town – The old city area of Riga is quite large, but unlike Tallinn, automobiles are permitted on many street. And there are also a few modern buildings that have been allowed. But for the most part, this is the historic core of Riga located between the river and Kronvalda Park where once a city wall and moat protected Riga. The streets are safe, clean and a delight to explore. And there are dozens of restaurants and cafes in which to refresh yourself.

The Old Town skyline seen from across the river

** Riga Ghetto and Latvian Holocaust Museum - This small museum tells the grim story of life in the Riga Ghetto and then of the Nazi occupation of the city and the ultimate extermination of the Jewish population. Unlike visiting holocaust museums in North American or Western European cities, here you are visiting a museum in a city that witnessed the horrors of the genocide. Both Latvia and Lithuania contained large Jewish populations.

The city of Riga was once a major cultural center for the Jewish population. Today this museum, like those in other cities of Eastern Europe with similar former ghettos, is a very well visited site, especially for American visitors.

The museum is just south of the Old Town at Maskavas iela 14A, Latgales priekšpilsēta, easily reached by taxi. The museum is open daily from 10 AM to 6 PM, but closed on Saturday.

A small Old Town souvenir market behind Saint Peter's Church

The Riga Ghetto Museum brings to life the horrors of the Holocaust

** **Rumbula Forest Memorial** - If one of the ship tours does not include this rather grim, yet vital memorial, you can reach it by either a privately reserved car and driver/guide or local taxi. This is a memorial in what is now a peaceful forest clearing. But once Jews were brought here and slaughtered during the Nazi occupation of Riga.

This memorial is located on Highway A-6 about 25 miles southeast of the city. It is a very somber site to visit, but it is an important part of learning about the horrors of the holocaust. Visiting is a sobering experience similar to that of one of the concentration camps in Poland, but it is a sobering reminder of the horrors of the Holocaust. For many guests on board ship there is a reluctance to visit such sites, but they are a stark reminder of the dark side of modern European history and should not be overlooked.

** **Saint Peter's Church** - This is the main Lutheran church for Old Town, and its tower is quite famous for having a viewing platform that can be reached via an old fashioned elevator. The views of the city are most dramatic, especially on a clear day. It is open from 10 AM to 6 PM weekdays and Saturday, but closed Monday. Sunday it is open from Noon until 6 PM.

** **Town Hall Square of Old Town** - Around the main square you will see many examples of the medieval and Hanseatic architecture of Riga. This is the heart of Old Town. Quite often there will be musicians or dancers performing, dressed in traditional costumes.

The commercial core of Riga

* **MODERN RIGA:** Most visitors do not see the major commercial and residential

sections of Riga unless they have a private tour in either a private car with a driver/guide or taxi.

The commercial heart of Riga contains a mix of buildings from the late 18th century through to the early post-Soviet Era. There are just a handful of 20th century buildings in the city center. However, across the Daugava River there is a beautiful string of ultra-modern high rise commercial and residential buildings that represent the dynamic growth of the new Riga in an era of prosperity as part of the European Union. Most of these buildings line the south bank of the Daugava River and can be seen from onboard your cruise ship. They stand in contrast to the Old Town and the commercial heart of the city, but are a reflection of a newly emerging modern Latvia.

The high rise towers of modern Riga across the Daugava River

* **OTHER VENUES OUTSIDE THE CITY:** Some cruise lines will offer journeys out into the countryside for those who want to experience the rural flavor of Latvian life. You can also plan a journey for all or part of the day into the countryside with a private car and driver. The Latvian countryside is very idyllic and peaceful and affords you an opportunity to experience a way of life that seems to still be rooted in the past. But unless you have been to Riga before, you will miss the beautiful architecture and flavor of the city.

If the weather is nice and you want to enjoy the beach, I highly recommend going to the main Riga railway station and taking the short 30-minute train trip to Jūrmala, the popular Riga beach resort on the Gulf of Riga. Jūrmala was once a favored seaside playground for high-ranking Soviet officials who would come from as far away as Moscow. There are many fine examples of wood 18th and 19th century architecture plus a few reminders of the rather boxy Soviet style used for public buildings such as hotels. The beach at Jūrmala is composed of a beautiful white quartz sand that sparkles in the summer sun. And the beach extends as a thin strand for over 20 miles, backed up by marshes and woodland. Once again I only recommend this option if you have already been to Riga on a previous trip.

LATVIAN CUISINE AND DINING OUT: For those who enjoy experiencing the food culture of a country, the Public Market at the south end of the Old Town is highly recommended. Here you will find displays of the produce, meats, seafood, cheese, breads and other delicacies in the Latvian diet. If you wish to do more than sample the cuisine, there are many restaurants located in the Old Town area. I have not expanded my horizon, so I have a few that I recommend. They are typically Latvian and are quite excellent:

* **Aleks Restaurant** - This is definitely not a restaurant that you would find on most lists for visitors. This is a small restaurant attached to an equally small hotel on aside street where you can savor the local architecture. The menu offers a variety of local dishes including appetizers, soups entrees and desserts. The quality and freshness are outstanding and the service is very gracious, but not at all pretentious. The address is 24 Jauniela and the restaurant is open from Noon to 10 PM Tuesday thru Saturday, closing extended to 11 PM Friday and Saturday. Sunday hours are from 2 to 10 PM. You will need to have one of the local reps on board the ship mark this obscure location on one of the maps of the old city area of Riga. You can have the ship's tour desk call +372 30 035 705 to book a table.

* **Bar & Restaurant Petergāilis** – In the heart of Old Town at Skarmu Ilea # 25, this is a beautiful and engaging traditional restaurant serving a wide variety of Latvian and other Eastern European dishes. The cuisine, service and atmosphere are all at a high standard that is sure to please. This is a rather small and somewhat eclectic restaurant so it is best to have the ship's concierge make a booking even for lunch since the restaurant has a good local following. The restaurant is open daily from 10 AM to Midnight. The phone number is +372 67 212 888 and it is a good idea to book a table ahead of arriving.

* **Folklubs Ala Pagrabs** – Located in the Old Town at Peldu # 19, this very traditional restaurant has very high standards of cuisine and service. The atmosphere is cozy and charming. The menu is diverse and offers many selections among seafood, meat and poultry entrees with all of the traditional accompaniments. Desserts are also quite delicious, so save room. Their hours of service are open from Noon Monday to 4 AM Tuesday, from Noon Tuesday until 4 AM Wednesday and from Noon Wednesday until 5 AM Thursday. They reopen at Noon on Thursday and remain open until 7 AM Friday. They open again at Noon Friday and remain open until 7 AM Saturday. They reopen at 2 Pm Saturday and are open until 7 AM Sunday. And finally they open at 2 PM Sunday and remain open until 4 AM Monday. Clearly they have a nighttime following. Call to book a table at +371 27 796 914.

* **Lido at Atputas Center** - Just southeast of the city center along the Daugava River, this recreation center hosts wedding parties and special events as well as having several restaurant choices from sit down menu service to buffet. There is a beer cellar, children's playground, small lake and an overall atmosphere conducive to enjoying an afternoon or evening. The cuisine is a combination of Latvian and Eastern European fare, and the quality is excellent. This is the largest of three Lido restaurants in Riga, and worth the drive out of the city center, but you do need a car and driver/guide, as a taxi there and back would cost just as much and not give you the flexibility of your own vehicle. It is located along Krasta Iela 76. The hours are from 11 AM to 11 PM seven days per week. The phone number to call for booking a table is +371 67 700 000.

* **Lido Old City** - There is also a small Lido Restaurant in the old city located on Tirgonu Iela 6 open from 10 AM to 9 PM, but it is small and often very crowded. I recommend going late for lunch at around 2 or 3 PM to avoid the lunch crowd. Bookings are not necessary.

* **Milda** – Located in the heart of the Old Town at Kungu Ilea # 8, this is a very traditional Latvian and Eastern European restaurant with a refined and elegant atmosphere. The cuisine is very traditional and the menu is quite varied with offerings in seafood, meat and poultry and a wide array of side dishes. The restaurant is open Tuesday thru Sunday from Noon to 10 PM. Call +371 25 713 287 to book a table.

* **Riits** – This fine restaurant is located beyond the confines of the Old Town, about four blocks east of the Freedom Monument in the city's central district, but easy walking from the ship. The address is Dzirnavu Ilea # 72 and should not be hard to find. You may wish to have the local tourist representative mark it on a city map. The atmosphere is casual and the vibe is that of being out in the Latvian countryside. The cuisine is traditional and well prepared. The menu includes a variety of grilled meats, poultry and fresh seafood. They have a wide variety of starters, soups and salads prior to their entrees, most of them grilled over natural oak charcoal. And they are open Monday from Noon to 11 PM and Tuesday thru Sunday from 9 AM to 11 PM. Phone +371 25 644 408 to book a table.

SHOPPING: There are literally hundreds of small souvenir and craft shops located in the Old Town area of Riga, but I cannot recommend one or the other because I have never patronized any of them. Latvian crafts include embroidery, dolls and many household items, but I would be reluctant to speak to quality or artistry. For regular shopping, there is a Stockmann Department Store located in the new city center on Satekles Iela. It is part of a large center that also contains one of the city's major cinemas.

I realize that my information regarding shopping is limited to just the major department store, but I do not wish to provide information I have not personally verified.

The one item many visitors to both Estonia and Latvia wish to purchase is amber jewelry. From my personal limited knowledge of shopping for amber, I have noticed that the majority of what is sold in Tallinn is very tourist oriented in that the amber jewelry does not have that elegant or substantial look that it does in Riga. However, unless you have personal knowledge or the ship's representatives refer you to a reputable shop, buying amber would be a gamble as to its authenticity. And unfortunately I have never been advised as to which shops sell the best quality.

As a geographer, I do know that amber, especially pieces that contain the preserved bodies of an insect that was initially trapped inside the sticky sap, are considered to be highly valuable mainly for their fossilized remains that can be hundreds of thousands of years old.

You will see large displays of amber in Old Town shop windows in Riga

A FINAL NOTE: Riga is a city that is just now starting to become more of a household word among people who have cruised the Baltic Sea. As more cruise lines include this beautiful city on their itinerary, Riga may become as well-known as Tallinn. The architecture, parks and friendly people will win over visitors and this will help to spread the word about visiting Riga. Initially cruise lines were bypassing Riga because the port fees being charged were supposedly too high relative to other Baltic ports. At least that was the answer I had received from several companies.

For anyone who had family living in Latvia during World War II, there is a strong interest in seeing the city that for many will hold sad memories, thus making the visit somewhat of a pilgrimage. This would also hold true for anyone who is a direct descendant of those who lost a relative in Riga during the Nazi occupation of the city. At one time Riga was a major center of culture for the Jewish community.

During the long period of Soviet domination, Latvia along with its neighbors Estonia and Lithuania, was a part of the Soviet Union. There was a strong emphasis placed upon subverting the local culture, but over the years it only brought strong resistance and today the Latvian culture is thriving.

RIGA MAPS

THE CENTRAL CITY

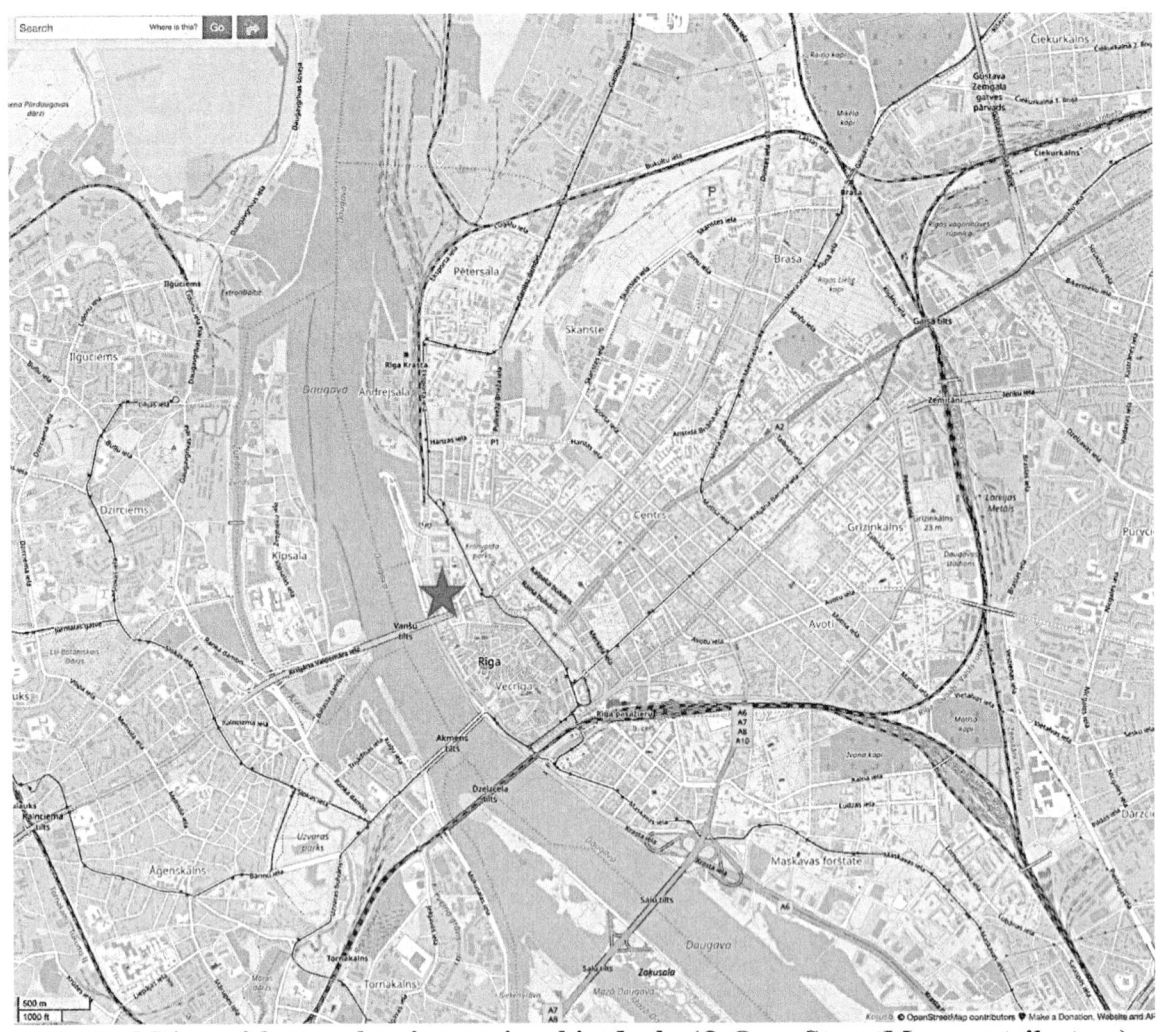

Central Riga with star showing cruise ship dock, (© OpenStreetMap contributors)

This map is best viewed directly from OpenStreetMap.com on your personal device where it can be expanded or one specific area can be enlarged. Given the format of this book, it is impossible to display maps with the level of detail you might wish to have while actually out exploring the city. But the OpenStreetMap maps used directly are the tool I always rely upon.

THE RIGA OLD TOWN

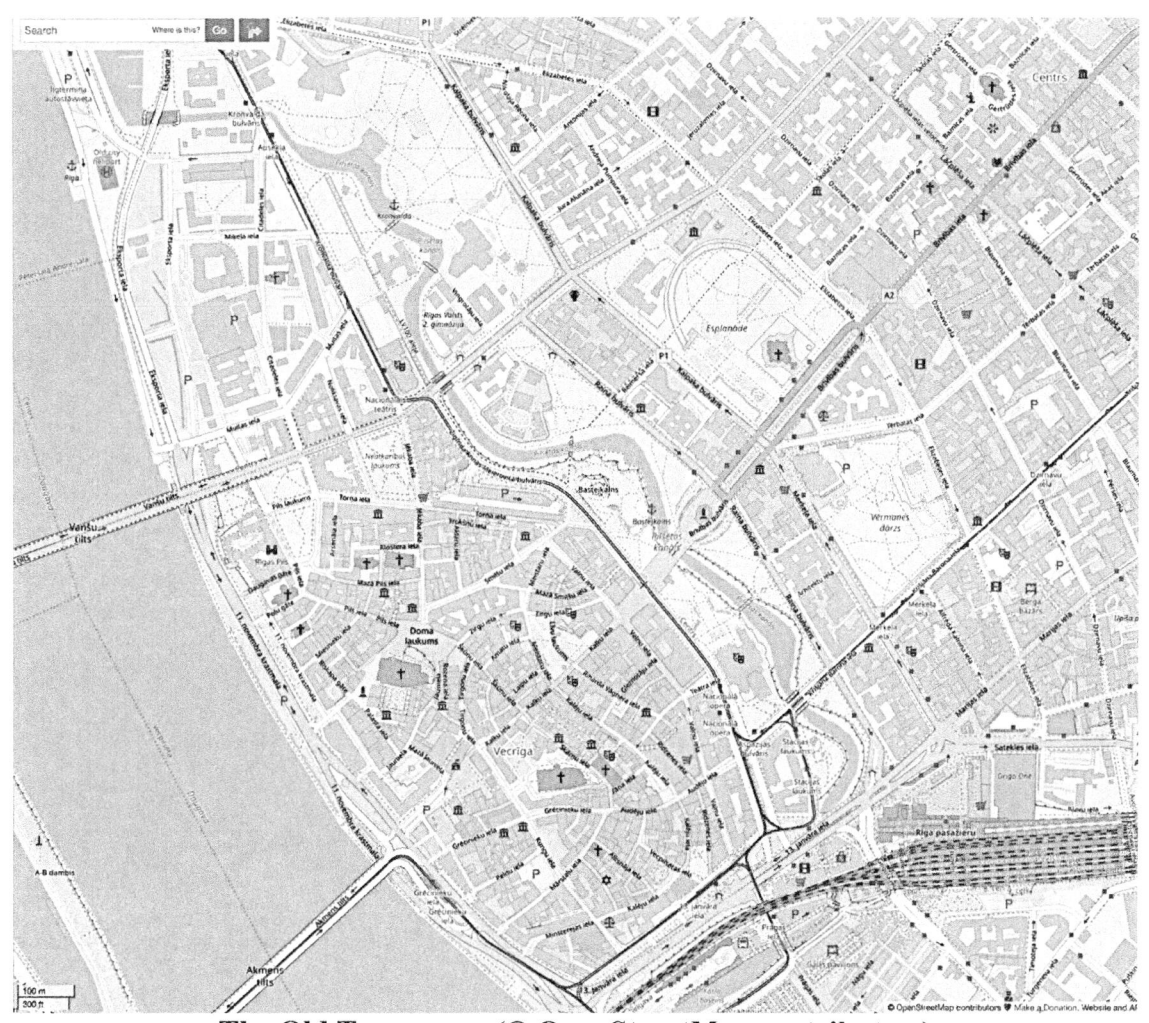

The Old Town area, (© OpenStreetMap contributors)

This map is best viewed directly from OpenStreetMap.com on your personal device where it can be expanded or one specific area can be enlarged. Given the format of this book, it is impossible to display maps with the level of detail you might wish to have while actually out exploring the city. But the OpenStreetMap maps used directly are the tool I always rely upon.

THE ART NOUVEAU AND DOWNTOWN AREAS

Art Nouveau (upper left) and downtown Riga, (© OpenStreetMap contributors)

This map is best viewed directly from OpenStreetMap.com on your personal device where it can be expanded or one specific area can be enlarged. Given the format of this book, it is impossible to display maps with the level of detail you might wish to have while actually out exploring the city. But the OpenStreetMap maps used directly are the tool I always rely upon.

KLAIPÉDA, LITHUANIA

A map of greater Klaipéda (© OpenStreetMap contributors)

The majority of cruise itineraries, especially for the large mega ships, do not include a stop in Klaipéda, Lithuania. I believe the main reason that Lithuania is avoided is because of the nature of the population distribution. The main center of population and cultural activity is in the far eastern corner of the country, too far from the Baltic Sea coast for access during a one-day port call. Even though this is also true for Poland and Germany, the conditions are different. In Poland the port cities of Gdańsk and Gdynia combined have over 1,000,000 residents and are historically very significant. In Germany the port cities of Warnemunde and Rostock combined have nearly 400,000 residents and are rich in history. And in addition, Berlin is easily accessible during the long one-day port call made by all cruise lines given the high speed Autobahn system that links the country together. In Lithuania the heart of the country is over on its eastern border around the capital city of Vilnius, too far from Klaipéda for a return journey in one day.

THE NATURAL SETTING: Klaipéda is the only seaport for the nation of Lithuania. Unlike Estonia or Latvia, Lithuania is not blessed with a seacoast that is amenable to trade. The long sand bar, known as the Curonian Spit, blocks most of the coastline from direct access. The bay inside this bar is very shallow and needs to be dredged for ships to be able to enter the mouth and reach Klaipéda. Thus although it is a Baltic Sea nation, Lithuania has turned more inland as evidenced by the fact that its capital and largest city of Vilnius is located closer to the border of Belarus than it is to the sea. And when ships dock in Klaipéda it is normally for eight hours or less, thus not providing time for a visit to Vilnius, as road and rail routes are not designed for high-speed travel.

The sandy Curonian Spit guards the shallow Klaipéda waters.

Lithuania is the largest of the three Baltic Sea states with 65,298 square kilometers or 25,212 square miles, making it just slightly larger than Latvia. It only has a population of 3,600,000 people. Its population matrix is such that the Lithuanian people comprise over 80 percent of the total, with the remainder being from surrounding countries, including 8 percent being of Russian origin, far less than in Latvia or Estonia.

Most of the land in Lithuania is rather low in elevation, slightly hilly to flat, again showing the result of glacial action during the ice age. There are over 3,000 lakes that dot the countryside, which in its natural state is a mix of broadleaf and needle leaf woodlands. Unlike its other neighbors, the coastline of Lithuania has few natural harbors, most of it containing marshes and sand dunes, but this unique landscape is quite scenic, a potential now becoming realized. Sand dunes are found scattered around the Baltic Sea, but along the Lithuanian coast, the combination of ocean currents and winds worked together to create a long, narrow sand bar along what was a shallow coastline. Today the Curonian Spit is both a Lithuanian National Park and a UNESCO World Heritage Site, attracting more visitors each year, as word of its existence becomes more widely disseminated.

The green woodlands surrounding Klaipeda

Winter is once again the dominant season, but being farther south it is not quite as severe as in Estonia or Latvia. This is still a relatively poor nation with regard to resources, one in which agriculture is an important part of the economy. Dairy farming and the raising of pigs and cattle are important. Industries are somewhat developed with shipbuilding and food processing being key to the country's trade balance. Lithuania relies heavily upon trade with Russia from where it obtains most of its raw materials.

A BRIEF LOCAL HISTORY: Lithuania is an old nation, having developed as an amalgamation of semi-nomadic Baltic tribes dating back before our modern calendar. Linguistically the Lithuanian and Latvian people are similar, forming a distinct grouping among Indo European speakers, yet each language is totally unique. Culturally speaking, the Lithuanian people have been heavily influenced by Germans, Poles and Russians and their culture exhibits traits that are a fusion of the three major traditions.

The earliest evidence of a Lithuanian state comes from the 9th century. By 1250, the country was united with Belarus into the Grand Principality of Lithuania. By 1341, the Grand Duke Gediminas had expanded the empire as far south as Kiev, and his dynasty ruled until 1572. Initially a pagan state, the Lithuanians fought off German Teutonic

Knights with an intense ferocity. But eventually the Lithuanians accepted the Catholic faith, which today accounts for 90 percent of the people.

In 1569, Lithuania united with Poland as a commonwealth with each nation having its respective leaders and identity. At its peak, its dominion extended from the Baltic to the Black Sea. During the years from 1772 to 1792, Lithuania disappeared from the map, its vast holdings divided between Prussia, Austria and Russia. What we recognize today as Lithuania was totally absorbed into Russia and the Tsar even was given the title as Grand Prince of Lithuania.

Being a neighbor of German East Prussia brought Lithuania under total control of Germany at the start of World War I. At the end of the war, the Lithuanians declared their independence as a republic, as did Latvia and Estonia. In 1940, the Soviet Union invaded Lithuania and absorbed it as a Soviet Socialist Republic. But when Nazi Germany attacked Russia in 1941, Lithuania came under Nazi control. It was not liberated until 1945, but it was then reabsorbed into the Soviet Union.

It was not until the Soviet state collapsed at the end of 1990 that Lithuania finally once again emerged as an independent republic. The country joined the European Union in 2004 along with Estonia. The Euro became the official currency at the start of 2015, replacing the short-lived Litu, which had been the currency since 1991. Today the country is seeing the economic benefits of European Union membership and increased tourism.

Klaipéda's Old Town only dates to the 16th century

THE PHYSICAL LAYOUT OF THE CITY OF KLAIPÉDA: Klaipéda is not physically very large, and the Dané River splits the city in half. The street pattern is surprisingly regular with all major streets oriented on a north to south and east to west axis. North of the Dané River is the city center, which has a strong Soviet Era architecture with the exception of two dominant high-rise towers. The central core is relatively small and many of the buildings house both shops on lower floors and apartments above. There is a lack of any feeling of being in a major city. There are few shops and no major stores in the central core. It is as much residential as it is commercial.

The small Old Town area is located south of the Dané River, but even here the streets form essentially rectangular blocks. But this area of about half a square kilometer has many buildings that date back to the 17th and 18th centuries and most of the streets are cobbled. Klaipéda has been restoring its Old Town, the core area of the city that features cobblestone streets, antique lampposts and old buildings that represent centuries of history. Many of the old buildings exhibit what is called "fachwork," timber-framed architecture, a style seen in German coastal communities. There are no monumental churches, palaces or other buildings of significance.

Beyond the Old Town, the architectural flavor is Soviet Era in nature with large apartment blocks and few single-family houses until you reach the outer edge of the city. But there are a few quite tall and modern apartment blocks in this area that reflect the growing prosperity in the post-Soviet period.

Fishing is a weekend pastime on the Dané River

Around the mouth of the Dané River is the port area, which occupies both the north and south shores. The port is not very large, but it does handle all of the country's import and export traffic that is done by sea. There are also small shipbuilding and repair facilities.

Opposite the port, across the water is the Curonian Spit and facing the city are some rather elegant homes that can only be reached by ferryboat. Most of the spit is either cloaked in scrubby pine forest or stands as raw sand dunes. It is this natural landscape that has attracted campers, hikers and beachgoers in recent years. And its unusual character is what has given it both national park status by the Lithuanian government and UNESCO World Heritage Status.

BRIEF COMMUNITY HISTORY: Klaipéda is Lithuania's third city in population, but its primary port, dating back to its origination in 1252. There is a strong feeling of being in Germany when one looks at the architecture of Klaipéda, and German is the most commonly spoken language apart from native Lithuanian.

The original name of the town was Memel, a truly Germanic name. During the 17th century, the Swedes devastated the city, and later during the 18th century, the Russians occupied it for a five-year period. In the early 19th century, Klaipéda became the temporary capital of Prussia when Napoleonic forces occupied Berlin. Throughout its history, this city has been tied closely to, if not a part of the German state.

The mouth of the Dané River separates Old Town (right) from the modern city center of Klaipéda

In the late 19th century, this northern part of Prussia was turned into an international zone, occupied by French troops, but in 1923, the new nation of Lithuania forced the French out and incorporated it into their own country. Klaipéda gives one more the flavor of Germany than they would have traveling inland to Vilnius, the national capital and the true core city of Lithuanian culture.

During World War II, Klaipéda served as a major submarine port for the German Navy, thus it came under attack from allied forces, being liberated by the Red Army in 1945, but at the expense of severe devastation. After the war, Lithuania, like its neighbors Latvia and Estonia, was absorbed into the Soviet Union where it remained as a Soviet Socialist Republic until 1991, the Russians claiming that the territory had once been theirs. Although the Soviet system brought industrial infrastructure, it also kept the people from expressing their own cultural traditions.

Today Klaipéda is undergoing a major revitalization. Lithuania is now a member of the European Union, and with the country's heartland located to the interior around the capital city of Vilnius; Klaipéda is the country's gateway to the sea. The city is also home to a major fishing fleet, and it is considered to be the most important fishing port on the entire Baltic Sea. A major maritime museum, housed in an old German fort on the Neringa Peninsula, now depicts the marine life and maritime heritage of the region.

Modern Klaipéda has sharp, angular lines

Lithuania's coastline offers few good anchorages, but here between the Dané River and the Curonian Lagoon, the city was able to cater to ships bringing trade goods and carrying away the country's exports. The city is separated from the open sea by a narrow sandy spit, facing the shallow inside lagoon that needed to be dredged to deepen it for major cruise vessels. The sand spit known as the Kursiu Nerija is today a national park, preserving the sandy dunes and thick woodlands. This is also a recreational area that is far more rural than urban. As ships sail into Klaipéda, the pass along the inside edge of this natural parkland, having the city itself on the port (left) side. The entire Lithuanian coastline is hidden behind this barrier, thus offering little access to the sea for trade.

Before World War II, Klaipéda had a thriving Jewish population that amounted to over 17 percent of the city's population. Most either fled the city prior to German occupation, and the remainder along with the rest of Lithuania's 235,000 Jews, were exterminated in Nazi concentration camps. Today only a handful of Jews live in Klaipéda, but the city does maintain one small synagogue, a reminder of its past history.

CRUISE SHIP DOCK: Ships will sail through the entry channel into the harbor for Klaipéda, passing along the edge of the Curonian Spit. There is a long docking area capable of handling the larger cruise ships, but there is no terminal building. Motor coaches and private vehicles as well as taxis wait just beyond the gate, only a few steps from the ship's gangway. Some of the more upmarket cruise lines may offer a shuttle bus into the Old Town, but it really is not necessary because the distance is very short and it only takes five to 10 minutes to be in the heart of town on foot.

SIGHTSEEING IN KLAIPÉDA: Of the few monuments in Klaipéda, most were desecrated by the Soviets when they captured the city from Nazi control in the later years of World War II, and then continued their degradation of Lithuanian culture during the occupation that lasted until 1991. Those seen today are actually reconstructions of older works, based upon old photographs. The city's old Theatre Square houses a neoclassical theatre, but this is a reproduction of the original structure, which burned in a fire during the 19th century. Southeast of the square, the History Museum of Lithuania is a venue that offers many of the typical costumes and artifacts of the region. Most guest will simply walk the old and modern sections of the city, as cruise ships dock at the mouth of the Dané River mere blocks from the heart of the city.

* **SIGHTSEEING OPTIONS:** There are fewer options for seeing the sights of Klaipéda than in the larger more tourist oriented ports. These include:

** **Ship sponsored tours** – Many cruise lines offer just brief sightseeing tours of Klaipéda by either motor coach or as a walking visit. But if you are staying in town, it is so easy to get around on your own. All you will miss is the narration, but with my book or any other major tourist guide, you will have all you need to know. Some of the more upscale cruise lines will offer a half or full day tour out into the Lithuanian countryside, which is a nice opportunity to get away from the port.

** **Private car and driver** – Your shore excursion desk can arrange for a private sightseeing excursion with your own car and driver, but personally I do not believe it is worth the greater expense unless you have strong feelings about or need for a private tour. For price and service comparison you may wish to check with the following two companies:

*** **JND** at *www.jnd.lt* to see what they can offer.

*** **OsaBus** at *www.osabus.com* for further comparison.

** **Rental cars** - I highly recommend against driving in Klaipéda because of the limited number of automatic transmission vehicles, if any and also the language barrier. There are no English language road signs in Lithuania. Many older signs are still bilingual but the second language is Russian.

** **Hop on hop off bus service** – Klaipéda is too small to have any hop on hop off bus service. And it does not receive that many cruise visitors per summer season to warrant such service.

** **Taxis** will be available at the dock, but be sure your drive is able to communicate with you in English or another language you speak, as few are competent in other languages. Also negotiate a price prior to starting out. Amber Taxi at *www.ambertaxi.com* may be able to arrange a pre booked tour.

** **Walking** is the option most guests tend to opt for, as it is easy to see the major sights of the city, which are not that many in number. It is more a matter of just absorbing the flavor of this small city to be able to garner a feel for the culture of Lithuania.

* **SIGHTS TO EXPLORE**: The few sights worthy of special note are listed below, and are generally included on any ship tours of the city, or can be accessed on your own if you choose to visit privately (shown in alphabetical order):

** **Drama Theater** - Facing the Dramatic Theater Square, the theater was initially developed in 1935, under strong German influence. This was during the brief period after breaking from the Russian Empire and before the Nazi invasion that brought all three of the Baltic nations under German control. It is a beautiful building, but tours are not given. Unless there is a daytime performance when your ship is in port, there is no way to view the interior.

If there happens to be a performance during the afternoon of your visit, you can attend providing tickets are available. It would be rare, however, for any performance to be held in English, but an all musical presentation of either classical or folk music would be a rewarding experience. The music and costumes are both memorable and thus making such a performance wowrthwhile.

Local artists display their wares in the Dramatic Theater Square

** Dramatic Theater Square - Generally when a ship is in port, local craftspeople and artists will set up their wares around the Annchen Tharau Fountain adjacent to the city's small dramatic theater. Some of the craft items or art work pieces are quite good even though they are the work of amateurs. Over the years I have purchased a beautiful hand embroidered tablecloth and two small oil paintings at very reasonable prices. And as an art collector, I consider the work to be quite excellent.

** Klaipéda Old Town - You can walk the entire Old Town in less than 30 minutes. The architecture is far from monumental, but it does give you a good look at what life was like in this once primarily Germanic city. At the south end of Old Town is an open air public market, but it is not very large.

** Kursiu Nerija National Park - Located across the lagoon on the Curonian Spit, this is the most important tourist attraction in Klaipéda. Tours are offered in either all-terrain vehicles or by bicycle for those who want to enjoy a taste of this natural landscape, which is unique to the Baltic Sea area.

A local ferry operates across the lagoon on a regular basis from adjacent to the cruise dock. But without renting a bicycle or participating in a local all-terrain tour, the most you can do is take a short walk through the woods and dunes to the open seaside.

Kursiu Nerija National Park is just across the channel from the cruise ship dock

** Lithuanian Clock and Watch Museum - This is a rather strange small museum, as it is devoted to timepieces, their history and the art of watchmaking and repair. We all use clocks and watches, but few of us give much thought to the delicate nature of their mechanisms and how they are made. I would only recommend it to those who have a specific interest in the subject or who are collectors of timepieces.

It is located in the city center at Liepug. #6. It is open Monday thru Saturday from Noon to 6 PM every day except Monday.

** Martynas Mazvydas Sculpture Park - A short walk east of the city center, this small, but well-manicured park is home to 116 sculptures by 67 Lithuanian artists, but of contemporary origin. The oldest of the sculptures only dates to the late 1970's, but it is still a nice way to spend half an hour taking in the work of Lithuanian sculptors.

There are also sculptures representing the Soviet Era when Lithuania was one of the republics of the Soviet Union. These rather controversial statues depict the idealized vision that was dictated by the Kremlin and are today considered to be an anachronism.

Being located along the river starting at the second bridge and running for two blocks, it is always open and there is no admission fee.

Soviet Era sculptures in the Martynas Mazvydas Sculpture Park

CUISINE: Lithuanian cuisine is strongly influenced by Russian and Polish traditions, which means lots of cabbage, potatoes and beets, with pork being the most popular meat. For lunch during summer a cold, creamy beet soup served with cold boiled potato or hard-boiled egg is a popular dish, and is essentially very Russian or Polish. The national dish is called "Zeppelin," named for the large German airships. It is an elongated potato dough stuffed with meat or cheese and then baked or fried. It is covered with crumbled bacon. The Lithuanians brew up a Czech style lager that is considered to be very good. Also there are a few local wines available.

There are several small restaurants in Klaipéda. Most of the restaurants are quite casual, but there are a couple in my listing that are more upmarket. As a small city with a limited number of outside visitors, it is hard to find a large array of quality restaurants. I have listed what I consider to be the best:

* **Momo Grill** - Located in the newer city north of the Dané River at Liepu Str. 20 and open from 11 AM to 11 PM Tuesday thru Friday and from Noon to 11 PM on Saturday, this is also an outstanding rather elegant restaurant. It is very small and only has less than ten tables, but the food and service are surprisingly quite excellent. Bookings are not required.

* **Monai** – At Liepu G # 4 in the city center, this traditional restaurant features Lithuanian dishes along with many representing other cultures of Eastern Europe.

They also serve vegetarian entrees as well. The entrees are beautifully prepared and served in a warm and friendly atmosphere. Their hours are from 11:30 AM to 10 PM Tuesday thru Friday, Saturday from 11 AM to 10 PM and Sunday from 11 AM to 4 PM. You will not need to book a table.

* **Stora Antis** - A small, upmarket restaurant and hotel. It serves traditional cuisine with much care as to freshness and flavors. The location is south of the Dané River at Tiltų g. #6. It is only open for dinner from 5 to 11 PM Tuesday thru Saturday, which is only going to work if your ship is staying into the mid evening hours. To book a table call +370 250 25020.

Local talent is being used to restore very old mosaic streets and walkways

SHOPPING: If the artists have set up their wares in the square outside of the Dramatic Theater, those of you interested in local crafts may find some treasures. Lithuanian women are known for their embroidery, generally on linen. Tablecloths or runners are often available at very reasonable prices for hand-made work. There are a few local landscape artists that have not been discovered. They are older men and women who either paint as a hobby or to supplement their retirement. But the work is moderately good, and you can buy a miniature oil painting of acceptable quality for around €20 or a larger 10 x 14 inch oil for €40.

There are a few arts and crafts shops in the Old Town, but I have found their prices to be higher and the quality no better than that found in the square. Over the years I have purchased two oil paintings, as noted above, that represent the work of highly talented, but from unknown artists in the square. The quality of the work is outstanding. So I advise you check the marketplace in the square prior to spending money in one of the shops. You may make a great find at far less expense.

FINAL WORDS: Klaipéda offers just a glimpse into Lithuanian culture, especially due to the fact that this city has a decidedly more German heritage. But its prosperity reflects the rapid growth of the overall nation now that Lithuania has become a member of the European Union. Many cruise guests often ask why the ship stopped here for the day, not realizing that even though this is not an exciting port of call, it does offer a somewhat rare opportunity to visit a country that is not on most traveler's agendas.

Many cruise lines pay to have local Lithuanian musicians perform on the dock when guests are leaving the ship

Clearly Lithuania is on track to become an important trading partner within the European Union. The national economy is expanding at a healthy rate, and the city of Klaipéda accounts for a share of that expansion. Once the highway infrastructure of Lithuania reaches the standard of its Scandinavian neighbors with the development of more divided expressways, it would become possible for cruise ship passengers to visit

Vilnius when ships dock for the day in Klaipéda, just as it is possible to visit Warsaw or Berlin from Baltic Sea ports when ships dock

The city of Klaipéda exhibits many touches of summer color

KLAIPÉDA MAPS

THE CITY OF KLAIPÈDA

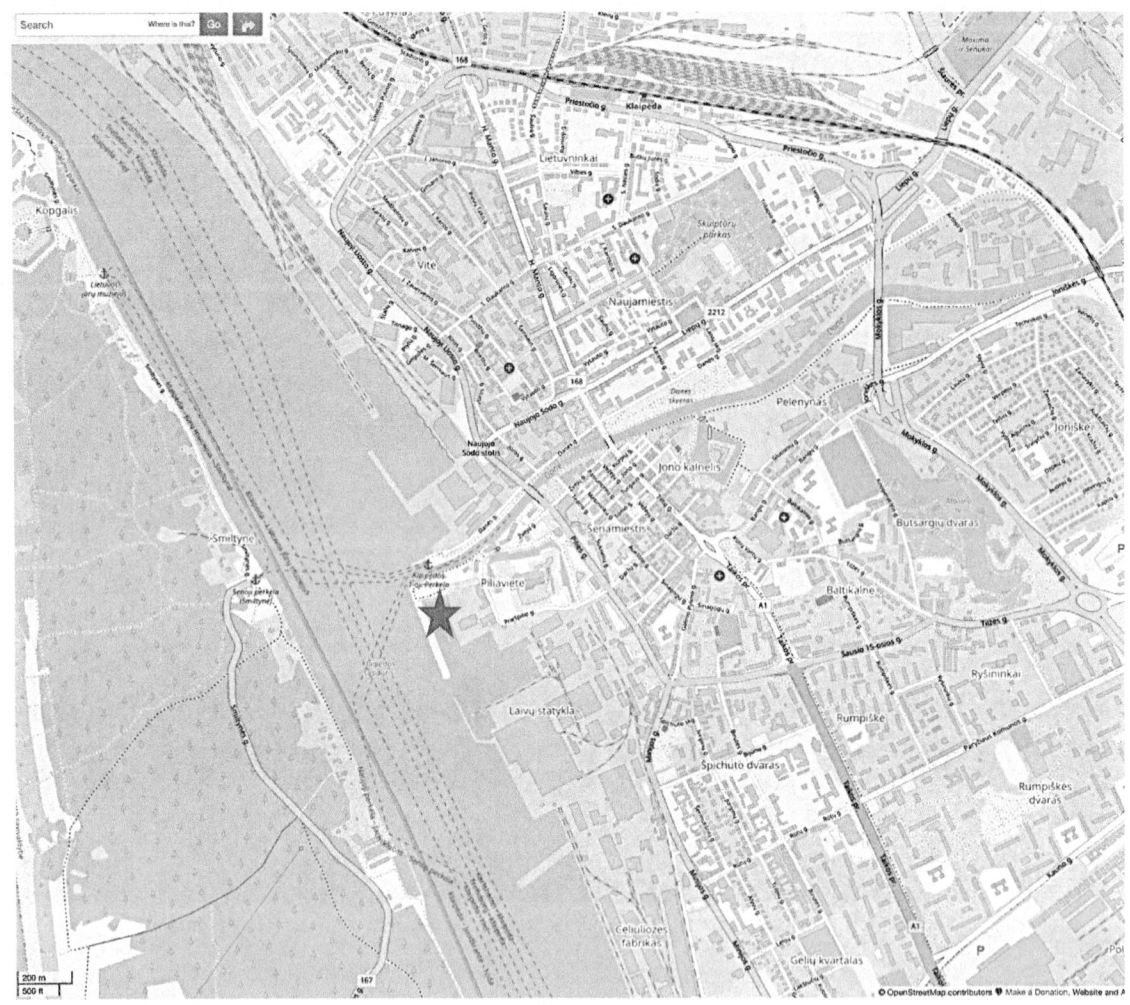

The city of Klaipéda with star showing cruise ship dock, (© OpenStreetMap contributors)

This map is best viewed directly from OpenStreetMap.com on your personal device where it can be expanded or one specific area can be enlarged. Given the format of this book, it is impossible to display maps with the level of detail you might wish to have while actually out exploring the city. But the OpenStreetMap maps used directly are the tool I always rely upon.

THE HEART OF KLAIPĖDA

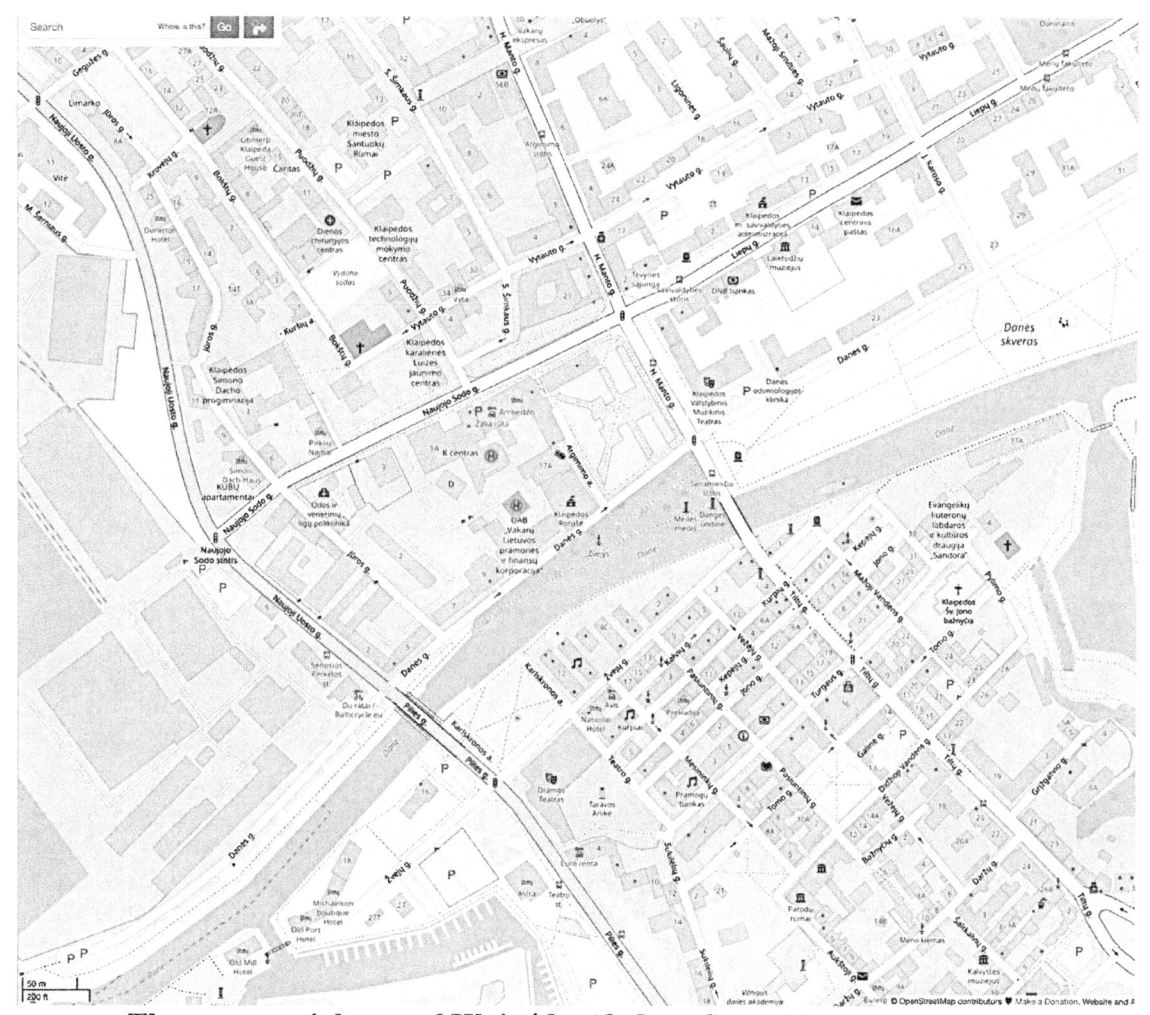

The commercial core of Klaipėda, (© OpenStreetMap contributors)

This map is best viewed directly from OpenStreetMap.com on your personal device where it can be expanded or one specific area can be enlarged. Given the format of this book, it is impossible to display maps with the level of detail you might wish to have while actually out exploring the city. But the OpenStreetMap maps used directly are the tool I always rely upon.

GDAŃSK, POLAND

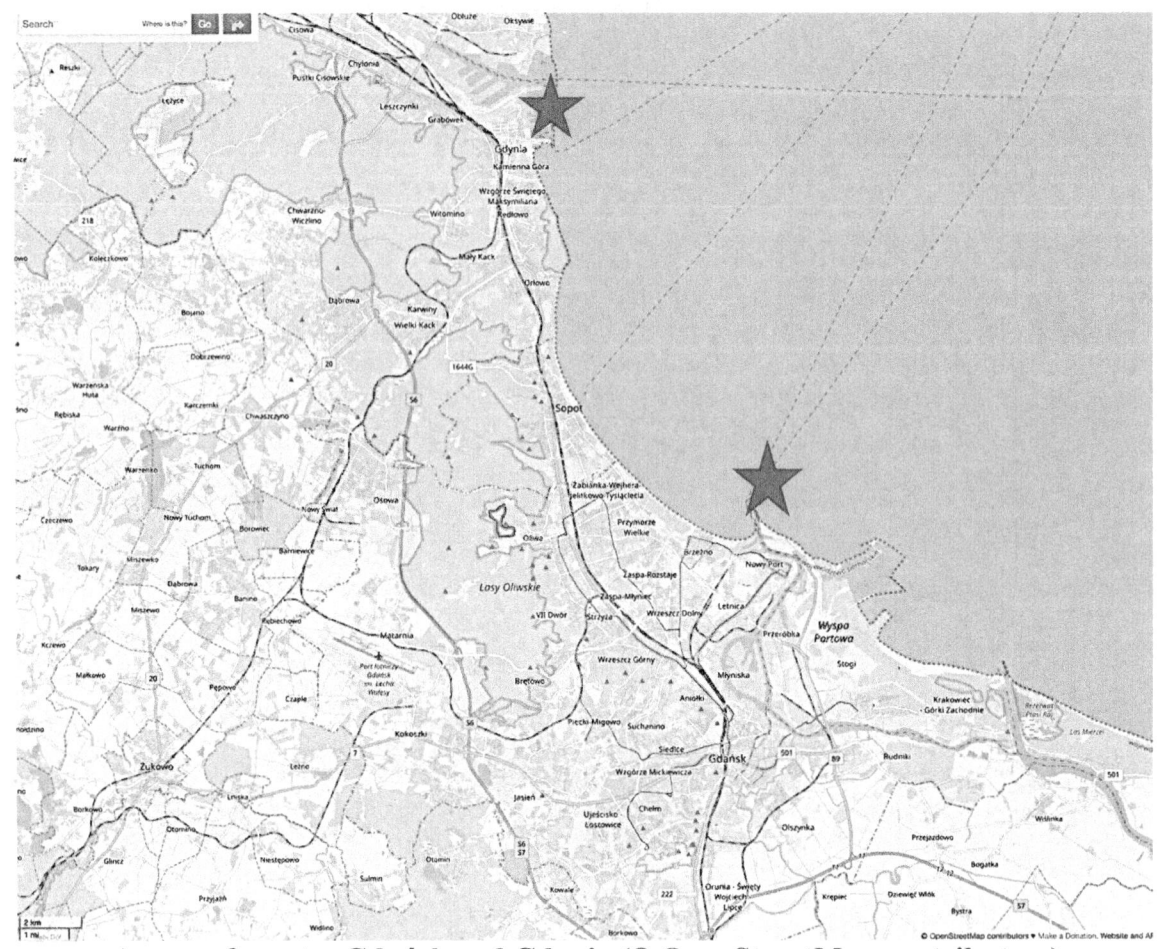

A map of greater Gdańsk and Gdynia (© OpenStreetMap contributors)

The coast of Poland is home to one of the larger Baltic Sea urban centers - the city of Gdańsk. It is today the center of a metropolitan region of over 1,000,000 people and a major industrial center as well as the most important port for Poland. Many Baltic Sea itineraries include Gdańsk, with the large mega cruise ships docking in Gdynia, as it has better facilities to accommodate them while the smaller cruise liners can dock in the main harbor of Gdańsk. Gdynia is part of the overall metropolitan region of Gdańsk, but it is about 45 minutes by motor coach or automobile from the old heart of Gdańsk, making it a bit less convenient for guests since Gdańsk is the major attraction.

THE NATURAL SETTING: Poland is one of the largest and most important nations to share its coastline with the Baltic Sea. But despite the economic and political significance of modern-day Poland, the country's history has been one of here today, gone tomorrow. Throughout the history of Europe, Poland has appeared on the map for a period of time, only to later be carved up by its more aggressive neighbors, Germany to the west, the former Austro-Hungarian Empire to the south and the Russian Empire to the east. But in spite of its absorption into its giant neighbors, the

Polish spirit and culture have lived on, a tribute to the will of her people. There is an old expression among the Polish people that is very meaningful - "There will always be a Poland!"

The beautiful northern Polish countryside with a faint touch of autumn color

Poland occupies 312,601 square kilometers or 120,696 square miles, approximately the size of the American state of New Mexico. Its shape is roughly oval. From the Baltic Sea on the north, Poland stretches south to the margins of the Carpathian Mountains where it shares a border with the Czech Republic and Slovakia. To the east and west, the borders are open, as most of Poland is flat to gently rolling land. Thus its history of invasions from both east and west is one that gave the Polish people little comfort. The land has exceptionally good fertility, as it is part of the North European Plain, a region of glacial till not unlike the country around the North American Great Lakes. Many rivers drain out of the Carpathian Mountains, all flowing north. The Odra River forms the border with Germany while the Vistula drains through the heart of the country. The capital city of Warsaw is located on the Vistula, and Gdańsk is situated adjacent to its delta.

The natural vegetation cover is one of beautiful broadleaf forests, but to the south there are evergreen woodlands, as the land rises into the Carpathian Mountains. Essentially Poland is lush, green and very attractive. It is also quite productive despite the moderately cold winters. Poland has always been able to feed itself, and today that is important with a population of nearly 40,000,000 people. The country has also been blessed with a variety of minerals and deposits of coal in the southwest, thus giving rise to heavy industry and manufacturing. Essentially Poland is both an agricultural and industrial giant among European nations.

Being farther south than the Scandinavian countries, Poland has longer and warmer summers, adding to the productivity of its agriculture. One might expect the winters to be milder, but being farther inland from the moderating influence of the Atlantic Ocean, Poland's winters have been historically long and cold with heavy quantities of snowfall. Today they are slightly more moderate, as is true for much of northern Europe with the impact of climatic change.

A BRIEF LOCAL HISTORY: The Polish people have a great spirit in spite of the many hardships the nation has endured as a result of outside invasion and occupation. But unlike the more somber Russian personality, Polish people have a decidedly more cheerful outlook. The people are outgoing, gregarious and welcoming. This is also a very religious nation, with 95 percent of the population being rather devout Roman Catholic. The late Pope John Paul II came from southern Poland, a source of pride to the citizens of the country even now after his passing. Prior to World War II, Poland also had the largest Jewish population in Europe, but as a result of the Holocaust, that population has been reduced to a mere handful, primarily in the cities of Warsaw and Kraków.

Numerous historic castles dot the Polish countryside

It is important to understand the essentials of Polish history, because the city of Gdańsk has played a pivotal role in the 20th century drama of Poland's independence and that of the rest of the former Soviet bloc of nations formed after World War II. You will be visiting a city that has gone from a German to a Polish persona in less than the last 100 years. But today it is decidedly Polish.

The people of Poland are of Slavic origin, related closely to the Russians, but descendants of western tribes that settled the region around the 6th century. History shows a Polish Principality having been established in 966, turning into the Polish Kingdom in 1024. There is a period of disunity when Poland broke into small principalities from 1138 until it was reunited into one kingdom in 1320. Poland and Lithuania were united in 1569 and their combined power spread as far south as the Black Sea, but between 1772 and 1792. Prussia, Austria and Russia ultimately carved up the united commonwealth, taking both countries off of the map.

During the Napoleonic Wars, the French used Polish soil as a staging ground for their invasion of Russia. The Duchy of Warsaw was established in 1807, essentially as a puppet state to France. But in the Treaty of Vienna in 1815, the Russian held portions of Poland became the Polish Kingdom, but subordinate to the Russian Tsar. Southern Poland, known as Galicia remained within the Austro-Hungarian Empire, but Kraków held on to its status as an independent republic until 1848. The western part of what is modern Poland remained a part of the Prussian Kingdom, which later became Germany.

During World War I, Poland was occupied by German troops, but in 1918, after the collapse of the German war machine, and with Russia in turmoil, Poland declared itself an independent republic. However, that status would not last for very long, and that has been the fate of Poland since its first inception. But it is important to note that despite the changes in political domination, the Polish people have culturally and spiritually always been one. Remember that saying that translates to, "There will always be a Poland!" The critical issues in the Treaty of Versailles, which ended World War I, were how to draw the borders of Germany and East Prussia, hopefully giving Poland more access to the Baltic Sea. Poland received more territory to the west at the expense of Germany, but in the east, most of East Prussia went to the Russians, and the southeastern border with the Ukraine (then a part of Russia) was not drawn favorably to the Poles. In 1920, the Poles united with rebellious Ukrainians in attempting to wrest that region away from Russia while she was engaged in her civil war. The Russians were defeated and in the Treaty of Riga in 1921, Poland was able to annex more territory along its eastern frontier.

Gdańsk, which had long been a part of Prussia and known as Danzig, was designated as a free city administered by the League of Nations but with its external affairs handled by Poland. A Polish military garrison was established and Poland was guaranteed free use of the harbor since the nation had essentially been landlocked. A small corridor of land had been given directly to Poland, cutting off Eastern Prussia physically from Germany. Here the Poles created their own port city of Gdynia, which today is part of the greater Gdańsk region. By 1933, the Nazi Party had gained control of the city administration since a majority of the residents were German and supported the new regime in Germany. And they agitated to have the city returned to German control.

In early 1939, Germany and the Soviet Union negotiated the Ribbentrop-Molotov non-aggression pact in which both powers secretly agreed to divide Poland between them. On September 1, 1939, German gunboats opened fire on the port of Gdańsk, which was nominally controlled by Poland under false pretext that Polish border guards had fired into Germany the day before. Germany also had contended that free access through the Polish Corridor to Gdańsk was vital to the maintenance of East Prussia. World War II essentially began that day, as France and the United Kingdom had pledged to aid Poland in the event of German military action. Thus it can be said that the opening shots of World War II began in Gdańsk and some ship tours will actually take visitors to the exact spot that was fired upon in September 1939.

The first shots of World War II were fired by Nazi forces here in the Gdańsk Shipyards where many cruise ships now dock

The German invasion was swift and brutal, a blitzkrieg type of war that did not enable the Poles to even mount a counter offensive. At the same time, the Red Army advanced from the east. The Polish government fled to Paris and later to London while an underground resistance movement attempted to work from within. In the spring of 1941, Germany advanced across the rest of Poland and began its full invasion of Russia, which then put all of Poland under Nazi control.

The war was brutal for Poland. The Germans had considered the Poles along with the Russians as "unter menschen," meaning second class or sub human. As for the Jews and Gypsies, they were not even considered worthy of survival. Massive roundups took place, first herding them into ghetto areas, and ultimately into extermination camps. Among the more than 6,000,000 Jews eliminated by the Nazi, more than half were Polish. Some of the most notorious concentration camps such as Auschwitz and Treblinka were located on Polish soil. Today only about 10,000 Jews remain in Poland, primarily in the two major cities of Warsaw and Kraków. But today among Poles there is a strong identification with Jewish culture. Each year in Warsaw there is a Jewish music festival but the vast majority of participants and attendees are non-Jews.

During the war, over 400,000 Poles fought with the Red Army and an estimated 200,000 fought with western forces. However, when German forces announced in 1943 that they found mass graves of murdered Polish military officers, the Soviet Union broke off relations with the Polish government in exile. One year later, the Red Army marched into Poland on its way to Berlin. This spelled the end of Polish freedom, as the Soviets install a puppet Communist government that for decades would answer to Moscow.

Monument to the fallen in World War II in Gdańsk at the mouth of the harbor

The war saw the death of more than 6,000,000 Poles, including the 3,000,000 Jews plus another 2,500,000 Poles deported to Germany as slave labor. Many of those deported never lived to return to Poland. Of all the countries that suffered during World War II, for its size and population, Poland suffered the most. And then it lost its freedom, as it became a satellite of the Soviet Union. But all during the Cold War period, the Catholic Church defied the Polish Communist government, keeping the faith alive. When Pope John Paul II was elected in 1979, it was a strong message for Communism, and he did his utmost to keep that message of hope alive. The Pope worked tirelessly to keep the

Communist government in check and this enabled the practice of religion to a greater degree than in other satellite countries.

The war also brought changes to the map, as Poland was essentially pushed westward by almost 160 kilometers or 100 miles. The Poles lost territory in the east, but the Odra River became its western border, putting Poland's western frontier within only 120 kilometers or 75 miles of Berlin. The Germans living in this corridor were forced to flee, as Poles were given farms and villages at the expense of their former German residents. Where once Gdańsk sat close to the border of Germany and East Prussia on both sides, Poland now ended up with an extensive coastline on the Baltic Sea, placing Gdańsk somewhere in the middle. The land that is now Poland was previously part of Germany. Many older Germans still feel a degree of resentment toward Poland for the loss of the territory.

The Polish people never fully supported the Communist Party, and there were periods of violence when workers went on strike, and of course the Church gave tacit support. The government could not crush worker strikes because of the power of the Church, as was done in other Eastern bloc nations. In 1980, shipyard workers in Gdańsk went on strike and this was the start of the Solidarity labor movement. The strength of the worker's movement led by Lech Walesa caused the government to declare martial law, and it was careful not to ask the Soviet Union for troops. Most of Solidarity's leaders were arrested, but by 1985, they were released because the government saw that the movement would not die. In 1988 the government recognized Solidarity and one year later, the Communist dominated government agreed to allow one third of the seats in the Polish congress to be open to non-Communist parties. Solidarity won nearly all of those seats. The military leader of Poland, General Jaruzelski, allowed the labor union leaders to form a government, the first led by non-Communists in 40 years. By 1990, Communism was dead in Poland, and Lech Walesa became the first popularly elected president since before World War II.

Poland has been one of the leading nations of the former East European bloc to become an integral part of western economics and politics. The country has been very successful, and it has thrown open its doors to visitors and the several million Poles who had immigrated over the decades prior to the war. There is a free exchange of ideas and commerce both, making Poland a very modern nation. The final capstone was when Poland joined the European Union and NATO. But like the United Kingdom, Denmark and Sweden, it has chosen not to use the Euro, remaining with its own national currency.

A BRIEF CITY HISTORY: The city of Gdańsk is a very historic and important Polish city. It dates to the 10th century. Its history during the medieval period is one of contest between local knights and the Polish crown, but in the mid 14th century, it became a part of the prosperous Hanseatic League. By the start of the 15th century, the city was under the control of the Polish king, however, the history of Poland has been one that has been closely tied to that of Prussia, and for long periods the country was ruled by the Germanic crown rather than its own. During the years of the renaissance,

Gdańsk became a rich and important trading port, and this period is often seen as its golden age. There was much ethnic mixing as Germans, Poles, Jews and Dutch people mingled in its streets and markets. By 1772, Gdańsk had declined, as Poland was partitioned between the German, Austro-Hungarian and Russian empires and Gdańsk became a part of Prussia, and ultimately part of the united German Empire in 1871. Other German ports such as Rostock and Hamburg overshadowed its importance.

A view of Old Town Gdańsk from the Green Bridge

Throughout so much of the city's later history, it was known as Danzig – the Germanic name that some people still use in reference to the port. It was only after World War I that Poland was allowed a narrow corridor to the Baltic and the city of Danzig was put under nominal authority of the League of Nations with Poland controlling its external affairs. And the Poles renamed it Gdańsk.

During the interim between the two world wars, Poland emerged as an independent nation, and Gdańsk uneasily became a major seaport along with Gdynia. It was here that German gunboats opened fire upon the port on September 1, 1939, thus igniting World War II. And as noted above, it was Poland that was totally overrun by both German and Russian forces over the next six years. The country paid a terrible price in blood and destruction of its infrastructure. Since Polish liberation from Germany, and with a readjustment of the borders, Gdańsk again became a major center for trade as well as for shipbuilding. It also then became a thorn in the side of the Communist authorities, as it was here that Solidarity began its agitation for a free Poland.

Because of its long association with the Hanseatic League, and its importance as a seaport, Gdańsk is a city richly endowed with great historic attractions. It has become one of the most popular tourist sites for those who cruise the Baltic Sea as well as among visitors who tour the major cities of Poland. Most of the important sites are located within the Old Town, which is much larger and more impressive than that of any other city in the eastern Baltic Sea region. And it is especially important when one considers that it was nearly all destroyed during World War II, yet lovingly and faithfully rebuilt after the war. Old photographs taken at the end of the war show the Old Town as simply a mass of rubble with a few crumbling walls. Yet it was restored faithfully and is a testament to great Polish pride.

The destruction of Gdańsk in World War II shown on a plaque

I strongly urge everyone who will be visiting Gdańsk by cruise ship to sign up for one of the ship's walking tours of the Old Town. This is the best way to learn about the city through seeing its dedicated monumental buildings. Yes you can walk the Old Town on your own, but you will miss so much of the fascinating history that can only be related by one of the many guides.

THE PHYSICAL LAYOUT OF THE CITY OF GDAŃSK: Gdańsk and its neighboring port of Gdynia represent Poland's window on the Baltic. Today it is the fourth largest urban complex in Poland with a metropolitan population of just over 1,000,000 people. It is Poland's gateway to the world with regard to maritime pursuits, thus making it a major seaport city. Gdańsk Bay serves as the outlet for the Motlawa River, but the upper end of the river is connected ultimately to the Vistula so that barge traffic can carry goods from Warsaw to the coast. Thus it is the major port city for

Warsaw, which is about 383 kilometers or 240 miles to the south of Gdańsk.

Gdańsk is quite a large city physically, as its suburbs do spread outward into the surrounding countryside. Between Gdańsk and Gdynia, a distance of 22 kilometers or 14 miles there is a string of suburban communities with the resort town of Sopot situated in the middle. These suburbs are not totally contiguous, and some are dominated over by large apartment blocks some of which date to the Communist Era mixed with small single-family homes.

Most of Gdańsk is quite modern, as seen here in the commercial center

The heart of Gdańsk lies along the Moltawa River with the historic Old Town right at its center. Although there is no actual wall around Old Town, its historic architecture dating back to the Hanseatic League is markedly different from the more modern structures beyond. And there are two dramatic old gates that do mark each end of the elegant Long Street that runs through the historic district. Despite its apparent antiquity, every bit of it was lovingly and carefully rebuilt after it was heavily bombed into rubble during World War II, not by its liberators but rather at the time it fell to Nazi forces in 1939. Remember it was here that the first battle of World War II was fought.

Few visitors ever leave the historic Old Town, as this is the main attraction of Gdańsk. The new city center is located just to the north of the historic center and it is a mix of Communist Era buildings with a handful of modern high-rises. Given the population of Gdańsk, it is not what one would expect because the suburban sprawl of the city has come with localized shopping districts and malls.

The main railroad lines all converge from north, south and east into a massive band of track that separates the Old Town and new city center from the spreading suburbs to the south and west. There is a very grand railway station built in the 19th century, but looking much older with its grand brick and stone facade.

The extensive port area lies to the northeast of the Old Town along the mouth of the Moltawa River. The Moltawa is actually a distributary of the Vistula River, which drains north from southern Poland, passing through the capital city of Warsaw. The geographic term distributary means that it is a branch of the lower end of a river that helps to drain the main river out to the sea or whatever larger body of water is the final destination. The harbor is very extensive and contains the shipyards that provide a great source of income for the city. And it was in the main shipyard that the Solidarity movement began the liberation of Poland from Communism.

The rival port for Gdańsk is the suburban city of Gdynia, located about 22 kilometers or 14 miles north along the coastline. The Polish government has spent a lot of money in building the infrastructure for the port, which is exceptionally modern and efficient. Prior to World War I, Gdynia was Poland's only window on the Baltic Sea while Gdańsk, still called Danzig, was a free trade port under the auspices of the League of Nations, yet claimed by Germany as theirs, and heavily populated with Germans. The narrow strip of land around Gdynia was often referred to as the Polish Corridor, and Germany was not pleased with the arrangement. Thus it was understandable that when the Nazi government decided upon an invasion, Gdańsk would be the first target, the opening salvo of the war on September 1, 1939 in the harbor of Gdańsk.

Like Gdańsk, Gdynia is also an old city, dating back to 1253 as an ancient fishing village. By the late 19th century, the city was a popular tourist spot with small guesthouses and cafes along its waterfront. The initial development of the seaport began in 1920, but the predominantly German residents of Gdańsk were hostile to the Polish authorities being so close to their territory. The Germans occupied the port of Gdynia in September 1939, as Nazi forces advanced across Poland. It became an important German naval base, and its shipyard served the Third Reich. There was once a concentration camp located just outside of Gdańsk, but it never developed an infamous reputation.

When the German withdrew in the face of the allied advance, they destroyed much of the port facilities in both Gdańsk and Gdynia. The Soviet Union saw to it that the borders of Poland were re adjusted to give the country an expanded window to the Baltic, thus making Gdynia and its larger neighbor Gdańsk a major economic and port center.

The modern city itself began to develop after the port was established, and by 1938, Gdynia was the most modern seaport on the Baltic Sea. Gdynia is still heavily industrialized and its architecture still reflects a strong measure of Communist Era development. For those whose ships dock in Gdynia, you will get an opportunity to see the size and scope of greater Gdańsk while traveling from the ship to the Old Town.

There is massive suburban sprawl between Gdańsk and Gdynia seen here from the sea

CRUISE SHIP DOCKS: The large cruise ships visiting Gdańsk find it necessary to dock in Gdynia, as its port facilities are larger and easier for ships to navigate. In the Gdańsk harbor the main channel is relatively narrow and a large cruise ship would not be able to turn around after entering without the aid of tugs and even then it would be quite difficult. The Gdańsk harbor is more oriented toward the shipbuilding activities than trade while the Gdynia harbor is the main commercial port.

Small to medium cruise ships, mainly those of the more upmarket cruise lines are able to enter the Gdańsk harbor, sail well into the channel and then turn around and dock very near the entry point, under the hill that contains the impressive World War II memorial. There is no terminal, but the dock is capable of serving the need of tour coaches, taxis and private cars. It is approximately a 15 minute drive to the edge of the Old City.

In Gdynia there are large docks capable of mooring the largest cruise ships, and again there is no cruise terminal facility. But as in Gdańsk there is plenty of room for tour coaches, taxis and private cars. Gdynia offers nothing of interest for the visitor, thus it is imperative to plan a tour into Gdańsk or be prepared for a long day with essentially nothing to do. The main downtown of Gdynia is nice, but is not oriented toward providing for visitor needs other than basic services. The drive into Gdańsk will take approximately 45 minutes. It is also possible to travel into the city by commuter rail, but from the dock it is not easy to access the station without first taking a taxi.

TOURING GREATER GDAŃSK: The large mega size cruise ships will dock in Gdynia, which means approximately a 45 minute motor coach or automobile ride to the Old Town of Gdańsk, which is the focus of tourism.

You will only see Gdynia if you are on board one of the large cruise ships, as this is where your ship will dock. But there is absolutely nothing in the city that is of interest to the average visitor. And the more upmarket cruise lines will offer shuttle bus service to the Old Town area of Gdańsk for those guests who are not going on group tours that would be leaving from the docks in Gdynia.

For those of you cruising on a smaller upmarket ship, you will dock just inside the entrance to the massive harbor and shipbuilding yards in Gdańsk, which is only a 15 minute motor coach or automobile ride to the historic Old Town. You will actually dock in the shadow of the World War II War Memorial. The distance is not walkable, so if you are not going on a group tour, you will need to take a shuttle bus, which the upmarket cruise lines all provide.

* SIGHTSEEING OPTIONS FOR GDAŃSK: Once in Gdańsk, there are numerous ways to get around and see all the sights. However, I must reiterate that the majority of what visitors come to see is in the relatively compact Old Town. The ways to see greater Gdańsk are:

** **Ship sponsored tours** – These can be either by coach or on foot. Most of the Old Town can only be seen on foot. But many tours include the Solidarity Shipyards, the historic old religious site in Oliwa and the resort community of Sopot. These are generally full day tours and most will include lunch.

** **Private car and driver** – If you wish to have the privacy and freedom of your own car and driver, the cruise line can arrange that for you, but at a relatively steep cost.

To arrange for a private car and driver/guide on your own you can contact:

*** SIXT My Driver at *www.mydriver.com* for further information, rates and booking.

***You may also wish to try Blacklane, one of Europe's largest sources for chauffeur driven cars. Their web page is *www.blacklane.com/chauffeur-service-Gdansk.*

*** You should also look at Greetings from Poland for localized service at *www.greetingsfrompoland.com* and follow the links to driver/guide services.

** **Rental cars** – I do not recommend attempting to rent a car in Gdańsk, as most of what you want to see is in the older historic district that is mainly pedestrian oriented.

And parking is very, very difficult to find. Also remember most rental vehicles do not have automatic transmission. And all traffic signs are written in Polish only.

** **Hop on hop off bus** service exists in Gdańsk. If your cruise ship docks in Gdynia, you will need to take a ship shuttle bus into Gdańsk to board the hop on hop off bus. For ships docking in Gdańsk harbor you will still need to take a ship sponsored shuttle into the Old Town, but that is a short ride taking a few minutes. The two routes (blue and red) begin and end their service at the Railway Station, which is a short distance to the northwest beyond the Old Town. The best information is at City Tour Gdańsk which is to be found at www.sightseeinggdansk.com and click on the British flag for English. .For further information you can also contact www.visitgdansk.com for information, rates and booking.

** **Taxis** – If your ship docks in Gdańsk you will find taxis waiting on the dock. And many post their rates for sightseeing, quoted in Euro. And many of the drivers speak English and are good guides. If your ship docks in Gdynia there will be taxi service to the main railway station in Gdańsk, but it is doubtful you will find a driver who will wish to spend a whole day taking you sightseeing in Gdańsk. So it is best to take the ship shuttle into the Old Town area of Gdańsk and then attempt to arrange for touring with a taxi.

** **Commuter train** service between Gdynia and Gdańsk runs every half hour, and the walk to the railway station is short on both ends. There are two different rail systems. You want the fast InterCity train, so look for the route to Gdańsk Glówny, which will take about 25 minutes each way. The local train makes many stops and you will have less time to spend in Gdańsk.

** **Ship shuttle** – Many choose to simply take the ship shuttle from the dock into the Old Town and walk if they are on a ship docking in Gdańsk. It is a very enjoyable way to see Gdańsk. You can walk from the Old Town into the modern city center, which is immediately to the north, between the railway tracks and the river. And you will find public washroom facilities and plenty of restaurants and cafes in the Old Town area to make for a pleasant day.

* **MAJOR SIGHTS TO SEE IN GDAŃSK**: There is much to see in Gdańsk, most of the venues in the Old Town. Among the many sites that make greater Gdańsk popular are (shown in alphabetical order):

* **Gdańsk War Memorial** - This absolutely moving memorial is built on a slight hill overlooking the entrance to the Gdańsk Harbor. Like all war memorials in Eastern Europe, this one is very poignant and evokes both a sadness and respect for the Polish people. If you are cruising on one of the small up market lines, your ship will dock adjacent to the memorial.

If you are visiting off one of the mega ships, you will have to check and see if the memorial is part of any of the tours, otherwise it can only be reached by means of a private car, taxi or local tour. This memorial is generally included on any Westerplatte tour. If your ship docks in Gdańsk it will be tied op opposite the war memorial, however, because of the fences, it is a fair walk to get into the memorial on your own, but you can obtain excellent views from the ship's upper decks.

The Golden Gate

** **Golden Gate** - The arched entrance to the Old Town from the landward side, it is not as large as the Green Gate, but it is still a dynamic structure. It offers a dramatic entry into the Old Town and by itself, it is a magnificent piece of Hanseatic architecture having been built between 1642 and 1644, capable of being viewed 24-hours per day. During World War II it was destroyed and then faithfully rebuilt following the war, as of course the entire Old Town was rebuilt.

** **Green Gate** - This arched building stands as the gateway to the Old Town when coming from the riverside. It was once an aristocratic residence, but today it is the primary entry into the Old Town. If you are on one of the smaller, upmarket cruise ships docking in Gdańsk, your shuttle bus will drop you off right at the walkway in through the Green Gate.

You can tour the former residence Tuesday thru Saturday from 10 AM to 5 PM or simply enjoy its magnificent façade and walk through its passage onto the Long Street. The Green Gate is older than the Golden Gate, having been built between 1564 and 1571. It was also destroyed by bombing during World War II and was faithfully rebuilt.

The Green Gate

Strolling the Long Street

** Long Street and Long Market – This is the most beautiful sight in Gdańsk, starting at the Golden Gate and ending at the Green Gate. This was once home to the richest residences in Gdańsk, many of the buildings dating back to medieval times. The architecture is one in which there are narrow facades and steep gables and parapets atop each building. The Long Street is the main feature of any guided walking tour of Old Town. Keep in mind that at the end of World War II the Old Town of Gdansk was destroyed and what you see now has all been faithfully and lovingly been reconstructed.

** National Maritime Museum - The museum consists of three distinct parts, the main museum, the granary and the crane. It details the importance of Gdańsk as a major port in the 18th and 19th centuries. The museum can be reached on foot from the Old Town by walking along the Moltawa River to Tokarska 21/25. The museum is open from 10 AM to 7 PM daily thru August, then from 10 AM to 4 PM Tuesday thru Friday and from 10 AM to 6 PM on weekends thru November.

The famous Neptune Fountain

** Neptune Fountain – Located in the heart of the city, this fountain was cast in 1615 and symbolizes the city's bond with the sea. The fountain stands in front of the Town Hall and is a main feature of the Long Street.

** Oliwa Cathedral – A magnificent cathedral dating to the 13th century, originally built in Gothic style, but later rebuilt with baroque design after being destroyed by a major fire. This is one of the most magnificent of cathedrals in Poland. It is located about 6 miles from the city center in the small suburban town of Oliwa, and is often visited by tours offered by the major cruise lines when the motor coach is in transit from Gdynia to Gdansk.

If you are not on a tour, you may reach the cathedral by taxi, as Oliwa is a well-recognized destination. The cathedral is open from 9 AM to 5 PM weekdays, 9 AM to 3:30 PM Saturday and 2 to 5:30 PM Sunday. No visitors are permitted during mass.

** **Saint Mary's Cathedral**, one of the city's old cathedrals reflecting the impact of the Roman Catholic faith upon Polish culture. It was built over the period of 1343 to 1542 and is the world's largest brick Gothic church. The cathedral in Uppsala, Sweden is second in size. Brick was generally not considered as a prime building material for cathedrals in the Gothic Era, but in the absence of the right type of stone, these are two unusual examples.

The church dominates the skyline of the Old Town and you will have no difficulty in finding it if you choose to visit on your own. There are many tours offered by the various cruise lines where much of the sightseeing is done on foot, and the Saint Mary's Cathedral in the Old Town is always included. The church is open to visitors from 9 AM to 8:30 PM daily.

Saint Mary's Cathedral towers over Ulitza Mariacki

** **Sopot** - The town of Sopot located between Gdańsk and Gdynia is a very important part of the combined urban region. This is the Baltic Sea playground for all of Poland, having many hotels, spas and broad sandy beaches. Some cruise lines offer a half-day tour to Sopot, but I do not recommend it because you miss so much of the history and architectural beauty of the city itself. Only visit Sopot if you want to enjoy a beach resort and if you have been to Gdańsk before.

** Ulitza Mariacki – Saint Mary's Street is one of the most beautiful streets in the city, lined with many old houses that possess a rich architectural heritage, some dating to the Hanseatic League, and all beautifully restored after the end of World War II. Again this street will also be featured in any guided walking tour.

** Westerplatte – This is the most important site in Gdańsk when it comes to contemporary history. It was on this narrow peninsula in Gdańsk Bay that German naval guns fired upon the city on the morning of September 1, 1939, supposedly in response to what the Nazi government claimed were Polish border incursions into Germany. As a result of this action, World War II officially began. There is really not a lot to see here, but it is very poignant to stand on the spot where the opening salvo of World War II was fired. You can only reach Westerplatte either on a tour, private excursion with your own car and driver/guide or taxi. There are several small private tour operators in Gdańsk but it is too far from where the ship's shuttle bus will drop off guests for guests to be dropped off.

The small museum is open from 10 AM thru 4 PM daily until October. The outdoor exhibit on the spot where World War II began is open during daylight hours as is the great World War II memorial.

CUISINE OF GDAŃSK AND DINING OUT: Despite its long association with Germany and the large number of German people who lived in Gdańsk, its cultural heritage is now very much Polish. And as a part of that heritage, food plays a major role. Polish cooking is rich in its diversity, elegant in its presentation and also includes some of the best-baked goods you will find anywhere in Europe. Many types of soup are popular in Poland. Borsch is similar to that of Russia, yet it has a definite Polish twist. And Zhurkek is considered a national soup, made with milk, fermented rye, carrots and spicy sausage. Rolled cabbage stuffed with pork or chicken and rice is cooked in a savory broth that has a both sweet and sour taste. There are also small stuffed pastry dumplings known as pirogue, which can be filled with meat, potato or cheese and covered with onions sautéed in butter or with fresh sour cream. Rich and savory sausages are served with cabbage and noodles as another popular dish. And to top off the meal, there are delicate strudels stuffed with apple, cherry or poppy seed and raisin that just melt in the mouth. All are a part of Polish cuisine, which though similar to Russian, has a greater degree of finesse. Every visitor should sample the cuisine and is sure to enjoy the flavors of Poland.

Gdańsk is filled with restaurants because of the number of visitors who come to the Old Town. There are dozens of restaurants lining the Long Street and also along the waterfront. As usual, I have my favorites, and they are based upon my combined Polish and Russian heritage. The best restaurants in Gdańsk that are truly Polish are to be found outside of the Old Town in various residential districts of the city. But these are impossible to get to without either knowledge of the language or the services of a car and driver/guide. The restaurants inside the Old Town definitely cater to tourists and the majority does not expect return guests.

The charm of a traditional Polish restaurant

Of the restaurants in Old Town that I have tried, there are only a handful I feel comfortable recommending:

* Barylka - Located along the Moltawa Embankment and open for lunch and dinner, Barylka pays careful attention to presenting traditional Polish cuisine in an atmosphere that is both sophisticated, yet has the feel of a country inn. Their menu is complete and offers all of the traditional dishes I noted above. They do not have an extensive dessert menu, but by the time you are finished with the meal, you will not have much room. They are open for lunch and dinner daily, serving daily from 10 AM to 11 PM. Bookings are not needed.

* Pieroarnia Mandu Centrum – Located at Ulitsa Elzbietanska # 4-8, in the heart of Old Town, this is a must if you have never tried Pierogi, those small dumplings that are to Polish cuisine what fish and chips are to British cuisine. There are so many types of pierogi and they can be boiled, baked or fried. This restaurant is a magnet for those who love the national dish. The food and service are incredible. If you have no preference, I recommend cheese pierogi smothered in sour cream – high in cholesterol, but you are on vacation. They are open daily from 11 AM to 10 PM. Booking a table is not necessary.

* **Pomelo Bistro** – In the heart of Old Town at Ulitsa Ogarna 121-122, this is a very popular and genuine Polish restaurant. Their diverse menu covers quite an array of Polish dishes, all expertly prepared and served in an impeccable manner. Like all Polish dishes, the food is quite hearty and not light if you are watching your diet, but oh so good to the taste. It would be a shame to visit Gdańsk and not try the mouth-watering cuisine. And this is a good choice. They are open daily at 9 AM. Closing times vary from 9 PM Sunday thru Tuesday to 10 PM Wednesday and Thursday and 11 PM Friday and Saturday. Table bookings are not needed.

* **Restauracja Bazar** – Located across the Motlawa River from the Green Gate, at Ulitsa Szafarnia # 6, which is facing the island in the middle of the channel at the north end. Their diverse menu will provide you with a great selection of Polish dishes from which to choose. The cuisine is genuine, well prepared and nicely served. They are open daily from 1 PM to 10 PM Monday thru Thursday and from Noon to 10 PM Friday thru Sunday. Call ahead to +48 58 354 58 14 to book a table.

SHOPPING: Within Old Town there are dozens of shops and stalls selling a mix of tourist kitsch and local handcrafts. Polish lace, embroidery and dolls are traditional items that can range in price from a few dollars into hundreds depending upon size and quality.

There are also artists who will be selling small to medium size watercolors, but you must be careful to make certain that you are not buying a print, but an original instead.

The most commonly purchased item by visitors is amber jewelry. Once again the old motto of buyer beware applies, as fake amber looks as good as real amber to the untrained eye. It is best to purchase amber in a reputable looking shop and charge your purchase so as to have grounds for entering the amount into a dispute if you later determine that you have been sold something that is not as represented. I personally have no interest in amber. It is nice to look at, but it does not entice me, and thus I have no real opinion as to whether it is a worthwhile purchase. I do know it is relatively rare and that the Baltic Sea region is where most quality amber is to be found.

There are two shopping centers in Gdańsk, but both are outside of Old Town, necessitating a taxi ride or if you have a car and driver/guide you then can reach either or both. One is a traditional marketplace and the second is the largest modern mall in central Gdańsk:

Wonderful bakeries entice you to bring something back to the ship for later

* Galeria Handlowa Madison - This is the largest of the modern shopping malls in the city of Gdańsk, and it is located in the heart of the new central business district at Rajska 10, due north from Hala Targowa about half a mile. This mall contains four floors of shops and cafes, open from 9 AM to 9 PM every day except Sunday when it closes at 2 PM. The shops carry a variety of European and Polish brands at a range of prices to please every budget.

* Hala Targowa - This is the old public market of Gdańsk. It sells a mix of fresh produce, meats, breads and baked goods along with clothing and has a few shops that do sell local handcrafts. But it is a fun place to visit because you will be mingling with locals and seeing how they shop. Surprisingly many guide books do recommend Hala Targowa as a place to at least be seen. It is walking distance from the Long Street in Old Town. Just walk north from Old Town to Plac Dominkański. It is open from 9 AM to 6 PM weekdays, 9 AM to 3 PM Saturday and closed Sunday.

FINAL NOTES: For most people who do not have any Polish heritage, Gdańsk will be your first impression. And it should be a positive one. The city's Old Town has been lovingly rebuilt to the look of medieval and Hanseatic times, a level of authenticity hard to match. Yes it is somewhat commercialized, but there is a definite attempt to present folk dancing, local crafts and good Polish food with an air of graciousness.

If you want to experience a more realistic aspect of life in Gdańsk or of Poland in general, then you need to walk beyond the Golden Gate out into the modern downtown of the city. Here you will be outside the normal tourist area and therefore mingling with Polish people as they go about their everyday lives. You will find that Poland is a modern country, but one where traditional values have not been lost.

A visit to Warsaw, Poland's vibrant capital and largest city is not possible during the normal eight to 10-hour visit of most cruise ships. But many guests on board ship who have a Polish heritage, and those seeking to explore one of the major countries of Eastern Europe will often add onto their holiday by taking a trip to Warsaw or Kraków after their cruise ends.

I have considered adding additional chapters on Warsaw and Kraków to accommodate those guests who may be planning a trip after their Baltic Sea cruise, but it goes beyond the theme of this book, which concentrates on the Baltic Sea. For that matter, I could add a chapter on Moscow since the more high end cruise lines do offer a one day tour by rail or air from Saint Petersburg, but again it goes beyond the theme of the book. However, I do add Berlin in the final chapter because the cruise port call in Warnemunde is specifically designed with the intent of enabling such a visit to Berlin, which is only a maximum of three hours by motor coach and the majority of ship passengers do make the journey.

GDAŃSK MAPS

THE CITY OF GDAŃSK

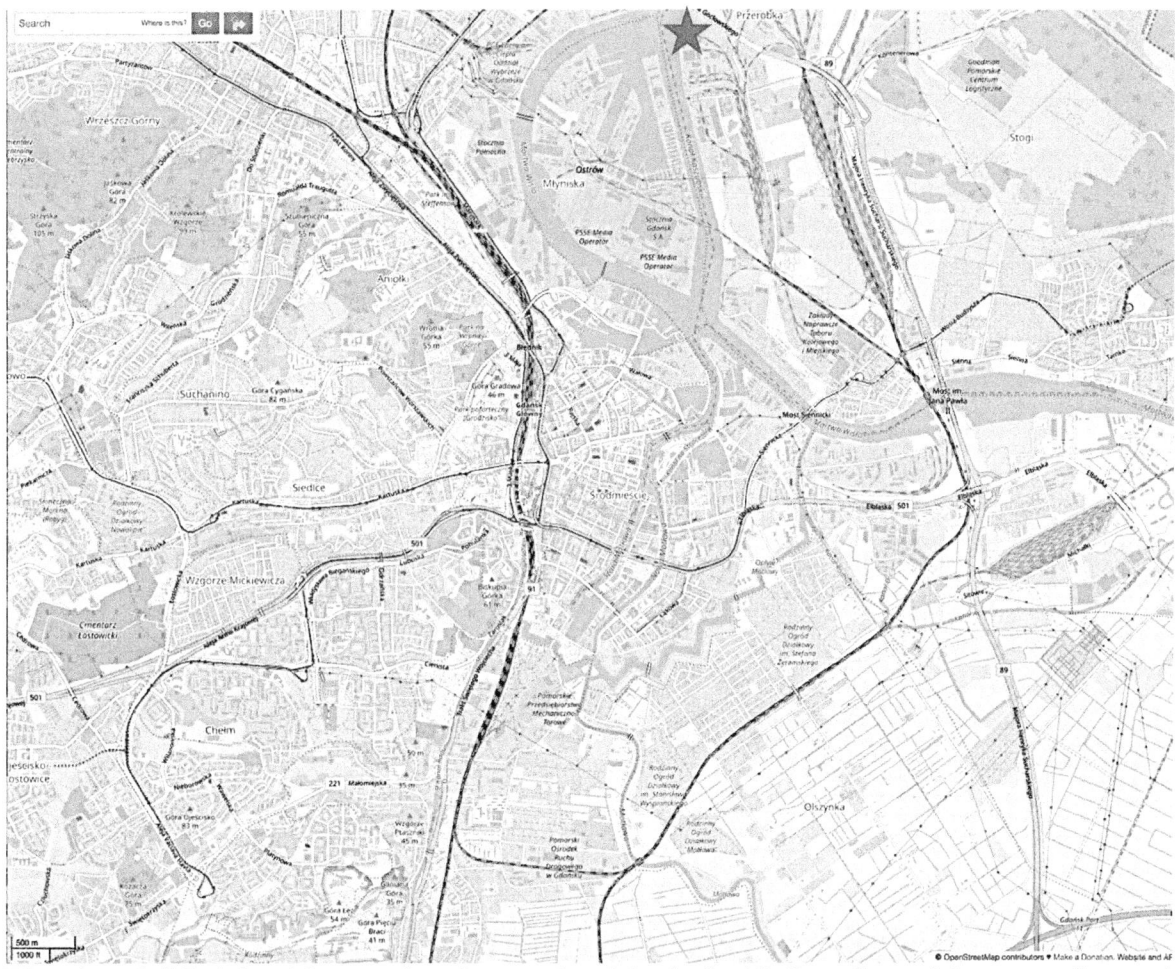

The city of Gdańsk with star showing cruise ship dock, (© OpenStreetMap contributors)

This map is best viewed directly from OpenStreetMap.com on your personal device where it can be expanded or one specific area can be enlarged. Given the format of this book, it is impossible to display maps with the level of detail you might wish to have while actually out exploring the city. But the OpenStreetMap maps used directly are the tool I always rely upon.

OLD GDAŃSK

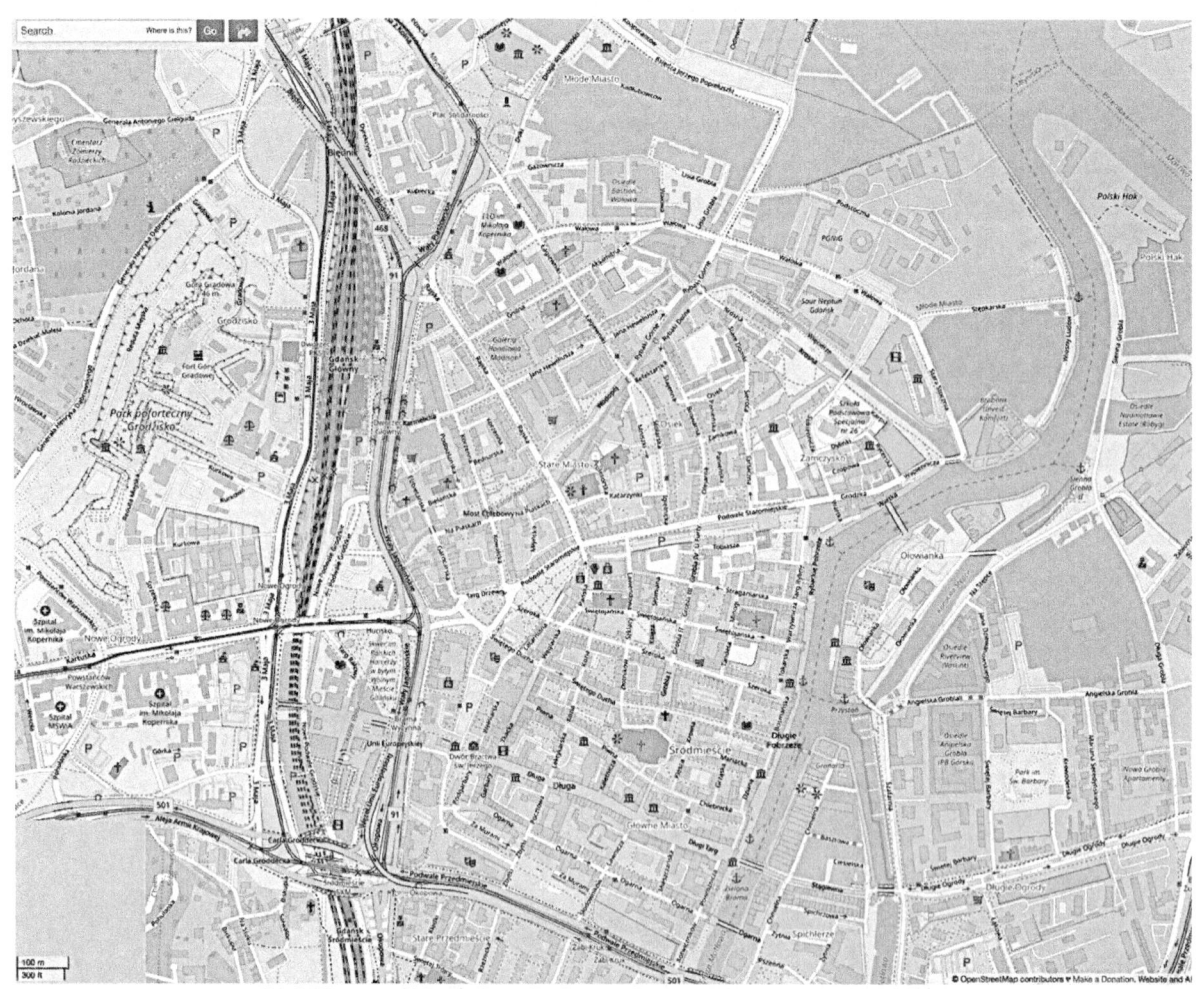

Old Town Gdańsk, (© OpenStreetMap contributors)

This map is best viewed directly from OpenStreetMap.com on your personal device where it can be expanded or one specific area can be enlarged. Given the format of this book, it is impossible to display maps with the level of detail you might wish to have while actually out exploring the city. But the OpenStreetMap maps used directly are the tool I always rely upon.

THE CITY OF GDYNIA

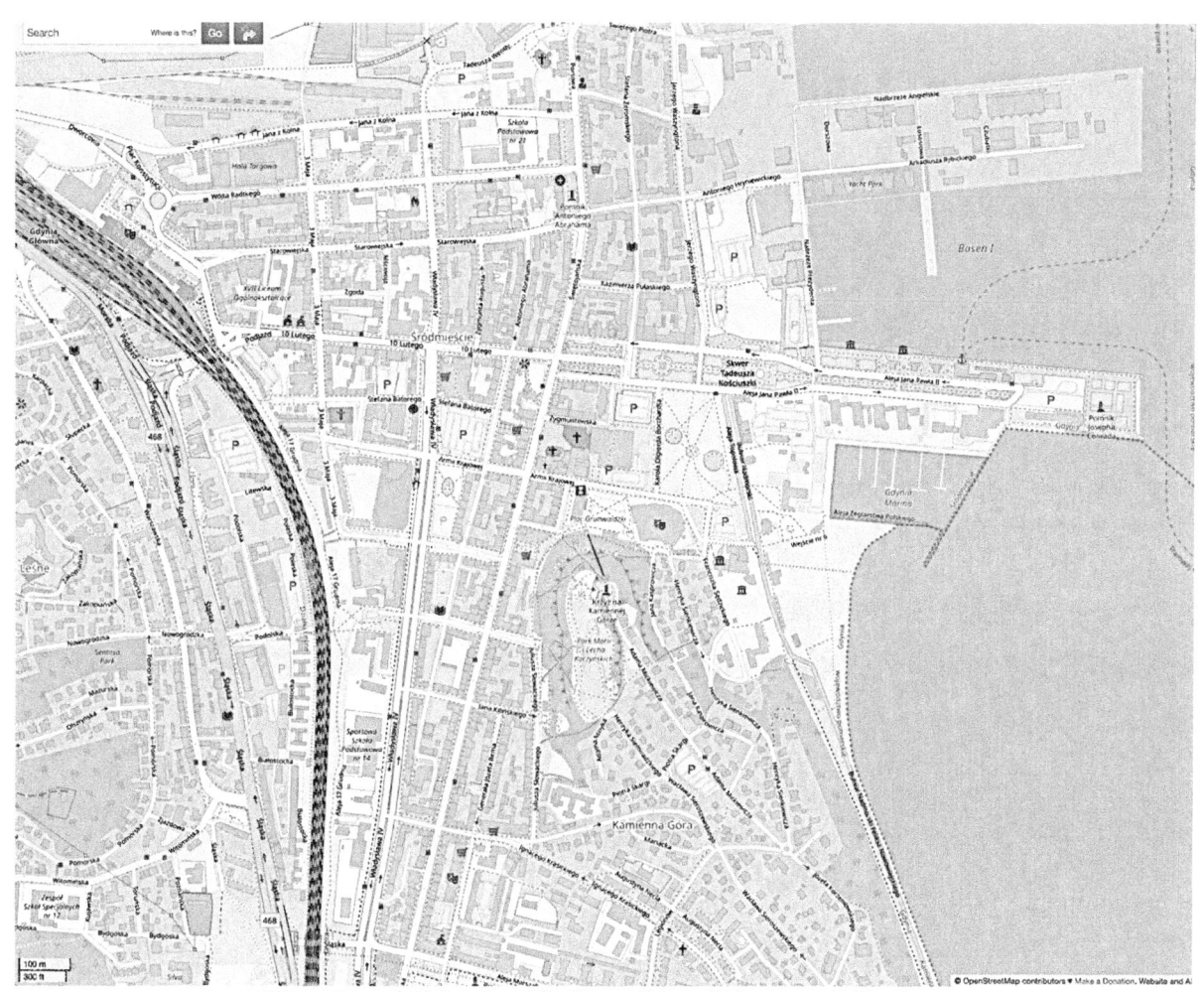

The city of Gdynia, (© OpenStreetMap contributors

This map is best viewed directly from OpenStreetMap.com on your personal device where it can be expanded or one specific area can be enlarged. Given the format of this book, it is impossible to display maps with the level of detail you might wish to have while actually out exploring the city. But the OpenStreetMap maps used directly are the tool I always rely upon.

WARNEMUNDE & BERLIN, GERMANY

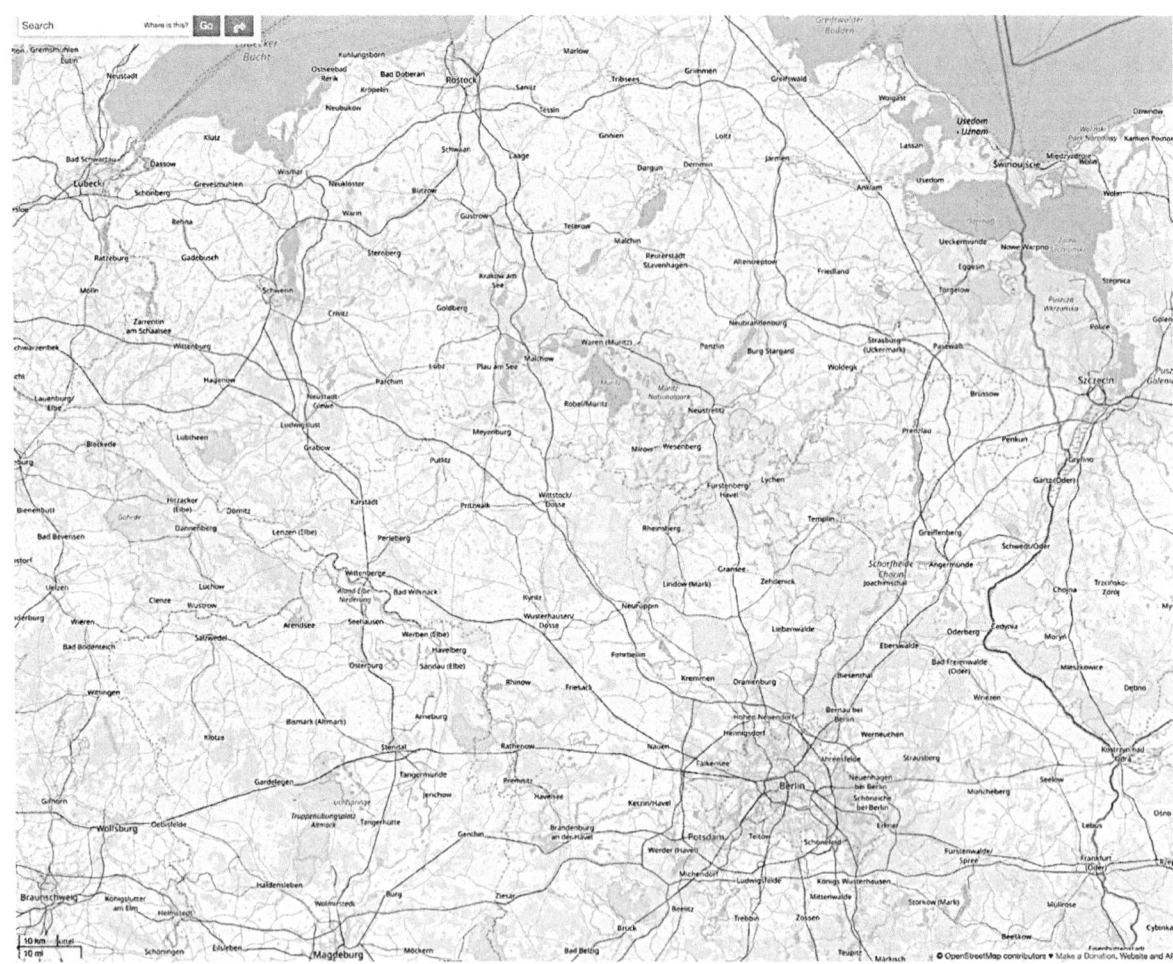

The route between Warnemunde/Rostock and Berlin (© OpenStreetMap contributors)

Warnemunde and its larger neighbor Rostock are the major German seaports that serve the inland capital city of Berlin, one of Europe's truly great cities. Berlin is located 209 kilometers or 130 miles to the south of Warnemunde via the Autobahn, Germany's superb and not to be rivaled system of divided express highways. The Autobahn is the original expressway first built by the Nazi regime back in the 1930's. One needs to be prepared for a fast ride if traffic is light, as in Germany there are few speed limits and drivers travel along principal roads at high speed. Depending upon traffic of the day, a trip into the heart of Berlin should only take an average 90 to 120 minutes.

I do not recommend attempting to rent a car in Warnemunde and drive to Berlin on your own. The Autobahn is no place for a foreign visitor who is not familiar with the rules of the road in Germany nor the customary manners concerning driving, passing or giving way to faster drivers. Frankly, if you are not familiar with driving conditions you place yourself and others in danger of a collision. Please accept my words as valid, as I am very familiar with driving in Germany. You are much safer with an experienced German driver behind the wheel or by utilizing one of the organized tours offered by your cruise line.

THE NATURAL SETTING OF GERMANY: Germany, known as Deutschland, contains 357,022 square kilometers or 137,847 square miles and has a population of over 80,700,000. The reunited country's landmass is about the size of the American state of Montana, slightly larger than Poland. But it is a more densely populated nation containing many major cities. It is the most populous nation in Europe apart from Russia, which of course spans both Europe and Asia. Germany is essentially the powerhouse of Europe, its most prosperous and highly industrialized nation.

On the Autobahn between Warnemunde and Berlin

Part of the German success lies in its land. Southern Germany borders the Alps. This is a beautiful region, known as Bavaria, rich in minerals, timber and a favored tourist destination. From the Alps, the Rhine River flows through the western part of Germany. With its tributaries, the greater Rhine Valley is a fertile region that offers many agricultural riches. Central Germany possesses a mix of forest and farmland in country that is gently rolling. Along the eastern border with the Czech Republic is the famous Black Forest, one of Europe's natural gems. Northern German is part of the North European Plain, that glacial till that gives most of Poland its great fertility. The climates vary from mild and wet in the northwest to cold and snowy in winter along the Polish border to moderately cold and wet in the south, with snow at higher elevations. The key word is wet, meaning that Germany is a luxuriant country. This means that it is highly productive, especially when one adds the German technology and drive to make itself productive. Approximately 30 percent of the country is under cultivation, but given the large population, imports of many foodstuffs are still important. Germany is one of the world's industrialized nations, and like Japan, it must import many of its raw materials. But German technology and precision quality have combined to make her products in demand worldwide.

Germany has been also blessed with large reserves of coal, which fueled the industrial revolution of the 19th century. Today's German industries rely more upon oil, hydro power and wind energy, so its coal deposits are of less value, especially with the impact of climate change and the ongoing move toward renewable energy sources. Apart from coal, the country is not overly rich in minerals, but it has made up for its lack of raw materials by possessing a highly skilled and innovative population. Both Germany and Japan have used their brain power to compensate for the lack of natural resources, and as a result they are the powerhouses of their respective continents.

Berlin is located in the North European Plain, situated along the River Spree, which bisects the city. A mix of woodland, glacial lakes and well-developed agricultural land surrounds Berlin, and the entire region is essentially flat to just gently rolling. Being located in the northern part of the country and some distance from the Atlantic Ocean, Berlin still does receive a significant amount of winter snow. Summers are generally mild, but there can be periods of very warm and humid weather.

A BRIEF GERMAN HISTORY: Visiting Berlin without an understanding of the history of Germany and the role the city has played will take away much of the meaning of what you will see. The city's overall flavor, its many fine buildings and the distinct architectural differences between what was from 1945 until 1990 East Berlin can better be appreciated with a basic knowledge of modern history and how it is rooted in Germany's past.

Many visitors often see Germans as somewhat aloof, even arrogant. But if this perception has any merit, it is in part because they are a highly creative nation. German education is rigid and places emphasis not only upon the sciences, but also upon literature, art and music as well as psychology and philosophy. Think of the great scholars, composers, musicians, doctors and scientists that have come from Germany. The list is most impressive. On a personal level, Germans are very gracious and helpful to visitors. They are also very welcoming.

Visitors often think of the Germans as one people with a long history as nation. This is not true on either account. Germans are somewhat unified in purpose and they have possessed a strong nationalism since the late 19th century, but there are intense regional differences in daily customs and even in dialect. And since World War II, Germany has seen the influx of many workers from Italy, Turkey and Greece. Today in 2018, there has been a massive influx of refugees and those looking to better their lives, people coming from Africa and the Middle East. The tide of this influx is massive and is causing problems for many of the nations southeast of Germany where the refuges land by boat and then attempt to make the journey northward with Germany as their goal.

The nation retains very strong regulations regarding citizenship, primarily aimed at not diluting the cultural identity of Germany. Yet based upon humanitarian grounds the government indicated in the refugee crisis of 2015-16 it was willing to absorb up to 1,000,000 refugees and asylum seekers. This has not been meeting with the full support of the populace, as many Germans fear diluting their culture. It was this ethnic nationalism, fueled by Adolph Hitler's concept of "Deutschland uber alls," translated to mean Germany over everyone, that got the country into so much trouble. There is a pride in being German that is justified, but today it is tempered with reason. It is hard to overlook the great spirit of the people and their ability to have risen from the ashes of World War II to become Europe's most powerful economic force.

The Germanic tribes were rather warlike during the days of the Roman Empire, but around the start of our calendar, the Romans conquered much of southern Germany. Following the fall of Rome, the Franks, the southern Germans, formed an empire that extended well into France and as far north as the Netherlands. The famous Charlemagne becomes Holy Roman Emperor in 800, uniting most of the Franks under his domain. By 843, the Frankish lands were divided into three kingdoms, the eastern kingdom becoming Germany in 919. But Germany was essentially nothing more than a loose confederation of semi-independent principalities, however, calling itself an empire.

The market square in Rostock dates to medieval times

By 1438, Austria emerges as the dominant Germanic kingdom, and by 1648 the

Netherlands and Switzerland secede. Prussia emerges by 1756 as the second great power after Austria, but eventually becomes the dominant Germanic force militarily, and during the mid 1700's, under Frederick the Great it grew to be a major power, having great influence over the lesser Germanic principalities. As a result of the Napoleonic War, the German Empire degenerated into a loose confederacy with no one kingdom being the dominant member, Prussia and Austria remained somewhat apart.

Berlin in the late 19th century

When Napoleon was defeated, the Vienna Congress in 1815 unified all of the German states, but this did not last long, as Austria and Prussia fought in 1867, resulting in Bavaria and Austria remaining outside of the newly formed state. In the 1870-71 Franco Prussian War, Prussia successfully united the various principalities into a united German Empire. From this point on, Germany took an aggressive stand in terms of expanding and building its world influence. Colonies were established in Africa, the South Pacific and Germany began to take an active role as one of the trade powers dominating China. Although a monarchy, Germany developed a parliament and Otto von Bismarck became the powerful chancellor. While Bismarck was establishing a German power base, winning respect and improving trade, the Kaiser (German word for Caesar) worked toward building up the German military. By 1914, Germany seized upon the assassination of the Austro-Hungarian archduke, siding with Austria in a war against Serbia. This drew in Italy on the German-Austrian side and Britain and France on the Russian side. World War I began. Later the United States joined the allies to help defeat Germany.

Germany was left in chaos after the war. The Treaty of Versailles stripped Germany of its colonies, forced it to pay reparations and it was not allowed to station any military troops west of the Rhine River. The country went into depression, the Deutschmark plummeted in value and the government became very unstable. The Kaiser was forced to abdicate, leaving the country in a state of near anarchy. The country also lost territory to France and Poland, taking away valuable industries and agricultural lands.

As social unrest and economic failure plagued the country, Adolph Hitler and his Nazi Party began to take advantage of the situation. At first Hitler was put down by the government and even spent time in prison, but ultimately he used the powers of both persuasion and brutality to rise to dominance. In 1933, the Nazi Party won the election and Adolph Hitler was sworn in as Chancellor by the aging president Paul von Hindenburg. Once in power, Hitler and his advisors set about to turn Germany into a dictatorship based upon the concepts of racism and nationalism. To foster these strong ideals, rooted in Nordic mythology, the Jews became the major target of German ire, blamed for all the post war ills. Other ethnic groups such as Poles and Gypsies were also singled out for persecution, as were the infirm and mentally handicapped.

Hitler sent German troops across the Rhine in 1935, reclaiming the Saar region that had been given to France. The French and British did nothing to stop him. Reports of oppression and persecution were not totally believed outside of Germany, and Hitler had a free hand to carry out his actions. During the 1936 summer Olympic games held in Berlin, Hitler snubbed African-American superstar Jessie Owens by refusing to present him with his gold medal, giving everyone outside of Germany some insight into his attitudes toward the outside world. But the United States did not even protest.

In 1938, German troops marched into Austria, claiming that it was truly German. Many Austrians welcomed the union with Germany, but most feared the consequences. The following year, Hitler demanded the western part of Czechoslovakia, the region in which many Germans lived. The British Prime Minister Neville Chamberlain conceded based upon a promise of friendship. Then on September 1, 1939, Germany used the pretext of the Polish forces having fired upon a German border outpost and invaded Poland and World War II began because Britain and France had pledged to defend the Polish people.

Suffice it to say that Germany reaped a whirlwind of destruction, as the Allies advanced from both east and west. The country was left utterly devastated. Berlin was nothing more than a bombed out ruin with few buildings remaining unscathed. The fighting in the streets of Berlin in the last few weeks of the war was of terrible ferocity, and it was the Red Army that ultimately claimed the victory of capturing the city. And this partly strengthened their claim to much of the territory of what would become East Germany. The Berlin you visit today is a totally rebuilt city, but many buildings were lovingly restored to their old nature, thus making it hard to believe that in 1945 they lay in ruin. Even the Reichstag has been totally rebuilt and once again serves as the German Parliament. This did not occur until after the 1990 reunification, and symbolizes the new Germany.

After World War II Germany was a divided nation, occupied by the Allied Powers that defeated the Nazi Regime

The post war recovery in West Germany under American, British and French protection was rapid. East Germany became a Soviet dominated state with typical Communist oppression. The victors divided the city of Berlin, but the western half of the city was unified under its own government. But being behind the Iron Curtain, Russia forced a blockade of rail and highways in 1948, which the Allies broke by a massive airlift, keeping the people of West Berlin supplied with all of their basic needs.

By 1949, the west was unified into the Federal Republic of Germany while the east became the German Democratic Republic. The Soviet Union had troops stationed in the east, and in 1961 they began construction on a wall to ring West Berlin and keep the people of the GDR prisoners in their own country by not allowing them an escape route via West Berlin. The wall became a notorious landmark of oppression. When John F. Kennedy visited Berlin, he stood near the wall and declared that, "Ich bin ein Berliner," saying he was a Berliner. America would not abandon the people of this surrounded city.

The year 1990 brought about the collapse of the GDR, and the wall began to come down. At last Germany could be reunited as one country. But the cost to the West in Deutschmark was tremendous, as the prosperous West had to share its wealth in the rehabilitation of the east. There was a lot of resentment regarding having to spend so much of the German GDP to rebuild the eastern part of the country, which had languished under communism.

The 1990 reunification with former Communist East Germany was costly to the economy of West Germany and did foster some resentment. As a reunified nation, the country has been able to expand its industrial and agricultural output greatly, and it is now the most important economic power on the continent. Germany's economy sets the stage for the European Union, and in today's time of economic troubles with countries such as Greece on the verge of bankruptcy, it has been the German government that has played the most major role in holding the European Union together.

The role of Germany as the leader of the European economy combined with its government's generosity in allowing almost 1,000,000 displaced refugees from the Middle East and Africa to settle has caused quite a bit of dissention within the general populace. The current government of Angela Merkel has come under severe criticism for its actions. There is quite a backlash today from those who want the government to consider Germans first and refugees second, similar to the attitudes being seen in the United States.

Warnemunde is both a small resort town and also major shipbuilding center

THE PHYSICAL LAYOUT OF WARNEMUNDE AND ROSTOCK: The beachfront town of Warneumnde and the industrial city of Rostock, which is about 20 kilometers or 12 miles farther up the wide, broad Unterwarnow River forming the harbor combine to create one significant urban landscape with around 250,000 residents. Warnemunde is a small town that is primarily a Baltic Sea beach resort, though its history dates back to 1200 when it was founded as a small fishing village. Today with a resident population of just over 8,000, it plays host to thousands of visitors, mainly German, who come for summer holidays. Being that it is at the point

where the harbor begins combined with its many restaurant and commercial amenities, it was the perfect location to build a cruise ship terminal. It is here that ships dock generally for a long day starting at around 7 AM and lasting until 10 or 11 PM. This gives the cruise lines sufficient time to operate a variety of tours to Berlin, which is the main focus of the port call. Some cruise lines charter a private train for the trip into Berlin, as the railway station in Warnemunde is directly opposite the cruise terminal. But other cruise lines have chartered busses, since via the Autobahn the travel time is quicker than by train.

Rostock is connected to Warnemunde by a local commuter rail train that leaves about every 20 minutes, the journey taking about the same amount of time. Rostock is a major industrial and port city with over 200,000 residents. Much of the residential portion of the city was built in the post-World War II period under Communism and is still rather uniform and drab. But the inner city of Rostock, which saw extensive rebuilding after the war, is faithful to its earlier centuries of history dating all the way to the Hanseatic League.

The port cities of Warnemunde and Rostock were once within the German Democratic Republic. A visitor there three decades ago would have found them rather drab with massive, gray apartment blocks. Shops were few, and goods were scares. The government was repressive and personal liberties limited. These would not have been interesting cities to visit. Rostock was once the only major port city for the German Democratic Republic, sharing the same harbor as Warnemunde. Rostock became a major manufacturing center while Warnemunde saw a significant amount of shipbuilding. During the Nazi build up leading to World War II, Rostock was an important ship building center and was also home to the Heinkel Nord airplane manufacturing plant where one of the earliest prototype jet aircraft was developed.

Today these two cities are still major ports, and shipbuilding and other industrial activities are still important. But there is a new spirit that has taken over. Warneumnde has returned to its original role as a summer seaside resort with many hotels, guesthouses and restaurants. It bustles with thousands of visitors, especially on the weekend, as it is an easy journey by car from Berlin or Hamburg. And on days when cruise ships dock, additional thousands of visitors crowd its small streets with people eager to spend their money. Rostock is still a major manufacturing center, but it is also an important academic center as well as being the major retail hub for northeastern Germany. During the German Democratic Republic era, Rostock was the major port for East Berlin and a center for diversified manufacturing. It was during this era that many of the old Hanseatic and later old buildings were faithfully restored because during World War II Rostock suffered severe damage from aerial bombing

CRUISE SHIP TERMINAL: All cruise ships visiting Warnemunde dock at the modern cruise ship terminal located just a short distance into the harbor. The main terminal can accommodate any size cruise ship and there is a semi-permanent second terminal facility adjacent that can also accommodate small to relatively large ships. Up to three ships can be accommodated at one time between the two adjacent facilities. If for some reason more ships have requested berthing at the same time a fourth ship can be accommodated in Rostock at Seehafen, but there is no terminal facility and such usage is relatively rare. And docking at Seehafen requires a shuttle bus into Rostock or shuttle ferry over to Warnemunde if the cruise line has chartered a train for Berlin.

WHAT TO SEE AND IN WARNEMUNDE: Today Warnemunde is a thriving beachfront city with an inner town center that is typical architecturally of a small German seaside community. There are many fine restaurants, bakeries and gift shops catering to those who come to enjoy its beach and small pleasure boat harbor. But apart from taking a walk around, browsing the shops or having a meal, there is essentially nothing for ship passengers to do in Warnemunde that warrants the long period of the port call. The length of the port call is to facilitate the journey to and from Berlin, which most guests opt for.

A few of the more up market cruise lines do offer bus tours to the beautiful and historic Schwerin Castle, a two-hour journey to the west. Schwerin is the ancient capital of Mecklenburg, one of the northern states of Germany. And its castle plus the beautiful lake around which the city of Schwerin is built makes for a way to spend five to six hours on tour. This tour appeals to people who do not want to spend a long day going to Berlin, but yet would like to see something of interest that is closer to the ship.

The vast majority of ship passengers generally opt for one of the various one-day tours to Berlin. Some cruise lines charter a train for the journey while others use motor coaches. The vast majority of trips to Berlin are long, leaving just after docking and returning to the ship around 10 PM. But guests find the trip rewarding and do not complain about the long day's activity.

* OPTIONS FOR EXPLORING WARNEMUNDE OR ROSTOCK: There is absolutely little or no need for expending money for a private car and driver to explore Warnemunde or Rostock. The commuter rail line connecting Warnemunde with the larger and industrial city of Rostock does give those not visiting Berlin or any other venue outside of the port a chance to at least see a bit more of the metropolitan area. Most of the cruise lines do offer a four-hour bus tour into Rostock, often returning by small tour boat. But for those who wish to sightsee on their own, it is very easy to take the train into Rostock and then explore the older quarter of this comfortable city

Here are details regarding the options that are available to you:

** **Ship sponsored tours** are offered by all cruise lines. There are generally two types of tours, one being a motor coach tour into Rostock and the second being a combined motor coach and river ferry tour where you go one way by water. There are no tours of Warnemunde offered by the majority of cruise lines since your ship is docked virtually in the heart of this small resort town.

** **Private car and driver/guide** option is available from most cruise lines, but frankly it is not worthwhile to just tour around Warnemunde and Rostock.

** **Commuter train service is excellent.** If on your own, you can take the commuter train from the Warnemunde train station opposite the docks into Rostock and return. Tickets are purchased on the platform from an automated machine and trains run continuously. To purchase your rail ticket ahead of time visit *www.thetrainline.com* and follow the prompts to find the Warnemunde-Rostock link. It is also possible to travel by comfortable passenger ferry one way or both, enjoying the sights of the busy harbor. Boats run on a frequent schedule. For more information on using the harbor ferry check on line at *www.blaue-flotte.de* and then you can plan either a combined rail-ferry transfer or use one or the other for the round trip.

The Warnemunde-Rostock commuter train

** **There are no hop on hop off bus services** in either Warnemunde or Rostock, as neither city offers sufficient sights to make such a service worthwhile.

** **Walking** is an absolute joy in Warnemunde, as much of this small beach resort is essentially pedestrian oriented. Having a personal car would actually limit you since there are few streets upon which you could drive. And in Rostock the commuter train brings you into the heart of town with a short connecting tram ride into the old market square. Rostock is more oriented toward pedestrian traffic within its central core.

Warnemunde is very much of a German holiday destination and its small downtown core is filled with restaurants, cafes and small shops catering to weekend visitors, but it also welcomes cruise ship passengers during the summer, as there is at least one major cruise ship in port every day.

* **WHAT TO SEE AND DO IN ROSTOCK:** Rostock dates back to the days of the Hanseatic League and its city center contains several streets with buildings that date back to the as early as the 14th century when it was the largest city in what is now northern Germany. This Old Town district merges with the new and modern buildings of the Rostock city center. There are two major medieval churches, and part of the town wall and one main tower still remain.

Modern Rostock has overcome its former drab Soviet Era flavor

For those who chose to visit Rostock on their own it is a simple matter of walking from the cruise terminal to the railway station and taking the commuter train, which runs about every twenty minutes. Then from the Rostock Banhoff (train station) a local tram takes you into the city center at no extra charge. But apart from walking around the Old Town center, there are only a few venues to visit in Rostock. These include (in alphabetical order):

** **Das Kulturhistorische Museum** – In the city center as Klosterhof # 7, this former historic old convent now houses the city's history museum. It is definitely worthy of a visit because it does provide you with a background as to the history and growth of Rostock. The museum is open Tuesday thru Sunday from 10 AM to 6 PM.

** **Karls** – This is a rather special strawberry farm located just about 30 minutes by car or coach east from Rostock on Highway 196. What you visit is a rather interesting combination shop, museum and large restaurant featuring the importance of the growing of strawberries. It in many ways is similar to what was once a popular stop in Southern California known as Knott's Berry Farm before it was turned into a large amusement park. Karls is open daily from 8 AM to 7 PM. A visit to Karls is only possible if it is part of a motor coach tour or if you have a private car and driver/guide. But this destination is too far to the east to be considered as a part of any ship sponsored tour of the Rostock area.

Fresh strawberries at Karls, which is famous for the fruit

** Neuer Markt – This is the central market square in the heart of Rostock. It is surrounded by a collection of very beautiful buildings from the Hanseatic period of the city's history when it was a major trade center and includes the Town Hall and numerous shops and cafes. It is where the tram will stop when you come from the railway station upon arrival.

** Sankt Mariem Kirche – This is the 13th century brick cathedral that has been beautifully restored. It also has a fascinating astronomical clock on display. It has been quite faithfully restored and represents the role of the Catholic faith in this part of Germany. The church is located at Am Ziegenmarkt # 4 just north of the market square where most people alight from the tram to visit the city center. No specific hours are posted, but it is open during daylight hours unless a special service is being held.

* **WHAT TO SEE AND DO IN WARNEMUNDE:** Warnemunde is technically a part of the greater city of Rostock, yet because it is located on the other side of the large harbor, it maintains its separate identity. This small beach resort has been popular among German visitors for the past two centuries, and it is where the cruise ships dock just inside the entrance to the main harbor. During the Communist Era, the residents of East Germany had no other resort on the Baltic other than Warneumnde. There are few actual sights of significance, but it is a delightful place in which to walk around if you plan to stay close to the cruise ship.

** **The Lighthouse** – The only significant landmark worthy of note is the dominant lighthouse that sits at the entrance to the harbor. This lighthouse is 36 meters or 118 feet high and offers spectacular views over the surrounding coast and town. It was built in 1896 and dominates the skyline. The lighthouse is open to those who want to climb to the top between 10 AM and 7 PM daily.

DINING IN ROSTOCK OR WARNEMUNDE: Rostock is not specifically oriented toward catering to large numbers of foreign visitors. Therefore, its restaurants are quite genuine, but you may have a bit of a language problem. If you are willing to overcome this possibility, it is a nice place for lunch when you visit on your own. I recommend the following:

* **Rathskeller12** – Located in the Neuer Markt, or market square at # 1. It is a superb traditional German restaurant serving a variety of dishes prepared following time honored lines. You can choose from seafood, meat and poultry dishes. The service is very good. They are open weekdays from 4 PM to Midnight, Saturday and Sunday they are open from 9 AM to Midnight. Reservations are not necessary.

There are so many cafes lining the boardwalk in Warnemunde that the selection is infinite. The main specialty is fresh seafood, but other German dishes are offered. Most, however, have their menus written in German and many waiters do not speak English, but will be as helpful as possible. And the food is great. My favorite is:

** **Restaurant Carls** located Muenlenstrasse # 28 in the central shopping district. This is a traditional German restaurant, but it also offers healthy vegetarian dishes. They offer fresh seafood, Weinerschnitzel and an assortment of other popular entrees. The restaurant is open daily from11:30 AM to 10 PM. Reservations are not necessary

Warnemunde's main walkway along the small boat harbor is lined with cafes all displaying their menu, some with English translation

ROSTOCK-WARNEMUNDE MAPS

THE ROSTOCK REGION

The Rostock region, (© OpenStreetMap contributors)

This map is best viewed directly from OpenStreetMap.com on your personal device where it can be expanded or one specific area can be enlarged. Given the format of this book, it is impossible to display maps with the level of detail you might wish to have while actually out exploring the city. But the OpenStreetMap maps used directly are the tool I always rely upon.

THE PORT OF WARNEMUNDE

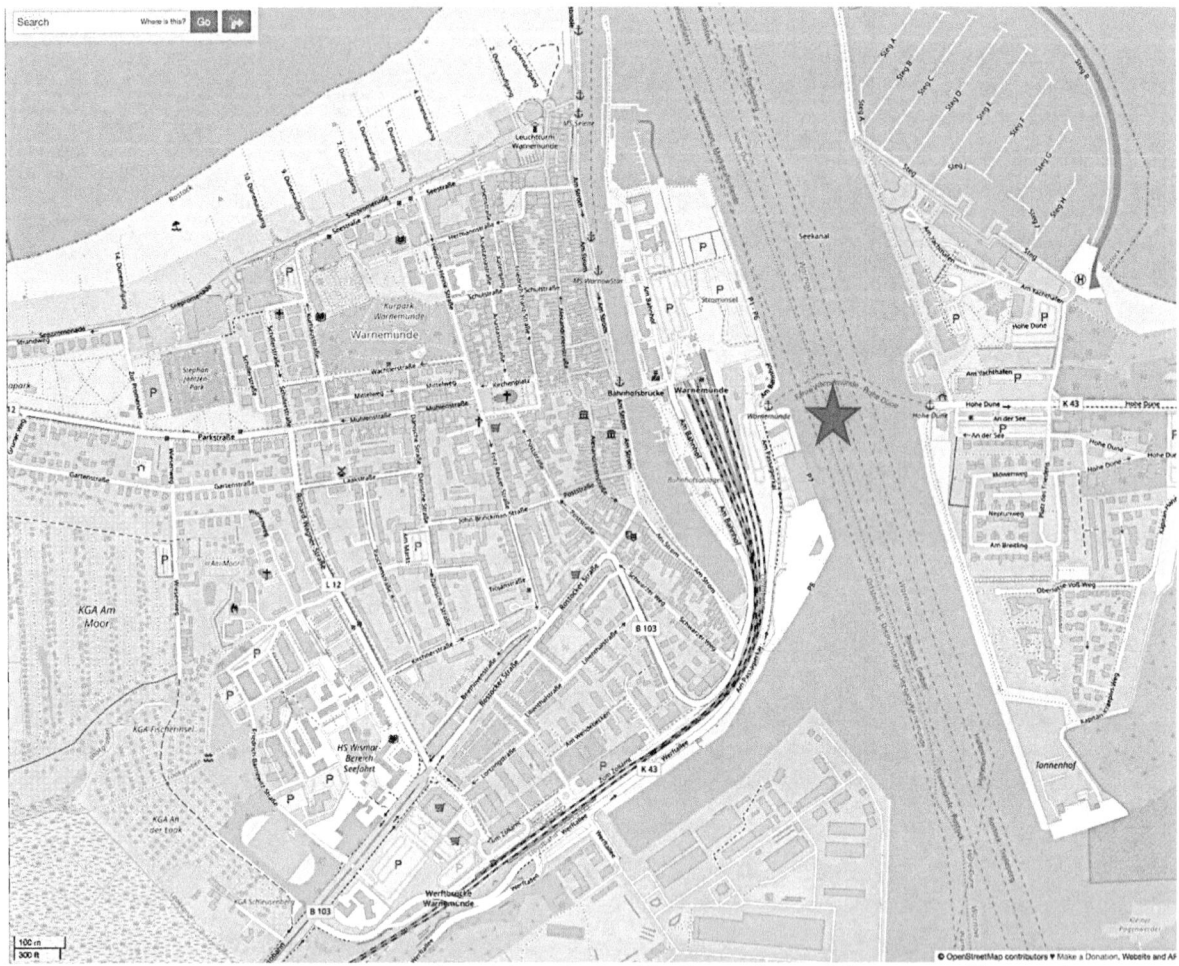

Warnemunde where cruise ships dock, (© OpenStreetMap contributors)

This map is best viewed directly from OpenStreetMap.com on your personal device where it can be expanded or one specific area can be enlarged. Given the format of this book, it is impossible to display maps with the level of detail you might wish to have while actually out exploring the city. But the OpenStreetMap maps used directly are the tool I always rely upon.

THE CITY OF ROSTOCK

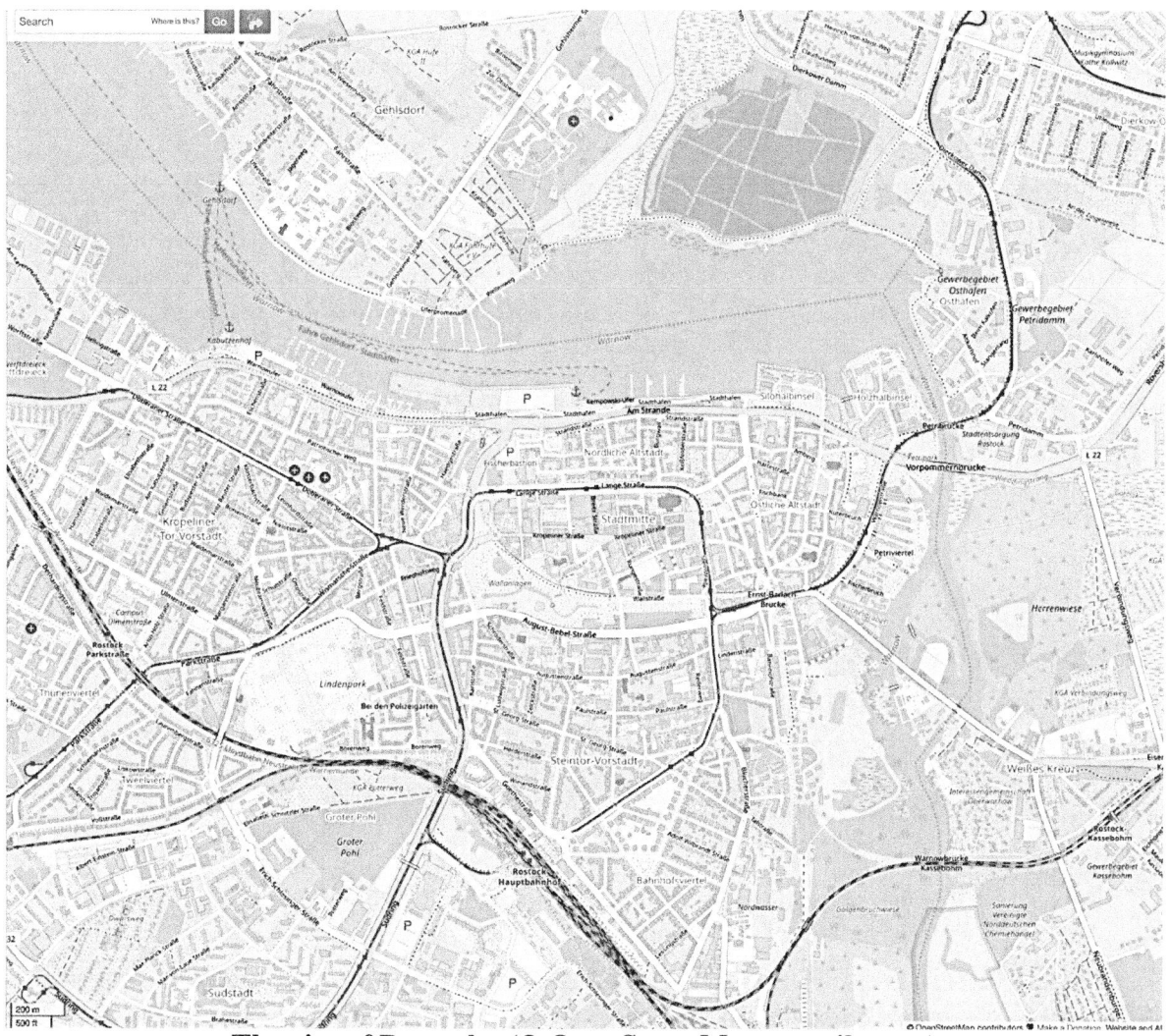

The city of Rostock , (© OpenStreetMap contributors)

This map is best viewed directly from OpenStreetMap.com on your personal device where it can be expanded or one specific area can be enlarged. Given the format of this book, it is impossible to display maps with the level of detail you might wish to have while actually out exploring the city. But the OpenStreetMap maps used directly are the tool I always rely upon.

THE JOURNEY TO BERLIN

The greater Berlin area, (@ OpenStreetMap contributors)

THE PHYSICAL PLAN OF BERLIN: Berlin dates to the mid 15th century, but it did not become a significant city until the rise of the Prussian realm during the 17th century. Slowly King Frederick William II who was known as Frederick the Great expanded the city, adding important boulevards such as Unter den Linden and important public buildings and monuments. When Germany became a united country in 1870, the capital of the Kingdom of Prussia, which was Berlin, became capital of a united Germany. As political and economic power became consolidated here, the city grew into a great metropolis, a city of culture and vitality. As Germany became an industrial nation, Berlin became the hub of the country's railroad network and road system as well as an important industrial city in its own right.

Adolph Hitler had grand plans for the rebuilding of Berlin into a showplace of Nazi power. He had his chief architect Albert Speer develop master plans and models of a city that was going to be imposing through its monuments and public buildings, making it a model for the Nazi concept of autocratic rule of a united people. As the war deepened and bombs began to fall on the city, Hitler proclaimed that Berlin needed to be destroyed so it could be rebuilt. But the total destruction of the city at the final stage of the war, and the great loss of life that accompanied it was surely more than he had ever envisioned. As a part of the plan not only to rebuild Berlin, but to make Germany a strong country in which its military could move freely, the Nazi government did invent the Autobahn, or what are now called the Freeways or Interstate highways. And at one point early in his reign, he had a small car designed for the common folk, and in German, the name was Volkswagen – the people's car.

Berlin is once again the capital of a unified Germany. It has been totally rebuilt, especially the former Communist dominated east. With a metropolitan population of over 3,500,000 people, it is the largest city in Germany and the second largest city in the Baltic Sea region after Saint Petersburg, Russia. The city spreads out along both banks of the River Spree in a flat to gently rolling landscape that exhibits a mix of broadleaf woodland and farms. It has a temperate summer weather pattern, but on occasion temperatures can reach the low mid 30's Celsius or 90's Fahrenheit. Winters are cold and there can be heavy accumulations of snow, but in recent years with global warming the winters have been less severe.

Looking across the Great Tiergarten, (Work of Chiara Mazzocchi, CC BYSA 4.0, Wikimedia.org)

There is still a distinct difference between former West and East Berlin with regard to architecture and urban function. The former heart of prewar Berlin was the massive park known as the Great Tiergarten. The Brandenburg Gate at the eastern end of the park led to the beautiful tree lined boulevard known as Unter dem Linden. This area was the commercial heart of the city. But after the war came the division of Berlin into what would essentially become two cities.

West Berlin developed its own city center along the Kurfurstendam, a street that followed a northeast to southwest direction leading out from the Great Tiergarten. This became a glittering commercial street, and still is to this day. West Berlin was redeveloped with beautiful apartment blocks on tree-shaded streets interspersed with localized shopping areas. There was no regularized street pattern, and is not to this day, but the major boulevards do at least divide the area into large tracts. Few high-rise buildings were developed, the city keeping a relatively even profile. And apart from local administration, this was not a capital city. Bonn had become the capital of West Germany since Berlin was behind the then known Iron Curtain, surrounded by Communist East Germany.

The Kurfurstendam is still the grand shopping street for all of Berlin

East Berlin became the official capital of the Democratic Republic of Germany, what the West simply called Communist East Germany. It was developed along Soviet lines with rather massive blocks of apartments and government buildings similar in design to those found in the Soviet Union -gray and drab. Many bombed out areas were simply cleared of rubble and left vacant. Overall East Berlin was a somber city with only a few streets fully developed in the Communist vernacular to showcase the so-called grandeur of the state system.

With the reunification of the country, Berlin became one city, but the West Berlin city

center known as Kurfürstendamm was unable to provide space for all the new development. Most of the new construction has taken place in Mitte, the former city center district of East Berlin. Today there are in effect two great city centers in Berlin, each with its own distinct character. Mitte has seen massive redevelopment with modern high-rise apartment blocks, hotels and office buildings representing the latest in design. There is a vibrant downtown shopping area along Friedrichstraße that now rivals the Kurfurstendam in former West Berlin. A classic example of buildup in the east is Potsdamer Platz, a few blocks to the south of Friedrichstraße, which until 15 years ago was a vacant clearing, and today is a vibrant development of shops, offices and residences where several underground and above ground transport lines cross. Modern Berlin in effect has two downtown cores with the Great Tiergarten separating them. The Kurfürstendam architecturally represents the 1950's and 60's while Mitte is definitely 21st century.

Friedrichstraße is now the second major shopping street for all Berlin

Where once the Brandenburg Gate was behind the Berlin Wall erected by the Communists to keep the two cities apart, today it is the proud symbol of a united Berlin. And opposite the gate is the German Parliament, which once again serves as the heart of modern government. The Reichstag stands as a proud symbol of a united Germany. After it was set afire by Nazi forces before the war, it stood as a grim reminder of that terrible period in German history, and the Berlin Wall was immediately to its east.

Present day Berlin is considered to be a city-state within Germany, what Europeans would simply call a province. A Senate of eight members, the chief of which is the Regierender Bügermeister or mayor governs the city. The city government is housed

in the Abgeordnetenhaus, or what in English would be a city hall. The city-state itself is divided into 12 boroughs, known in German as Bezirke. These are essentially self-governing neighborhoods, not unlike the boroughs of New York City or London. Each borough's mayor works in consort with the overall mayor who heads the city's senate as noted above. Although it is a massive city, Berlin is quite compact for its size, owing to the fact that most residents live in apartment blocks. Only in the outer suburbs will one find single-family housing. But despite this closeness, there are many green spaces and Berlin does not feel overly crowded.

The Brandenburg Gate now is a symbol of a reunited Berlin

Berlin's neighborhoods or boroughs are each quite distinctive. Before the Berlin Wall came down, this was not only a divided city, but each side represented a different political system. East Berlin was capital of the German Democratic Republic. It was a rather grim city and contained many neighborhoods that were still partly destroyed from World War II. Only the principal streets showed any signs of modernization and vitality, but still with a measure of austerity. West Berlin was semi-autonomous as a city-state, but militarily supported by the United States, Britain and France. It recovered rapidly, sprouting modern apartment blocks, office towers and shopping centers. And East Berlin was guarded by Red Army troops from the Soviet Union.

Although Germany is a fairly homogenous country population wise, there has been immigration permitted for the purpose of filling factory jobs in the country's expanding industry. As a result, Berlin does have about 12 percent of its population comprised of Poles, Turks and other foreign nationals. This has caused some consternation and occasional violence against outsiders, especially against the Turkish populace. With the plans to house more refugees from Syria, Iraq, Afghanistan and eastern Africa, tensions and possible violence may flare in the future.

The restored Great Synagogue of Berlin

Once Berlin was home to one of the largest Jewish populations in Europe. Jews were an integral part of the city's business, medical and educational life, but Nazi persecutions and eventual exterminations destroyed this community. Today only a handful of Jews live in Berlin, a shadow of the once great community. Jews only account for .4% of the overall population, or some 14,000 people. But large numbers of Turkish and Polish workers have made their home in Berlin. They do live in self-segregated neighborhoods, partly because often choose not to culturally integrate into the nation. Some Germans criticize these immigrants as not meeting the national standards for cleanliness. These attitudes are not unlike those that Adolf Hitler used to fan the flames of resentment against the Jews and other non-Germans. However, today's German people are far more enlightened and such madness could not happen again. American, Canadian, Australian and British residents or visitors, on the other hand, are very welcome and treated with great kindness and respect. If one can speak a bit of German it makes the welcome that much greater. I am quite fluent in German and have found the people to be incredibly friendly and helpful.

WHAT TO SEE AND DO IN BERLIN: When coming to Berlin as a visitor there is much to see in both the eastern and western sectors so as to see the major redevelopment that has taken place in what was once behind the Berlin Wall. And there are major sites that are considered the hallmarks of the city's history.

* **OPTIONS FOR SEEING BERLIN:** When your ship docks in Warnemunde, you will have various options with regard to the long trip to Berlin. These options are very important to understand before making your decision as to how you will visit the German capital. Here are the possibilities:

** **Cruise line tours by motor coach** – Most cruise lines offer different Berlin itineraries, but all first involve getting to and returning from the city, which is over 200 kilometers or 130 miles away. The majority of cruise tours will be by motor coach and you can count upon approximately two hours of driving time each way. If the Autobahn is not crowded, the drive can be made in about one hour and 40 minutes, but that cannot be guaranteed.

** **Cruise line tours utilizing a train to and from Berlin** – Some of the large cruise lines with several thousand passengers on board will charter a train for the journey between Warnemunde and Berlin. This may seem like a more comfortable way to travel, but unfortunately these are not high speed ICE trains and the journey each way will take four hours. Motor coaches will be waiting at the Hauptbanhoff in Berlin for the various tours.

** **Hiring a private car and driver/guide** is my preferred option although costly. A car can make the journey in around 90 minutes under good conditions. And once in Berlin, a car is more maneuverable and can get you around the city to see and do more in the time allocated. And you do not need to wait for straggling guests to return to the motor coach, which in a large city with many diversions often happens. I found that to charter a private car in Warnemunde or Rostock on your own for the round trip to Berlin plus a day of sightseeing will cost as much or more than what the cruise line could arrange. It is also vital to keep in mind that if you charter a car and driver on your own and if for some reason you are delayed by traffic or other problems and return to the ship late, you may find that the ship will have sailed without you. However, if you have the cruise line make the arrangements, the ship is then obligated to wait for you no matter how long you are delayed. For this reason alone it is best not to try and arrange a charter on your own and I am not providing any recommendations as to other companies.

** **The self -guided motor coach option** – Some cruise lines offer transportation into the city and provide you with maps and information regarding a self-guided tour. I highly recommend against this option unless you have been to Berlin before. The city is too large and spread out and the public transport system too complex for a novice to accomplish much on his/her own. It simply will be a wasted day. But if you are adventurous or experienced and should choose this option, there are ways to get around the city far more effective than simply walking from where your transport from the ship brought you. These include:

*** **Hop on hop off Bus** – This can be an effective means of getting around the city in the time allotted to you when taking the self-guided motor coach option. Hop on hop off bus service - there are multiple routes and these busses can take you to most of the important sights that most visitors want to see. And there are narrations and maps provided. You first need to carefully check out the service on line at *www.bigbustours.com/Berlin/Bus_tours* also check *www.berlincitytours.com*.

*** **The U Bahn and S Bahn** - these are the two major systems of underground and above ground rapid transit. The two systems integrate to provide a multiplicity of routes around the city. Day passes can be purchased, but you need to study the map carefully to determine the best routes to use. It can be a bit daunting to use these rapid transit systems if you are not able to read or speak German, but you will always find someone who speaks English and willing to assist. For information regarding the various fare zones and travel passes on the network check on line at *www.freetoursbyfoot.com* and then click on Navigate Berlin Public Transport. Also check *www.berlin.de* and then go to public transportation.

*** **Taxis** are plentiful, but relatively expensive per kilometer. You can ask a taxi driver regarding an hourly rate to do touring. Prior to visiting you may wish to check on line with Radio Cab Berlin 26 10 26 or visit their web page for information at *www.funk-taxi-berlin.de*.

*** **Walking** is not an option other than in each part of the city you visit, but the various districts where you find the major tourist venues are simply too far apart for walking.

* **MAJOR SIGHTS TO SEE**: The following descriptive list represents only the most major of Berlin's important monuments since your time will be limited (listed in alphabetical order):

** **Alexanderplatz** – This was the central business district of old East Berlin, but it has undergone westernization since reunification. It is here that the Berlin Tower is located. Shops here also maintain a variety of opening and closing hours.

** Alexander von Humboldt University - Located on Unter den Linden, this famous academic institution is where Albert Einstein once taught. It was also the site of the infamous Nazi book burning, memorialized in the university's central quadrangle.

Alexander von Humboldt University main courtyard

** Berlin Television Tower – If the weather is clear, this tower offers the best observation platform from which to view the city. From the open-air deck one can have a 360-degree panorama of all Berlin from an observation deck 203 meters or 665 feet above the city street level. This is the tallest vantage point in Berlin, as the city does not possess many tall buildings to rival or block the view.

It is located at Alexanderplatz. If the tower is included on one of the organized ship sponsored tours you will be taken as a group to the head of the line and straight up to the top without waiting. However, if you are touring on your own the wait to first purchase tickets and then ascend the tower can be over an hour. You can prior tickets on line, and this will cut your wait time considerably. The tower is open daily from 10 AM to Midnight. To purchase advanced tickets for the tower go to _www.tv-turm.de_ .

** Berlin Dom - This massive cathedral located along Unter den Linden is the largest of the Lutheran cathedrals in Berlin. Its organ is one of the largest in Europe and some of the up market cruise lines arrange for a brief organ recital during their visits to the cathedral. Guided tours are offered from 9 AM to 8 PM Monday thru Saturday and from Noon to 8 PM on Sunday.

Sitting in the Royal Box at the Berlin Dom

** Brandenburg Gate – This is one of the city's most cherished monuments, standing at the end of Unter den Linden, the city's broad and once fashionable boulevard. The gate dates to the 18th century Prussian Empire, commissioned by Emperor Frederick Wilhelm II. The Emperor had it commissioned to commemorate the restoration of order following the Batavian Revolution, which occurred in The Netherlands. Prussian forces helped to restore order.

The gate was heavily damaged during World War II. It stood behind the Berlin Wall until the reunification of the city, and is now once again the symbol of Berlin. It marks the start of Unter dem Linen where the grand boulevard meets the Tiergarten Park. Most of the trees along Unter dem Linden and many in the Tiergarten Park were cut down for firewood during the darkest days of World War II.

Cars may not drive through the gate. It is only open for pedestrian pass through, and it is considered a must do activity by all Berliners. A certain mystique has developed where walking through the Brandenburg Gate is supposedly to bring a certain amount of well-being to those who do so.

The iconic symbol of Berlin is the Brandenburg Gate

** Checkpoint Charlie – After the construction of the notorious Berlin Wall in the early 1960's, this became the most important crossing between allied West Berlin and Communist East Berlin. It is found at Friedrichstraße and Zimmerstraße, This is one of the most photographed venues in Berlin.

During the years following the Berlin Blockade, this became the major crossing, and at times the only one the Communist forces would allow. Crossing was a harrowing experience for thousands and many people lost their lives attempting to be smuggled through Checkpoint Charlie often concealed in the trunk or wheel wells of cars.

Young actors dress in uniforms representing the American and East German guards and stand for photos during the day. For a few Euro you can have your picture taken with these actors and the guard house behind.

The museum adjacent on Friedrichstraße #43-45 is open daily from 9 AM to 10 PM. At times there are people asking to stamp your passport with old stamps from the days when crossing the wall meant crossing a true border. But for most nations it is illegal to have what are now bogus stamps placed in your passport. Although it would be a nice souvenir, it can cause trouble when you arrive in your home country since East Germany is no longer a country.

Actors portray soldiers at Checkpoint Charlie

** **East Side Gallery** – This is the last surviving section of the Berlin Wall complete with its graffiti, now preserved in a park like setting, but standing in the exact spot where it once was part of the infamous wall. It is located at Mühlenstraße #3-100 and is open 24-hours daily. This has become a very important symbol of the years when Berlin was so physically divided.

** **Gendarmenmarkt** – The Gemdarmenmarkt Square is the most beautiful of Berlin's public squares, graced by two of the city's major cathedrals and its concert hall. It is located in the heart of Mitte in former East Berlin. This is a major gathering place for people who take the Hop on Hop off bus around the city. It is so well situated for sightseeing in the former eastern sector of the city.

This square is often the drop off location for the self-guided excursions where the motor coach from the ship leaves you. Many cruise lines offer a self-guided tour where a motor coach ferries you from the ship in Warnemunde to the Gendarmenmarkt and while en route a guide presents ideas and information so you can establish a self-guided route for your day in Berlin.

The Gendarmenmarkt

** **Hakescher Markt** – A district of small boutiques, cafes and galleries that once was the heart of the Jewish quarter of the city. It is located north of the River Spree on Rosenthaler Straße and shops maintain a variety of opening and closing hours.

The very distinctive Holocaust Memorial

** **Holocaust Memorial** – A stark reminder to the 6,000,000 murdered Jews of Europe, this memorial just opened in May 2005, and it is a reminder to the world of what can happen under dictatorship gone astray. The memorial is located south of Unter den Linden and the Brandenburg Gate at Cora Berliner Straße #1 and open from 10 AM to 8 PM Tuesday thru Sunday. The memorial is closed Monday.

** **Jewish Museum** - Unlike the Holocaust Memorial, this museum provides a detailed history of the Jewish people in Germany as well as in the rest of Europe. It is located on Linden Straße #9-14 in former East Berlin. The museum is open from 10 AM to 8 PM daily, with extended hours to 10 PM on Monday. And tours are offered.

** **Kurfürstendamm** – This became the main commercial street of the western sector of Berlin. It is still the liveliest street in Berlin, brightly lit with neon at night. The bombed ruin of the Kaiser Wilhelm Memorial Church sits at the top end of the street as a symbol of the destruction wrought upon the city in 1945. Most shops on the Kurfurstendam do stay open late each night. The most important store is the massive Ka DaVe Department Store, an elegant shopping venue.

** **New Synagogue** – This reconstructed building once housed the largest Jewish congregation in all of Europe. The synagogue is just across the River Spree from Mitte on Oranienburger Straße # 28-30. The visitor center is open Monday thru Friday from 10 AM to 6 PM and on Sunday from 10 AM to 7 PM.

Potsdamer Platz, (Work of Tanweer Morshed, CC BY SA 4.0, Wikimedia.org)

** **Potsdamer Platz** – This square was once used as a military parade ground. Today it is the heart of a maze of skyscrapers, representing the new face of Berlin. It is located just to the southeast of the Reichstag and is one of the examples of how former East

Berlin has become so modern. It is an interesting and quite photogenic plaza surrounded by ultra-modern buildings. The S-Bahn and U-Bahn both can take you to Potsdamer Platz.

** **Rathaus Schöneberg** – The site of John F. Kennedy's famous "Ich bin ein Berliner" speech. It is the old town hall for the borough of Templehof that stood next to the former East Berlin Wall. It is appropriately located at what is now called John F. Kennedy Platz #1 and is open daily except Monday from 10 AM to 5 PM/

** **Reichstag** – The German Parliament has been fully restored and now serves as the legislative building for the nation. In 1933, it was burned, which gave Adolph Hitler the excuse he needed to declare himself as dictator. It stands at the eastern end of the Tiergarten and faces the Brandenburg Gate.

Visitors are permitted to view the interior of the parliament from the glass dome above the legislative chamber. Guided tour of the building are also provided. Tours and visits to the dome are permitted from 8 AM to Midnight daily, but tickets must be purchased first. And there is relatively tight security upon entering the building. In my restaurant section, I will make special note of the Reichstag's elegant rooftop restaurant. You will need to show your passport at security if you visit the Reichstag.

The Reichstag – Parliament of Germany

** **Schloss Charlottenburg** – The largest of the surviving historical palaces in Berlin that date back to the glory of the Kingdom of Prussia. It was last home to Kaiser

Wilhelm II until the end of World War I. It is located in the suburban district of Charlottenburg to the west of the Kurfürstendamm. The palace is open and guided tours are offered between 10 AM and 6 PM Tuesday thru Sunday. The palace is closed on Monday.

** **Tiergarten** – The largest park in Berlin, the Tiergarten is a masterpiece in park design with its beautiful landscaping and numerous walking paths. The neighborhood to the north, also known as Tiergarten, became the middle-class sector of the city, housing academic and professional families. The Tiergarten stands between the former heart of West Berlin in the days of division. To the east beyond the Brandenburg Gate is Mitte, which was once the business center of former East Berlin.

** **Topography of Terror** – This museum located adjacent to the former Berlin Wall at Niederkirchnerstraße # 6 is dedicated to presenting the horrors of the former Nazi SS and gestapo through a series of photographic exhibits. It is quite graphic and disturbing, yet important in helping people understand what happened during that period of German history. It is an important exhibit despite its chilling ramifications and one that all visitors should see. It is open from 10 AM to 8 PM daily.

The Topography of Terror Museum

Berlin is a city that once was the center of culture for all Germany. After World War II, with the division of Germany by the victors, Berlin fell within the Soviet controlled zone that became the Democratic Republic of Germany. As noted previously, the city was not a part of East Germany, but rather divided among the allied powers and occupied up until German reunification. The eastern portion of the city became the capital of the austere and dictatorial regime of East Germany, and became separated from West Berlin by the infamous Berlin Wall. The capital of the Federal Republic of Germany, better known as West Germany, was located in Bonn and much of West German culture became rooted in Frankfurt or Munich. Once reunification was completed and Berlin became whole again, it once more became the national capital and the focus of importance. It is once again a city with a rich and vibrant nightlife, major symphony orchestras and many fine museums and galleries. Once again, Berlin has become the center for the German film industry and for its radio and television broadcasting. But Frankfort has remained as the financial hub of the nation. And Hamburg, as a port city, has developed as a major economic and cultural center. Berlin no longer has the star role among German cities.

The dynamic East Berlin skyline today reflecting reunification

DINING OUT: You will only have time for lunch during your one-day visit to Berlin. And on all of the organized tours, lunch will be provided so you will not have a choice of restaurants or a wide range of menu selections. Any visit to Berlin should become a gastronomic experience if you have the free time, which only a few of you will.

Like in Poland, the food of Germany is rich, substantial and very delicious. Roasted meats and chicken are served with crisp potato pancakes, sweet and sour red cabbage and washed down with heavy, dark beer. At lunch, Germans also like sausages and sauerkraut or fried veal or pork cutlet, known respectively as Wienerschnitzel or Schweineschnitzel. Spaetzle, small egg noodles covered in melted butter and parsley are a popular side dish.

Bread plays a major role in the German diet and there is a great variety of breads and rolls in any bakery. For dessert, Germans love rich chocolate cakes with whipped cream and brandied fruits or crispy apple strudel or thin tortes made up of many layers of cake, nut fillings and butter cream icing. As a treat, marzipan candies are a popular snack. Marzipan is made from ground almond paste and has a most distinctive flavor, but many say it is an acquired taste.

If you are traveling to Berlin in a private car or going about on your own after arrival by either train or bus, I recommend the following few as possible venues for lunch because they best represent German cuisine at the midday meal (shown alphabetically):

* **Boulevard Friedrichstraße** – Located in Mitte at Friedrichstraße # 106c, this is a locally popular restaurant for traditional German cuisine at both lunch and dinner. It has a good reputation for consistent quality and a nice atmosphere with indoor or outdoor service. It is conveniently located in the former East Berlin downtown, close to many tourist venues. They are open daily from Noon to 11 PM. Bookings for lunch are not needed.

Bakeries are found everywhere in Germany brimming with delectable

* **Fassbender and Rausch** - This famous chocolate shop also has an upstairs cafe where light meals are served for lunch since they open as early as 10 AM. The soup, sandwich and other light items give you the needed protein and energy that will then

allow you to indulge in their decadent sweets. The shop and cafe are located at Charlottenstraße 60, just south of the Deutscher Dom in the Gendarmenkarket of former East Berlin. They are open from 11 AM to 7 PM Monday thru Saturday and from 1 to 7 PM on Sunday. Bookings are not essential.

* **Gasthaus Kater Alex** – Located west of the Kurfürstendamm shopping area, you will need to have your own car and driver or take a taxi to reach this gem of a restaurant. It is at Kaiser Friedrich Straße # 29. This is one of the finest restaurants serving traditional German cuisine in a superb atmosphere with impeccable service, one of the best dining establishments in the city. I highly recommend that you have the ship's concierge call to book a table or you can call them to book your table at +49 30 34709065. Their serving hours are Monday thru Wednesday from 11 AM to 10 PM, Friday from 11 AM to 10PM and Saturday from 2 to 10 PM. They are open Sunday from 1 to 10 PM. Reservations are not necessary.

* **Häppies** - This is a small restaurant where the service and the quality of the food are hard to beat. Open from Noon to 8 PM, this is a good place to sample German cooking for lunch. It is located on Dunckerstraße 85 in the part of the city known as Prenslauer. It is not close to any of the main attractions, but worth taking a taxi just for lunch. To book a table call +49 1511 4984140.

KaDaWe is one of the most beautiful as well as being the largest upmarket department store in all of Europe except for London.

* **Ka DaWe 6th Floor** - This impressive restaurant will insure that you visit the

famous Ka DaWe Department Store if for no other reason than to have lunch. The food is authentic and the selection is quite large. You can truly sample a taste of Germany in this one restaurant. Table bookings are not needed.

* Käfer Dachgarten-Restaurant – This unusual restaurant is located on the roof terrace of the Reichstag, or parliament building. I cannot think of any other gourmet public restaurant located inside a national parliament or legislative building and open to the public.

Gourmet cuisine with a view out over Berlin is the hallmark of this unusual restaurant inside a national capitol building. Reservations are an absolute must and you will need to register in the lobby and be cleared by security before going up to the restaurant. To book a table go to their web page at *www.feinkost-kaefer.de* a few days prior to your visit. The restaurant is open for breakfast and lunch from 9 AM to 5 PM and for dinner from 7 to 11 PM. Reservations are essential and can be made at +49 3300 2262990.

The River Spree meanders through Berlin and small cruise boats offer tours

SHOPPING: When going to Berlin for the day, generally on an organized tour, there is little or no time for shopping. Even if you are going on your own, there is so much to see that shopping become irrelevant other than buying a few souvenirs, which you will find available at most major scenic sights.

There is one major department store that will sometimes be included on tour itineraries, or that you can briefly visit on your own. Located on the Tauentzienstraße, the continuation of the Kurfürstendamm you will find KaDaWe, properly known as Kaufhaus des Westens. This is the Harrods of Berlin - the most upscale department store in the city. If you visit the Kurfurstendamm, this store is a must-see venue.

FINAL WORDS: The portions of Germany that were under the domination of the Communist regime have been fully integrated into a united Germany. Scars of World War II and the grim architecture of the Communist Era are fast fading. Potsdamer Platz in Berlin is without exception the classic example of this transformation. Berlin is the most dynamic example of the strength of this reunification, and it is a city rich in history yet committed to building its 21st century image as a great European city.

The pride of the city and of the entire nation is the Reichstag, the German Federal Parliament, which is located just west of the Brandenburg Gate. The Reichstag sat as a derelict building from the day it was ordered burned by Adolf Hitler until after the reunification of Germany. Millions of Deutschmark were spent to restore the building and once again it serves its original purpose. But more than just being a renovated building, it is a reminder of the tribulations of the nation from the end of World War I until the reunification in the ending years of the 20th century.

Souvenir military items from the former East Germany

BERLIN MAPS

THE TIERGARTEN AREA

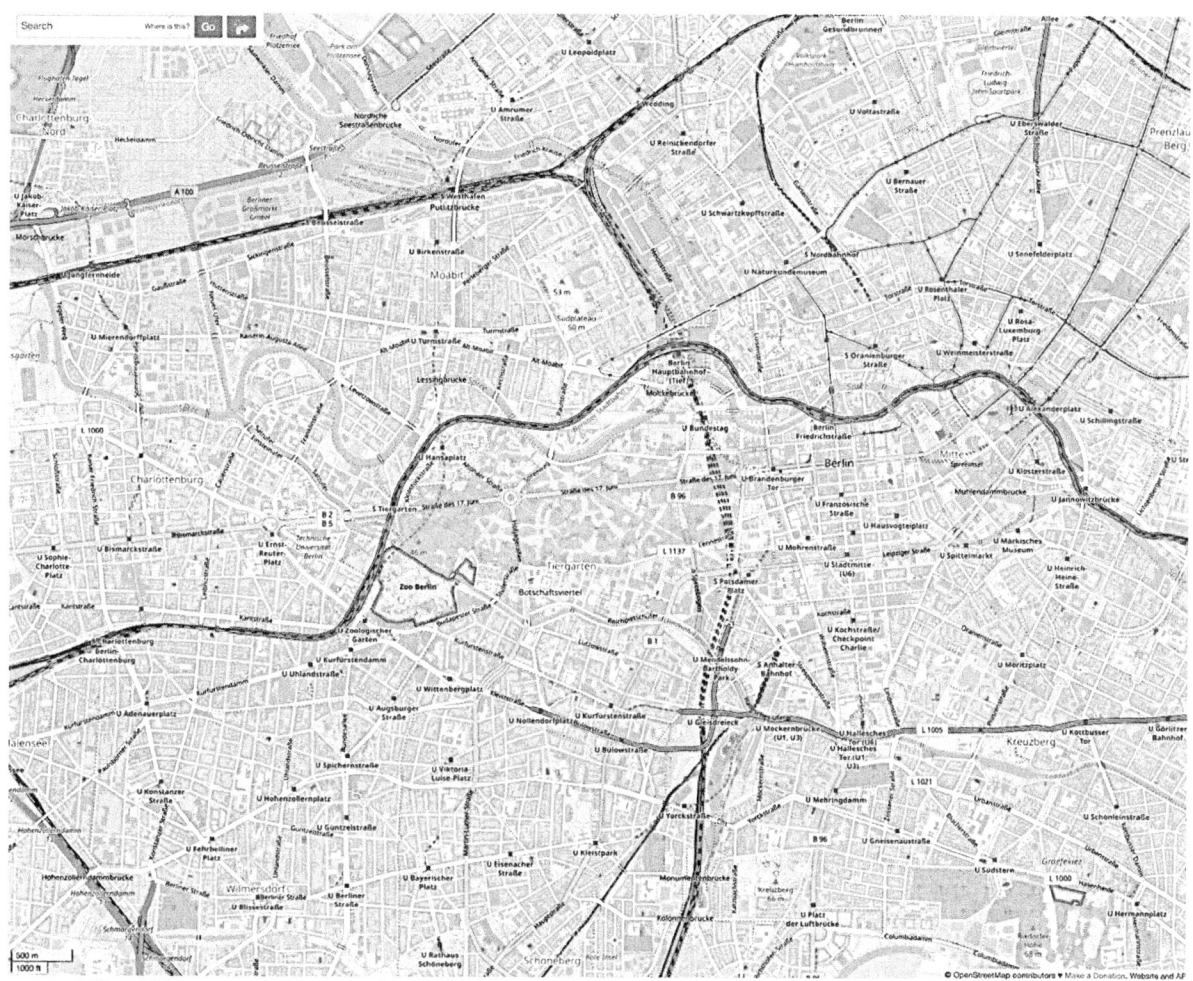

The Tiergarten – meeting of east and west Berlin districts, (© OpenStreetMap contributors)

This map is best viewed directly from OpenStreetMap.com on your personal device where it can be expanded or one specific area can be enlarged. Given the format of this book, it is impossible to display maps with the level of detail you might wish to have while actually out exploring the city. But the OpenStreetMap maps used directly are the tool I always rely upon.

THE KURFURSTENDAM

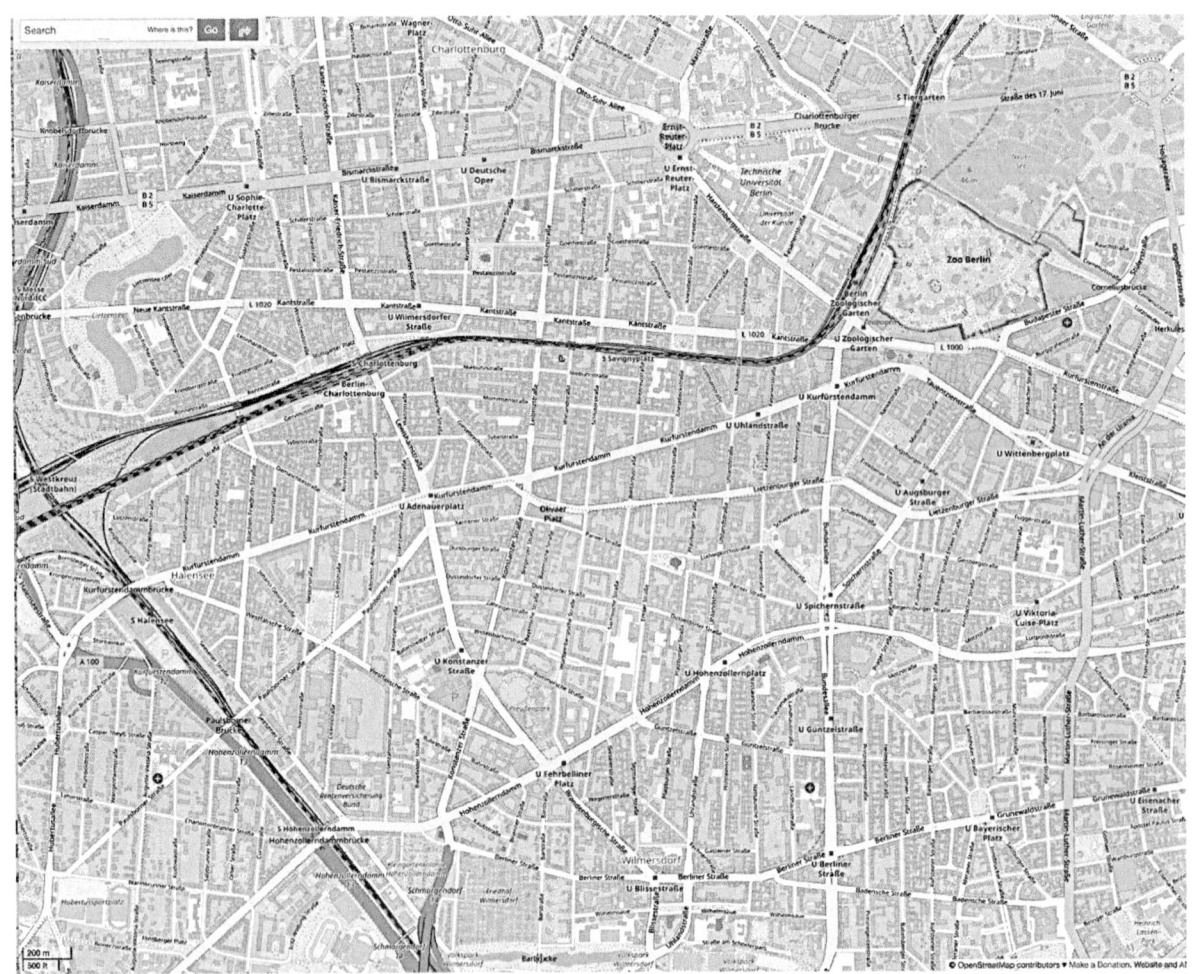

The Kurfurstendam – former West Berlin, (© OpenStreetMap contributors)

This map is best viewed directly from OpenStreetMap.com on your personal device where it can be expanded or one specific area can be enlarged. Given the format of this book, it is impossible to display maps with the level of detail you might wish to have while actually out exploring the city. But the OpenStreetMap maps used directly are the tool I always rely upon.

MITTE

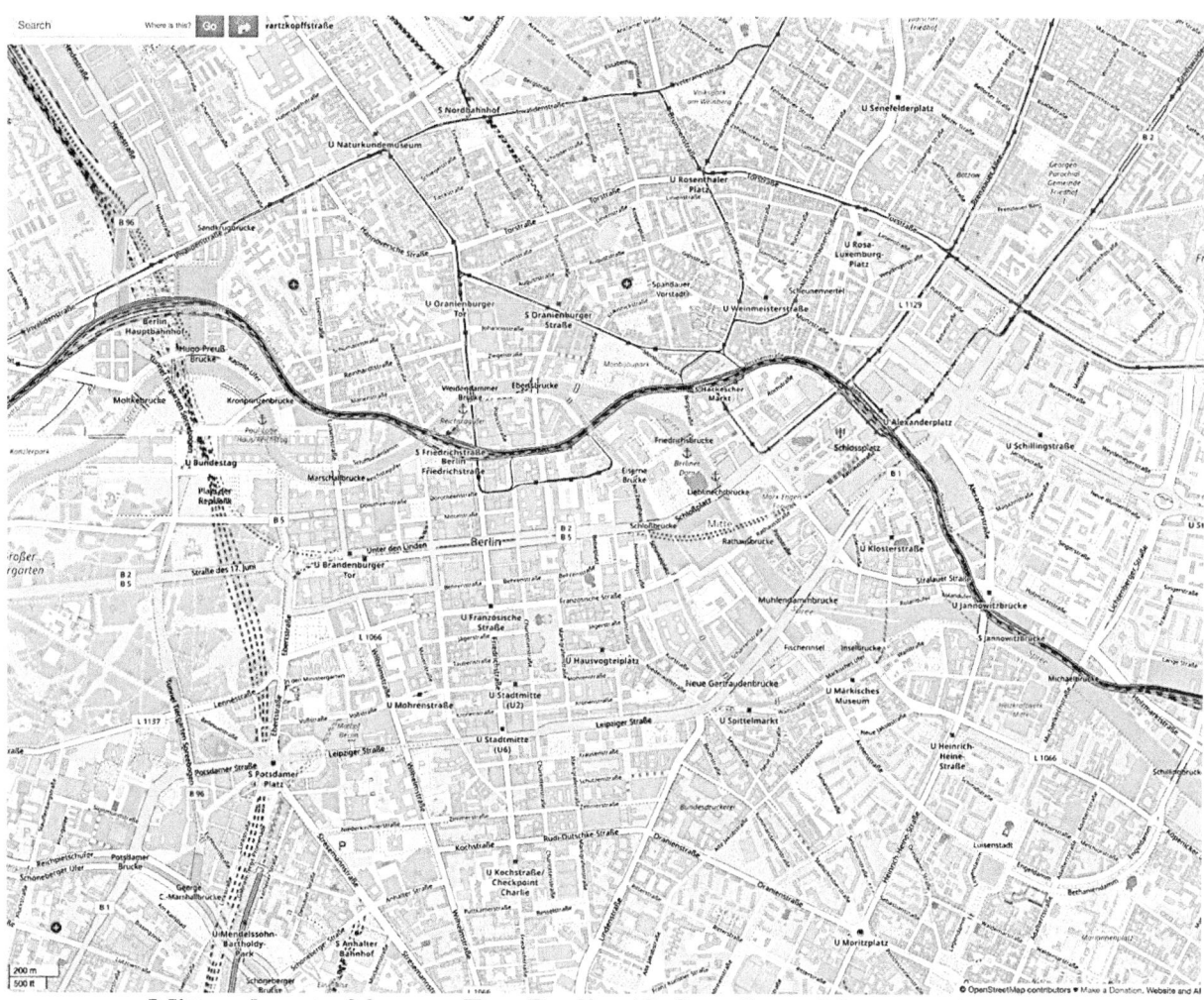

Mitte – heart of former East Berlin, (© OpenStreetMap contributors)

This map is best viewed directly from OpenStreetMap.com on your personal device where it can be expanded or one specific area can be enlarged. Given the format of this book, it is impossible to display maps with the level of detail you might wish to have while actually out exploring the city. But the OpenStreetMap maps used directly are the tool I always rely upon.

AROUND THE GULF OF BOTHNIA

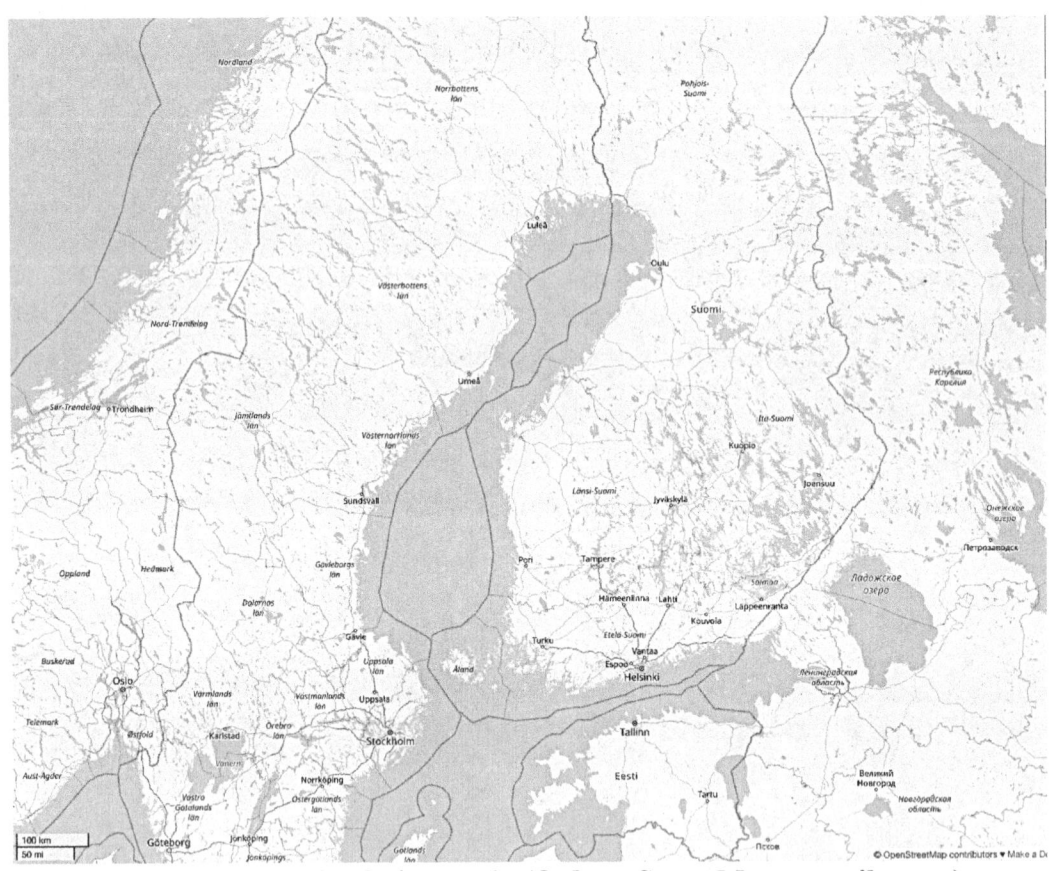

Map of the Gulf of Bothnia (© OpenStreetMap contributors)

It is rare for a cruise line to offer an itinerary that circumnavigates the Gulf of Bothnia. In the past two years there have only been a handful of such cruises, primarily by small to medium size ships belonging to the upmarket five-star cruise lines.

This large arm of the Baltic Sea that extends northward between Sweden and Finland almost to the Arctic Circle is not well populated on either shore. There are few cities or towns of any significant size and for that reason combined with the distances involved, most itineraries transit between Stockholm and Turku or Helsinki, leaving this large body of water and its shores unexplored. But for the benefit of those of you who may be fortunate enough to have booked a cruise that does include the Gulf of Bothnia I have added this section to the book. The detail in the following chapters is not as extensive as in the book to this point simply because these small towns and cities for the most part are not as relevant to the passage of time in the Baltic Sea region. Yes, many date back to Viking or medieval times, but they were considered to be minor players in the unfolding history of the northern Baltic Sea.

Few of you who buy the book may have an opportunity to visit these small ports, but I value all of my readers and therefore have made information available on Sundsvall, Luela, Kemi, Vaasa, Marienhamn and Turku, which are the primary stops on Gulf of Bothnia itineraries.

The Swedish Archipelago extends west from the Gulf of Bothnia

As noted above, the chapters are shorter and the amount of detail is not as extensive as in the major chapters. Also there are fewer photographs for each port of call, again because there is far less to be shown.

If you are on a cruise to the Gulf of Bothnia, any suggestions you might wish to submit to my web page (*www.doctorlew.com* will be greatly appreciated for future editions.

SUNDSVALL, SWEDEN

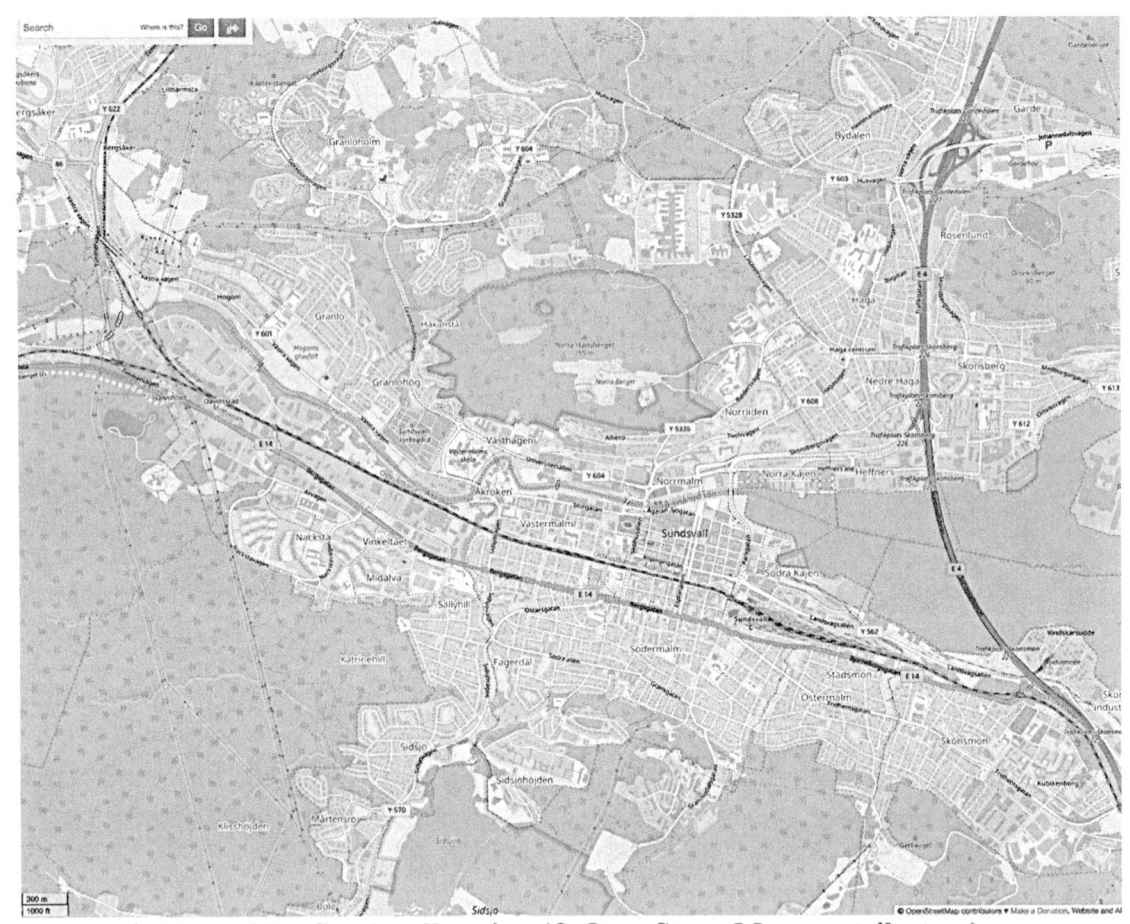

Map of the Sundsvall region (© OpenStreetMap contributors)

Sundsvall is a small Swedish city located 343 kilometers or 213 miles north of Stockholm. It has a city population of approximately 52,000 and nearly 115,000 residents in its immediate service area. This is an old city dating back to the early 1600's and it is a very pleasant community set along the Gulf of Bothnia. It is rare for a cruise ship from any of the major companies to visit Sundsvall or for that matter any of the ports around the Gulf of Bothnia. And most tourists visiting Sweden on their own, traveling either by rail or automobile seldom come this far north unless they have a particular interest such as getting all the way into the homeland of the Sami.

THE NATURAL SETTING: Sundsvall is built on a series of hills surrounding a small bay extending west from a deep water channel that separates the mainland of Sweden for hundreds of offshore islands, some of them quite sizeable. The entire area was heavily glaciated during the last ice age, and it was glacial scour that created the deep channels, separating pieces of the coastline from the mainland and creating the islands, similar to the archipelago in the vicinity of Stockholm.

The land is thickly forested primarily in spruce, but with groves of willow and other broadleaf deciduous trees. And in wetland areas there are marsh grasses and open meadows. Winter in these northern reaches is quite severe with bitter cold and heavy snow. Summer is mild and days are often misty or overcast. Sunshine and blue skies are a precious commodity.

The verdant landscape surrounding Sundsvall

A BRIEF LOCAL HISTORY: Although Vikings may have briefly occupied sites in this area, but their impact was minimal and the city of Sundsvall does not owe any of its history to them. The town was created under charter in 1621. During its first two centuries, the predominantly wooden town experienced four disastrous fires sweeping through most of the community. Only one fire was the result of war, and occurred in 1721 when the Russians set fire to Sundsvall after first looting it of any of its valuables. Russia and Sweden were quite bitter foes at this time, especially after Peter the Great had established his new capital in Saint Petersburg. The worst fire in Swedish history occurred in 1888 during an extremely dry summer when once again much of the city burned. This blazer left over 9,000 residents homeless. Today in central Sundsvall you will find a great use of stone and brick with wood relegated to suburban residences. This is many ways is the result of that great fire.

What put Sundsvall on the map and still plays a major role in its economy is forestry. It is often claimed that the Industrial Revolution came to Sweden via Sundsvall when one of the mills started to use steam power rather than manual labor. And with plenty of wood in the surrounding forests, a portion could be used to generate the steam power.

Along with industrialization came labor disputes and strikes, and in 1879, Sundsvall experienced a major shutdown due to workers walking off the job. Eventually Sweden became heavily committed to labor movements, and many say Sundsvall paved the way to increased sympathies for blue-collar workers. Thus in the labor history of Sweden, Sundsvall has its important place.

On the street in Sundsvall in the late 1920's

Today Sundsvall remains an important center for wood product industries, but there is growing IT and telecom development. The city is also a major commercial and financial center for much of the northern coast of the Gulf of Bothnia and the northern interior. It is also an important regional educational, cultural and medical center, being the most important city in the far northern region.

THE PHYSICAL LAYOUT OF SUNDSVALL: Surprisingly Sundsvall is relatively spread out around its bay and the shoreline of the main channel. The heart of Sundsvall is south of the Selongerson River at the point where it empties into the bay. The city center has a distinct grid pattern, but with the main line railroad running through it, separating the commercial downtown area from the southern residential section that rapidly climbs the forested hills.

Looking over central Sundsvall, (Work of M3lith1306, CC BY SA 3.0, Wikimedia.org)

Extending east from the core, there is a significant residential area that follows the railroad to the main channel and then clings to the waterfront where there is a mixture of residential and industrial sectors. The main E-4 Motorway runs along the coast and then crosses the bay to the north, essentially staying out of the city center. Residential and industrial development extends west from the city core along the river and then becomes rather fragmented out into the surrounding forest land.

North of the river there are two distinct nodes of residential development, the largest being to the east and extending north along the E-4 Motorway. The Norra Stadsberget Park that is a protected small forest covered mountain rises 155 meters or 460 feet above the river and separates the more fragmented residential districts to the west and north of the river.

CRUISE SHIP DOCK: There is no actual terminal in Sundsvall, as so few cruise ships visit. Ships dock in the industrial port, which is located along the southern shore of the harbor five kilometers or three miles east of the city center, too far for most guests to walk. The port authority provides a shuttle bus into the center of town, as passengers are not permitted to walk through the port area for safety reasons.

WHAT TO SEE AND DO IN SUNDSVALL: For a visitor, it is the city center that will be the most interesting part of the city to visit. All tours will leave from the dock immediately adjacent to the ship, making it very convenient. There is not much to do in Sundsvall, but guests normally find this a very pleasant stop, as it is a very typical northern Swedish city that is exceptionally clean and well ordered.

* **SIGHTSEEING OPTIONS IN SUNDSVALL:** There is not a significant tourist infrastructure in Sundsvall. The number of options available to you is not as widespread as in major ports of call, but you will find this to be true of the majority of the ports of call around the Gulf of Bothnia, as tourism here is still in a more developmental phase. Here are the options open to you:

** **Ship sponsored tours** – The few cruise ships that do stop may only offer a half day overview tour of the city and its surroundings. The tour will at least give you a chance to familiarize you with the layout of this small city so that you can later explore on your own.

The central square in front of the town hall, (Work of Hans Lind qvist, CC BY SA 4.0, Wikimedia.org)

The Storgatan is the main street of Sundsvall (Work of Åsa Grip, per Wikimedia.org)

** Private car and driver option – Unless you have strong geographic interests and want to do some major exploring of the Sundsvall area I do not recommend spending money on a private car and driver/guide since there is not that much of great interest to be experienced. But some guests do want or need the convenience and privacy of having their own vehicle. Apart from having the shore excursion desk arrange for a car and driver, which is quite expensive, you may also wish to look into Knopka Transfer at *www.knopkatransfer.com* for comparison on price and service.

** Rental cars are available from the major car rental agencies. However, take note that they will all have manual transmission, as vehicles with automatic shift capabilities are not widely used. Also note that all traffic signs are written in Swedish, which may pose a problem for most visitors who are not multilingual. Fortunately traffic in this city is not that heavy, but still be very careful if you do your own driving.

** There is no hop on hop off bus service offered in Sundsvall, as the city is too small and not a major tourist hub.

** Taxi services - There is always the option of hiring a taxi if you wish to see more of the city than what can be accomplished on foot. In Sundsvall, the majority of the taxi drivers do speak English and can show you around the city. Be sure to negotiate an hourly rate prior to departure. You may wish to check on line with Taxi Sundsvall at *www.taxisundsvall.se* to see what they can offer in advance. Your computer will need to be able to translate the site written only in Swedish.

** **Walking** is the best way to enjoy the city center, and the port provided shuttle bus service drops you into the heart of Sundsvall. This is a small city and people are very friendly and helpful. If the weather is nice, walking is a very enjoyable activity. For those more active, bicycles can be rented. Check on line with *www.velomesto.com* for more details.

* **IMPORTANT SIGHTS TO SEE**: The major highlights of visiting Sundsvall include (shown in alphabetical order):

** City center on foot or bicycle, which is a pleasant way to spend a few hours. There are small parks, plenty of shops, restaurants and coffee shops where you can simply experience the hospitality of a small Swedish city. Despite its small population, Sundsvall's downtown core is quite extensive because it is the regional trade center.

** **Galstroms Bruk** - This small museum is located on the edge of the city and does require a taxi in order to visit. This was once a place where small iron tools were manufactured. It gives you a chance to both enjoy an idyllic rural setting and also learn about how people lived and the tools they made as far back as the 1600's. There is also a nice restaurant on site. Overall it is a pleasant way to spend a few hours outside of the city. It is open daily from Noon to Midnight. Although few foreign guests generally visit, you will always find someone available who does speak English.

** **Himlabadet Water Park** - I recommend this venue only if you have a young family that wants to spend a day having fun at a very fascinating water park. There is a wave pool, water slide and steaming outdoor baths for the adults. This water park is located along the north shore of the river walking distance from the city center east along Universitetsallen. Generally the weather in Sundsvall is very mild and for many visitors it may be too chilly for children to enjoy a water park.

The park is open Monday thru Friday from 10 AM to 7 PM, Saturday and Sunday from 9 AM to 6 PM. It is not at all difficult to find a taxi in the city center to take you to the water park.

** **Kulturmagasinet** - This small museum in the center of Sundsvall, located at Packhusgatan #4 offers a glimpse into the history and cultural flavor of this part of Sweden. The museum has a small library and cafe as well as nicely planned exhibits. For most foreign visitors it may not be of great interest, as the majority of visitors have little or no background in Swedish history.

It is open Monday thru Thursday from !0 AM to 7 PM, Friday only until 6 PM and on weekends from 11 AM to 4 PM.

The Kulturmagasinet, (Work of Sendelbach (talk), CC BY SA 3.0, Wikimedia.org)

** **Norra Berget** - This mountain park across the river to the north of the city center is a very popular local venue, especially on a nice sunny day. The park combines an open air museum with a chance to take one of the many walking trails through the woods with panoramic views out over all of Sundsvall. And there are no charges to enjoy this lovely amenity. The open air museum represents old Sweden through its collection of buildings, very similar to the larger such park in Stockholm called Skansen. There are small restaurants where you can also have a light meal. Overall it is easy to spend a few hours in Norra Berget. The park is open daily, but each individual venue has its own set of hours. Normally everything is open during daylight hours. It is best to check their web page at *www.norraberget/se* for specific details.

DINING OUT: You will only be in Sundsvall for a few hours, and there are many places open for lunch both in the downtown and at the venues noted above. I have chosen my three favorites where the emphasis is upon Swedish cuisine:

* **Opus Piano Bar** - Located on Storgatan #12 in the city center. This restaurant is both classic with regard to its ambiance and its menu. Here you will dine on traditional Swedish dishes all served with that special flair and an air of friendliness. The average price for a full meal will be more expensive than most restaurants in

Sundsvall, but well worth the charge. The restaurant is open Monday thru Thursday from 2 to 10 PM, Friday remaining open until 1 AM and on Saturday open only from 5 PM to 1 AM. They are closed on Sunday. I would call to make certain regarding a table available at +56 60 15 08 00.

* **Restaurang 180 Grader** - A restaurant with a view over the city from its perch in the Hotel Sodra Berget. This is located just south of the city center up in the forested hills. It offers the combination of great views along with traditional Scandinavian dishes that are well prepared, but a bit expensive. The restaurant is open Monday thru Friday 11:30 AM to 11 PM and on Saturday for dinner only from 5 to 11 PM. They are closed on Sunday. You can call to book at +46 60 67 10 00.

* **Tant Anci & Froken Sara** - Located at Bankgatan #10 in the city center, this restaurant serves excellent food with a definite Swedish flair. It also has vegetarian dishes and many items are organic. You will find a wide array of hot and cold entrees, salads and desserts, many compatible with vegetarian or vegan tastes. It is open from 11 AM to 8 PM weekdays, It is open from 11 AM to 6 PM Saturday. Reservations are not usually necessary, but are accepted. Call +46 60 785 57 00.

SHOPPING: I have no specific recommendations for Sundsvall with regard to where to shop. This is not really a tourist destination where you will find a large supply of souvenir items from which to choose. However, if you need a shopping mall, the Birsta Mall on Gesällvägen #1 is the largest center in Sundsvall. It has 90 shops, a grocery and several cafes. It is normally open weekdays from 10 AM to 8 PM and from 10 AM to 6 PM on weekends.

FINAL WORDS: Sundsvall is not one of the major Scandinavian cities, so please do not expect Stockholm or Copenhagen. There are only a few interesting venues, but the city will give you the overall flavor of a small Swedish city that is not a major tourist destination. And the scenery should make up for the lack of urban excitement.

On those few cruises that circumnavigate the Gulf of Bothnia visitors should expect to see more of a natural landscape that is quite serene and beautiful without being spectacular like the fjords of Norway. And the ports of call are not among the major cities of the Baltic Sea region, but they are still fascinating in their own manner.

MAP OF SUNDSVALL

INNER SUNDSVALL

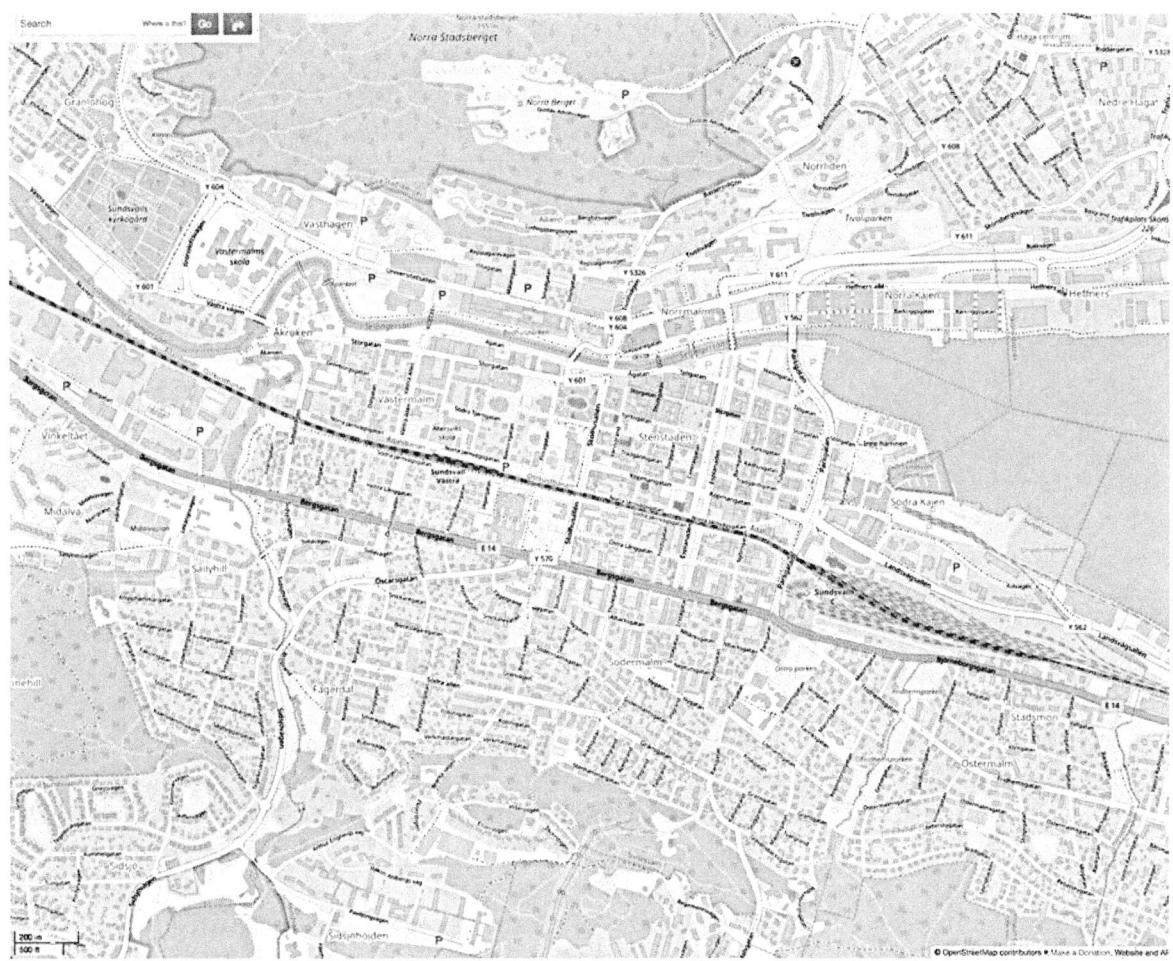

The inner heart of Sundsvall

This map is best viewed directly from OpenStreetMap.com on your personal device where it can be expanded or one specific area can be enlarged. Given the format of this book, it is impossible to display maps with the level of detail you might wish to have while actually out exploring the city. But the OpenStreetMap maps used directly are the tool I always rely upon.

LULEÅ, SWEDEN

Map of the City of Luleå, (© OpenStreetMap contributors), the star showing where cruise ships dock

The small northern city of Luleå is located on the far northern Swedish shore of the Gulf of Bothnia, 901 kilometers or 540 miles north of Stockholm. The city is only 109 kilometers or 58 miles in a straight line from the Arctic Circle, giving it a very harsh climate. With a population of nearly 75,000 in its metropolitan area, it is the largest Swedish city this far north. Being this far north during summer while you will be cruising, Luleå will give you the longest day of your cruise, almost total daylight. During June and early July, it will have just about 23 hours of daylight, and it will never get completely dark when the sun just touches below the horizon. Norway does have one major city above the Arctic Circle, which is Tromsö and Murmansk, Russia is the world's largest urban center north of the circle. It has over 500,000 residents.

THE NATURAL SETTING: Luelå will be for many of you a highlight because of its far northern geographic location. Unless you have actually been above the Arctic Circle, this will be your most northerly destination. The Arctic Circle represents that line that encircles the globe at the point where the northernmost ray of sunlight reaches during winter and only for very short periods of time each day from early December until mid-January will all lands north of that line be in total darkness. Then of course in summer, there is about a six-week period of total daylight for everyone living north of that somehow magical line. Luleå is almost there, but just falls short. During winter, its weather conditions are bone chilling and the days are dark for up to 23 hours. There is not a great quantity of snow, but what falls then sticks through to spring. Summer can be very mild to even warm on occasion. And there is almost perpetual daylight.

The midnight sun outside of Luluå in July

The surrounding landscape is one of glacial scour where the hard bedrock is fragmented into numerous offshore islands and mainland peninsulas that create many deep bays that are not quite what can be called fjords. Luleå is located on a deep channel, but it is not a true fjord. The countryside is covered primarily in spruce with a few willows and other deciduous trees. Unlike Sundsvall, here the forest cover is thin and farther north the landscape turns into true Arctic tundra.

One unique bit of geology shows how active the land has been in rebounding since it was covered in glacial ice over 10,000 years ago. When Luleå was founded in 1621, the land had already been rising back up after the weight of glacial ice had been removed for nearly 10,000 years. Within a few decades, Luleå had to be moved because the harbor was becoming too shallow due to the land rebounding at a more rapid rate in the later years.

Luleå is very close to the top end of the Gulf of Bothnia and if your cruise is moving in a clockwise direction, your next port of call will be in Finland. There is one major road that does follow the Swedish coast past Luleå and then crosses the border into Finland, proceeding all the way to the southern end of the country. And there is a parallel rail line extending around the top of the Gulf of Bothnia into Finland. Luleå also a rail link to the city of Kiruna, Sweden's iron mining center close to the Norwegian border and this continues on to Narvik, Norway. With its deep and extensive harbor, Luleå is a center for both the manufacturing and export of steel products.

A BRIEF LOCAL HISTORY: Luleå is an old city, dating back to 1621 when King Gustavus Adolphus granted a Royal charter, but it does not date back far enough to have any Viking history. The Old Town quarter, located approximately 12 kilometers north of the present city center is today a UNESCO World Heritage Site, especially its beautiful old church and other wood buildings from the 17th century. As noted earlier, the geological uplift common in much of Scandinavia following the last glacial advance made the upper end of the harbor too shallow. Thus in 1649, present day Luleå was founded, but it was not until the King issued a decree that everyone moved south.

During the 18th century Luleå stagnated because of two events. When Peter the Great secured his new capital of Saint Petersburg, he sent troops against Sweden to assert Russian dominance. Luleå was one of those coastal towns to have been attacked. In addition to this depredation, the predominantly wooden town suffered numerous disastrous fires similar to those that plagued Sundsvall.

Economically the city did see some development apart from timber and fishing. Two shipyards were developed in the late 18th century to produce sailing ships, but by the mid 19th century, the steamship had curtailed this industry. But the future of Luleå was to be in iron ore, which was found in several deposits on the hard rock lands of Lapland to the north and west of Luleå. By 1906, the Norrbotten Ironworks had been established in Luleå and is today a major factor in the city's growth, known now as Swedish Steel Company, Limited. The ore is brought from Kiruna in the northwest for processing into finished steel products. But some ore does end up being shipped west into Norway for export abroad.

Modern Luleå has become quite a high-tech research and educational center despite its distance from the core of the country. Luleå University of Technology is well recognized as having one of Europe's finest engineering schools. The university also has excellent music, education and business programs The Luleå Science Park is another important component of the city's high tech development. And Facebook located its very first data center in Luleå because of the beauty and peaceful nature of its environment and its educational institutions.

Luleå is also home to the Norbottens Air Force Base, one of the major bases for the Flygvapnet, the Swedish national air force. There is a museum on base, which I note under things to do.

THE PHYSICAL LAYOUT OF LULEÅ: The way in which the city has grown is rather complex for the visitor to comprehend without first studying the map, or possibly being fortunate enough to fly into the city on a clear day. Luleå spreads along the eastern shore of a deep water bay or fjord, and its central core developed on a small peninsula that juts westward into the water. The map at the start of this chapter will help in establishing a mental image of the city plan. The bay has two arms extending north from the city center and a small part of Luleå has developed on the intervening peninsula.

Flying over the city center, (Work of Tortap, CC BY SA 3.0, Wikimedia.org)

East of the main heart of the city there are several glacial lakes that interrupt the spread of the urban landscape, but there are several residential districts beyond this string of lakes.

To the south, there is a long narrow peninsula that exists because of a smaller indentation into the land, which the locals call Hertsöfjärden. This peninsula is primarily industrial land, as the steel mills and other fabricating plants are located here.

Outside of the immediate central city core known as Luleå proper there is no semblance of a grid pattern. The city core does exhibit a nice rectangular pattern, but it is only a small part of the overall city.

SHIP DOCKING: Today the pier that was once used for loading iron ore is today used by government icebreakers during winter and for the few cruise ships that stop during the summer season. There are no terminal facilities at this pier, but the distance into the city center is relatively short and can be walked in approximately 20 to 25 minutes. Most cruise lines do, however, offer a shuttle bus service.

WHAT TO SEE AND DO: Luleå is similar in nature to Sundsvall in that it does not have a well-developed tourist infrastructure. There are no hop on hop off busses and most cruise lines that do stop for a few hours do not offer any tours. Thus you are essentially on your own with regard to getting around. But this does not mean you cannot enjoy your visit, as the city is easy to get around in and people are very friendly.

An aerial over central Luleå, (Work of Tortap, CC BY SA 3.0, Wikimedia.org)

* **OPTIONS FOR SIGHTSEEING IN LULEÅ:** There are still a few options open to you despite Luleå not having a well-developed infrastructure for tourism. Here are my recommendations:

** **Ship sponsored tours** – For those who wish to see the most possible with the least expenditure, I do recommend the tour(s) your cruise line will offer. If you are not into group touring, there are other options.

** **Private car and driver** – Having your cruise line arrange a private car and driver/guide is difficult because there are few available and the cost will be substantial. But if you plan ahead it is possible. You may also wish to check with VIP Limousine at _www.vip-limo.se_ to compare price and service.

In the heart of Luleå, (Work of Gerrit, CC BY SA 3.0, Wikimedia.org)

** **Rental cars** – There are rental car agencies, but as in Sundsvall I wish to remind you that almost all vehicles will have manual shift and road signs are all written in Swedish. So unless you feel comfortable and have an adventurous nature, you should consider these factors.

** **There is no hop on hop off bus service** available in Luleå, as the city is too small.

** **Taxi service** – There will be taxis on the dock and you can negotiate with a taxi for a tour around the city at an agreed upon price. Drivers for the most part do speak English. But do not be hesitant, as someone else will seize the opportunity given the small supply. If you wish to try and book ahead, I recommend checking with Luleå Taxi at *www.luleataxi.se* .

** **Local bus service** – There is a local bus line in Luleå, and I suggest you ask the local hospitality representative that will either come on board your ship or greet guests on the pier. Gammelstead, which is the number one attraction, can be reached by local city bus, as it is far out of the city and not easily reachable on foot. The city bus ticket office is in the center of town at Smedjegatan 13H and is open weekdays from 10 AM to 5 PM. You can be given directions on reaching any location in the urban area.

** **Walking** – This is a good option if you just want to remain in the city center, but you will only gain a narrow view of this charming northern community.

* **SIGHTS TO SEE IN LULEÅ:** Here are my recommendations as to the major attractions in Luleå that you should concentrate upon (shown in alphabetical order):

In historic Gammelstead, (Work of Zairon, CC BY SA 4.0, Wikimedia.org)

* **Gammelstead Church and Town** - This is without question the prime destination for all visitors since it is a declared UNESCO World Heritage Site. Located 12 kilometers north of the city center, it can be reached by taxi. This town centers upon its old church. There are several hundred preserved wood buildings, as the town was forcibly abandoned when the land rose and the harbor became too shallow. You can walk the town and absorb the feeling of what it was once like. Guided tours are offered during summer daily at 11 AM 1 PM and 3 PM seven days per week. As of September tours are given at 1 PM weekdays and 3 PM weekends.

* **Flygmuseet F-21** - Located on the Norbottens Air Force Base, this museum is a must for any aviation enthusiast. The Swedish Air Force is one of the finest and best trained in Europe. And Saab built fighter jets are the primary aircraft, today the JAS Gripen being its major fighter. The exhibits illustrate over 60 years of air force activities and aircraft. Sweden although being a neutral nation does have a formidable jet fighter capable air force. The museum can be reached by city bus or taxi. The museum is only open on from 10 AM to 4 PM Tuesday thru Friday during the summer months. The rest of the year it is only open on Thursday.

* **Hägnan Open Air Museum** - This museum is part of the overall Gammelstead complex and it offers a variety of activities that help bring the old cultures to life. From mid-June until mid-August the museum is open from 11 AM to 5 PM daily.

* **Kulturens Hus** - This cultural center is located at Skeppsbrogatan #17 near the city center. It is where all cultural activities such as concerts, dance performances and drama are held. If you happen to be in Luleå when there is a performance that would be of interest, you simply need to go to their box office and hope you can get in. Or if you are a theater oriented person, check their web site for advance purchase at www.kulturenshus.com.

* **Norbottens Museum** - In the city center at Storgatan #2, this museum represents all of the natural and cultural aspects of the region, which happens to be the largest of Sweden's counties in area. It is interesting if you have a great love of local geography and history, but frankly most visitors seem to come away less than impressed. I believe this is because they are holding out too high an expectation. It is open Tuesday thru Friday from 10 AM to 4 PM and Saturday and Sunday from 11 AM to 6 PM.

* **Tekniksens Hus** - This is the city's technology museum that chronicles all of the technical developments since the days of early iron and steel production through to today's varied high-tech activities. There is also a planetarium, gift shop and restaurant on the site. This is an excellent venue for children or any adult with a scientific interest. The museum is open Tuesday thru Sunday from 10 AM to 4 PM Tuesday thru Sunday. It is located on the Luleå Technical University campus a bit of a walk north from the city center, but a short taxi ride.

WHERE TO DINE: You will only be in Luleå for a few hours, thus my recommendations are for those restaurants open at lunch and serving traditional Swedish food since I strongly believe in sampling the local flavors. Here are my few choices, as unfortunately this port is not noted for its fine cuisine. In Luleå, there is not a very great selection when it comes to having a traditional Swedish lunch:

* **Bistro Norrland** - Located on the water in the city center at Norra Strandgatan #3-6, this is another excellent restaurant where the emphasis is upon the dishes popular here in Norrland County. Seafood is definitely the star in this restaurant. Open Monday thru Thursday 11 AM to 10 PM, Friday until 10:30 PM, but dinner only on Saturday from 4 to 10:30 PM. You can book a table at +46 920 52 31 00.

* **Hemmagastronomi** - Located at Norra Strandgatan #1 on the water but in the city center, this is an outstanding restaurant that serves gourmet Swedish cuisine along with dishes from elsewhere. Both the atmosphere and food are outstanding, be it in seafood, poultry or meat. If you are in a hurry, you can order in their deli department where service is quick, but the atmosphere is not as conducive to a leisurely meal. Open for lunch from 11 AM to 4 PM, Monday, 11 AM to Midnight

Tuesday thru Thursday, 10 AM to 1 AM Friday and Saturday. Call to book a table at +46 920 22 00 02.

* **Restaurang CG** - In the city center at Storgatan #9, this is one of the best overall restaurants in Luleå. The cuisine is top notch whether you choose a seafood dish or reindeer, which is very traditional. Everything is well prepared and beautifully served. However, if you are in a hurry, I would say go elsewhere. This is a restaurant where gracious dining is the rule, so take time and enjoy. I am listing this because it is so good. They serve Monday thru Thursday from 5 to 11 PM and Friday and Saturday from 5 PM to Midnight. These hours will only work when your ship is in port into the evening hours, which many will be doing. Call +46 920 20 07 00 to book a table.

SHOPPING: As in Sundsvall, Luleå is not a city where you will find a large variety of souvenir items. For regular shopping, Luleå, I do recommend Shopping Galleria on Stordgatan at #51. It claims to be the world's first indoor shopping mall, first opened in the 1950's. It is open Monday thru Friday from 10 AM to 6 PM, Saturday from 10 AM to 4 PM and Sunday from Noon to 4 PM.

Inside the modern Shopping Galleria in Luleå, (Work of Andreas Lakso, CC BY SA 4.0, Wikimedia.org)

FINAL WORDS: You will find Luleå to be a very delightful small city despite it not having many major venues for visitors or a great selection of restaurants. However, once again you have the opportunity to visit one of the more isolated cities of northern Sweden and experience how comfortable it is despite its northerly location.

MAP OF LULEA

THE CENTRAL AREA OF LULEÅ

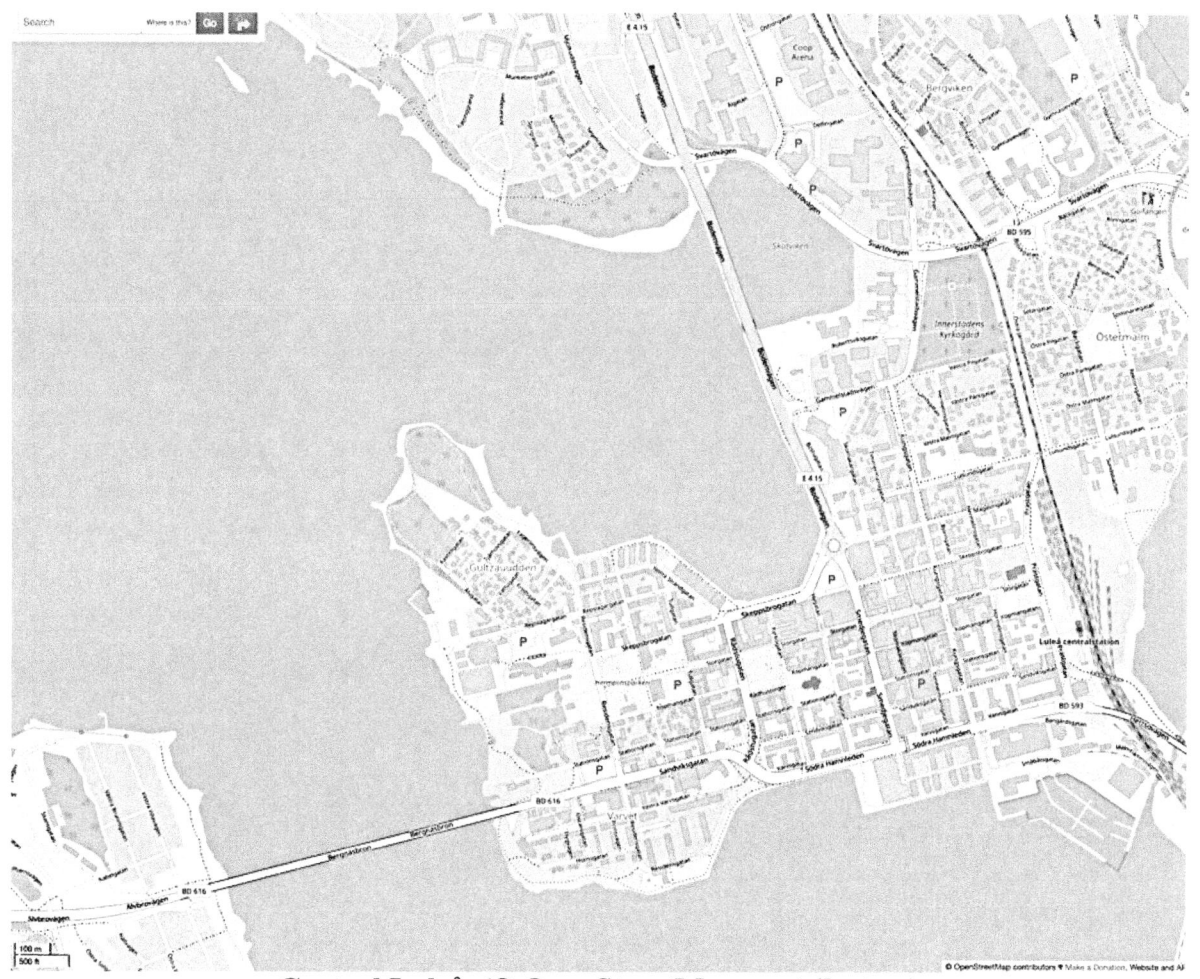

Central Luleå, (© OpenStreetMap contributors)

This map is best viewed directly from OpenStreetMap.com on your personal device where it can be expanded or one specific area can be enlarged. Given the format of this book, it is impossible to display maps with the level of detail you might wish to have while actually out exploring the city. But the OpenStreetMap maps used directly are the tool I always rely upon.

KEMI, FINLAND

A map of greater Kemi showing the Swedish border and the port area where you dock, (© OpenStreetMap contributors)

The port of Kemi is located in the upper half of Finland, approximately 711 kilometers or 442 miles from Helsinki via the main inland road. From Kemi to Turku, Finland's second city, which is also one of the major ports on the Gulf of Bothnia the distance is 722 kilometers or 449 miles. Kemi is a small city with a metro area population of only 25,000 and it is only minutes by road from the border with Sweden. Like other ports around the Gulf of Bothnia, Kemi does not see cruise ships very often and its tourist infrastructure is still minimal, but this is what gives the city its charm in that it is not overrun by outside visitors.

THE NATURAL SETTING: Kemi is located in north central Finland, a region that has been well scoured by past glacial ice. There are outcroppings of hard continental rock and the landscape is one of thousands of lakes interspersed with forests of spruce, willow, birch and other small deciduous trees. It is a scenic landscape, but not a spectacular one.

There are fast flowing rivers that come from the interior to the Gulf of Bothnia, and they are excellent fishing sites. The main land animal is the reindeer, and from Kemi north into the tundra of Finland, this is Sami country. The Sami are better known as the Laplanders. The Sami are ancient reindeer herding people who roam from Norway across Scandinavia and into western Russia.

The thick forests around Kemi

Winter is a long and harsh season. Snowfall is quite prodigious and temperatures fall to well below the freezing mark. And this far north, the days are quite short. The winter landscape of Sea Lapland, the region in which Kemi is located, also typifies Siberia. In the 1960's when Hollywood was filming the great epic Russian novel *Doctor Zhivago,* Finland was chosen for the winter scenes since at that time the Soviet government would not allow those portions of the movie to be filmed in the Soviet Union. But the movie was filmed closer to Helsinki rather than in the somewhat forbidding northland.

A BRIEF LOCAL HISTORY: Kemi is not an old city with a history dating back into medieval times. It was actually the result of orders from Russian Tsar Alexander II in 1869 that a city be created on a deep water harbor for the purpose of being able to tap into the rich timber of the interior for export. I often wonder why the Tsar considered this to be important since Russia is the largest country in the world and has forests identical to those around Kemi that stretch for thousands of kilometers. Kemi's only possible advantage was its proximity to western

European markets during the brief summer season when the Gulf of Bothnia was not frozen.

By the early 20th century, Kemi was known for its wood processing into a variety of products including paper. Because of the vitality of this industry, a railroad line was pushed north in 1902, connecting Kemi with Turku.

Finland gained its independence from the Russian Empire in 1917, but after the creation of the Soviet Union, the Communist powers looked to Finland as a prize to be recaptured. The long coastline combined with the wood processing industries, many developed with Russian capital, made a prize that they wanted. In 1939, the Red Army invaded, but the smaller Finnish Army was able to hold them off. Fortunately, Kemi was far enough away from the front and was not bombed. Finland was offered help by Nazi Germany to fend off further Soviet encroachment, and they accepted. Military action continued until 1944 and the Finns ultimately did lose a strip of eastern territory to the Soviet Union after first gaining it back. For more information on this aspect of the war, refer back to the historic detail in the main chapter on Helsinki.

Finnish troops defending Kemi in the Lapland War against Nazi forces

The Finns wanted the Germans out of their country since they did not consider World War II to be their war. They made peace with the Soviet Union. The Germans resented what Finland had done, and they feared that the Red Army would ultimately decimate their forces. In their retreat to the north toward Norway, they did blow up bridges, burn towns and they attempted to leave a wake of destruction behind them. Kemi stood in the way and the crossing of the Kemijoki River was considered strategic to Germany. The Finns essentially were forced into this war, as otherwise the Soviet Union would consider them as an enemy force and it would have given them justification to retake the country. The Nazi troops had captured over 200 civilians from Kemi and Rovanimi, and threatened to kill them unless they released the German forces the Finns had captured. The Finns threatened to kill the German troops if harm came to the civilians. Fortunately for Finland, the German forces crossed back into Norway, which they already held, and then both sides released their prisoners. Because the Finns had confronted the Germans and had suffered localized devastation, the Soviet Union did not retaliate by occupying the country. But they did demand reparations for the earlier Finnish and German conflict along Finland's eastern border even though they had been the original aggressors.

From the end of World War II until 1991, Finland always had to tread lightly in dealing with the Soviet Union. Today the country has good relations with Russia and tourists from Saint Petersburg and Moscow add significantly to the Finnish economy.

Kemi has continued to prosper and is today still an important center for wood products, especially wood pulp and paper production. Chromium, a vital mineral in today's high-tension metals production has also been mined in the vicinity of Kemi. However, in 1949, a major strike among timber workers did end in a mass demonstration that turned violent and caused the deaths of two people. But since that period, Kemi along with the rest of the country has seen ongoing prosperity. Finland is actually one of the most idyllic countries in the world with regard to the overall welfare and education of its people. In the last two years, UNESCO reported that the public education in Finland ranked as the world's best. This is a great source of national pride.

Today the city of Kemi is quite cultured. It has fine museums a good public library, a music school and the Kemi-Tornio University of Applied Sciences. There is also a technology center that specializes in a variety of high-tech endeavors.

THE PHYSICAL LAYOUT OF KEMI: The port city of Kemi is quite small and easy for visitors to explore. There are few taxis and no hop on hop off bus since tourism other than winter skiers is rather limited.

Kemi is spread along the shore of a deep water bay that is filled with numerous rocky islands that are forest covered. It also sits on the southern bank of the delta of the Kemijoki River, which is a relatively wide and fast flowing waterway. Part of the city does extend across to the northern bank of the river, including settlement on a broad island at the mouth of the river. There is also quite a bit of industrial development along the river bank. Also on the southern bank there is a large island that is likewise heavily industrialized. It is here that the pulp and paper mills are located.

A view over central Kemi, (Work of Lijonama45, CC BY SA 3.0, Wikimedia.org)

The heart of Kemi consists of a square kilometer block of land that has a regularized grid street pattern. The main railroad line runs parallel with the main north to south expressway (Finnish Route 4) and both separate the city core from the residential areas that extend into the forested hills beyond to the east.

A narrow isthmus connects the southern shore to a large island that is home to the main seaport for Kemi. It is here that the mills can export their product, as all are interconnected by spur railway lines.

Like most Finnish cities, Kemi contains many apartment blocks with single family houses being found all around the city center in distinct residential nodes on curvilinear streets showing a degree of urban planning.

SHIP DOCK: When cruise ships visit Kemi, they dock in Ajos Port, which offers four different moorings. The port is ten kilometers or six miles south of the city on a forested island that contains the small suburban town of Ajos. The location is based upon the deep draught capability for cruise and cargo vessels. Most cruise lines will offer a shuttle bus into the center of Kemi and there will be local taxis plying the route all day.

SIGHTSEEING IN KEMI: There is very little in the way of a developed summer tourist infrastructure in Kemi. This is a city where winter tourism is far more important to the local economy. Most cruise lines do not offer any major tours, if any, as this area does not have a developed infrastructure. Depending upon where your ship will dock, a shuttle bus into the town center may or may not be required.

In the town center of Kemi

* **SIGHTSEEING OPTIONS IN KEMI:** The options are rather limited, as Kemi does not have a well-developed infrastructure for tourism.

** **Ship sponsored tours** – This is your best option if your cruise line offers an overview tour of greater Kemi, usually for only four hours. Some cruise lines simply leave you on your own for the visit.

** **Private car and driver** – This option may not be readily available, as there are very few private vehicles and driver/guides. So book early with your shore excursion desk if this is what you would prefer. You should also check on line with Limo Finland to see what they can provide by going to *www.limofinland.com* .

** **There is no hop on hop off bus** service in Kemi, as it is too small a city to support such service.

** **Taxis** will be at the dock and you can try to negotiate an hourly or daily rate for sightseeing. You can also contact the local taxi service on line to see if it is possible to book in advance for sightseeing. Kemi-Torino Taxi can be reached at *www.finavia.fi* for further information.

** **Walking** is the option many guests opt for, especially if your cruise line offers a shuttle into the city center or if your ship docks within walking distance. The few attractions are in the heart of the city.

Older residential buildings in central Kemi reflect a strong Russian flavor

* **MAJOR SIGHTS TO SEE IN KEMI:** The following major sights to see during the summer when cruise ships visit include (shown in alphabetical order):

* **Ice Breaker Sampo** - This once mighty ice breaker that helped keep the Baltic Sea open during winter is now docked in Kemi. During winter it does offer tours through the ice covered Gulf of Bothnia, giving visitors a chance to experience what it may be like to go on a polar expedition. During summer special tours are often given, especially when arranged by visiting cruise ships. Some tours may even include a short harbor area cruise, all dependent upon what your cruise line arranges.

Kemi Church, (Work of Matthewross, CC BY SA 3.0, Wikimedia.org)

* **Kemi Church** - This is the largest and most imposing of the city's churches. Although an early 20th century building, it is constructed in a pseudo-Gothic style and is an interesting piece of architecture. It is located in the heart of the city at Kirkkopuistokatu #9. It is open for visitors daily except when services are being conducted. No specific hours are available at the time of this writing.

* **Kemi Downtown** – The small city center is quite pleasant and does reflect the very modern and well-ordered nature of Finnish communities. The focal hub is the beautiful Lutheran church whose tower dominates the city center. Normally visitors can enter the church during daylight hours. A stroll through the downtown area does give you an introduction to the prosperity, yet conservatism of the Finnish way of life, which is one of the highest in quality in the world.

When walking around the city of Kemi's central district, be sure to also visit the adjacent residential streets to get some idea as to the Finnish home life.

* **Kemi Gemstone Gallery** - This small museum features a sizeable display of gemstones from all over the world. It is primarily of interest to those who find looking at displays of gemstones to be a worthy experience, thus it is not for everyone. It does have on display a crown made for a Finnish king, however, when Finland gained its independence in 1917, it became a republic. It is located in the city center at Kauppakatu #29. The gallery is open between 10 AM and 4 PM Monday thru Friday.

* **Merike** - This small company offers scheduled and chartered tours of the archipelago around Kemi on cruises that last up to 90 minutes. Their scheduled sailings are only between mid-June and mid-August, and they operate only on Friday and Sunday with several sailings each day. If your ship happens to be in port on either day and the weather is nice, this is one way to enjoy the countryside and the surrounding waters. They are located at Luulajantie, which is on the downtown waterfront. You can contact them at *www.merike.fi* for more information and to make bookings.

* **Snow Castle** - Each year a Finnish architect, and there are many excellent ones, designs and supervises the building of a massive snow castle that is quite famous. the snow and ice castle covers over 20,000 square meters with walls up to 1,000 meters long and turrets as high as 30 meters. The castle contains a restaurant, hotel and wedding chapel. It now attracts several hundred thousand visitors from all over the world. It is only mentioned here in the event that it may last into the late spring months, but most often it is gone before cruise season.

DINING OUT: There are several small restaurants in the central core area of Kemi that do serve lunch. I have chosen only two that I recommend for both serving some traditional Finnish cuisine and having acceptable standards of quality. The restaurants in Kemi are not of the highest standard you will find across Scandinavia, but a few are relatively good.

Finnish cuisine includes a bounty from the sea, especially the use of salmon during the summer months. One of the most traditional is a soup made with salmon, potatoes, carrots and fresh dill. It is served either in a clear fish broth or in with a milk and butter stock, which is my favorite. There is another milk soup that is vegetarian and contains carrots, onion and barley among other vegetables. Reindeer is a very popular source of meat protein, especially here in Kemi and other northern cities. And the Finns are outstanding bakers when it comes to quite a variety of delectable pastries and cakes.

Here are my two recommendations for lunch in Kemi, as unfortunately other than pizza, Thai or Indian, there is nothing else noteworthy:

* **Pursiseura** - Located in the city center on the water at Luulajantie #11, this restaurant provides a mix of European and Scandinavian dishes served in a very casual atmosphere. On warm days you can eat out on their terrace facing the water. They are open Monday thru Thursday from 11 AM to 8 PM, Friday from 11 AM to 10 PM, Saturday from 1 to 10 PM and Sunday from 1 to 7 PM. Call if you wish to book a table at +358 40 6853559.

* **Restaurant Merihovi** - Located at Keskuspuistokatu #6-8 on the edge of the city center is open for lunch and dinner. Its hours are from 10:30 AM to 2 AM Monday thru Friday and from Noon to 2 AM Saturday. Sunday hours are from 2 PM to 2 AM. This restaurant serves a mix of European, American and

Scandinavian dishes. And yes they do specialize in the traditional salmon soup. But their dessert selection is very limited. Call to book a table at +358 40 6853500.

SHOPPING: There are no special shops or malls to recommend in Kemi, as essentially this is a blue collar community with a small population. The city center does offer a selection of small, locally owned shops that have souvenirs and a handful of local crafts.

The local Stockmann Department Store

As in most Finnish cities, there is a branch of the famous Stockmann Department Store, but this one does not offer a broad selection of merchandise as you would find in the larger cities of Finland. No opening or closing hours are posted for this particular store, but you can be sure it will be open during normal business hours every day of the week.

FINAL WORDS: Kemi is located in a part of Finland known for its beautiful scenery, and as you sail in and out of its harbor, you will be treated to some nice views of its offshore islands. The city's main focus is the pulp and paper industry, but its tourist infrastructure is definitely oriented toward winter activities.

Consider a visit to Kemi as a chance to see what life is like in this remote northern portion of Finland. You will find that despite its isolation from the heartland of the country, life in Kemi is actually not one of deprivation but rather is quite comfortable.

MAPS OF KEMI

THE CITY OF KEMI

Central Kemi, (© OpenStreetMap contributors)

This map is best viewed directly from OpenStreetMap.com on your personal device where it can be expanded or one specific area can be enlarged. Given the format of this book, it is impossible to display maps with the level of detail you might wish to have while actually out exploring the city. But the OpenStreetMap maps used directly are the tool I always rely upon.

THE CENTRAL A\REA OF KEMI

Central Kemi

This map is best viewed directly from OpenStreetMap.com on your personal device where it can be expanded or one specific area can be enlarged. Given the format of this book, it is impossible to display maps with the level of detail you might wish to have while actually out exploring the city. But the OpenStreetMap maps used directly are the tool I always rely upon.

OULU, FINLAND

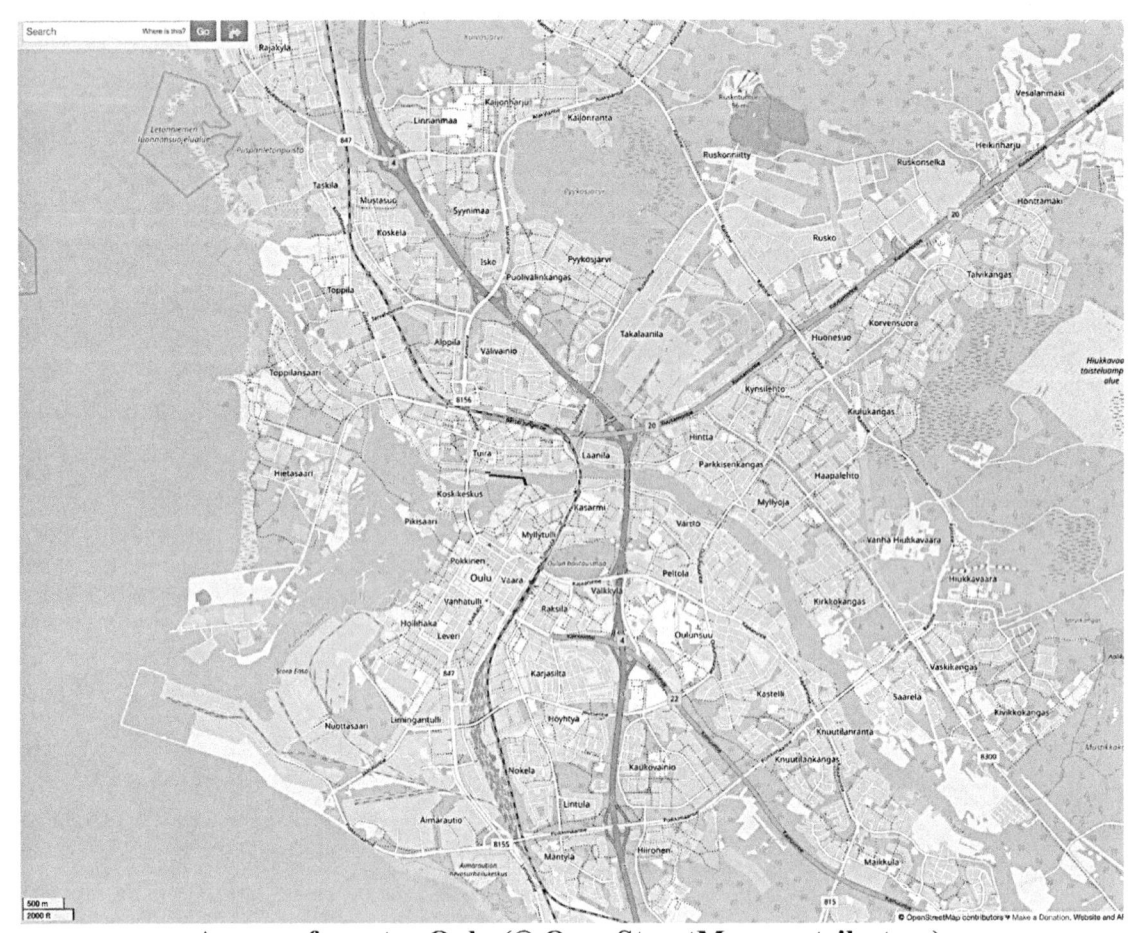

A map of greater Oulu (© OpenStreetMap contributors)

If cruise ships visit Kemi, they are unlikely to visit Oulu because it is only 90 kilometers or 56 miles to the south. But Oulu is a larger and more interesting city, yet less often visited than Kemi, a fact I find hard to understand. It has a metropolitan population of just over 201,000 residents, making it second only to Turku in population on Finland's Gulf of Bothnia coast. It is the largest Scandinavian city at this northerly latitude, larger than Tromsø, Norway and only exceeded by Murmansk and Norilsk in Russia. Yet I ask why some cruise ships stop in Kemi when they have a larger city with better port facilities and more sights of interest to see.

THE NATURAL SETTING: Oulu wraps around a large bay on the northern Bothnian coast of Finland. The bay is fed by the fast flowing Oulujoki River, which flows right through the city, coming from a beautiful glacially created lake to the east. The bay is filled with numerous offshore islands that are composed of hard rock like the mainland, all the result of past glacial scour, as are all of the inland lakes. The land is moderately hilly and covered in thick spruce forest with groves of willow and birch on the more fertile, damp ground. In late summer and early fall, the willows and birch trees turn a golden yellow, providing for a beautiful backdrop to the city.

The thick spruce and birch forests around Oulu

The serenity of the shoreline around Oulu

The regional climate is similar to all of the other ports surrounding the Gulf of Bothnia in that it is sub polar with long, dark winters where temperatures can and do drop well below freezing. The snow that falls remains and builds up through at least five months until the spring thaw. Summer is mild to sometimes warm, but of short duration. It is a harsh landscape, but the Finns have been masters at adapting to their climate, and the vast majority actually accept winter as a season that can be enjoyed.

A BRIEF LOCAL HISTORY: The prehistory of Oulu actually dates back to a peace accord between the Swedish kingdom and ancient Novgorod (early Russia) in 1323. This part of what is now Finland was ceded to Novgorod and the Russians built a fort at the mouth of the Oulujoki River to protect the territory against Swedish domination. No trace of the fort can be seen today. In 1590, The Swedes established a castle at the river's mouth to assert their dominance over the region. Five years later in a new peace treaty, Russia surrendered its rights to the territory.

Oulu before World War II

What is today Oulu was settled by order of King Charles IX of Sweden in 1605 to consolidate his hold against Russia even though peace had been established. But Peter the Great was intent upon taking all of Finland from Sweden by the early 18th century and his forces began in the north since Helsinki had a massive fort protecting it, which did not fall until the early 19th century. From 1714 until 1721,

Oulu was attacked and burned numerous times, and Oulu and its surroundings were almost abandoned.

After peace was established in 1721, Oulu began to develop as an important port for trade in timber products, fish and furs, partially aided by a shift in the river, creating a deep inlet. By 1765, Oulu was given permission to accept foreign trade, but not foreign ships.

Ultimately Russia managed to take control of all Finland in 1809, but trade with Sweden continued from Oulu because of its strong ties through both the merchant and noble communities.

The aftermath of Soviet air raids on Oulu

Like so many cities in Scandinavia during the 19th century, Oulu experienced a massive fire that destroyed most of the community in 1822. This later prompted the use of stone or brick for public buildings, especially the town's main church. Another fire in 1882 burned much of the town center, this fire having started in a batch of tar waiting to be exported.

During the Winter War with the Soviet Union in 1939-40 and the Continuation War in 1941-44, Oulu was bombed by the Soviets on two occasions. German forces had been stationed in Oulu. It was the second air raid in 1844 that did the most damage in the Russian attempt to route Nazi forces.

In the post-World War II era, Oulu has continued to grow and prosper. Today it is home to a fine university, many cultural venues, including both a winter and summer music festival, and it also is a major center for light manufacturing, wood processing and fishing.

THE PHYSICAL LAYOUT OF OULU: The city is quite spread out, occupying both banks of the Oulujoki River whose mouth splits into two channels around a significantly large island devoted to residential districts, parkland and industrial and port facilities at its southern end. Across the river channel from the southern end of the island is the main port and industrial area of the city, and it is quite significant. The river also makes a large loop first eastward and then to the southeast, and urban development is found on both the southern and northern margins (see the detailed map at the end of the chapter).

The city center occupies the shoreline along the southern half of the river delta and has a well-defined grid pattern canted at a northeast to southwest angle following the riverbank. The main railroad line backs up the city center, with significant yard facilities located at the southern end.

In the city center of Oulu

Beyond the railroad line is a large residential area extending to the east and southeast. Here the street pattern is one that exhibits distinct residential nodes often separated from one another by parkland, a common practice in Finland. Expressway 4 runs on a north to south axis right through this residential area, then after crossing the river, it turns to the northwest.

North of the river and west of the expressway there is a significant residential district through which the railroad line runs. This area also lacks a cohesive pattern and shows a mix of residential communities separated by parkland. Closer to the shore of the northern branch of the river there is significant manufacturing development. A large manufacturing area served by a spur line of the railroad lies to the east of the expressway and north of the major boulevard known as Kuusamontle, which is somewhat of a controlled access route. To the south of this main route is another extensive residential area that again is broken by extensive parkland.

Looking down upon modern residential Oulu surrounded by thick forest

In all Finnish cities, the residential areas exhibit a mix of apartment blocks and single-family homes. But the development is quite organized, exhibiting a great degree of fore thought and planning. This is a hallmark of the quality of residential life in Finland.

SHIP DOCK: The port facility in Oulu is located approximately four kilometers or two and one half miles southwest of the city center. There is no cruise terminal, but the docks are capable of handling small to moderately large cruise ships. The surrounding area is not conducive to cruise passengers walking, as it contains numerous railway spurs and cargo storage facilities. Thus most cruise lines will provide continuous shuttle bus service into the town center. And there will be local taxis available dockside as well.

Like most Finnish cities much of residential Oulu consists of apartment blocks

SIGHTSEEING IN OULU: In all likelihood your cruise line will operate a shuttle bus to the city center, as the docks where a cruise ship can tie up are not easy walking distance from the heart of Oulu. Given that this is a larger city, I would expect your cruise line to offer group coach excursions either around the city or to one of the beautiful rural sites outside.

* **SIGHTSEEING OPTIONS FOR OULU:** These are the options available to you with regard to spending time exploring Oulu and its surroundings:

** **Cruise sponsored tours** – Most cruise lines that stop in Oulu do offer as a minimum a half day motor coach tour around the city. Depending upon your itinerary and the company you are with there may be a walking tour of the city center or possibly an all-day excursion.

The more upmarket cruise lines may offer a half day tour into the surrounding countryside, which gives you a chance to enjoy the scenery of northern Finland.

** **Private car and driver** – As a major city, your cruise line should be able to organize private cars with driver/guides. As an alternative, and possibly a cost savings, I recommend contacting Limo Finland at *www.limofinland.com* for further details or bookings.

** **Local tour trolley** – There is a tour service that is somewhat like a train on wheels operating around the city, starting at the city hall. It is the Oulu equivalent of a hop on hop off bus. There are two routes to choose from. For more details check out their web page at *http://otptravel.fi/potnapekka* for schedules and details. This is an inexpensive way to see the major highlights of Oulu.

In late fall the old railway station is reminiscent of the movie *Doctor Zhivago*

** Taxi touring – There will be taxis waiting at the dock. Most drivers speak English and you can negotiate a price for sightseeing services. I recommend that you contact Taxi Kadenius at *www.kadenius.fi* for service and rate information or to book a taxi in advance. In Finland the vast majority of taxi drivers are very helpful and actually enjoy showing visitors around.

** City bus services – Oulu maintains a city bus service that is not difficult to use as a visitor. If you choose to get around the city using local busses, I recommend that you first ask the local hospitality representative either who will either board your ship or be at the dock or go on line to the city bus service at *www.ouka.fi* for further details. However, you will find that many bus drivers do not speak much English and you could easily get yourself lost.

** Bicycle option is risky – Despite the long snowy winters, the people of Finland embrace the bicycle as a means of daily transport and many cities are bicycle friendly. Bicycle touring is great if you are up to it. If the weather is good and you enjoy riding a bicycle, Oulu has some of the most extensive bicycle paths of any city in Scandinavia. This is a truly bicycle oriented city. For detailed rental information visit Outdoors Oulu Oy website found at *www.outdoorsoulu.fi* . Another popular operator is Mustosen Pyörä Oy whose web page is at *www.mustosenpyora.fi* .

Oulu offers a fine network of bicycle and walking paths and this is a great way for seeing the city

* THE MAJOR SIGHTS TO SEE AND THINGS TO DO: As a major city on the Gulf of Bothnia, Oulu has developed an excellent park and walking or bicycle trail system that is typical of the Finnish interest in outdoor activities. This is a very pleasant city to visit and it gives you a fine example of the high quality of life that Finland is noted for having. In many global surveys of the best countries in which to live, Finland always rates quite high, often being in first or second place. And part of that high rank is the result of the urban amenities Finnish cities offer for their residents.

It is also important to note that Finland ranks among the top five countries in the world for the quality of its public education system. Finnish people have a relaxed lifestyle and are very easygoing, but this belies their strong attachment to the work ethic and learning.

Here is my listing of sights to see and places to visit in the city of Oulu (shown in alphabetical order):

** Botanical Gardens – This site is located on the University of Oulu campus, which is in the northern part of the city and requires using either a taxi or public bus to reach. The exact address is Pentti Kaiteran katu #1. Here is a chance to see almost all of the northern vegetation of the taiga and tundra in one beautiful setting that is open to the public at no charge. If your cruise line is offering a motor coach tour of Oulu, there is a strong likelihood that the Botanical Gardens will be included in your tour.

Hours are Tuesday thru Friday from 8 AM to 3 PM and Sunday 11 AM to 3 PM. The gardens are closed Monday and Saturday. During summer afternoon hours are usually extended. If the weather is favorable, this is a very restful and inspirational place to visit.

The beautiful Botanical Gardens at the University of Oulu in early spring

** Hupisaaret Islands Park - This is a major park developed on several tightly grouped islands immediately adjacent to the heart of the city. Much of the vegetation in the park is totally natural, giving you a feel for the surrounding countryside. It is one of the most important and well patronized parks in the city, and it offers a nice respite when one is in the city center.

Because of its proximity to the central business district, Hupisaaret Island Park is often a favorite picnic spot for those working in the city center, especially on a warm summer day. Although centrally situated, this park offers one the feeling of being out into the local countryside well away from Oulu without the need to travel by motor coach to explore the countryside.

The park was created in the 1860's and is open daily without any visitor fees.

On the Hupisaaret Islands

** **Museum of Northern Ostrobothnia** - Located in Ainolanpolku #1, which is a city parkland. The museum is open Tuesday and Wednesday from 10 AM to 4 PM and Thursday thru Sunday from 10 AM to 5 PM. This museum spread over four levels presents the regional history in a series of excellent exhibits that help you truly understand where you are. There is a detailed scale model of early Oulu as it was in 1938.

** **Oulu Cathedral** - Located on Kirkkokatu #3a on the northern edge of the city center, this is a beautiful church built in what is called the empire style and dates to 1777, but was later destroyed by fire in 1822 and then rebuilt. As a Lutheran house of worship both its interior and exterior are rather plain, but with very elegant lines. Unfortunately hours when it is open to the public are not posted on the cathedral web page.

** **Oulu City Art Museum** - Located at Kasamintie #7, which is walking distance from the city center. This fine museum is extensive and specializes in contemporary works of art, many by Finnish artists. It is open Wednesday thru Sunday from 10 AM to 5 PM.

** **Pohjois-Pohjnmaan-Museo** - This is the local cultural museum located just north of the city center, not too far to walk in nice weather. The museum is open from 10 AM to 5 PM Tuesday thru Sunday. It contains costumes, furniture and artifacts from all the surrounding cultures of northern Finland. And it also has exhibits on trade and economic activities. The museum also has a small gift shop offering locally handmade craft items. It is well worth a visit.

** **Rapids Center** - This is a grouping of three small residential islands that sit in the estuary of the Oulujoki River. They are interconnected by small bridges. These islands are rather beautifully planned with numerous fountains and green spaces. One area contains a grouping of apartment blocks designed by Alvar Aalto, one of Finland's best-known architects. You may not be aware of the fact that Finland is quite noted for its rather revolutionary architectural designs in the 20th century, and the influences can be found in many countries abroad where Finns have made a name for themselves.

** **Rotuaari** - In the city center, this is the main pedestrian street and during the summer months there are often street entertainers who will be performing. It is a lively street and gives you a good feel for the city and its people. You will find that on a summer afternoon or evening the city center is quite lively.

** **Science Center Tietomma** - This is one of the prime destinations in Oulu. It is located at Nakhatehtaankatu #2 and is open daily from 10 AM to 7 PM. It offers many fascinating exhibits and some hands on activities. It is said to be the first public science museum in the world.

Turkansaari Museum

** Turkansaari** - This open air museum is located on an island in the main channel of the Oulujoki River about ten kilometers south of the city center. The museum reconstructs what rural life was like in Finland one to two centuries ago. It is an interesting place for visitors who have a strong historic interest. The museum is open from 10 AM to 4 PM daily during the summer months. Most of the organized motor coach tours offered by the cruise lines visiting Oulu will include the Turkansaari Museum.

DINING OUT: Most cruise itineraries that include Oulu will only enable you to spend a few hours in port. If you are out on your own, then you will find the restaurant listings in this section most helpful. However, if you are on a long organized motor coach tour lunch will be provided at a restaurant chosen by the tour operator.

I have listed my favorite restaurants in Oulu that I consider good for lunch or dinner if your ship is staying late because they offer a traditional Scandinavian menu. I have always believed that as visitors we should be trying the local food and thus all my restaurant choice are based upon that major criteria. For lunch and dinner in Oulu I recommend the following:

* **Café Hertta** – This tearoom is popular with locals, located at Rautatiekatu, just a short way from the center of town, near the railway station. It offers light meals and desserts with a selection of teas and coffee And it is especially well rated for good service. They are open weekdays from 10 AM to 6 PM and weekends from 10 AM to 4 PM. Reservations are not required or necessary.

* **Ravintola Hella** - This very popular restaurant with an in depth Scandinavian menu is outstanding. Located at Isokatu #13 in the city center, it offers expertly prepared salmon in several ways, excellent duck and a variety of vegetables and sides.

It is open Monday thru Thursday from 10:30 AM to 10 PM, Friday and Saturday from 4 to 11 PM. You can call +358 8 371189 to book a table.

* **Ravintola Merhiovi** – It is located just to the north of the town center at Keskuspuistokatu # 6 8, this is a popular restaurant, many claim to be the best in Kemi. The menu is essentially Scandinavian with many other European dishes to offer a broad selection. Their hours are from 10:30 AM to 2 AM weekdays and from Noon to 2 AM Saturday. Their Sunday hours are from 2 PM to 2 AM and reservations are not necessary.

* **Ravintola Sauraha** – It is located at Asemakatu # 10 and open Monday thru Friday from 10:30 AM to 10 PM and on weekends from Noon to 10 PM. The cuisine is traditionally Finnish and the service is excellent. You will need to take a taxi

because the restaurant is not in the city center, but well worth the effort. To book a table call them at +358 45 3550358.

* **Ravintola Uleåborg 1881**- This traditional Finnish restaurant is located at Aitattori # 4-5 along the waterfront in the city center. Their beautiful menu is diverse in presenting the finest in Finnish dishes along with some vegetarian specialties. The quality of the food, service and atmosphere make this one of the nicest dining establishments in the city.

Their dining hours are 5 to 11 PM Monday thru Thursday and 5 PM to Midnight on Friday and Saturday. Some ship itineraries stay into the evening thus enabling you to have dinner in town. You can call +358 8 8811188 to book.

The unique barn like architecture of Ravintola Uleåborg

* **Skoeri-Jussen Kievari** - Located at Pikisaarenti # 2, a short distance from the city center on the residential island of Pikisaarenti Island, this fine restaurant offers traditional Finnish cuisine and also the dishes of Lapland, including reindeer. Here in an old house, you will be treated to the flavors of Finland that are fading from memory. They are open 11 AM to 10 PM Monday thru Saturday and from Noon to 10 PM on Sunday. Call to book a table at +358 8 376628.

* **Viikinkiravintola Harald** - This very authentic Scandinavian restaurant with a Viking flavor is located at Kirkkokatu #16 in the city center. Their fish, meats and accompanying dishes are excellent, but the only complaint I have heard is that their prices seem to be a bit high. They are open Monday from 11 AM to 9 PM, Tuesday until 10 PM, remaining open until 11 PM Wednesday thru Friday and Saturday from Noon to 11 PM. Sunday hours are from 3 to 9 PM. You can book a table by calling them at +358 44 7668000.

SHOPPING: Despite its larger size, Oulu does not offer a great degree of shopping that will be of interest to visitors. There are a few gift shops that sell typical souvenir and some craft items, all located in the city center. But I have no specific recommendations to make.

FINAL WORD: Oulu is a significant port city, but it still does not have a well-developed tourist infrastructure. There is the somewhat limited hop on hop off bus/train that does take you around the city. And the local bus system is not hard to master. But by simply walking around the city center you will get a good feel for Oulu. This is a pleasant town and its small museums and parks can hold your attention for the day.

MAPS OF OULU

THE CITY OF OULU

Central Oulu, (© OpenStreetMap contributors) with the star showing the port area

This map is best viewed directly from OpenStreetMap.com on your personal device where it can be expanded or one specific area can be enlarged. Given the format of this book, it is impossible to display maps with the level of detail you might wish to have while actually out exploring the city. But the OpenStreetMap maps used directly are the tool I always rely upon.

THE CENTRAL AREA OF OULU

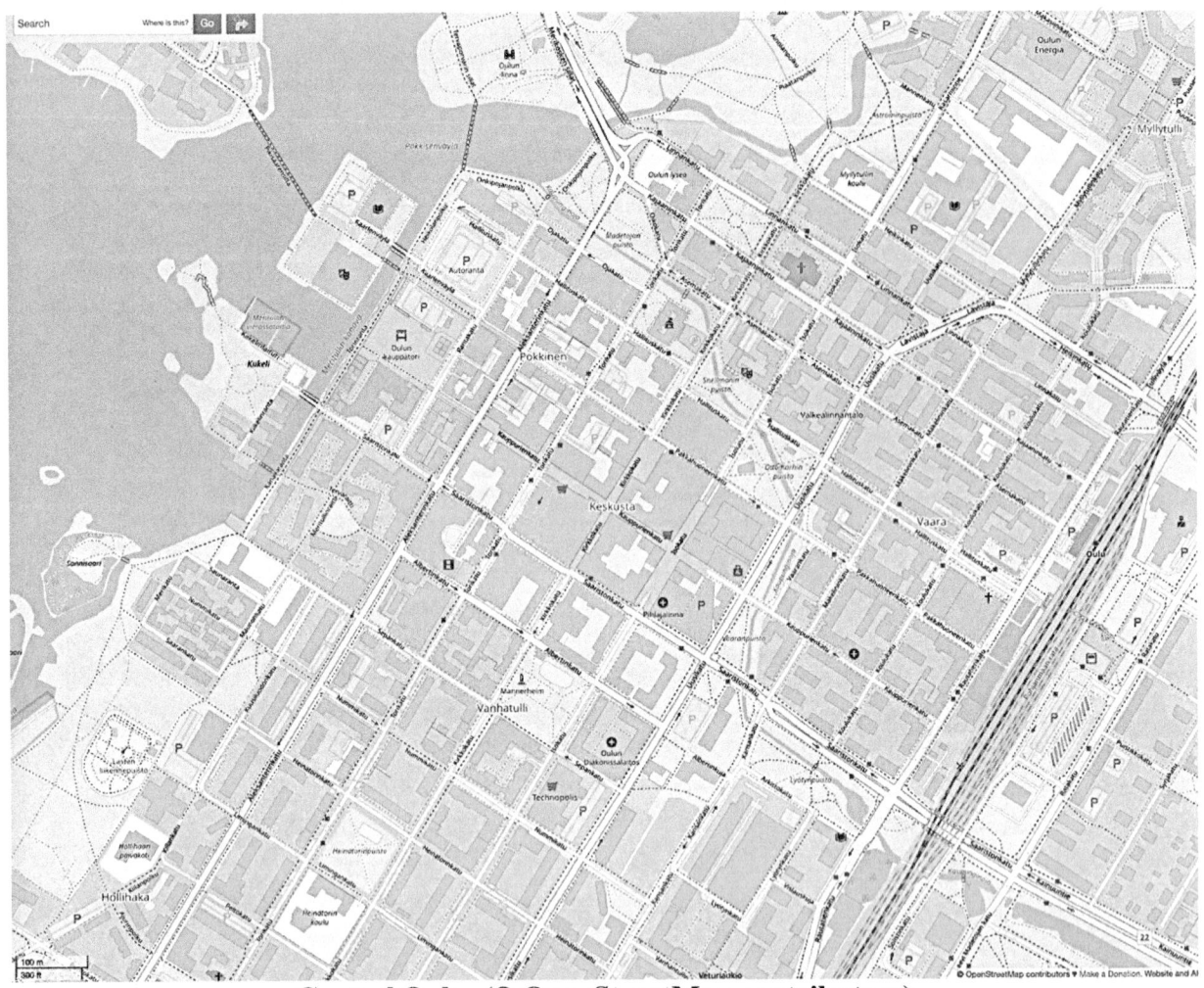

Central Oulu, (© OpenStreetMap contributors)

This map is best viewed directly from OpenStreetMap.com on your personal device where it can be expanded or one specific area can be enlarged. Given the format of this book, it is impossible to display maps with the level of detail you might wish to have while actually out exploring the city. But the OpenStreetMap maps used directly are the tool I always rely upon.

VAASA, FINLAND

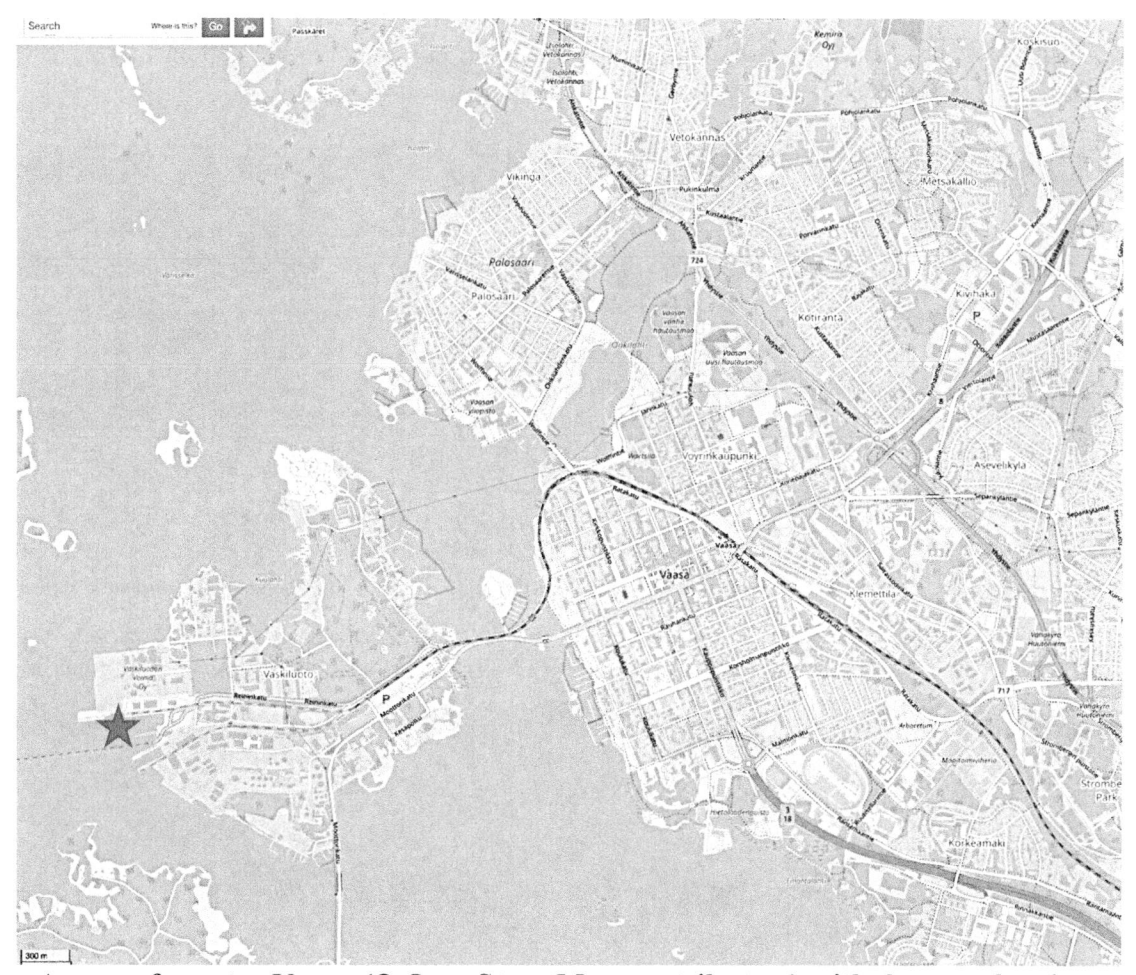

A map of greater Vaasa (© OpenStreetMap contributors) with the star showing the port area

Vaasa is the third largest city to be visited on the Finnish coast of the Gulf of Bothnia. It has approximately 125,000 people in its metropolitan area, but only 67,000 within its corporate limits. It is located 420 kilometers or 252 miles from Helsinki via the direct inland route. It is also 331 kilometers or 198 miles south of Oulu via the coast route. With its irregular coastline resulting from past glacial action, any travel along the coast is much more convoluted than taking inland routes between these cities and towns and the capital city of Helsinki.

THE NATURAL SETTING: Like all of the other ports on the Finnish coast, Vaasa is built around a bay with numerous offshore rocky islands. But there is no river flowing through the city to empty into the bay. The landscape was heavily glaciated as evidenced by numerous small to medium size glacial lakes, rocky outcrops and little deep soil.

The vegetation cover is essentially that of taiga with spruce dominating and groves of willow and birch in the more fertile pockets. The Kvarken Archipelago is located just outside of the bay on which Vaasa is built, and it today is a UNESCO World Heritage Site for its natural beauty. On clear, calm days the reflections of these rocky islands into the surrounding waters is quite striking.

Walking in the thick forests outside of Vaasa, (Work of Anna Katrina Puikko, CC BY SA 4.0, Wikimedia.org)

Weather conditions are as in the other ports so far discussed for the Gulf of Bothnia. Winters are long, cold and blustery with snow being the dominant precipitation. And summer is the mild season. It can get quite warm on days when a high pressure system dominates. Winter is brutally cold, quite dark for at least two months and snowfall can be extensive. There are no specific remarkable features to the surrounding landscape, but when visiting in summer, you will note it is especially green.

A BRIEF LOCAL HISTORY: One observation visitors have almost immediately is that Vaasa has a very strong Swedish flavor. Of all the cities in Finland, Vaasa has the highest percentage of its population of Swedish descent and still speaking the language, approximately 25 percent of Vassa's residents.

The region was settled in the 14th century by the Swedes who built Korsholm Castle outside the village of Mustasaari, which became what is the present day city of

Vaasa. Mustasaari was the Finnish name for the region that the Swedes called Korsholm, and today this is the name given to the surrounding municipality that encircles Vaasa, but Mustassari became Vaasa to honor the Swedish Royal House of Sweden when given its royal charter in 1606. If that name is somewhat familiar, it is the name of the great wooden royal warship that sunk upon its launching in 1628, having been commissioned by the Vaasa royal house.

Between 1808 and 1809, during the Russian conquest of Finland, taking it away from Sweden, there was a significant battle in Vaasa, as over 1,600 Swedish forces attempted to dislodge the 1,700 tsarist forces occupying the town. The town came under fire and suffered much damage. Because the local citizens had supported the Swedes, after the Russian victory, the commandant allowed his men to loot and plunder the town.

Ruins of Saint Mary Church in Old Vaasa, (work of Htm, CC BY SA 4.0, Wikimedia.org)

After a great fire in 1852, the result of it having been a community of ramshackle wood buildings, Vaasa was moved about ten kilometers or six miles to the shore where its core sits today. The current city center reflects the distinct grid pattern with wide avenues that was deliberately laid out in advance of settlement. Under Russian rule between 1855 and 1917 it was called Nikolaistad, named in honor of Tsar Nicholas II. Under tsarist rule, it became a major port for shipping timber and furs.

When Finland declared its independence in 1917 after the Russian Revolution, the country did see some limited occupation by the Red Army in a halfhearted attempt to hold on to the territory. Vaasa became for a brief period the capital of Finland, protected by forces loyal to the White Army, which was fighting the Communist forces in Russia.

In modern times, Vaasa has become an important manufacturing center, as Finland has developed many high-tech industries. The electronics industry is a major force in Vaasa. And the city has several universities, especially ones dedicated to applied science and technology.

THE PHYSICAL LAYOUT OF VAASA: The old city core of Vaasa, the one laid out by the Russians when the town was moved after the 1852 fire, has a perfect grid pattern, but the rest of the city has no regularized street pattern. The old inner city is surrounded by a chain of parks that separate it from the primary residential and industrial sectors that lie beyond. One major motorway reaches the city center, coming up from the south along the coastline. Branching off from the motorway is a major boulevard part of which has controlled interchanges, and it extends northwestward to a large interchange and then sharply turns to the right and continues out of the city in a northeasterly direction.

The main street of central Vaasa, (Work of wwikgren, CC BY SA 20, Wikimedia.org)

Various residential and manufacturing sectors lay in a rather disarrayed pattern around the city, all interspersed with woodlands that have been left as parkland, a pattern seen in most Finnish and Swedish cities. This gives Vaasa a larger physical framework, but it also keeps the city from becoming congested.

The main railroad line comes into Vaasa, circles east and north of the city core and then continues on to Vaskiluto Island where the major harbor facilities are located. The city is not on the main line railroad that links Helsinki or Turku with points to the north. Rather it is located on a spur line that branches from the city of Seinäjoki some 100 kilometers or 60 miles to the south.

The old Vaasa Railway Station reflects its Russian roots, (Work of Junafani, CC BYSA 3.0, Wikimedia.org)

SHIP DOCK: Cruise ships and ferryboats both dock in the Vaasa main port, which is located approximately ten kilometers or six miles west of the city center. There are two major piers that are capable of accommodating small to moderately large cruise ships, but there are no terminal facilities. The main street of Vaskiluoto Island where the port is located does terminate at the dock and it is possible to walk into the city center without having to cross extensive loading areas. And once leaving the immediate port, the footpath runs along the edge of a small residential area and a woodland before crossing the bridge into the city center. However, most cruise lines will provide a shuttle bus service and there are also taxis waiting on the dock.

SIGHTSEEING IN VAASA: The city of Vaasa does not have a well-developed tourist infrastructure, as seems to be the case with most of the ports around the Gulf of Bothnia. But despite the lack of a defined infrastructure, it is an interesting port and there are several venues within walking distance of the city center. As with other ports around the Gulf of Bothnia the options open to you for sightseeing are limited.

* **Ship sponsored tours** – Most cruise lines offer either very limited motor coach or small boat tours in and around the city or none at all. Many of the cruise lines that do not offer any tours simply expect guests to make their own way around the city center.

* **Private car and driver** – You should be able to order a private car and driver if that is your choice, but be sure to make your request to the shore excursion desk early, as supply is limited.

** For a comparison on price and service Go Limousines can provide that service. Contact them at www.golimousines.com for details and bookings.

** You can also check Limo Finland at www.limofinland.com for comparison.

* **Rental cars** – I would caution against renting a car in Vaasa, as in other ports of the area the supply is limited and automatic transmissions are hard to come by. And all road signs are written in Finnish with some also in Swedish, the second language of the country.

* **Hop on hop off bus** – Vaasa is not large enough to have a hop on hop off bus service for visitors.

* **Taxi services** – There should be a handful of taxis at the dock and you can check with the drivers about hourly sightseeing. Taksi Vaasa can provide guided tours of the city. I recommend you check out their web page at www.taksivasa.fi for further information, rates and bookings.

* **Bicycles** are available in the central district of Vaasa and if the weather is favorable, this is an enjoyable city in which to ride a bicycle and explore the various neighborhoods, parks and vistas. There is one bicycle rental service that makes bicycles available for a few hours or the full day. Check on line for details with www.rekola.su to see if this is a means of touring you may wish to engage.

* **Walking** – The city center is rather small, and if you do not wish to do any major touring, it is a pleasant area for walking and self-exploring. But you will be limited to just a small part of the overall community.

* **IMPORTANT SIGHTS TO SEE**: Vaasa does not have a great array of special venues, but the few I list are what give the city character. These are my recommendations as to what are the important sights to see in Vaasa, shown in alphabetical order:

** **Kaupungintalo - Town Hall** - Located at Senaatinkatu #1, the town hall of Vaasa is a beautiful old building whose architecture is reminiscent of public buildings from tsarist times in Russia when it was constructed. It is reminiscent of many of the public buildings found in Helsinki from the same period of Tsarist rule.

During normal business hours the building is open and visitors are welcome to stroll through, but no tours are given.

The Vaasa Market Square, (Work of Santeri Vinamäki, CC BY SA 4.0, Wikimedia.org)

** **Meteoriihi** - Here just outside of Vaasa is the site of a meteor impact. Although very ancient, the crater makes you realize just how insignificant we are in the cosmos. You will need to hire a taxi for the approximately 30 minute drive to this site. There is a museum at the crater, but you need to check with the local tourist office since the hours it is open are somewhat erratic. The latest information I have regarding their hours shows them open Wednesday between 6 and 8 PM and Sunday between 2 and 8 PM only.

** **Pohjanmaan Museo - Osterbottens Museum** - In the city center at Museokatu #3, this museum combines geographic, historic and fine art depictions of the Vaasa region. It is well organized and very user friendly, giving people a chance to see how Vaasa has developed. The museum hours are from 10 Am to 5 PM Tuesday thru Sunday.

** Ruins of Old Vaasa - Located in a park, the ruins of the St. Mary's Church and a few other buildings date back to the great Vaasa fire of 1852 and give a glimpse into what the city once looked like. You will need to take a taxi to reach the site, which for a nominal fee will take you there and return you to the city or ship. It is open at all times.

Old Vaasa ruins (Jonund, CC BY SA 4.0, Wikimedia.org)

** Terranova - This is essentially a natural history museum and it also covers the Arctic and the role of glacial ice and its impact upon Scandinavia. The museum is also located at Museokatu #3. Its hours are from NOON AM to 5 PM Tuesday and Thursday thru Sunday as well as from NOON to 8 PM on Wednesday.

DINING OUT: With limited time, you will only be in Vaasa during the day, so lunch is always a good option. I have chosen three excellent restaurants that serve traditional Scandinavian food in a nice atmosphere. There are many more traditional restaurants in Vaasa, but quite frankly their cuisine and service are mixed and inconsistent, thus I find it hard to recommend them The three I have chosen include:

* Ravintola 1H+K - Located Hovioikeudenpuistikko #13, which is in the city center, is a perfect place for a good lunch with true Scandinavian flavor. Their food has a home cooked flavor and is beautifully served. There is a strong emphasis upon freshness, especially their seafood dishes and soups. They are open Monday from 11 am to 2 PM. Tuesday thru Friday from 11 AM to 11 PM. Saturday hours are from 4 to 11 PM. You can call to book a table if during the main lunch hour at +358 50 5668338

* **Seglis Restaurant and Brewery** – Located on Vaskiluoto Island just a short walk from the city center, at Niemelaentie #14 on the harbor, this is a casual restaurant with a diverse lunch menu. You have the option to eat indoors or out on their patio overlooking the water. They are open Monday from 11 AM to 3 PM, Tuesday thru Thursday from 11 AM to 9 PM. Friday from 11 AM to 10 PM and Saturday from Noon to 10 PM. To book a table call +358 10 3203779 or go on line to www.seglis.fi .

* **Strampen** – On the north side of the city center at Rantakatu # 6, Strampen is a traditional Scandinavian restaurant that also does serve vegetarian friendly dishes. Their cuisine, service and atmosphere are quite good, and you cannot go wrong dining here for lunch. They are open Monday thru Thursday from 10:30 AM to 2PM and Thursday from 6 to 11 PM for dinner in the event your ship is staying into the evening hours. Friday they are open from 11 AM to 3 PM and again from 6 to 11 PM. Saturday they serve from 6 to 11 PM. It is best to call and book a table at +358 41 4514512.

SHOPPING: There is one small shopping mall in Vaasa called Rewell Center located at Ylätori #2b. It is in the city center and is open daily from 7 AM to 11 PM. There are other small shopping centers and several outlet stores in the downtown area with a variety of clothing and household items. And there are a few shops that sell souvenir items and crafts.

FINAL WORLD: Vaasa may not be the highlight of your cruise around the Gulf of Bothnia, but it is a friendly and charming small city that reflects the wholesome values that make Finland such a fine country for its citizens. So enjoy its simple pleasures.

MAP OF VAASA

THE CENTRAL AREA OF VAASA

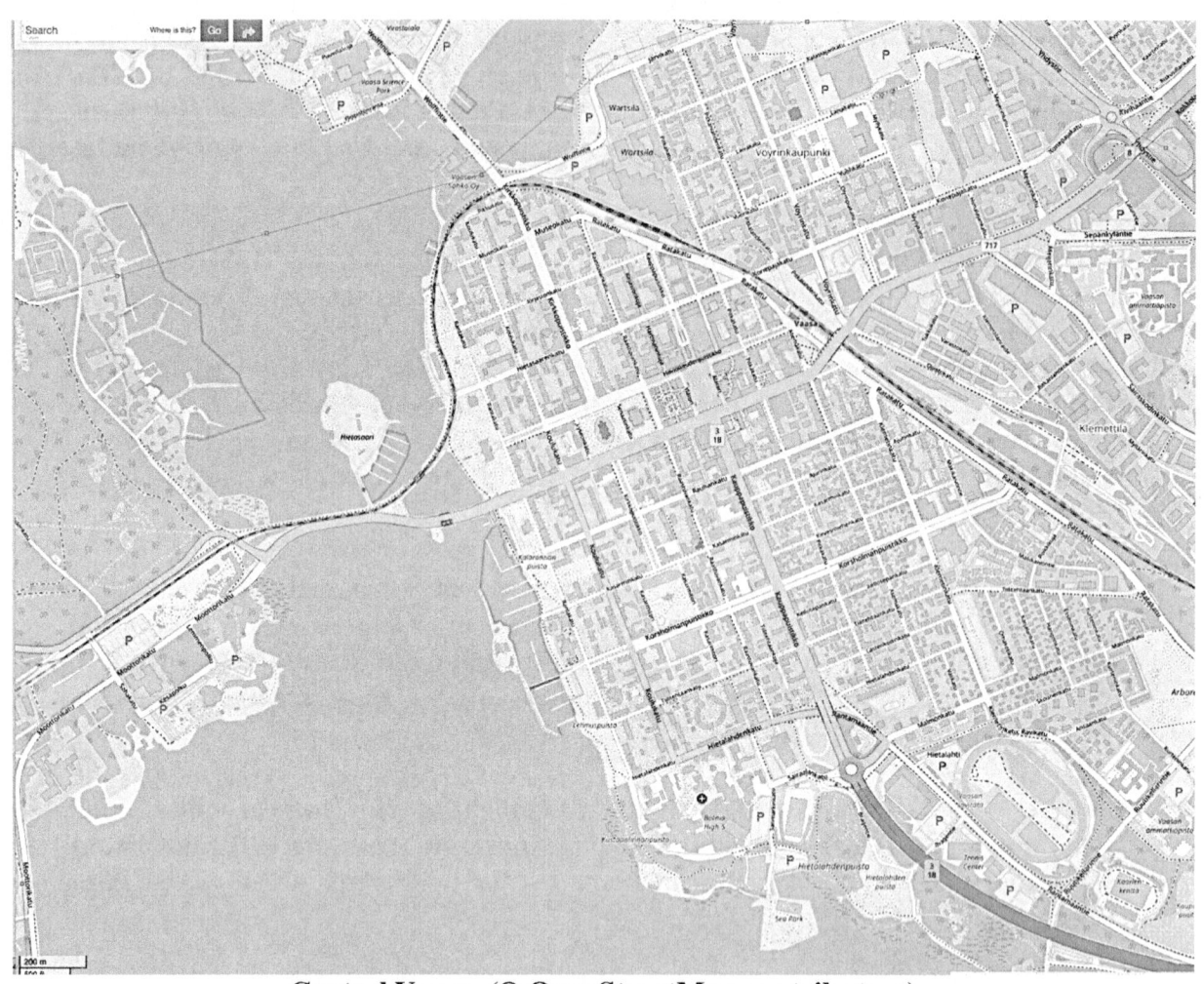

Central Vaasa, (© OpenStreetMap contributors)

This map is best viewed directly from OpenStreetMap.com on your personal device where it can be expanded or one specific area can be enlarged. Given the format of this book, it is impossible to display maps with the level of detail you might wish to have while actually out exploring the city. But the OpenStreetMap maps used directly are the tool I always rely upon.

MARIEHAMN, ÅLAND, FINLAND

Greater Mariehamn, (© OpenStreetMap contributors)

Mariehamn is located on the Finnish island of Åland, part of the larger Åland Archipelago that is made up of almost 300 small islands, some of them mere rocks. It is located off the southwest coast of Finland close to the major port city of Turku.

THE NATURAL SETTING: Mariehamn is located among a grouping of islands geographers call an archipelago, here just along the outer edge of Finland's Gulf of Bothnia shore. The collection of the Åland Archipelago has a total land area of just 600 square kilometers or 1,550 square miles and the highest elevation only reaches 129 meters or 419 feet. These are hard granitic rock islands that were heavily glaciated, partly seen by the striations on the rock surfaces and the small ponds and lakes. The shorelines are quite irregular with many indented bays, some almost large enough to be classed as fjords if this were a mountainous environment, all resulting from intensive glaciation during the period known as the Pleistocene or more popularly called the Ice Age.

There are a few pockets of soil left behind by the retreating glaciers. The islands are covered in a mix of spruce, pine and birch forests with open meadows and small bogs. But the limited soil means that the practice of agriculture is very limited and the people have turned more toward fishing, timber and today to tourism.

Sailing amid the Åland Archipelago, (Work of Kenny McFly, CC BY SA 3.0, Wikimedia.org)

The beauty of Åland landscapes, (Work of Kenny McFly, CC BY SA 3.0, Wikimedia.org)

The climate of Åland is moderated by it being a group of islands just off the coast, thus tempered by the waters of the Gulf of Bothnia. Summers are cool and moist, but winters see a mix of rain, sleet and significant amounts of snowfall, but they are spared the bitter temperatures found inland in central Finland. The climate is more akin to the Archipelago region of greater Stockholm, which is essentially on the other side of the Gulf of Bothnia.

Most of the islands are uninhabited with the majority of the population living on Fasta Åland, the island that is home to Mariehamn, capital and largest city of the archipelago.

A BRIEF LOCAL HISTORY: This island archipelago has a very long and interesting history, important to understand so as to appreciate the nature of the port of Mariehamn that you will be visiting. I can never stress enough how important history is to the understanding of the visual landscapes you see when on a cruise or any visit to a specific location.

Kastleholms built by the Swedes in 1388, (Work of Janneman, CC BY SA 3.0, Wikimedia.org)

Åland has a long prehistory of settlement dating back at least 7,000 years when primitive hunting and fishing tribes occupied the islands. By the time of the modern calendar, early farmers had come to the islands and were scattered, living in the more favorable locales. By the 10th century, there is evidence of small villages at the time Christian teaching reached Åland. And by the 13th century, the islands and much of the mainland of what is now Finland came under Swedish domination. By 1388, Kastelholm Castle had been built by a Swedish counselor to the king to secure this part of the expanding kingdom. Most of the people who had been settling the archipelago had come initially from Sweden and not Finland.

During the period of 1397 to 1523, Sweden was linked to Denmark and Norway in the Kalmar Union, and toward the end of that union, Swedish and Danish forces did fight over the archipelago since Sweden maintained a strong hold on Finnish territory. Ultimately more Swedes settled on Åland than Finns and to this day, Åland is predominantly Swedish in culture and language and many locals would prefer to politically be a part of Sweden.

The Åland Parliament Buildings, (Work of Johannes Jansson, CC BY SA 2.5, Wikimedia.org)

When Russia ousted Sweden from Finnish territory in 1809, Åland then came under Russian occupation. But during the Crimean War fought between Russia and both Britain and France, Åland was briefly captured and occupied by the two allies even though the Baltic was not the theater of war. At the end of the war in 1856, Åland Archipelago was declared as demilitarized territory, a factor Russia was not pleased with because these islands were seen as a potential stepping stone to Sweden.

Mariehamn is a relatively young community, as it was founded in 1861 by Russia, its very name taken from the Empress Maria Alexandrovna, the wife of Tsar Alexander II. Despite its name, the majority of residents that ultimately settled were Swedish in origin. The town was preplanned and much of its older architecture strongly reflects the more rural side of the Swedish and Russian use of wood.

When Finland broke away from Russia during the 1917 Revolution and later civil war, the people of Åland indicated that they wanted to unify with Sweden and not remain a part of Finland. There was fighting on the main island of Farsta Åland between tsarist loyalist and Communist forces, and Sweden sent troops to attempt to avert more bloodshed. Ultimately at the end of World War I, the League of Nations gave Finland jurisdiction, but the Finns have given the archipelago its own degree of internal sovereignty. Åland has its own flag and issues its own postage stamps even though it is nominally part of Finland. It also issues its own special automobile license plates that contain the island flag in the upper right corner. When Finland joined the European Union, special recognition of Åland was given and it is treated as extra territorial land but still recognized as a part of Finland. As extra territorial land, a duty free policy has been maintained, which does encourage more tourist based upon the shopping motive.

THE PHYSICAL LAYOUT OF MARIEHAMN: The town of Mariehamn has a population today of 11,700 and it is built on a narrow peninsula that fronts to the west on the Gulf of Bothnia and on the east to a small inlet or what locals consider to be a fjord. The main harbor is the one facing west and it receives a lot of ferry traffic, primarily because of the duty free shopping incentive, which encourages people from Sweden to visit, especially during summer weekends.

Mariehamn from the deck of the ship, (Work of Kenny McFly, CC BY SA 3.0, Wikimedia.org)

The peninsula is just over a kilometer in width, and Mariehamn has a regular grid pattern for the town center, extending from its western main harbor to the smaller eastern docks, which handle more private traffic during the summer. The southern end of the peninsula is somewhat hilly and still well forested, but there are residential enclaves tucked into the woodlands along with a bit of open parkland. The main road down the southern margin of the peninsula continues on and connects Mariehamn with small residential islands that are interconnected with short bridges and extending about 20 more kilometers or 12 miles to the south.

The main shopping street in Mariehamn, (Work of Bahnfrend, CC BY SA 4.0, Wikimedia.org)

Significant residential and small manufacturing enclaves continue north of the town center where a major east to west road connects Mariehamn with the much larger part of Farsta Åland Island.

SHIP DOCK IN MARIEHAMN: Visiting Mariehamn by cruise ship is very comfortable, as the ships dock along the western side of the narrow peninsula that comprises the city. There is a terminal facility and it also offers rest facilities and tourist information services. Only small to medium size cruise ships can be docked in Mariehamn, the maximum length of a ship being 210 meters or 689 feet. If a larger ship were to visit Mariehamn it would be necessary for guests to tender to the shore, but such a visit would be relatively rare. The distance from the dock to the center of town is only 900 meters or approximately half a mile. Despite this small distance, shuttle bus service is provided.

WHAT TO SEE AND DO IN MARIEHAMN: There are several interesting sights and things to keep the visitor occupied while spending the day in Mariehamn. Not all cruise itineraries provide organized motor coach or boat tours in or around

Mariehamn, but the majority of visitors do find that they can keep occupied during the daytime stop.

* **SIGHTSEEING OPTIONS IN MARIEHAMN:** Here are my local recommendations for Mariehamn:

** **Ship sponsored tours** – There are usually several local tours offered by every major cruise line visiting Mariehamn. The standard tour is by motor coach around the city and its accompanying islands, which are all connected by a series of bridges. Some cruise lines also offer tours by small boats capable of holding up to 100 people and visiting several adjacent island locations.

** **Private car and driver** – This option can be arranged through the shore excursion desk, but should be booked well in advance. It is a relatively costly option, but of importance to many guests. You can also check with Show Around for their private option at *www.showaround.com* and entering Mariehamn as your search parameter. There is very limited service so book ahead of arrival.

In the heart of Mariehamn, (Work of Mikael Parkvall, CC BY SA 3.0, Wikimedia.org)

** **Rental cars** – There are rental cars available, but as in other Gulf of Bothnia ports keep in mind that the vehicle will have manual transmission and that all traffic signs are written only in Finnish and Swedish.

** **There are no hop on hop off busses** in Mariehamn.

** **Taxi service** – There are local taxis available and will offer various sights at predetermined rates. Mariehamn Taxi can provide hourly rates for explorations in town or to the surrounding islands since they are interconnected by bridges. I suggest checking their web page at *www.mariehamn.com* for further information, rates and booking.

Residential Mariehamn is very beautiful, (Work of Kenny McFly, CC BY SA 3.0, Wikimedia.org)

** **Boat touring** – There are small boat excursions offered out of Mariehamn. If this is something you would like then look at *www.visitaland.com* and follow the prompts to boat excursions.

** **Bicycle rental** service is available and given the low density of traffic and the small size of the community, Mariehamn is an ideal place in which to tour on a bicycle given good weather. For more details on rental of a bicycle for the day in Mariehamn visit on line at *www.rono.ax* or send an email to *rono@aland.net*.

** **Walking** - If you are not interested in doing any motorized sightseeing or riding a bicycle, you can enjoy many of the important venues through walking the town center, which can occupy you for much of the day. Mariehamn is very friendly and tourists are a major factor in the summer economy.

* MAJOR SIGHTS IN MARIEHAMN: There are several places of historic interest in Mariehamn worthy of your time. Here are my recommendations for specific sights to see in Mariehamn (In alphabetical order):

** Åland Konstmuseum - This is the local art museum that showcases contemporary artists whose work reflects the combination of Swedish, Finnish and Russian influences. You will find the artwork to be quite interesting and with a very distinctive style.

The museum is in the same building as the Cultural History Museum, so it is possible to see two totally different exhibits each with its own focus at one time. It is located at Storagatan #1 in the center of town and is open daily from 10 AM to 5 PM during the summer months. The Cultural History Museum has as its main focus the various people and cultures that have combined over time to make Mariehamn the community it is today.

Traditional Finnish wood houses in Mariehamn, (Work of Kenny McFly, CC BY SA 3.0, Wikimedia.org)

** Åland Maritime Museum - Located at Hamngatan #2 on the western shore of Mariehamn, this museum chronicles the importance of sailing and shipping to the history of Mariehamn. It is an important and interesting stop that all visitors should make because it brings to light the importance of maritime activities to this semi-autonomous region of Finland that is like a country within a country. During the summer the museum is open from 10 AM to 5 PM, but after September it is only open from 11 AM to 4 PM daily.

** **Lilla Holmen** - This is a small island park and beach that is close to the city center of Mariehamn. It offers enticing walking or bicycle paths to enable you to enjoy the out of door environment.

There are many types of waterfowl to enjoy, and the park is famous for its peacocks, which are of course an introduced species. This park is at its best if you happen to be visiting on a nice sunny day, and it is easy to spend a couple of hours just soaking in the views.

** **The Maritime Quarter** - Located along the eastern shore at Osterleden #110, this collection of old buildings and docking facilities harkens back to the early years of Mariehamn. It has a collection of exhibits related to the sea, including boatbuilding, maritime handcrafts, a museum shop and cafe. It is an easy place in which to spend a couple of hours. It is open weekdays from 10 AM to 4 PM and on weekends from 11 AM to 4 PM during the summer months.

The famous sailing vessel Pommern

** **Museumship Pommern** - Located close to the maritime museum and sharing the same address is this beautiful four mast schooner that enhances your appreciation of the days when wood sailing vessels kept the Swedish Empire together and extended its trade far out to sea. There is a majestic quality to old sailing schooners and this particular one is quite special to the people of Mariehamn. The opening hours are between 10 AM and 5 PM during the summer months, but are shortened to between 11 AM and4 PM after the start of September with the shorter length of days and the cooler weather.

DINING OUT: As in most of the ports you will visit, dining out applies to having lunch since it is rare for a cruise ship to remain into the evening hours or overnight except in St. Petersburg. Here in Mariehamn there are a few restaurants where you can enjoy a traditional Finnish meal at lunchtime. I have listed those four that I believe are outstanding, as so many of the local restaurants receive mixed reviews. These are my personal choices (Alphabetically listed):

ÅSS Paviljongen – Located at Sjopromenaden, this is a popular Scandinavian restaurant with a strong emphasis upon fresh ingredients combined into tempting dishes with a Swedish influence. They serve lunch weekdays from 11 AM to 2 PM and dinner 2 from 5 to 8 PM. Saturday they are only open from Noon to 8 PM And Sunday from Noon to 8 PM. Call them to book a table at
+358 18 19141.

* **Indigo Restaurang and Bar** - In the center of the city at Nygatan #1, this is definitely an upscale restaurant with a strong emphasis upon fresh seafood served in Scandinavian style. At lunch they also have more casual dishes and you can even have a hamburger. They are open weekdays 11 AM to Midnight, remaining open until 4 AM on Friday. Saturday they are open from Noon to 2 AM. To book a table call the restaurant at +358 18 16550.

* **Kvarter5** – Located at Norragatan #10 in the center of town, this delightful restaurant serves traditional Scandinavian cuisine, but with a decidedly Swedish twist. Their menu is diverse, the cuisine quite good and the service is friendly and efficient. They do also offer vegetarian friendly items on the menu. Hours are between 2 and 9 PM Monday thru Thursday, remaining open until 10 PM on Friday and Saturday. To book a table call the restaurant at +358 18 15555.

* **Nautical** - Located in the heart of Mariehamn at Hamngatan #2, this is one of the finest restaurants you will find in the entire country. Their cuisine represents the Scandinavian and Finnish style, but served with a modern flair. There is an outdoor terrace looking out over the western harbor that is perfect on a sunny day. They are open Monday thru Friday from 11 AM to 11 PM, with extended closing at Midnight on Friday. Saturday they serve between 5 PM and 1 AM. Call to book at
+358 18 19931.

SHOPPING: Given the duty-free status of Mariehamn, the main pedestrian street Torggatan in the town is lined with a great variety of boutiques and distinctive gift shops selling a variety of products of Scandinavian and other European producers. Depending upon what you are looking for, I cannot recommend any particular store.

FINAL WORDS: Mariehamn is not all that historic, nor does it have a great many specific venues to visit, but it is a pleasant community that blends Finnish and Swedish cultures in a unique way. It is an example of a region within a country that in many ways functions as if it were an independent country.

Early morning calm in the Åland Archipelago

MAP OF MARIEHAMN

THE CENTRAL AREA OF MARIEHAMN

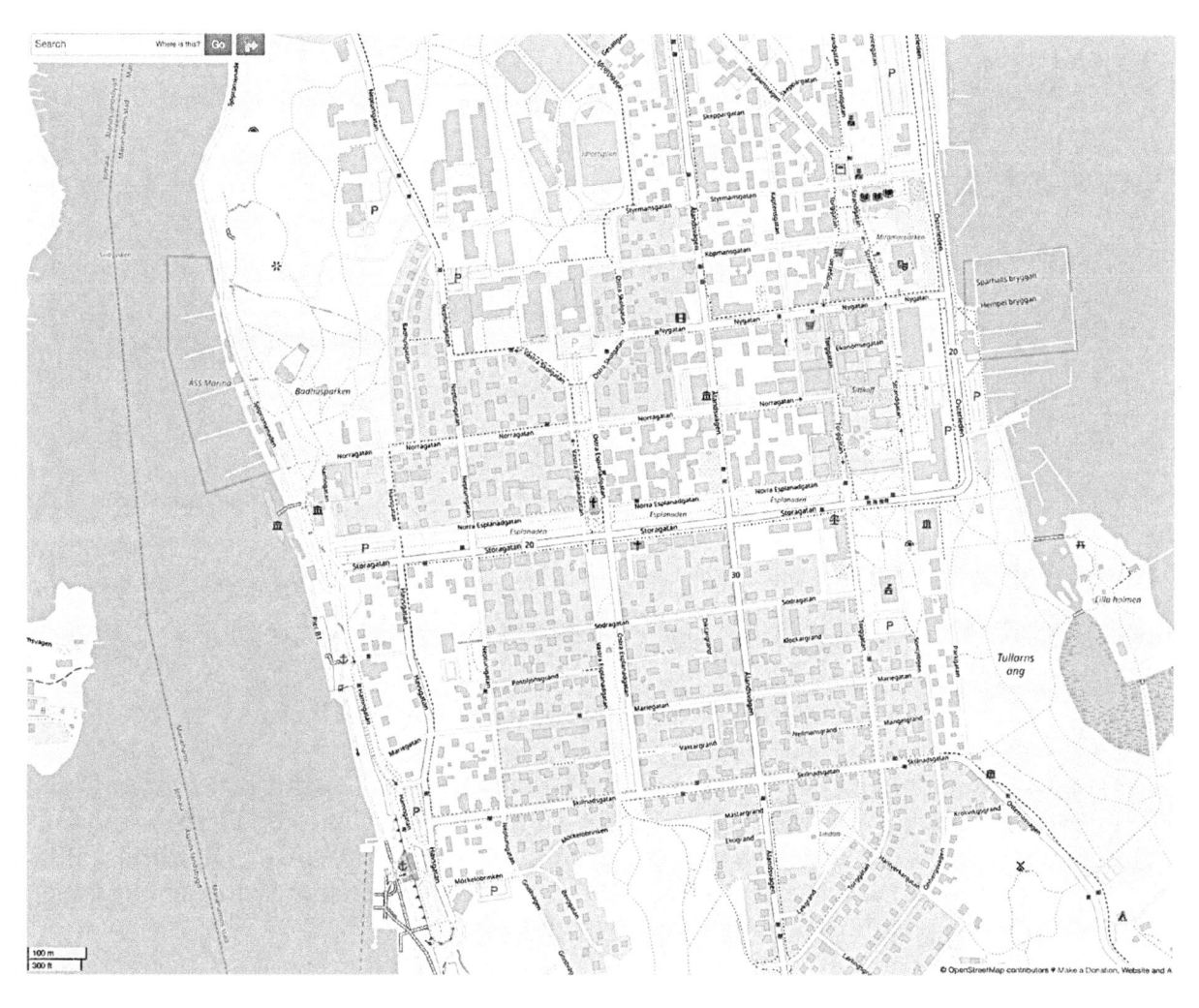

This map is best viewed directly from OpenStreetMap.com on your personal device where it can be expanded or one specific area can be enlarged. Given the format of this book, it is impossible to display maps with the level of detail you might wish to have while actually out exploring the city. But the OpenStreetMap maps used directly are the tool I always rely upon.

TURKU, FINLAND

A map of metro Turku (© OpenStreetMap contributors)

Of all the ports of call located around the Gulf of Bothnia, Turku is the largest in overall population, having over 252,000 residents in its metropolitan area. It actually is the third largest urban center in all of Finland following Helsinki and Tampere. Unlike the Mariehamn region, the Swedish component is only about five percent of the population, but once was much higher.

THE NATURAL SETTING: Turku is located on both banks of the Aura River where it empties into a complex network of islands that are the result of past glacial scour (see map above). The physical geography of the many waterways is very intricate with one broad channel trending from the mouth of the Aura River to the southwest, this being the main route of navigation between those islands closer to the shore and those at some distance. There are essentially hundreds of islands that shelter the city from the open waters of the Gulf of Bothnia, somewhat similar to the archipelago that one sails through to reach Stockholm, but most of the islands are not quite as large nor as close together. And this landscape is more linear in that it stretches all along the southern coast of Finland. Turku is about 100 kilometers or 60 miles from open water, making the entry by ship quite beautiful, again very similar to the entry into Stockholm.

The islands and the mainland are composed primarily of ancient hard rock scoured by glacial erosion, leaving large chunks of the land isolated from the mainland when sea level rose at the end of the last glacial retreat. The entire region is covered in thick forest or woodland primarily composed of spruce, pine, willow and birch. There are open areas where the land has been cleared for agriculture or where lenses of softer sedimentary rock have created soil that has formed marshes or bogs.

The surrounding countryside of Turku, (Work of Tomisti, CC BY SA 3.0, Wikimedia.org)

The climate of all southern Finland is dominated over by winter with cold Arctic blasts bringing heavy snow and bitter cold. However, in the Turku area there is some moderation of the winter condition by the effect of the Gulf of Bothnia. But even with the moderating influence of the sea, the far northern latitude does translate into short days and long nights.

Spring is short, but as the days blend into summer, they can be quite pleasant. Fall is also a transition season starting off with mild weather, but blends into winter by late November.

Summers are generally warmer inland, as once again the sea tends to moderate the climate. Turku has pleasant summers with long sunny days interspersed with cloudy or rainy weather. Again the far northern latitude does give Turku long summer days and what the Russians call the "white nights," where twilight extends until very late into the evening.

Late winter is a beautiful time in which to photography the parks and countryside, (Work of Användare LPfi på svenska Wikipedia)

A BRIEF LOCAL HISTORY: Turku has a long history, and it is very important to review it at this point because the entire urban landscape reflects the growth of the city through the centuries. This is one of the oldest cities in Finland. Remember that the landscape is the sum total of its history seen in what the human imprint is upon the natural surroundings.

Turku is cited as being the oldest city in Finland, the area having first been settled somewhere in the early 13th century, and the city dating to the 1280's when Turku Castle was built. Soon after, a Catholic bishop took up residence in the new church in 1300.

As the political and cultural center of Swedish Finland, the country's first university was the Royal Academy of Turku, established in 1640. The city became the most important center of worship and government in Finland under Swedish rule, and it was not until the Russians moved the capital of the new Grand Duchy of Finland to Helsinki in 1812 to have the seat of power closer to St. Petersburg. At first many Russian government offices remained in Turku, but a disastrous fire in 1827 destroyed most of the city center. But even after losing the seat of government, Turku remained the cultural center for most Finns, especially those with Swedish heritage. And it continued to be the largest city in Finland until 1850. Today

Helsinki is not only capital, but also the largest urban center in the nation, followed by Tampere and then Turku.

Post card from Turku around 1900

Finland never had a royal family of its own, but during the long period of Swedish occupation, Turku became home to many barons and dukes along with the appointed royal governors, giving it a level of prestige that Helsinki could not assume when the Russians made it their capital.

After Finland secured its independence following the collapse of the Russian monarchy, Turku strengthened its ties to Sweden, Denmark and other western capitals. Being so close to Stockholm meant that Turku was the easiest city to reach in Finland, and in the first half of the 20th century, there was even an ice road link across the Gulf of Bothnia to Stockholm until the winter temperatures ceased to be as cold with the onset of the global warming trend. But even today the closest ferryboat link to Sweden is through Turku.

Because of Turku's westward look, during the long Soviet Era, many students and business leaders studied in Turku. And following the fall of the Soviet Union, Russian entrepreneurs often looked to Turku as a place to come and study Western ways. Vladimir Putin even spent time studying in Turku in the early 1990's when he was only the deputy mayor of St. Petersburg. Even today, Turku is looked at as a model city of Western ways by many in the former Soviet Era block.

THE PHYSICAL LAYOUT OF TURKU: **The city center of Turku is quite well designed, this occurring after the fire in 1827. The street pattern on both sides**

of the Aura River exhibits a perfect grid pattern with several bridges crossing the river to connect both banks. The main railway line is found to the north of the grid pattern on the northern bank of the river. And to the immediate west along the mouth of the river is the major port and industrial district.

Central Turku, (Work of Kallerna, CC BY SA 4.0, Wikimedia.org)

The remainder of Turku exhibits a lack of any cohesive pattern. There is no semblance of a grid and residential, commercial or industrial districts are separate enclaves interspersed with parkland, natural woodland, especially on steeper ground and even limited agricultural land on the city margins. This is a pattern similar to that of both Helsinki and Stockholm. It is not necessarily random, but rather organized to keep such a large urban community from developing a feeling of being congested. The interplay between parkland and residential communities gives everyone a sense of space and comfort, especially given the large number of apartment blocks that a large number of people live in. This pattern has given Turku a large urban area, but without crowding or traffic congestion.

Turku has undergone quite a renaissance in its architectural development. What was once a city of mainly wood houses and stone buildings in its core, the post-World War II years have seen more application of brick and concrete, and the once rather quaint and almost nostalgic wood houses are now relegated to a few remnant structures. Today many local residents and architects alike have mourned the loss of so many of the old style buildings, saying that Turku has become too contemporary.

Turku Cathedral, (Work of Gary Bembridge, CC BY SA 2.0, Wikimedia.org)

CRUISE SHIP DOCK IN TURKU: Cruise ships dock very close to the city center at a dedicated cruise terminal adjacent to Turku Castle. It is approximately two kilometers or just over a mile to the main city square, easily walked by most guests not on tour. Most people choose the route along the Aura River, which is tree lined and quite beautiful. But shuttle bus service is also provided.

SIGHTSEEING IN TURKU: The city of Turku does offer many interesting sightseeing venues. As the third city of Finland and the largest city you will visit on the Gulf of Bothnia, as well as being the oldest major city in Finland, Turku offers a rich mosaic of architecture and the blending of Swedish and Finnish cultural elements.

* SIGHTSEEING OPTIONS FOR TURKU: As a major city you will find that Turku offers a greater number of options for sightseeing than in the prior ports of call so far evaluated. These options are:

** Ship sponsored excursions – Most cruise lines do offer tours either by motor coach or a combination of coach and boat, with a variety of itineraries. Some cruise lines may offer a full or partial day out into the countryside, with one popular destination being the very serene Ruissalo National Park where nature walks are possible in favorable weather.

** **Private car and driver** – Private car and driver/guide arranged through the cruise line is the most expensive yet most personalized way to sightsee in Turku. For those who do not wish to participate in organized group tours, and who like to have the opportunity to see what they want to and at their leisure this is always the best option. You may also wish to check on line for comparisons with regard to price and service.

***I recommend Amber Transfers at www.amber-transfers.com .

***Also check Osa Bus at www.osabus.com/chauffeur-service-turku-finland for comparison.

Central Turku does not have a high rise skyline, (Work of Samuli Lintula, CC BY SA 3.0, Wikimedia.org)

* **Rental Cars** – They are available at the Turku Airport or at downtown offices from major car rental agencies. Turku is not a difficult city to drive in with regard to congestion, but its street pattern outside of the city center is not all that easy for visitors to become acquainted with in a short time. And keep in mind that this is a relatively large city with limited congestion. Also remember that all traffic signs are written in Finnish and Swedish only.

** **Hop on hop off bus** – There is no hop on hop off bus service in Turku. However, a local sightseeing bus for a 1.5 hour tour of the city is available at the

Visit Turku Tourist Information Office located in the city center at Aurakatu #2. Tickets need to be purchased on site and the service runs from early June until the end of August For information check *www.visitturku.fi* and click on getting around Turku.

** **Taxi touring** in Turku – Taxi tours can be arranged. There are always taxis waiting at the pier and most drivers do speak English. The taxis do offer hourly rates for sightseeing. Unfortunately none of the taxi companies offer any on line information in any language other than Finnish. The major web page for the largest taxi service is *www.turunseuduntaksiyrittajat.fi* but it is in Finnish only.

** **Public transport** – Bus and tram service in Turku is quite efficient and many of the drivers and service personnel do speak English. Visit the public transport passenger web page at *www.foli.fi* for details.

Turku's modern light rail trams, (Work of Zache, CC BY SA 4.0, Wikimedia.org)

** I do not recommend bicycle rentals, as this is a major city with significant traffic. However, if you do wish to look into bicycle rentals check on line with Carfield Bike Rental at *www.carfield.fi*.

** **Walking** is always an option. Most cruise lines will offer a shuttle bus into the city center, but depending upon your walking ability there is just so much that you can see.

* **MAJOR SIGHTS TO SEE IN TURKU**: These are my recommendations as to the important venues in Turku not to be missed (Alphabetically listed):

** **Abora Vetus & Ars Nova** - This is a strange, but interesting museum in that it combines the archaeological history of Turku dating back to its earliest periods with a portion of the exhibition on modern art. If there are any two topics that are incompatible is placing the very old with the very new, but it does work for most visitors. I personally do not like modern art, so anyone like me can simply breeze through the art works and concentrate on the history. But those who like both, have it all under one roof. The museum is on the south bank of the river at Itaeinen Rantakatu #4-6 and it is open daily from 11 AM to 7 PM.

** **Forum Marinum Maritime Center** - This maritime and military history museum is located near the Turku Castle at Linnankatu #72, a bit of a walk from the city center, but a short taxi ride. The exhibits are well presented to give an insight into the maritime history of Turku, including old sailing ships on display as part of the museum. It is open daily from 11 AM to 7 PM, but closed for Midsummer Eve and Day.

Forum Marinum Maritime Center, (work of Jan-Erik Finnberg, CC BY SA 2.0, Wikimedia.org)

** **Kylämäki Village of Living History** - Although not widely recognized by many tourist sources, this unique outdoor museum presents early rural Finnish life as living history like the name implies. It is very similar to the more famous Seurasaari National Park in Helsinki, which is a recreated Finnish village located on an island north of the city center. Jannintaie #45 about 25 minutes by taxi east of the city center on the south side of the river. It is open during summer from Tuesday thru Sunday starting at 10 AM and closing at 6 PM.

Kylämäki Village, (J. Albert Vallunen, CC BY SA 3.0, Wikimedia.org)

** Luostarinmaki Handicrafts Museum - Located just across the river from the heart of the city at Vartiovuorenkatu #2, this was once the craftsman's quarters of the city, and somehow it escaped the great fire in 1827, thus preserving a taste of old Turku. Many of the buildings have been furnished with the living quarters and workshops, as they would have looked at the time just before the fire. It is a realistic look at what Turku was like in the past. During summer the museum is open from 10 AM to 6 PM daily.

** Turku Art Museum - Located just north of the city center at Aurakatu #26, this museum does not have a very worldly collection of art, but it does feature the works of Finnish artists who are quite accomplished. It is definitely worth a brief visit at the very least. The museum is open Tuesday thru Friday from 11 AM to 7 PM and on weekends from 11 AM to 5 PM.

** Turku Castle - This is the oldest castle in southwestern Finland, dating back to 1280, having been built to secure Sweden's hold on the land. It is a large and well-preserved castle and touring it does give you an appreciation for the life of the medieval period. There are many fine exhibits with some hands on opportunities within the castle rooms. The castle is located at Linnankatu #80 on the northern bank of the Aura River near its mouth just west of the city center. It can be reached on foot or by local bus or taxi. The castle is open daily from 10 AM to 6 Pm with extended hours on Monday to 8 PM.

Turku Castle, (Work of Grzegorz Jereczek, CC BY SA 2.0, Wikimedia.org)

** **Turku Cathedral** - Consecrated in 1300, this medieval cathedral is quite impressive with its semi-Gothic style of architecture. It is located along the south bank of the Aura River at Tuomiokirkkotori # 20. This church is not the original, as that one burned in the great fire of 1827. This is the second building of the cathedral, but it does offer a museum rich in the history of the city. The cathedral is generally open during the day to receive visitors unless there is a special event in progress.

** **Turun Kauppahalli** - The city's grand indoor market hall is a fascinating place to visit because it gives the observer a chance to see all aspects of Finnish cuisine under one roof. Finland is a country where good food is a very important part of life, so any visitor should take advantage of seeing a public market. Many of the vendors will give you a taste of various wares, so you can literally snack your way through the market hall. It is located right in the city center at Eeriekinkatu #16 and it is open weekdays from 8 AM to 6 PM and on Saturday from 8 AM to 4 PM. Closed on Sunday.

** **Turku University Botanical Gardens** - If the weather is nice and you want to enjoy both the fresh air and a very well organized botanical exhibition, I do recommend the botanical garden. It is located on Ruissalon Island about a 20 minute taxi ride from the city center at Puistotie #215 and it is open from 8 AM to 8 PM daily during summer.

There are many more interesting sights to see in Turku, but I have chosen what I know to be the most interesting and highly rated. The local tourist information office in Turku can offer an unlimited list of places to visit, but many will be farther out of the city center and difficult or expensive to reach without having your own personal transport. The ones I have presented are all very worthwhile and are close enough into the city to be accessed during a one-day port visit.

DINING OUT: Turku has many fine restaurants that are open during the day for lunch. Once again I have chosen from the best restaurants in the city, but limited my choice to those that serve traditional Finnish and Swedish cuisine to offer you a real taste of the country you are visiting. I have listed only three restaurants where past reviews have not had any negative comments and where I have personally sampled the cuisine. These are my choices for lunch in Turku (Shown alphabetically):

The market hall in Turku is brimming with delicacies, (Work of Hajotthu, CC BY SA 3.0, Wikimedia.org)

* **Mami** - Located in the city center at Linnankatu #3, this is one of the most popular and highly acclaimed restaurants in Turku. The menu is a feast of Scandinavian delights along with a variety of other European dishes. The presentation and service compliment the high quality of the cuisine and I doubt anyone would be disappointed. They serve Tuesday thru Friday from 11 AM to 10

PM and Saturday from 1 to 10 PM. You can book a table by calling the restaurant at +358 2 2311111.

* **Smör** - Located in the city center along the north bank of the river at Lantinen Rantakatu #3, this is another superb restaurant where the finest in Finnish and other Scandinavian cuisine is served. There is an emphasis upon those dishes that represent western Finland. Their quality, presentation and service are outstanding. They serve Monday thru Friday from 4 to 11 PM and on Saturday from 2 to 11 PM. Ships often stay well into the evening hours when in Turku. Call the restaurant at +358 2 5369444 to book a table.

* **Viikinkiravintola Harald** - This unique restaurant claims that much of its menu represents Viking times, which may be true. But the attention to detail and the presentation are exquisite and I doubt if Vikings had such a flair for fine cuisine. It may be Viking inspired, but meets a high level of modern standards that will please everyone. They are located in the heart of the city at Aurakatu #3 and serve from 2 to 10 PM Monday thru Thursday with extended closing at 11 PM Friday. Saturday they serve from Noon to 11 PM and on Sunday from 1 to 10 PM. Call the restaurant at +358 44 7668204 to book a table.

* There are many small restaurants in the central core of Turku that you may wish to look into. Most post their menu outside on display, however, few are written in any languages other than Finnish and Swedish. The ones I have recommended are based upon my years of personal experience in the Baltic Sea region.

SHOPPING: As a major city, Turku does offer some excellent shopping, especially in the areas of fine quality clothing and home accessories, two categories that include many Finnish and other Scandinavian brand names. My choices for good shopping in Turku are:

* **Stockmann Department Store** - In central Turku at Yliopistonkatu #22, this is one of the major department stores not only in Turku but in the eastern Baltic, its flagship store being in Helsinki. Stockmann is a very complete store with a broad selection in every area that encompasses the middle and upper range of products. They are open from 9 AM to 8 PM Monday thru Friday, closing at 7 PM Saturday and they are open from 11 AM to 6 PM on Sunday.

Stockmann (Department Store in Turku (Image courtesy of Stockmann Group)

* **Kauppakeskus Skanssi** - Located in the suburbs just a few kilometers south of the Aura River, this is a mid-size mall, but one that has a very complete and high quality selection of shops sure to please most tastes and budgets. It is not tourist oriented, but offers a good selection of quality merchandise in an unhurried atmosphere. Its exact address is Skannsinkatu #10 and can be reached easily by public bus using routes 9, 90, 99 and 221. It is open weekdays from 8 AM to 9 PM, Saturday from 8 AM to 7 PM and Sunday from 11 AM to 6 PM.734031 to book a table.

* **Ravintola Ludu** – Located in the heart of Turku at Linnankatu # 17, this delightful restaurant specializes in Scandinavian dishes with a great emphasis upon Finnish recipes. The food and service will please visitors by giving them a true local experience. They are open Tuesday thru Thursday from 5 to 11 PM and Friday and Saturday from 5 PM to Midnight. If your ship is staying into the evening hours, call ahead to +358 20

There are dozens of stores in the city center offering a wide array of merchandise, and yes there are those stores selling souvenirs that many visitors are seeking.

FINAL WORDS: Turku is a beautiful city and should be one of the highlights on any cruise around the Gulf of Bothnia. It has many of the same attributes as Helsinki and gives you the aura of what urban life is like in Finland, a country with one of the overall highest standards of living in Europe and one in which there is a great sense of contentment with what their society offers each individual.

TURKU MAPS

THE MAIN CITY AREA OF TURKU

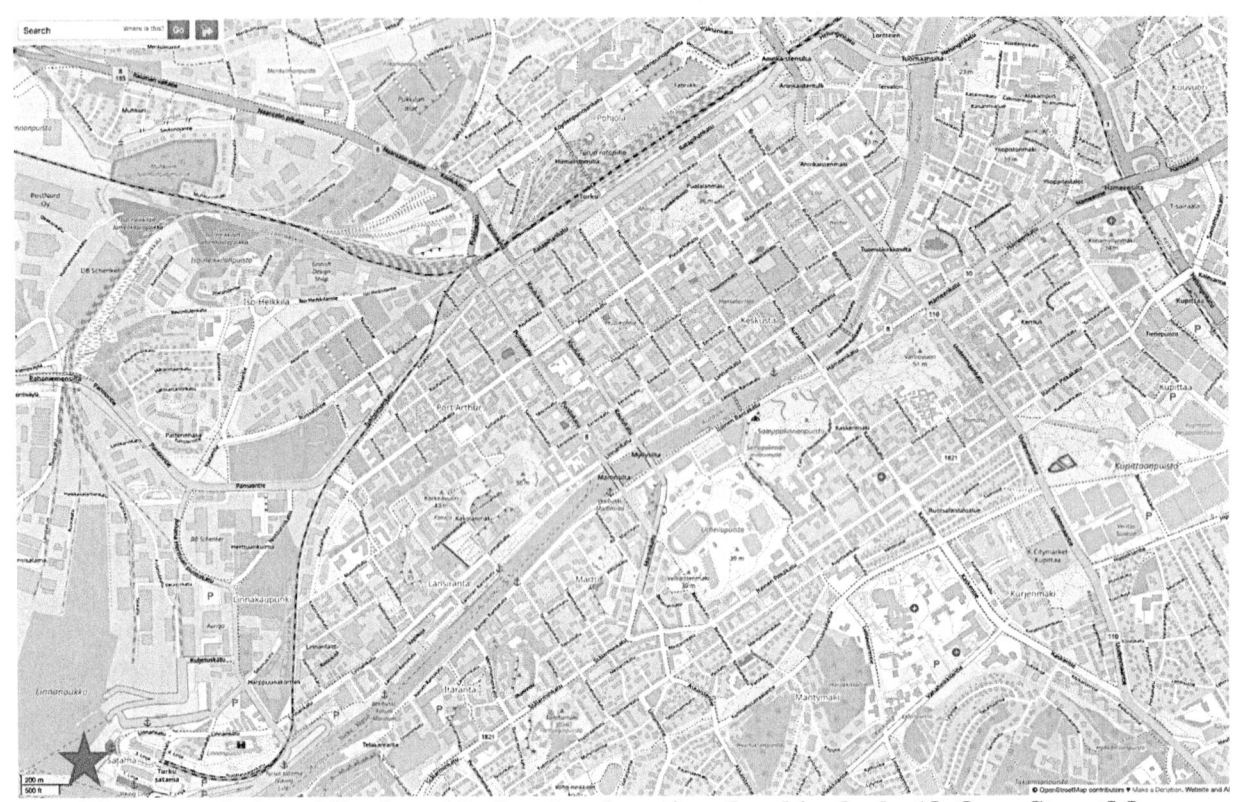

The central city of Turku with the star denoting the ship dock, (© OpenStreetMap contributors)

This map is best viewed directly from OpenStreetMap.com on your personal device where it can be expanded or one specific area can be enlarged. Given the format of this book, it is impossible to display maps with the level of detail you might wish to have while actually out exploring the city. But the OpenStreetMap maps used directly are the tool I always rely upon.

THE HEART OF TURKU

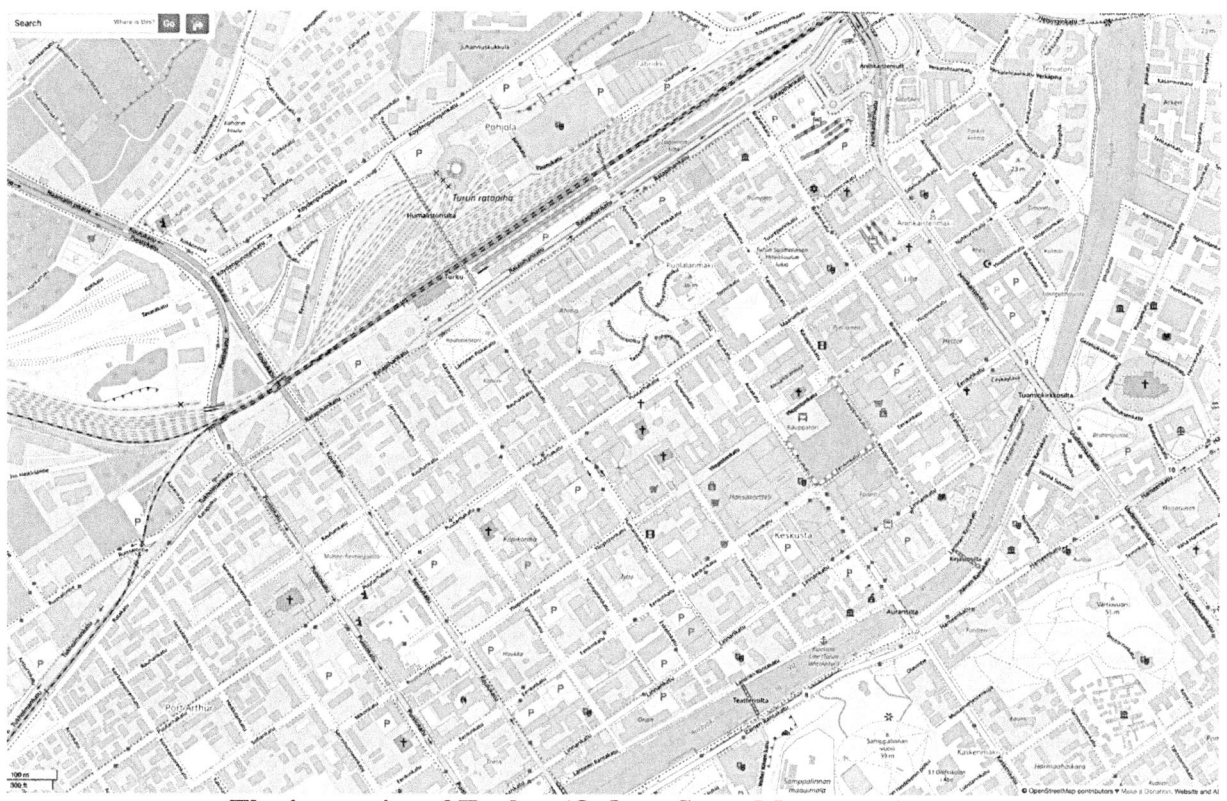

The inner city of Turku, (© OpenStreetMap contributors)

This map is best viewed directly from OpenStreetMap.com on your personal device where it can be expanded or one specific area can be enlarged. Given the format of this book, it is impossible to display maps with the level of detail you might wish to have while actually out exploring the city. But the OpenStreetMap maps used directly are the tool I always rely upon.

ABOUT THE AUTHOR

Dr. Lew Deitch

I am a semi-retired professor of geography with over 46 years of teaching experience. During my distinguished career, I directed the Honors Program at Northern Arizona University and developed many programs relating to the study of contemporary world affairs. I am an honors graduate of The University of California, Los Angeles, earned my Master of Arts at The University of Arizona and completed my doctorate in geography at The University of New England in Australia. I am a globetrotter, having visited 97 countries on all continents except Antarctica. My primary focus is upon human landscapes, especially such topics as local architecture, foods, clothing and folk music. I am also a student of world politics and conflict.

I enjoy being in front of an audience, and have spoken to thousands of people at civic and professional organizations. I have been lecturing on board ships for a major five star cruise line since 2008. I love to introduce people to exciting new places both by means of presenting vividly illustrated talks and through serving as a tour consultant for ports of call. I am also an avid writer, and for years I have written my own text books used in my university classes. Now I have turned my attention to writing travel companions, books that will introduce you to the country you are visiting, but not serving as a touring book like the major guides you find in all of the bookstores.

I also love languages, and my skills include a conversational knowledge of German, Russian and Spanish.

I was raised in California, have lived in Canada and Australia. Arizona has been his permanent home since 1974. One exciting aspect of my life was the ten-year period, during which I volunteered my time as an Arizona Highway Patrol reserve trooper, working out on the streets and highways and also developing new safety and enforcement programs for use statewide. I presently live just outside of Phoenix in the beautiful resort city of Scottsdale and still offer a few courses for the local community colleges when I am at home.

**TO CONTACT ME, PLEASE CHECK OUT MY WEB PAGE
FOR MORE INFORMATION AT:**
http://www.doctorlew.com

Printed in Great Britain
by Amazon